OLD LONDON

Highgate & Hampstead
to The Lea

THE
'VILLAGE LONDON'
SERIES
from
THE VILLAGE PRESS

THE VILLAGE LONDON SERIES

Other titles already published in hardback are:

VILLAGE LONDON Volume I
VILLAGE LONDON Volume II
LONDON RECOLLECTED Volume I
LONDON RECOLLECTED Volume II
LONDON RECOLLECTED Volume III
LONDON RECOLLECTED Volume IV
LONDON RECOLLECTED Volume V
LONDON RECOLLECTED Volume VI
VILLAGE LONDON ATLAS

Other titles already published in paperback:

VILLAGE LONDON Pt. 1 West and North
VILLAGE LONDON Pt. 2 North and East
VILLAGE LONDON Pt. 3 South-East
VILLAGE LONDON Pt. 4 South-West

OLD FLEET STREET
CHEAPSIDE AND ST. PAUL'S
THE TOWER AND EAST END
SHOREDITCH to SMITHFIELD
CHARTERHOUSE to HOLBORN
STRAND to SOHO
COVENT GARDEN and the THAMES to WHITEHALL
WESTMINSTER to ST. JAMES'S
HAYMARKET to MAYFAIR
HYDE PARK to BLOOMSBURY
BELGRAVIA, CHELSEA & KENSINGTON
PADDINGTON GREEN TO SEVEN SISTERS
HIGHGATE & HAMPSTEAD TO THE LEA

The above thirteen titles are extracts from the hardback edition of London Recollected.

OLD LONDON

Highgate & Hampstead to The Lea

by

EDWARD WALFORD

THE VILLAGE PRESS

British LIbrary Cataloguing in Publication Data

Walford, Edward, *1823–1897*
Old London: Highgate & Hampstead to the Lea.
I. Title II. Walford, Edward, *1823–1897:* London recollected
942.1

ISBN 1-85540-018-9

This edition published 1989

The Village Press Ltd.,
7d Keats Parade,
Church Street,
Edmonton,
London N9 9DP.

Printed and bound in Great Britain
by Biddles Ltd. Guildford. Surrey

CONTENTS.

CHAPTER XXX.

HIGHGATE.

PAGE

CHAPTER XXXI.

HIGHGATE (*continued*).

CHAPTER XXXII.

HIGHGATE (*continued*).

CHAPTER XXXIII.

HORNSEY.

CHAPTER XXXIV.

HAMPSTEAD.—CAEN WOOD AND NORTH END.

CHAPTER XXXV.

HAMPSTEAD (*continued*).—THE HEATH AND THE "UPPER FLASK'.

CHAPTER XXXVI.

HAMPSTEAD (*continued*).—THE TOWN.

CHAPTER XXXVII.

HAMPSTEAD (*continued*).—ITS LITERARY ASSOCIATIONS, &c.

CHAPTER XXXVIII.

HAMPSTEAD (*continued*).—ROSSLYN HILL, &c.

CHAPTER XXXIX.

HAMPSTEAD (*continued*).—BELSIZE AND FROGNAL.

CHAPTER XL.

THE NORTH-EASTERN SUBURBS.—HAGGERSTON, HACKNEY, &c.

CHAPTER XLI.

THE NORTH-EASTERN SUBURBS.—HACKNEY (*continued*).

CHAPTER XLII.

HOXTON, KINGSLAND, DALSTON, &c.

CHAPTER XLIII.

STOKE NEWINGTON.

CHAPTER XLIV.

STOKE NEWINGTON (*continued*), AND STAMFORD HILL.

CHAPTER XLV.

TOTTENHAM.

CHAPTER XLVI.

NORTH TOTTENHAM, EDMONTON, &c.

CHAPTER XLVII.

THE LEA, STRATFORD-LE-BOW, &c.

LIST OF ILLUSTRATIONS.

CHAPTER XXX.

HIGHGATE.

"The sister hills that skirt Augusta's plain."—*Thomson's "Seasons."*

Population of Highgate at the Commencement of the Century—The Heights of Highgate—The Old Roadway—Erection of the Gate—Healthiness of the Locality—Growth of London Northwards—Highgate Hill—Roman Catholic Schools—St. Joseph's Retreat—"Father Ignatius"—The "Black Dog" Tavern—Highgate Infirmary—The "Old Crown" Tavern and Tea-gardens—Winchester Hall—Hornsey Lane—Highgate Archway—The Archway Road—The "Woodman" Tavern—The Alexandra Orphanage for Infants—Asylum of the Aged Pilgrims' Friend Society—Lauderdale House—Anecdote of Nell Gwynne—The Duchess of St. Albans—Andrew Marvell's Cottage—Cromwell House—Convalescent Hospital for Sick Children—Arundel House—The Flight of Arabella Stuart—Death of Lord Bacon—Fairseat, the Residence of Sir Sydney Waterlow.

HIGHGATE, though now it has gradually come to be recognised as a parish, is the name of a district, or hamlet, embracing sundry outlying portions of Hornsey, Islington, and St. Pancras; and it is treated as such not only by older writers, but by Lysons, in his "Environs of London." It must, however, have been an important hamlet of the parish, for the Parliamentary Return of the Population in 1801 assigns to Highgate no less than 299 out of the 429 inhabited houses in Hornsey.

It may well be styled one of the "northern heights" of London, for its summit is about 350 feet above the level of the Thames, or twenty-five feet higher than Hampstead Heath; and—passing into the region of poetry—Garth has suggested that the heights of Highgate might put in a claim to rivalry with the mountain in Greece which was the fabled haunt of the Muses—

"Or Highgate Hill with lofty Pindus vie."

We have already seen* that the old highway between London and Barnet ran from the east end of St. Pancras Church, and thence to Crouch End, leaving Highgate considerably to the left; but in 1386, or thereabouts, the Bishop of London consented, on account of the "deepnesse and dirtie" passage of that way, to allow a new road to be carried through his park at Highgate, at the same time imposing a toll on all carts, wagons, and pack-horses; and that for this purpose there was erected on the top of the hill the gate which for five hundred years has given its name to the locality. In fact, until the fourteenth century there would seem to have been no public road at all over the top of Highgate Hill into the midland and northern counties.

The great northern road was, no doubt, very largely frequented in the Middle Ages, because it was the only means of access to the shrine of St. Alban, which from the Saxon days was a constant object of pilgrimage. The road at that time, however, did not lie over the top of Highgate Hill, but wound round its eastern slope, by way of Crouch End and Muswell Hill; but we have reason to believe that the country hereabouts through which it passed was densely covered with forest-trees and brushwood, and was the home and haunt of all sorts of "beasts and game," among which Fitzjames enumerates "stags, bucks, boars, and wild bulls;" to which "wolves" also must be added, if Matthew Paris is to be believed, who states that owing to such beasts of prey the good pilgrims were often in imminent danger of their lives and property.

Norden tells us, in his "Speculum Britanniæ," that "the name is said to be derived from the High Gate, or Gate on the Hill, there having been from time immemorial the toll-gate of the Bishop of London on the summit. . . . . It is a hill over which is a passage, and at the top of the said hill is a gate through which all manner of passengers have their way; so the place taketh the name of the High Gate on the hill, which gate was erected at the alteration of the way which is on the east of Highgate. When the way was turned over the said hill to lead through the park of the Bishop of London, as it now doth, there was in regard thereof a tole raised upon such as passed that way with carriages. And for that no passenger should escape without paying tole, by reason of the wideness of the way, this gate was raised, through which, of necessity, all travellers pass." The road here described, no doubt, as Mr. Prickett suggests, in his "History of Highgate," formed a junction with the northern private road between the bishop's palace and the common at Finchley. Other writers, including Mr. James Thorne, F.S.A., in his "Handbook of the Environs of London," suggest that the name denotes simply the high road or passage, the word "gate" being used almost in the same sense as the "gatt" or "gate" of our eastern counties, and preserved in Danish in the Catte*gatt*.

The gateway, which thus gave its name to the place, is described by Mr. Prickett, in his work above mentioned, as having been built, not at the

* See *ante*, p. 372.

side of the road, but across it, as an arch; and he tells us that it extended from the gate-house on the west side of the road to the old burying-ground on the east. "The rooms," he adds, "were approached by a staircase in the eastern buttress;" but they do not seem to have been of a very imposing character, as immediately before the removal of the gateway in 1769 they were occupied by a laundress. The cause of the removal of the arch was the fact of its crown being so low that even moderately laden stage-wagons could not pass under it; but whenever it was found that the wagon would not pass under the archway, the latter was taken round through a yard in the rear of the "Gate House Tavern," on the site afterwards covered by the Assembly Rooms. It may be added here that there was a corresponding gate at the other end of the episcopal demesne, at the "Spaniards," just at the north-east end of Hampstead Heath.

The newly-made way, no doubt, soon became the leading thoroughfare to the North of England, for we read that it was by way of Highgate that, in the reign of Mary, her sister, the Princess Elizabeth, was brought up to London from Ashridge, in Hertfordshire, to be imprisoned in the Tower.

Norden, whom we have quoted above, bears testimony to the healthiness of this locality. He writes: "Upon this hill is most pleasant dwelling, yet not so pleasant as healthful; for the expert inhabitants there report that divers who have long been visited by sickness not curable by 'physicke have in a short time repaired their health by that sweet salutary air." Indeed, the place is still proverbially healthy, and therefore has been chosen from time immemorial as the site of hospitals and other charitable institutions. It is worthy of note that Defoe, in his "History of the Plague," records not a single death from that fearful visitation having happened here, though it extended its ravages into and beyond the northern suburbs, and even as far as Watford and St. Albans; and his silence is corroborated by the fact that during the continuance of the plague only sixteen deaths are recorded in the register. Convalescent hospitals and infirmaries abound here in plenty; the earliest —except the Lazar House already mentioned— being a hospital for children, established on Highgate Hill in 1665.

THE GATE-HOUSE, HIGHGATE, IN 1820. (*From an Original Sketch.*)

HIGHGATE ARCHWAY GATE AND TAVERN IN 1825. (*From an Original Sketch.*)

So continuous are the lines of streets and roads between London and Highgate that the latter may now be reckoned quite as much a part of the great metropolis as Kensington or Chelsea. Indeed, not only have the prophetic lines of Mother Shipton, already quoted,* been to a certain extent verified, but the same, in a great measure, may be said of another curious prophecy, which appears in a collection of epigrams written by Thomas Freeman, a native of Gloucester, and published in 1614, under the title of "Rub and a Great Cast." The lines are headed "London Progresse," and run as follows:—

> "Why how now Babell, whilt thou build?
> The old Holborne, Charing-Cross, the Strand,
> Are going to St. Giles'-in-the-Fields:
> St. Katerine, she takes Wapping by the hand,
> And Hogsdon will to Hy-gate ere 't be long.
> London has got a great way from the streame;
> I think she means to go to Islington,
> To eat a dish of strawberries and creame.
> The City's sure in progresse, I surmise,
> Or going to revell it in some disorder
> Without the walls, without the liberties,
> Where she neede feare nor Mayor nor Recorder.
> Well, say she do, 'twere pretty, yet 'tis pity,
> A Middlesex Bailiff should arrest the citty."
>
> *Brayley's "Londiniana."*

The whole of the above prediction may be said to be accomplished, with the exception of the union of Hoxton with Highgate; but even that is in a rapid course of fulfilment. This extension of "modern Babylon" has, no doubt, in a great measure been mainly brought about by the easy means of transit northwards by the various lines of railway running thitherward. Perhaps no line has felt so rapidly the increase of the suburban traffic as the Great Northern. "There was a time, indeed," says the *North Londoner*, "when, in common with all the leading railway companies, it rather threw cold water upon it. It has now at least 4,000 season-ticket holders, and trains call at Holloway and Finsbury Park almost continuously during the working hours of the day, and every train is crowded with passengers. Speculative builders have been very busy in the north of London, which was till lately regarded by them as a *terra incognita*. Highgate Hill was an insurmountable difficulty. Nor did the Archway Road, which at the time of its construction was held to be the eighth wonder of the world, do much to remove it. A heavy toll most materially interfered with the traffic, and thus the north of London was almost as free, and airy, and untrodden as it was when the Gunpowder Plot conspirators (we merely quote a local tradition) stood on the hill between Hampstead and Highgate to witness the speedy exit to the upper regions of the British Solomon and his Parliament; or as when Dick Turpin, from his far-famed oak on Finchley Common, an oak which still defies the battle and the breeze, was in the habit, immortalised by Dickens, of accosting the passing traveller, and by means of a couple of balls in his saddle prevailing on him to stop. A fatal blow was dealt to this state of things by the connection of the Great Northern with the Underground Railway. All at once London discovered that there were no more salubrious breezes, no greener fields, no more picturesque landscapes, no more stately trees than could be shown in the district of country bounded by Highgate Hill on one side and Barnet on the other. The green lanes of Hornsey and Southgate ceased to be such. The lucky landowner who had purchased his lands at sixty or seventy pounds an acre sold them at a thousand pounds an acre. Ancient mansions, where City aldermen had lived, where lord mayors had dined, where even monarchs had deigned to shine, were pulled down; broad parks were cut up into building lots; and instead we have semi-detached villas—much better, as a rule, to look at than to live in—advertised as being in the most healthy of all neighbourhoods, and within half an hour's ride of the City."

From Holloway the transition to Highgate, morally speaking, is very easy, though the actual ascent of the hill which leads up to its breezy heights is tolerably steep, in spite of the causeway, the handy-work of the amiable hermit whom we have mentioned in the previous chapter. We must accordingly commence it, starting from "Dick Whittington's Stone."

On both sides our road is fringed by small cottages, some standing in dreary and unkempt gardens, and mostly belonging to laundresses and small shopkeepers. Norden says that the maker of the causeway was not only a hermit, but "poor and infirm;" and Dr. Fuller writes that it was a double benefit, "providing water on the hill, where it was wanting, and cleanness in the valley, which before, especially in winter, was passed with great difficulty." And to come to a far more recent time, that of the reign of Queen Anne, we find it stated, so lately as 1714, in a preamble of an Act for erecting turnpikes and making other improvements on the roads about Islington, Highgate, &c., that the highways were very ruinous and almost impassable for the space of five months in the year. It may be added here that the hill is a

---

* See *ante*, p. 313.

mass of London clay, crowned with a layer of sand and gravel.

Ascending the hill, we pass, at some distance up on the left-hand side, the Roman Catholic schools for boys and girls, belonging to the Passionist Community. The schools are spacious buildings of light-coloured brick, with ornamental string-courses, &c.; and the porch is surmounted by a turret rising high above the roof. Higher up the hill, and standing at the corner of Dartmouth Park Hill—which, by the way, is a continuation of the York and Brecknock Roads, which we have noticed in the preceding chapter, and like them, was till very recently known as Maiden Lane—is a large monastic establishment, called St. Joseph's Retreat. It occupies the site of a house formerly known as the "Black Dog Inn," and the grounds which adjoined it, enclosing altogether an area of about six or seven acres. Mr. Howitt, in his "Northern Heights of London," published in 1869, says: "Of late years the Catholics have established a large chapel and house for priests on the hill descending towards Holloway, by the entrance to Maiden Lane, under the name of St. Joseph's Retreat. The greater part of the priests there being foreign, and with a predominance of Italians, speaks pretty plainly of its origin in the Propaganda; and it seems to have succeeded greatly, its chapel being generally crowded, especially by the Irish living in Upper Holloway. For many years the Roman Catholic Church has instituted a system of perpetual prayer, which is carried on by priests and nuns, whose especial office it is to pray for the conversion of England; and the strange tendency evinced, especially amongst the established clergy, towards a reversal of the Reformation, looks as though these ceaseless prayers were in course of being answered."

The first superior of this monastery was the Hon. and Rev. George Spencer, brother of the Lord Althorp of Reform celebrity, and himself formerly a beneficed clergyman of the Church of England, but who had thrown up his preferment on becoming convinced of the claims of the Roman Catholic Church. He had been educated at Eton and at Cambridge, and as the brother of a cabinet minister he enjoyed the fairest prospects of advancement in his profession; but these he abandoned in order to assume the cowl and coarse gown and open sandals of a Passionist, and adopted instead of his hereditary title the name of "Father Ignatius." He died in 1864. The author of the "Life of Father Ignatius" writes shortly before his death:—"In 1858 we procured the place in Highgate now known as St. Joseph's Retreat. Providence guided us to a most suitable position. Our rule prescribes that our houses shall be outside the town, and yet near enough for us to be of service in it. Highgate is wonderfully adapted to all the requisitions of our rule and constitution. Situated on the brow of a hill, it is far enough from the din and noise of London to be comparatively free from its turmoil, and yet sufficiently near for its citizens to come to our church. The grounds are enclosed by trees; a hospital at one end and two roads meeting at the other promise a freedom from intrusion and a continuance of the solitude which we now enjoy."

The new monastery, designed by Mr. Francis W. Tasker, and erected in 1875–6, was solemnly blessed and opened in the latter year by Cardinal Manning. It forms three sides of a square, and is built in a broad Italian style, after the fashion of the monastic buildings of the Romagna and of Central Italy. The walls are faced with white Suffolk bricks with stone dressings, and the roofs, which project in a remarkable manner, are covered with large Italian tiles. The building contains guests' rooms, a choir or private chapel for the "religious," a community-room, library, refectory, kitchen and kitchen-offices, and infirmary, with forty "cells" or rooms for the monks. The chapel is on the north side of the monastery, and adjoining it is a room for the meeting of the members of religious brotherhoods or confraternities connected with the Passionist order.

We have stated above that the Retreat occupies the site of the "Black Dog" tavern; and we may add here that the dog, in one of its various kinds, has always been a common sign in England, and of all dogs the "Black Dog" would appear to have been the favourite; possibly, it has been suggested, because it means the English terrier, a dog who once "had his day" among us, just as the Scotch terriers and the pugs have now. The "Black Dog" here may have been chosen on account of his being the constant companion of the drovers who frequented this house. But it is also possible that the "Black Dog" may have been of a more poetical character, and have derived its name, as Mr. Larwood suggests in his "History of Sign-boards," from "the canine spectre that still frightens the ignorant and fearful in our rural districts, just as the 'Dun Cow' and the Lambton 'Worm' were the terror of the people in the Midland counties and the North of England in former times."

Be this as it may, the Passionist fathers now own not only the old "Black Dog" and its out-premises, but the adjoining property, a private house and grounds, and on the conjoined properties have constructed a monastery and chapel in which all traces of the "Black Dog" will be thoroughly "exorcised" in the course of time, if, indeed, that has not been done already.

It should be explained that while the St. Joseph's Retreat enjoys a long frontage on the west side of Highgate Hill, it is bounded in the rear by the steep and narrow lane mentioned above. On the right-hand side, as we go down the lane, is the Highgate Infirmary, a large modern building, of nondescript architecture, affiliated to one of the large London parishes. It was originally constructed as the infirmary of the St. Pancras Union. The foundation-stone was laid, in the year 1869, by Sir William H. Wyatt, chairman of the Board of Guardians, and at the close of the following year the management of the building was transferred to the Board of Managers of the Central London Sick Asylum District, representing the following unions and parishes:—St. Pancras, St. Giles-in-the-Fields, St. George's, Bloomsbury, Strand Union, and Westminster Union. The building, which covers a large space of ground, commands, at the back, extensive views over the fields—or what is left of them unbuilt upon—in the direction of Kentish Town and Paddington. It was erected from the designs of Messrs. Giles and Biven, and forms a square, the north side of which is occupied by the governor's house and offices, the principal entrance, &c.

On the east side of Highgate Hill, opposite the Passionist Monastery, is the "Old Crown" public-house, with its tea-gardens. The grounds, which are cut up into arbours, are not very extensive, and, notwithstanding its sign, the building has altogether a modern appearance. It is a favourite resort for London holiday-makers.

Close by the grounds of the above establishment is a narrow thoroughfare, running in an eastward direction, known as Hornsey Lane, an ancient cross-road, forming, in this place, the boundary line of Islington parish.

At the opposite corner of the lane, and adjoining the grounds of Cromwell House, stands a large, old-fashioned, red-brick mansion, called Winchester Hall, for what reason, however, it will puzzle the antiquary to explain.

Along Hornsey Lane we now pass on our way to the famous Highgate Archway. This structure, at the time of its erection in 1813, was considered an engineering triumph, though it is insignificant enough by the side of more recent constructions. It is simply a bridge carried over a roadway, which, as we have already stated, strikes off on the right at the foot of Highgate Hill, and which was formed in order to avoid the steepness of the hill itself.

In cutting this road various fossil remains were found, consisting of shells, crabs, and lobsters, the teeth and vertebræ of sharks and other fish, thus proving that there was a time when the hill held a far lower level, or else that the whole valley of the Thames was one large arm of the sea. The construction of this roadway cost something like £13,000, which was, perhaps, rather a large sum, seeing that its length is only a little more than a mile.

Previous to the formation of the roadway and the erection of the arch, a scheme was projected to construct a tunnel through the London clay at Highgate Hill, for the purpose of making a more easy communication between Holloway and Finchley. The attempt, however, failed, and the result was the construction of the open cutting which forms the present Highgate Archway Road. The failure appears to have arisen, in a great measure, from the want of experience on the part of the engineers who had charge of the work, more especially as they had such very difficult and heavy ground to work in as the London clay. The tunnel was nearly completed when it fell in with a terrific crash, in April, 1812, fortunately before the workmen had commenced their labour for the day. The idea of forming the tunnel, therefore, was ultimately abandoned, and the present arch constructed in its stead. The toll which was levied upon passengers along this road was of its kind unique, for not only was a toll levied upon the drivers of horses and vehicles, but one penny was also levied upon foot passengers; sixpence was the toll upon every horse drawing. When the subject of tolls was before the House of Commons in 1861, the "Holyhead Road Act" was passed, and in this the Highgate Archway Road was included. It is not an ordinary turnpike-road, belonging, in fact, to a company. The company in 1861 owed the Consolidated Fund Loans £13,000; but by the Holyhead Road Act the debt and arrear of interest were compounded for a payment of £9,000, in instalments spread over fifteen years. Then the tolls were to cease, and this happy time having at length come round, the year 1876 saw Highgate freed from the impost. Within the previous twelve years more than one hundred turnpike-gates had been removed from the thoroughfares of the metropolis; and before many years are passed we may expect to see all the toll-gates in our suburbs superseded.

The archway thrown across this thoroughfare is about thirty-six feet high, and eighteen feet in width. It is formed of stone, flanked with substantial brick-work, and surmounted by three semi-arches, carrying a bridge sufficiently wide to allow of the transit of two carriages abreast. An open stone balustrade ranges along the top. The only useful purpose attained by the construction of this archway is the continuation of Hornsey Lane. It is recorded on a brass plate, fixed to the southern entrance to the structure, that the foundation-stone was laid by Edward Smith, Esq., on the 31st of October, 1812; and above the arch is cut in Roman capitals the following inscription:—"GEO. AVG. FRED. WALLIÆ. PR. REGIS. SCEPTRA. GERENTE." The archway presents itself as a pleasing object to the traveller either leaving or entering London by this road; and from the pathway of the bridge on a clear day is obtained an excellent view of the surrounding country, and of many buildings in the metropolis, among which St. Paul's Cathedral stands finely displayed.

At the top of the Archway Road, where it is cut by Southwood Lane, is the "Woodman" Inn, a favourite resort for Londoners. The "Woodman" is a common sign in rural villages, but not often to be met with so near to a large city. The sign-board is almost always a representation of Barker's picture, and evidently suggested by Cowper's charming description of a winter's morning in "The Task." The sign-board at Highgate formed, and possibly forms, no exception to the rule.

On the slope of the hill, and turning out of the Hornsey Lane, a little to the east of the archway, is Hazelville Road. In this road are two very useful charitable institutions, places for the reception of the two extremes of the great human family—namely, of infancy and old age. The first hospital, which we pass on our left in descending the hill, is a neat and unostentatious red-brick building, called the Alexandra Orphanage for Infants. It was founded in 1864, and is a branch of the Orphan Working School at Haverstock Hill, which we have already noticed.* The other building referred to stands nearer to the foot of the hill, and covers a large space of ground. This is the asylum of the Aged Pilgrims' Friend Society; an institution established in 1807 for giving life pensions of five, seven, and ten guineas per annum to the aged Christian poor of either sex, and of every denomination, who are not under three-score years of age. The present asylum, which was opened in 1871, forms three sides of a quadrangle, and, as originally constructed, consisted of a centre and two wings, which afforded one room and a small scullery for each of the eighty inmates, besides committee-rooms, warden and matron's rooms, a laundry, and a beautiful chapel; but in 1876 the two wings were lengthened, thus giving space for forty additional rooms. The buildings are of two storeys, with the chapel in the centre of the north side; the south side, which was originally unbuilt upon, has now in the centre a large hall in which lectures and addresses are sometimes given, and festive gatherings among the aged inmates take place. The hall is connected with the wings of the building on either side by a covered pathway. The spacious central enclosure, owing to the steepness of the ground, forms two or three grassy slopes and terraces, connected with each other by flights of steps.

Since the foundation of this institution, in 1807, it has been the means of relieving upwards of 3,600 aged persons, and has distributed amongst them the sum of upwards of £116,900. The total number of the recipients of the charity in 1876 was 1,038, and the annual sum expended in pensions alone is upwards of £6,200. The pensioners are each provided with a comfortable home, together with a sufficient supply of coals, with medical attendance when sick, and other comforts. One of the earliest and best friends of this institution was Mr. John Box, of Northampton Square, who, in addition to many other gifts, bequeathed a sum of £12,000 towards the funds for the new building.

Retracing our steps to the top of Highgate Hill, the first building which we notice, on our left, is Lauderdale House, now the Convalescent Home to St. Bartholomew's Hospital. The house, said to have been erected about the middle of the seventeenth century, was formerly the residence of the Earls of Lauderdale, and at one time the home of Nell Gwynne. It has about it nothing in the way of architectural details to attract the attention of the passer-by. A high wall and iron gates, with a garden on either side of the stone pathway to the door, separate it from the high road. It has two fronts—one facing the highway, and the other looking down south-eastward towards Holloway. It has on each front a very simple pediment, and has been stuccoed, probably in very recent times. The upper storey on the side of the house overlooking the garden projects somewhat from the lower, and is supported by a row of columns. Much of the old gardens remain, though doubtless considerably altered from what they were when "poor Nelly" occupied the mansion. "Those who remember this house some years since," writes Mr. Prickett, in his "History of Highgate," "describe the internal arrangements as bearing testimony to its antiquity; indeed, the entrance-hall, which is pro-

* See *ante*, p. 315.

bably still in its primitive state, the delightful terrace on the southern side, and the walls of the garden, thoroughly testify to the remnants of ancient days."

This house is supposed to have been built about the time of the restoration of Charles II., "one of whose most active and detestable ministers Lauderdale was from first to last," says William Howitt, in his "Northern Heights of London." "Nay," he continues, "we are assured that he was a prominent man, even in the reign of Charles I., in Scotland, being then a Covenanter, and one of those who sold Charles I. to the English army. He turned round completely under Charles II., and became one of the most frightful persecutors of the Covenanters that existed, he and Archbishop Sharpe going hand-in-hand in their diabolical cruelties. He was not only an English minister, a leading one of the celebrated Cabal Administration, but Lord-Deputy of Scotland, where nothing could surpass his cruelty but his rapacity. Lord Macaulay draws this portrait of him: 'Lauderdale, the tyrant deputy of Scotland at this period, loud and coarse both in mirth and anger, was, perhaps, under the outward show of boisterous frankness, the most dishonest man in the whole Cabal. He was accused of being deeply concerned in the sale of Charles I. to the English Parliament, and was, therefore, in the estimation of good Cavaliers, a traitor of a worse description than those who sat in the High Court of Justice. He often talked with noisy jocularity of the days when he was a canter and a rebel. He was now the chief instrument employed by the court in the work of forcing episcopacy on his reluctant countrymen; nor did he in that cause shrink from the unsparing use of the sword, the halter, and the boot. Yet those who knew him knew that thirty years had made no change in his real sentiments; that he still hated the memory of Charles I., and that he still preferred the Presbyterian form of government to any other.' If we add to this picture Carlyle's additional touch of 'his big red head,' we have a sufficient idea of this monster of a man as he was at that time at work in Scotland with his renegade comrade, Archbishop Sharpe, with their racks, thumbscrews, and iron boot in which they used to crush the legs of their victims with wedges, so vividly described by Sir Walter Scott in 'Old Mortality' and in the 'Tales of a Grandfather;' whilst their general, Turner, was pursuing the

LAUDERDALE HOUSE, IN 1820.

flying Covenanters to the mountains and morasses with fire and sword." To complete his military despotism, as any reader of English history will know, Lauderdale got an Act passed in Scotland for the raising of an army there which the king should have the right to march to any part of his dominions; his design being, as Bishop Burnet stated at the bar of the House of Commons, to have "an army of Scotch to keep down the English, and an army of Irish to keep down the Scotch." "When Lauderdale was in Scotland on this devil's business," continues Mr. Howitt, "no doubt his indulgent master used to borrow his house at Highgate for one of his troop of mistresses; and thus it was that we find pretty Nelly Gwynne flourishing directly under the nose of the indignant patriot Marvell. If Charles had picked his whole harem, however, he could not have found one of his ladies less obnoxious than 'poor Nelly.' As for Lucy Walters, the mother of the Duke of Monmouth, she was dead. Lady Castlemaine, Duchess of Cleveland, the mother of the Dukes of Grafton, was a bold and fiery dame that kept even the king in constant hot water. Madame de Querouaille, created Duchess of Portland, mother of the Dukes of Richmond, was the spy of Louis XIV. of France, sent expressly to keep Charles to his obedience, and for this service Louis gave her a French title and estate. Moll Davis, the rope-dancer, the mother of the Radclyffes, had lost her influence, and Miss Stewart had got married. Of all the tribe Nelly was the best; and yet Marvell launched some very sharp arrows at her. He describes Charles as he might be seen walking in the Lauderdale gardens as—

> 'Of a tall stature and of sable hue,
> Much like the son of Kish, that lofty grew;'

and Nelly, as 'that wench of orange and oyster,' in allusion to her original calling; for she commenced life by selling oysters about the streets, and then oranges at the theatres."

MARVELL'S HOUSE, 1825.

In our account of Pall Mall we have spoken at some length of Nell Gwynne's career at Court,* but a little of her history still remains to be told. Though of the lowest extraction, "her beauty, wit, and extreme good nature," writes the author above quoted, "seem to have made her friends amongst

* See Vol. IV., p. 126

the actors; and her figure and loveliness raised her to the stage. There she attracted the dissolute monarch's attention by a merely ludicrous circumstance. At another theatre an actor had been introduced as 'Pistol' in a hat of extravagant dimensions. As this caused much merriment, Dryden caused Nelly to appear in a hat as large as a coach-wheel. The audience was vastly diverted, and the fancy of the king, who was present, was taken at once. But as she was already the mistress of Lord Buckhurst, Charles had to compound with him for the transfer of Nelly by an earldom, making him Earl of Middlesex. Nelly soon won the ascendancy among the mistresses of the king,

'Who never said a foolish thing,
And never did a wise one.'

"Though extremely gay and witty, poor Nell Gwynne seems never to have shown any hauteur in her elevation, nor any avarice, a prominent vice in some of her rivals. On the contrary, she made no secret of condemning her peculiar position, and was always ready to do a good action. Charles never endowed her with the wealth and titles that he lavished on other women, probably because she did not worry him; but on his death-bed his conscience pricked him for his neglect, and he said, 'Don't let poor Nelly starve!' a frail security against starvation for a king's mistress in a new court.

"The circumstance which connects her memory with Lauderdale House is the tradition that, as the king delayed to confer a title on her child, as he had done on the eldest son of others of his mistresses, she one day held the infant out of an upper window of Lauderdale House, and said, 'Unless you do something for your son, here he goes!' threatening to let him fall to the ground. On this Charles replied, 'Stop, Nelly; save the Earl of Burford!' Whether these words were said exactly as related or not, at all events, the story is very like one of Nell's lively sallies; and the child was created Earl of Burford, and afterwards Duke of St. Albans." An exquisite portrait of Nell Gwynne, by Sir Peter Lely, is in the National Portrait Gallery.

This story, it will be seen, differs somewhat from the version we have told in the volume above referred to, but the reader is at liberty to choose which he pleases as being the more reliable; perhaps the one is as truthful as the other. It is rather a curious coincidence that on the western slope of Highgate, a few years ago, lived a certain Duchess of St. Albans, the wife of one of Nell's descendants, who had also begun life, like her, as an actress. This was Miss Harriet Mellon, who married firstly Mr. Thomas Coutts, the banker, and who, after his death, became the wife of William Aubrey de Vere, ninth Duke of St. Albans. Of this lady we have spoken in our account of Piccadilly.* "Like Nelly," remarks Mr. Howitt, "she had, whether actress or duchess, a noble nature; and the inhabitants of Highgate still bear in memory her deeds of charity, as well as her splendid *fêtes* to royalty, in some of which, they say, she hired all the birds of the bird-dealers in London, and fixing their cages in the trees, made her grounds one great orchestra of Nature's music."

Lauderdale House of late years has been occupied as a private dwelling, and was for some time the residence of the first Lord Westbury before he reached the woolsack. In 1872 the house was converted to its present use, having been made over by its then owner, Sir Sydney Waterlow, to the governors of St. Bartholomew's Hospital for the purposes of a convalescent hospital, and it was opened in the above year as such by the Prince and Princess of Wales. The building contains beds for thirty-four patients. In its external appearance it is very slightly changed from what it must have been in the days of Lord Lauderdale and Nell Gwynne.

The house formerly occupied by Andrew Marvell, the poet and patriot, as we have intimated above, adjoins the grounds of Lauderdale House, on the north side. The house—or cottage, for it was scarcely anything more—was small, and, like Andrew Marvell himself, very unpretentious. It was built mainly of timber and plaster; and with its bay window, latticed doorway, and gabled roof, had about it all the attributes of the picturesque. In front were some old trees, and a convenient porch led to the door, in which its owner doubtless used to sit and look forth upon the road. Most of the old windows had been modernised, and other alterations had been made which the exigencies of tenancy had rendered necessary since Marvell's days; and in the end a large part of the building itself was demolished, all that remains being a few fragments of the lower portion of the walls, now profusely overgrown with ivy, and the stone steps leading up to the door. Of Andrew Marvell himself we have already had occasion to speak in our notices of the Strand and of St. Giles's Church.†

Mr. Samuel Carter Hall, in his "Pilgrimages to English Shrines," published in the year 1850, thus describes his visit to this interesting spot:—"We know nothing more invigorating than to breast the

* See Vol. IV., p. 280. † See Vol. III., pp. 64, 202.

breeze up a hill, with the bright clear sky above, and the crisp ground under foot. The wind of March is as pure champagne to a healthy constitution; and let mountain-men laugh as they will at Highgate Hill, it is no ordinary labour to climb it, and look down upon London from its height. Here, then, are we, once more, opposite the house where lived the satirist, the poet, and the incorruptible patriot. . . . The dwelling is evidently inhabited; the curtains in the deep windows as white as they were when we visited it some years previous to the visit concerning which we now write; and the garden is as neat as when in those days we asked permission to see the house, and we were answered by an elderly servant, who took in our message. An old gentleman came into the hall, invited us in, and presented us to his wife, a lady of more than middle age, and of that species of beauty depending upon expression, which it is not in the power of time to wither, because it is of the spirit rather than of the flesh; we also remembered a green parrot, in a fine cage, that talked a great deal, and was the only thing which seemed out of place in the house. We had been treated with much courtesy; and, emboldened by the memory of that kindness, we now again ascended the stone steps, unlatched the little gate, and knocked.

"Again we were received courteously and kindly by the lady whom we had formerly seen here; and again she blandly offered to show us the house. We went up a little winding stair, and into several neat, clean bedrooms, where everything was so old-fashioned that you could fancy Andrew Marvell was still its master.

"'Look out here,' said the old lady; 'here's a view! They say this was Andrew Marvell's closet where he wrote *sense;* but when he wrote *poetry*, he used to sit below in his garden. I have heard there is a private way under the road to Cromwell House opposite; but surely that could not be necessary. So good a man would not want to work in the dark; for he was a true lover of his country, and a brave man. My husband used to say that the patriots of those times were not like the patriots now; that then they acted for their country, now they talk about it! Alas! the days are passed when you could tell an Englishman from every other man, even by his gait, keeping the middle of the road, and straight on, as one who knew himself, and made others know him. I am sure a party of Roundheads, in their sober coats, high hats, and heavy boots, would have walked up Highgate Hill to visit Master Andrew Marvell with a different air from the young men of our own time—or of *their* own time, I should say—for *my* time is past, and *yours* is passing.'

"That was quite true; but there is no reason, we thought, why we should not look cheerfully towards the future, and pray that it may be a bright world for others, if not for ourselves; the greater our enjoyment in the contemplation of the happiness of our fellow-creatures, the nearer we approach to God.

"It was too damp for the old lady to venture into the garden; and, sweet and gentle as she was, both in mind and manner, we were glad to be alone. How pretty and peaceful the house looks from this spot. The snowdrops were quite up, and the yellow and purple tips of the crocuses were bursting through the ground in all directions. This, then, was the garden the poet loved so well, and to which he alludes so charmingly in his poem, where the nymph complains of the death of her fawn:—

> "'I have a garden of my own,
> But so with roses overgrown
> And lilies, that you would it guess
> To be a little wilderness.'

The garden seems in nothing changed; in fact, the entire appearance of the place is what it was in those glorious days when inhabited by the truest and the most unflinching patriot that ever sprang from the sterling stuff that Englishmen were made of in those wonder-working times. The genius of Andrew Marvell was as varied as it was remarkable; not only was he a tender and exquisite poet, but entitled to stand *facile princeps* as an incorruptible patriot, the best of controversialists, and the leading prose wit of England. We have always considered his as the first of the 'sprightly runnings' of that brilliant stream of wit, which will carry with it to the latest posterity the names of Swift, Steele, and Addison. Before Marvell's time, to be witty was to be strained, forced, and conceited; from him—whose memory consecrates that cottage—wit came sparkling forth, untouched by baser metal. It was worthy of him; its main feature was an open clearness. Detraction or jealousy cast no stain upon it; he turned aside, in the midst of an exalted panegyric to Oliver Cromwell, to say the finest things that ever were said of Charles I.

"Beneath Italian skies his immortal friendship with Milton seems to have commenced; it was of rapid growth, but was soon firmly established; they were, in many ways, kindred spirits, and their hopes for the after-destinies of England were alike. In 1653 Marvell returned to England, and during the eventful years that followed we can find no record of his strong and earnest thoughts, as they worked upwards into the arena of public life. One glorious fact we know, and all who honour virtue must feel its force, that in an age when wealth was never wanting to the unscrupulous, Marvell, a member of the popular and successful party, continued poor. Many of those years he is certain to have passed—

> "Under the destiny severe
> Of Fairfax, and the starry Vere,'

in the humble capacity of tutor of languages to their daughters. It was most likely during this period that he inhabited the cottage at Highgate, opposite to the house in which lived part of the family of Cromwell."

In 1657 he was introduced by Milton to Bradshaw, and shortly after became assistant-secretary, along with Milton, in the service of the Protector. After he had occupied this post for some time, he was chosen by the burgesses of his native town, Hull, as their representative in Parliament. "Whether under Cromwell or Charles," writes the author of the work quoted above, "he acted with such thorough honesty of purpose, and gave such satisfaction to his constituents, that they allowed him a handsome pension all the time he continued to represent them, which was till the day of his death."

Opposite the door of Marvell's house was the residence of General Ireton and his wife Bridget, the eldest daughter of Oliver Cromwell. The house, now the Convalescent Hospital for Sick Children, still bears the name of Cromwell House, and is thus described in Prickett's "History of Highgate:" "Cromwell House is supposed to have been built by the Protector, whose name it bears, about the year 1630, as a residence for General Ireton, who married his daughter, and was one of the commanders of his army; it is, however, said to have been the residence of Oliver Cromwell himself; but no mention is made, either in history or in his biography, of his having ever actually lived at Highgate. Tradition states there was a subterraneous passage from this house to the mansion house, which stood where the new church now stands, but of its reality no proof has hitherto been adduced. Cromwell House was evidently built and internally ornamented in accordance with the taste of its military occupant. The staircase, which is of handsome proportions, is richly decorated with oaken carved figures, supposed to have been those of persons in the general's army in their costume, and the balustrades are filled in with devices emblematical of warfare. On the ceiling of the drawing-room are the arms of General Ireton; this, and the ceilings of the other principal apartments, are enriched in conformity with the fashion of those days. The proportions of the noble rooms, as well as the brickwork in front, well deserve the notice and study of the antiquarian and the architect. From the platform on the top of the mansion may be seen a perfect panorama of the surrounding country."

The staircase above described is a remarkably striking and elegant specimen of internal decoration, broad and noble in its proportions; indeed, the woodwork of the house generally is everywhere equally bold and massive. There are some ceilings in the first storey which are in rich plaster-work, ornamented with the arms of Ireton, together with mouldings of fruit and flowers. The series of figures which stand upon the newels of the staircase are ten in number; they are about a foot in height, and represent the different soldiers of the Cromwellian army, from the fifer and drummer to the captain. It is stated that there were originally twelve of these figures, and that the missing two represented Cromwell and Ireton. In 1865, at which time Cromwell House was occupied as a boarding-school, the building was partially destroyed by fire, but it did not injure the staircase, or anything of historical interest. The building was thoroughly restored, and now presents much the same appearance that it did before. The front of the house is rather low, being only of two storeys, finished by a parapet, so that the roof, which is thrown backwards, adds but little to its elevation. It is of a solid and compact bright-red brickwork, and has a narrow cornice or entablature running the whole length of the front over each row of windows. Its doorway is arched, and faced with a portal of painted wood, in good keeping with the building. In front is a gateway, with solid square pillars surmounted by stone globes. At the lower end a lofty archway admits to the rear of the building. The mass of the mansion running backwards is extensive, and behind lies a portion, at least, of its ancient gardens and pleasure-grounds.

Ireton, one of the staunchest and bravest of Cromwell's generals, was a native of Attenborough, in Nottinghamshire, and, as stated above, married Bridget, the eldest daughter of Cromwell, who, after Ireton's death, became the wife of General Fleetwood. Ireton commanded the left wing of Cromwell's army at the battle of Naseby. He was constantly with the Protector when he was in treaty with King Charles, at Hampton Court, in 1647, and in the following year sat on the trial of the king, and voted heartily for his death. Morrice, in his "Life of Lord Orrery," declares that "Cromwell himself related that in 1647, at the time they were endeavouring to accommodate matters with the king, Ireton and he were informed that a scheme was laid for their destruction, and that they might convince themselves of it by intercepting a secret messenger of the king's, who would sleep that night at the 'Blue Boar,' in Holborn, and who carried his dispatches sewed up in the skirt of his saddle. Cromwell and Ireton, disguised as troopers, waited that evening, seized the saddle, and found letters of the king's to the queen in France, confirming all that they had heard. From that hour, convinced of Charles's incurable treachery, they resolved on his death." Clarendon describes Ireton as taciturn, reserved, and uncommunicative, and as being "never diverted from any resolution he had taken." Such was the son-in-law for whom this old mansion was built. There is a portrait of Ireton by Walker, in the National Portrait Gallery. It was formerly in the Lenthall collection.

In 1869, Cromwell House was taken as a convalescent establishment in connection with the Hospital for Sick Children, in Great Ormond Street, of which we have already spoken.* Fifty-two beds are here provided for the little ones on leaving the hospital. The number of admissions to the Convalescent Hospital, as we learn from the printed report of the committee of management, amounts annually to about 400, and the testimony of the medical officers who attend at Cromwell House, in reference to the progress of the children under treatment there, is of a most satisfactory character. The spacious play-ground attached to the house presents an attractive picture on fine days, when nearly all the children are out of doors at sport.

A little higher up the hill, or bank, as it is called, than Cromwell House, once stood Arundel House, the suburban residence of the Earls of Arundel. A few scattered remains of the old mansion and its garden-walls still exist. "Its site," says Mr. Howitt, in his "Northern Heights of London," "is now occupied by some modern houses, but its position may be known by its abutting on an old house, called Exeter House, probably also from its being once the abode of the Earls of Exeter; of this, however, there seems to be no record. It is not until towards the middle of the reign of James I. that we hear of the Earl of Arundel having a house at Highgate. When Norden wrote his 'Survey of Middlesex,' in 1596, the principal mansion was thus mentioned:—'Upon this hill is a most pleasant dwelling, yet not so pleasant as healthful, for the expert inhabitants there report that divers that have long been visited with sickness, not curable by physick, have in a short time repaired their health by that sweete salutarie air. At this place, —— Cornwalleys, Esquire, hath a very faire house, from which he may with great delight behold the stateley citie of London, Westminster, Greenwich, the famous river Thames, and the country towards the south very farre.' . . But the question here is, was the house of the Cornwallis family on what is called the Bank that which became the property of the Earl of Arundel? Lysons has remarked that there is in the Harleian Manuscripts a letter of Sir Thomas Cornwallis, dated 'Hygat, 16 July, 1587.' Sir Thomas, who was Treasurer of Calais, and Comptroller of the Household to Queen Mary, had been knighted as early as 1548, so that the Mr. Cornwallis mentioned by Norden in 1596, was doubtless his son William, who had taken up his residence there, while Sir Thomas had retired to his mansion at Brome, in Suffolk. It is said that this house at Highgate was visited by Queen Elizabeth in June, 1589. At all events, it is on record that the bell-ringers of St. Margaret's, Westminster, were paid 6d. on the 11th of June, when the Queen's Majesty came from Highgate.†

"It is certain, however, that James I., the year after his accession, visited the Cornwallises here. On May 1, 1604, the house was the scene of a splendid royal feast. Ben Jonson was employed to compose his dramatic interlude of *The Penates* for a private entertainment of the king and queen, given on Monday morning by Sir William Cornwallis, at his house at Highgate; and Sir Basil Brooke, of Madeley, in Shropshire, was knighted there at the same time. At the end of the same year, Sir Thomas Cornwallis died at his house at Brome—namely, on the 24th of December—aged eighty-five; and a writer in the *Gentleman's Magazine* for 1828 says that 'it is most probable that Sir William then removed to reside in the Suffolk mansion, as we hear no more of his family in Highgate. This residence, it is clear, from what has been already stated, had been the principal mansion in the place; and as we find the Earl of Arundel occupying a house of a similar description a few years later, whilst we have no information of his having erected one for himself, there appears reason to presume that it was the same mansion.'"

Arundel House numbers amongst its historical

* See Vol. IV., p. 560.

† Nichols's "Progresses of Queen Elizabeth," vol. iii., p. 30.

associations two very different and yet very interesting events: the flight from it of Arabella Stuart, in the reign of James I., and the death of the great Chancellor Bacon in the same reign, about

STAIRCASE OF CROMWELL HOUSE, 1876.

fifteen years afterwards. The story of the early life of Arabella Stuart, and how she was held in dread by King James, is told by Mr. Howitt at some length in his work above mentioned, but it will be sufficient for our purpose to extract that portion of the narrative which has special reference to Arundel House:—

"James might have permitted Lady Arabella to marry, and dismissed his fears; but then, instead of a poor pusillanimous creature, he must have been a magnanimous one. She was dependent on the Crown for fortune, and the pension allowed her was miserably paid. Under these circumstances she met with an admirer of her early youth, William Seymour, second son of Lord Beauchamp, the eldest son of the Earl of Hertford. Their juvenile attachment was renewed, and the news of it flew to James, and greatly alarmed him. Seymour,

VIEW IN HIGHGATE CEMETERY.

on his side, was descended from Henry VII., and there were people who thought his claim better than James's, for Henry VIII. had settled the descent, in case of failure of his own issue, on his youngest sister, Mary, and her line, which was that of the Seymours. James fiercely reprimanded Seymour for presuming to ally himself with royal blood, though Seymour's was as royal as his own, and forbade them, on their allegiance, to contract a marriage without his permission. But Love laughed at James, as it is said to do at locksmiths, and in 1610 it was discovered that they were really married. James committed Seymour to the Tower, and Arabella to the custody of Sir Thomas Parry, in Lambeth; but not thinking her safe there, he determined to send her to Durham, in charge of the bishop of that see. Refusing to comply with this arbitrary and unjustifiable order, she was suddenly seized by officers in her bed, and was carried thus, shrieking and resisting, to the Thames, and rowed some distance up the river. She was then put into a carriage, and conveyed forcibly as far as Barnet. But by this time her agitation of mind had brought on a fever, and a physician called in declared that her life must be sacrificed by any attempt to carry her farther. After some demur, James consented to her being brought back as far as Highgate. The account says that she was conveyed to the house of a Mr. Conyers; tradition asserts this house to be that now called Arundel House. Probably it belonged to a Mr. Conyers before it became the property of the Earl of Arundel, whose it was when Lord Bacon was its guest, fifteen years afterwards. Lady Arabella had leave to stay here a month, and this term was extended to two months, which she made use of to establish a correspondence with her husband in the Tower, and to plan a scheme for their mutual escape. This plan was put into effect on June 3, 1611, the very day that the Bishop of Durham had set out northward to prepare for her reception."

How the Lady Arabella made her way, disguised as a man, down to Gravesend, where she expected to find her husband on board a French vessel, which was in waiting to receive them—how the captain, growing impatient, put to sea before Seymour's arrival; and how the latter engaged a collier, and was conveyed safe to Flanders—are all matters of history. Poor Arabella, as we read, was not so fortunate as her husband; for no sooner had the escape of the two prisoners become known than there was a fearful bustle and alarm at Court. A number of vessels of war dropped hastily down the Thames in pursuit, and another put out of the Downs. The latter intercepted the boat carrying Lady Arabella in the Calais roads, and after a sharp struggle the Frenchman struck, and gave up the fugitive. The poor distracted Arabella was carried back to London and committed to the Tower, exclaiming that she could bear her own fate, could she but be sure of the safety of her husband. Her grief and despair soon deprived her of her senses, and after a captivity of four years she died in the Tower, on September 27, 1615. Seymour, who was permitted to return to England after his wife's death, did not die till 1660, nearly half a century after the above romantic adventure.

Mr. Thorne, in his "Environs of London," states that it was from the house of Mr. Thomas Conyers, at East Barnet, that the Lady Arabella made her escape, and not from Arundel House, as generally stated by biographers and topographers; but the latter tradition is too firmly grounded at Highgate to be lost sight of here.

Of the death of Lord Bacon, which occurred at Arundel House in April, 1626, the following particulars are given by John Aubrey:—"The cause of his lordship's death," he writes, "was trying an experiment, as he was takeing the aire in the coach with Dr. Witherborne, a Scotch man, physitian to the king. Towards Highgate snow lay on the ground, and it came into my lord's thoughts why flesh might not be preserved in snow as in salt. They were resolved they would try the experiment. Presently they alighted out of the coach, and went into a poore woman's house at the bottome of Highgate Hill, and bought a hen, and made the woman exenterate it [take out the entrails], and then stuffed the bodie with snow, and my lord did help to doe it himself. The snow so chilled him that he immediately fell so ill, that he could not return to his lodgings (I suppose then at Gray's Inn), but went to the Earl of Arundel's house, at Highgate, where they put him into a good bed, warmed with a panne, but it was a dampe bed, that had not been layn in for about a yeare before, which gave him such a colde, that in two or three dayes, as I remember, he (Hobbes) told me he died of suffocation."

Bacon was attended in his last illness by his near relative, Sir Julius Cæsar, the Master of the Rolls, who was then grown so old that he was said to be "kept alive beyond Nature's course by the prayers of the many poor whom he daily relieved." At the dictation of the great ex-chancellor Sir Julius Cæsar wrote the following letter to Lord Arundel:—

"My very good Lord,—I was likely to have had the fortune of Caius Plinius the elder, who lost his life by trying an experiment about the burning of the mountain Vesuvius. For I also was desirous to try an experiment or two touching the conservation and induration of bodies. For the experiment itself, it succeeded remarkably well; but in the journey between Highgate and London I was taken with a fit of casting, as I know not whether it was the stone, or some surfeit, or cold, or, indeed, a touch of them all three. But when I came to your lordship's house, I was not able to go back, and therefore was forced to take up my lodging here, where your housekeeper is very careful and diligent about me, which I assure myself your lordship will not only pardon towards him, but think the better of him for it. For, indeed, your lordship's house was happy to me; and I kiss your noble hands for the welcome which I am sure you give me to it."

This letter shows that at the moment when he dictated it Bacon did not suppose himself to be on his death-bed; but he must have died in the arms of his friend, Sir Julius Cæsar, very shortly after the epistle was penned.

Arundel House was originally a mansion in the Elizabethan style, with spacious windows commanding a magnificent view of the surrounding country. It was partially pulled down in the year 1825, but the present building still bears the name, and the walls which are left standing of the old house bear evidences of great antiquity.

On the opposite side of the roadway, and adjoining the remains of Andrew Marvell's cottage, is Fairseat, the residence of Sir Sydney Waterlow, Treasurer of St. Bartholomew's Hospital, whose gift of Lauderdale House to that institution we have mentioned above. Sir Sydney Waterlow was Lord Mayor of London in 1872–3; he was representative of the county of Dumfries in the House of Commons, in 1868–9; and in 1874 he was returned as one of the members for the borough of Maidstone. His mansion here was named after that of his late father-in-law, Mr. William Hickson, of Fairseat, Wrotham, Kent.

At the back of Sir Sydney Waterlow's house, and covering a greater part of the slope of the hill looking towards Kentish Town, is Highgate Cemetery, of which we shall give a description in the following chapter.

We find but very scanty mention of this neighbourhood (and, indeed, of all the northern suburbs) in the Diaries of Pepys and Evelyn. The former, however, incidentally states, under date January, 1660–1, that Highgate was for two or three days the head-quarters of sundry "fanatiques at least 500 strong," who raised the standard of rebellion, avowing a belief that "the Lord Jesus would come here and reign presently." They appear to have routed the king's life-guards and train-bands, and to have killed twenty persons, before they were captured and their outbreak suppressed. Again, Pepys mentions the fact that on the 4th of August, 1664, he and a friend went to see a play at "the King's House," one of the best actors of which, named Clun, had been waylaid, and killed in a ditch by the roadside between Kentish Town and Highgate. The following day the little secretary and his cousin Joyce, mounted upon two horses which had been lent them for this purpose by Sir W. Warren, rode out of town towards Highgate, to inspect the scene of the murder.

CHAPTER XXXI.

HIGHGATE (*continued*).

"They bury their dead in the fairest suburb of the city."

Swaine's Lane—Traitors' Hill, or Parliament Hill—St. Anne's Church, Brookfield—Dr. Coysh—Highgate Cemetery—Arrangement of the Grounds—The Catacombs—A Stroll among the Tombs—Eminent Persons buried here—Stray Notes on Cemeteries—Sir William Ashurst's Mansion—Charles Mathews, the Actor—Anecdotes of Mathews—Ivy Cottage—Holly Lodge, the Residence of Lady Burdett-Coutts—Holly Village—Highgate Ponds—The "Fox and Crown" Public house—West Hill Lodge—The Hermitage.

LEAVING the main street of Highgate by Dartmouth Park Road, of which we have made mention in the preceding chapter, and passing in a south-west direction, we find ourselves at the entrance of a narrow thoroughfare called Swaine's Lane (formerly Swine's Lane), which branches off from the Highgate Road just on the outskirts of Kentish Town. This lane runs along the base of that part of Highgate which was formerly known by the name of Traitors' Hill, from being the rendezvous, real or reputed, of the associates of Guy Fawkes. It is traditionally stated that it was upon this spot that the conspirators anxiously awaited the expected explosion on the 5th of November, 1605. It was called also Parliament Hill. "The more common tradition," says Mr. Thorne, "is that it was called Parliament Hill, from the Parliamentary generals having planted cannon on it for the defence of London." To the left of Swaine's Lane stands St. Anne's Church, Brookfield, a large and handsome edifice erected by a Miss Barnett to the memory of her brother. The fine peal of bells in the tower was the gift of Miss (since Lady) Burdett-Coutts. In Swaine's Lane lived the celebrated medical practitioner, Dr. Coysh, as is certified by the following memorandum from the Court Rolls of the Manor of Cantelowes:—"These very ancient copyhold premises were formerly in the possession and occupation of Dr. Elisha Coysh, who, at the time that the plague of London prevailed, in the year 1665–6, was very famed in his medical practice and advice in cases of that dreadful malady, and was much resorted to at this his copyhold residence (modernly called Swaine's Lane) formerly called Swine's Lane, Highgate." The house in which he resided has long since been pulled down, but a portion of the ancient garden wall is standing.

Passing up Swaine's Lane, we soon arrive at the entrance to Highgate Cemetery. This is a showy composition, in the pointed or Old English style; for the most part machicolated, and flanked with turrets and octagonal buttresses, pierced with windows or panelled, the former capped with cupolas and finials, and the latter surmounted with pinnacles and finials. In the centre is a Tudor-arched gateway, above which is an apartment, lighted at each end by a bay window; the roof terminating with two bold pointed gables, bearing in its centre an octangular bell-tower of two storeys, enriched with pinnacles, and surmounted with a cupola and finial. The right wing contains the lodge and clerk's office; and the left wing is appropriated as a chapel, the windows being filled with stained glass. The cemetery covered originally about twenty acres of ground on the southern slope of the hill, between the east and west bays; but a further extension has since been made, as we shall presently show. This cemetery possesses many natural beauties which are not enjoyed by any other rival of Père la Chaise in or out of London. The beauty of the situation would naturally lead to the supposition that it had been previously a park or garden of some nobleman; and such, indeed, we find to be the case, for in Mr. Prickett's "History of Highgate" it is stated that it comprises part of the grounds belonging to the mansion of Sir William Ashurst. The irregularity of the ground, here rising into a terrace, and there sinking into a valley, together with its many winding paths and its avenues of dark shrubs and evergreen trees, combine to impart to this hallowed spot a particularly charming effect.

The ground is the property of the London Cemetery Company, which was incorporated by Act of Parliament in 1839; and the cemetery itself was one of the first which was actually established by the Burial Act of 1835, which "rung the death-knell of intramural interments." The London Cemetery Company were among the early promoters of that reform which, as we have stated in our account of Kensal Green Cemetery,* was so long needed. It was founded by Mr. Stephen Geary, who also acted as architect to the Company, and who was buried here in 1854.

By the artist-like arrangement of the landscape gardener, Mr. Ramsey, the grounds are so disposed that they have the appearance of being twice their actual size; this effect is produced by circuitous roads, winding about the acclivity, and making the ascent more gradual. Besides the carriage road, the footpaths in all directions encircle the numerous plantations and flower-beds. On the left of the entrance is the chapel, a spacious and lofty building, well adapted and fitted up for its solemn purpose. The absence of all unnecessary ornament produces an effect of appropriate simplicity. A bier stands at the western end, which can be lowered through an aperture in the floor by hydraulic pressure. The object of this bier is to convey the coffin to a subterranean passage below, at the termination of the service in the chapel, so as to facilitate its conveyance to the new ground on the opposite side of the lane; for it may be here stated that the original ground being now fully occupied, an addition to the cemetery has been made, and this too is now being rapidly filled up. On leaving the chapel we pass by the lodge of the superintendent, and ascend a flight of broad stone steps which lead up towards the higher and more distant parts of the grounds. About half way up the hill, the roads gradually descend again to the entrance of a tunnel or passage, called the Egyptian Avenue. The angular aperture at the entrance of this avenue, with its heavy cornice, is embellished with the winged serpent and other Oriental ornaments; the Egyptian pillars and the well-proportioned obelisks that rise gracefully on each side of the entrance recall to the imagination the sepulchral temples at Thebes described by Belzoni. The group around this entrance is one of the most artistic points in the cemetery. The solemn grandeur of this portion of the cemetery is much heightened by the gloomy appearance of the avenue, which is one hundred feet long; but, as the road leading through it is a gentle ascent, the perspective effect makes it appear a much greater length. There are numerous square apartments, lined with stone, on each side

* See *ante*, p. 220.

of the avenue; these sepulchres are furnished with stone shelves, rising one above the other on three sides of the sepulchre, capable of containing twelve coffins, in addition to those which could be placed upon the floor. The doors of the sepulchres are of cast iron; they are ornamented with a funeral device of an inverted torch. At the termination of the avenue is a circular road five hundred feet in circumference; on each side of the road are sepulchres similar to those already described; the inner circle forms a large building, flat at the top, which is planted with flowers and shrubs; from the midst rises the magnificent cedar of Lebanon. The avenue, the sepulchres in the circles, with the elegant flights of steps leading to the upper ground of the cemetery, form a mass of building in the Egyptian style of architecture that, for extent and grandeur, is perhaps unequalled.

The lower parts of the grounds are striking, from their beauty of situation and tasteful arrangement; but the view of the upper plantations, on ascending from the sepulchre, is still more so. Here we have an architectural display of another character: a long range of catacombs, entered by Gothic doorways, and ornamented with buttresses, the whole surmounted with an elegant pierced parapet. Above the catacombs is a noble terrace, which communicates with the centre ground by an inclined plane and a flight of steps. The view from this terrace on a clear day is extensive and beautiful: the foreground is formed by the cemetery gardens, and the pleasure grounds of the suburban villas, beyond which are seen the spires, domes, and towers of the great metropolis, backed by the graceful sweep of the Surrey hills.

The Gothic Church of St. Michael at the summit of the hill, with its lofty spire rising from amid the surrounding trees, forms a prominent and interesting feature in the background as the cemetery is viewed from Swaine's Lane. On the upper terrace abovementioned is the long range of Gothic catacombs, immediately beneath this church, presenting one of the most ingenious points of design in the architectural arrangement of the cemetery, of which the church appears to be an integral part, though such is not the case. We may here remark, *en passant*, that catacombs are found in most parts of the world. The catacombs of Rome, at a short distance from the city, are very extensive, and have evidently been used as burying places and as places of worship. The catacombs of Naples are cut under the hill called Corpo di Monte; the entrance into them is rendered horrible by a vast heap of skulls and bones, the remains of the victims of a plague which desolated Naples in the sixteenth century. At Palermo and at Syracuse there are similar recesses. In the island of Malta catacombs are found at Città Vecchia cut into the rock in which that old town stands. They occur again in the Greek islands of the Archipelago. At Milo there is a mountain completely honeycombed with them. In Egypt they occur in all parts of the country where there is rock; and in Peru, and in some other parts of South America, catacombs have been discovered.

"Many names familiar to London ears," writes the author of "Northern Heights," "present themselves on the tombs as you wander through this city of decomposition; and some of considerable distinction. The French have found their Montmartre or Père la Chaise; Germans, their Friedhof; and natives of countries still more distant lie scattered here and there. Perhaps no tomb has ever, as already stated, attracted so many thousand visitors as that of Tom Sayers, bearing on it his own portrait and that of his dog.* Wombwell, with his lion standing over him, as if to say, 'Well, he kept me cramped up for many years in his vans, but I have got him safe under my paw at last,' was, in its newness, a thing of much note; but it never had a charm for the pugnacious populace of London like the tomb of the great boxer."

It would be impossible, and indeed superfluous, to give here anything like a complete list of the various personages who have been buried in this cemetery; but a few of the most important may be mentioned.

Here reposes Michael Faraday, the celebrated chemist and philosopher,† already mentioned by us in our account of the Royal Institution, and of North Marylebone. He died in August, 1857, and, being a Sandemanian of the mystic school, he was laid in his grave without any service, not even a prayer or a hymn. H. Crabb Robinson, the friend of Coleridge, Goethe, Wordsworth, Lamb, Flaxman, and Clarkson, and the author of a most interesting Diary, who died in February, 1867, aged ninety-one, was here interred. Here, too, lie Mr. and Mrs. John Dickens, the father and mother of Charles Dickens, together with the latter's little daughter Dora. Sir John Gurney, a Baron of the Court of Exchequer, was buried here in 1845. Sir Thomas Joshua Platt, also a Baron of the same Court, who died in 1862, lies here; here too repose the remains of Judge Payne, and those of John Singleton Copley, Lord Lyndhurst, thrice Lord Chancellor of Great Britain, who was buried here in 1863.‡ Admiral Lord Radstock was interred here in 1857.

Of the artists buried in Highgate Cemetery, we

* See *ante*, p. 370. † See Vol. IV, p. 297, and *ante*, p. 260. ‡ See Vol. IV., p. 322.

may mention Charles Turner, A.R.A., who died in 1857; Alfred Edward Chalon, who died in 1860, brother of the more celebrated John James Chalon, who also was buried here in 1854. He was a native of Geneva, and achieved his greatest reputation as a portrait painter in water colours, and that mostly by his sketches of courtly and well-born ladies. Charles Joseph Hullmandel, the lithographic artist, was interred here in 1850. Sir William Ross, whom Sir Thomas Lawrence declared to be the first miniature painter of his day, and who died at an advanced age in 1860, lies buried here. Near to the upper entrance gate lie the remains of Mrs. Bartholomew, an artist of some note, the wife of Mr. Valentine Bartholomew, the celebrated flower painter, who also rests here. Two other Royal Academicians, Abraham Cooper and George Jones, lie buried here; the former died in 1868, and the latter in the following year.

Among persons of literary note whose remains are interred here we may notice Mr. Alaric A. Watts, editor of the "Literary Souvenir;" Pierce Egan, author of "Life in London," "Boxiana," "Life of an Actor," &c., the veteran historian of the ring, and sporting journalist; Mr. Samuel Lucas, managing proprietor of the *Morning Star;* Mr. W. J. Pinks, the Clerkenwell antiquary; Mr. James Kennedy, M.R.C.S., author of a "History of the Cholera," &c.; Mr. Joseph Guy, author of "Guy's Geography;" "George Eliot," the novelist; and Mr. George B. Sowerby, the naturalist, author of "The Genera of Recent and Fossil Shells." Here, too, is buried the Rev. Frederick Maurice, the Founder and Principal of the Working Men's College in Great Ormond Street, of which we have spoken in a previous volume;* and also the Rev. Dr. Hamilton, a well-known author, and the successor of the great Edward Irving.

CROMWELL HOUSE, HIGHGATE. (*See page* 400.)

Of the miscellaneous interments we may mention those of Mr. John Vandenhoff, the actor; Lillywhite, the well-known cricketer, whose marble monument, erected by the members of the Marylebone Cricket Club, is carved with a wicket struck by a ball, representing the great cricketer as "bowled out;" of Colonel Stodare, the famous conjuror; and Atcheler, the horse-slaughterer, or knacker, to the Queen, whose tomb is marked by a rudely-carved horse, to show, it may be supposed, his fondness for his profession.

* See Vol. IV., p. 560.

As an appendage to an account of Highgate Cemetery, which appeared in the *Mirror*, shortly after these grounds were laid out, the writer thus observes :—"The most ancient cemetery we are acquainted with, and perhaps the largest in the large enclosure, having three hundred and sixty-five openings or sepulchres, answering to the days of the year, symmetrically arranged. The *campo-santo* or cemetery of Pisa is on every account worthy of attention. As a work of art, it is one of the first in which the classical style of architecture began to be revived in modern Europe. It was constructed by John of Pisa, being projected by Ubaldo, archbishop of Pisa, in 1200. The length of this cemetery is about 490 feet, its width 170, height 60, and its form rectangular. It contains fifty ships' freights of earth from

IVY COTTAGE, HIGHGATE, 1825. (*See page* 411.)

world, is that of Memphis; and of all the ancient burial places, no one conforms so nearly to modern ideas of cemeteries as that of Arles. In the early ages of Christianity the cemeteries were established without the cities, and upon the high roads, and dead bodies were prohibited from being brought into the churches; but this was afterwards abrogated by the Emperor Leo. The early Christians celebrated their religious rites in the cemeteries, upon the tombs of their martyrs. It was also in cemeteries that they built the first churches, of which the subterranean parts were catacombs. Naples and Pisa have cemeteries, which may be regarded as models, not only for good order and conveniency, but for the cultivation of the arts and the interest of humanity. That in Naples is composed of a

Jerusalem, brought hither in 1288. The whole of the edifice is constructed of white marble. The galleries are ornamented with various specimens of early painting. Fine antique sarcophagi ornament the whole circumference, raised upon consoles, and placed upon a surbase, breast high. The Turks plant odoriferous shrubs in their cemeteries, which spread a salubrious fragrance, and purify the air. This custom is practised also in the Middlebourg and Society Islands."

Cemeteries, or public burial-grounds planted and laid out as gardens, around the metropolis, are a novelty of our time, although they were suggested just after the Great Fire in 1666, when Evelyn regretted that advantage had not been taken of that calamity to rid the city of its old burial places, and establish a necropolis without the walls. He deplores that "the churchyards had not been banished to the north walls of the city, where a grated inclosure, of competent breadth, for a mile in length, might have served for a universal cemetery to all the parishes, distinguished by the like separations, and with ample walks of trees; the walks adorned with monuments, inscriptions, and titles, apt for contemplation and memory of the defunct, and that wise and excellent law of the Twelve Tables restored and renewed."

As we have intimated above, Highgate was once important enough to possess a "Mansion House," the grounds of which now serve as a part of the cemetery. The house itself stood at the top of the hill, as nearly as possible on the site now occupied by St. Michael's Church. The mansion was built by Sir William Ashurst, Lord Mayor of London in 1694, and, as may be imagined from its situation, commanded a most delightful prospect over the county for many miles on the one side, and an extensive view of the metropolis on the other. The chestnut staircase is said to have been executed from a design by Inigo Jones; some of the rooms were hung with tapestry, and the chief doorway was richly carved. The extensive pleasure grounds are said to have been laid out with considerable taste. The house was for some years occupied by Sir Alan Chambre, one of the Justices of the Common Pleas, and he was almost the last person who used it as a private residence. It was taken down in 1830. The stone doorway, with the coat of arms, has been placed as an entry to a house in the High Street; and some other armorial bearings, carved in wood, which once adorned the mansion, found a depository in the house of a local antiquary.

In Millfield Lane, in the hamlet of Brookfield, not far west from the spot where now stands St. Anne's Church, was the suburban retreat of Charles Mathews, the comedian, to which we have briefly referred in our notice of Kentish Town.* This celebrated humourist was the son of a well-known theological bookseller in the Strand, and was born in 1776. He used to relate, in his own amusing way, that he had ascertained from his nurse that he was "a long, lanky, scraggy child, very good tempered, with a face that could by no means be called regular in features; in fact," she said, she "used to laugh frequently at the oddity of his countenance." He received his education at Merchant Taylor's School, where the peculiar manners of three brothers, schoolfellows, incited his first attempts at mimicry, and which he afterwards embodied in one of his "entertainments." He could just remember Macklin, the centenarian actor, on whom he called when quite a young man, in order to ask his advice as to going on the stage. The old man, though he had then seen his hundredth birthday, frightened him so much that he was glad to beat a retreat.

In 1803 Mathews first appeared on the London stage in Cumberland's *Jew*. From this time the fame of the comedian was fully established; "never had broad humour been better represented." In 1818 he first resolved on giving an "entertainment" by himself, and in that year first announced himself "At Home" at the English Opera House. His success was signal, and such as to induce the managers of Old Drury and Covent Garden to attempt to interdict the performances; but in this they failed.

His "At Home," as we learn from Crabb Robinson's "Diary," was very popular in 1822, when he represented Curran, Wilkes, and other statesmen of the reign of George III. His imitation of Lord Ellenborough, indeed, is stated to have been so remarkable, that he was rebuked for the perfection with which he practised his art. In 1819 and three following years he resumed these profitable labours in the "Trip to Paris," "Country Cousins," &c. These "entertainments" have been given in almost every theatre in the United Kingdom. His last appearance in the regular drama was in *Hamlet*, when Mr. Young took leave of the stage, in 1832.

Charles Mathews' sense of humour, however, was so strong, that he was unable to restrain himself at any time from comic speeches. It is said that his residence at the foot of Highgate Hill was so situated that the wind when high blew with great violence on the house, and at times very much alarmed Mrs. Mathews. "One night, after they had retired to rest," as the story is told by Mr. Palmer, in his "History of St. Pancras," "Mrs. Mathews was awakened by one of these sudden gales, which she bore for some time in silence; at last, dreadfully frightened, she awoke her husband, saying, 'Don't you hear the wind, Charley? Oh, dear, what shall I do?' 'Do?' said the only partially-awakened humourist; 'open the window, and give it a peppermint lozenge; that is the best thing for the wind.' At another time, and when on his death-bed, his attendant gave him in

* See *ante*, p. 321.

mistake, instead of his medicine, some ink from a phial which stood in its place. On discovering his error he exclaimed, 'Good heavens, Mathews, I have given you ink!' 'Never, ne-ver mind, my boy, ne-ver mind,' said the mimic, 'I'll—I'll swallow——bit—bit—of blotting-paper.' Fun was in him by nature, and to the last he could not be serious."

Charles Mathews has been styled "the Hogarth of the English stage." His pleasant thatched cottage here, which looked down on Kentish Town, and commanded a distant view of London, was, as he was wont to say, his "Tusculum." It rose, not unlike a country vicarage, in the midst of green lawns and flower-beds, and was adorned externally with trellis-work fancifully wreathed and overgrown with jasmine and honeysuckles. In the interior of this retired homestead was collected a more interesting museum of dramatic curiosities than ever was gathered together by the industry of one man. Here he would show to his friends, with pride and pleasure, relics of Garrick—a lock of his hair, the garter worn by him in *Richard III.;* and also his collection of theatrical engravings, autographs, and portraits now in the Garrick Club.*

> "A merrier man,
> Within the limit of becoming mirth,
> I never spent an hour's talk withal.
> His eye begat occasion for his wit,
> For every object that the one did catch
> The other turned to a mirth-moving jest."

Charles Mathews, whose wit and versatility were proverbial, died at Devonport, June 27th, 1835, immediately after his return from America. Mrs. Charles Mathews wrote her husband's memoirs after his decease.

A view of Ivy Cottage, as the residence of Charles Mathews was called, is given by Mr. Smith, in his "Historical and Literary Curiosities." With it is a ground-plan, showing the apartments devoted to his theatrical picture-gallery, and the arrangement of his portraits, now in the possession of the Garrick Club. Among the treasures of the house also was the casket made out of Shakespeare's mulberry-tree at Stratford-on-Avon, in which the freedom of that town was presented to Garrick, on the occasion of his jubilee, in 1769. A sketch of this is also given in the same volume.

Holly Lodge, the residence of Lady Burdett-Coutts, stands in its own extensive grounds on Highgate Rise, overlooking Brookfield Church, Millfield Lane, and the famous Highgate Ponds, which lie at the foot of the south-western slope of the hill. The house—formerly called Hollybush Lodge—was purchased by Mr. Thomas Coutts, the well-known banker, of whom we have spoken in our account of Piccadilly,† and it was bequeathed by him, with his immense property, to his widow, who afterwards married the Duke of St. Albans. On her decease, in 1837, it was left, with the great bulk of her fortune, amounting to nearly £2,000,000, to Miss Angela Burdett, a daughter of Sir Francis Burdett, the popular M.P. for Westminster, who thereupon assumed the additional name of Coutts. As we have intimated in the chapter above referred to, the extensive power of benefiting society and her fellow-creatures, which devolved upon her with this bequest, was not lost sight of by its possessor, and her charities are known to have been most extensive. Amongst the chief of these have been the endowment of a bishopric at Adelaide, in South Australia, and another at Victoria, in British Columbia; also the foundation and endowment of a handsome church and schools in Westminster in 1847, and the erection of a church at Carlisle in 1864. Besides the above, she has been also a large contributor to a variety of religious and charitable institutions in London—churches, schools, reformatories, penitentiaries, drinking-fountains, Columbia Market, model lodging-houses, &c. Miss Burdett-Coutts also exercised her pen, as well as her purse, in mitigating and relieving dumb animals and the feathered tribe from the suffering to which they are often subjected, having written largely against cruelty to dumb creatures. In recognition of her large-heartedness she was, in the year 1871, raised to the peerage as Baroness Burdett-Coutts.

Holly Village, of which we have already spoken, stands on the southern side of the pleasure-grounds of Holly Lodge. It was built about the year 1845 by Lady Burdett-Coutts, as homes for families of the upper middle class. They comprise a group of about ten cottages, erected to add picturesque and ornamental features to the surroundings of Holly Lodge, and are surrounded by trim and well-kept gardens. They were also intended, in the first instance, to provide cottage accommodation of a superior description for the workpeople on the estate; this idea, however, was abandoned, and the houses are now occupied by a higher class in the social scale. The whole village has been erected with an amount of care and finish such as is seldom bestowed on work of this description, or even work of a much more pretentious kind. Some of the houses are single, and some comprise

* See Vol. III., p. 263.

† See Vol. IV., p. 280.

two dwellings. They are built of yellow, white, and moulded brick, some with stone dressings. Although bearing a general resemblance, and in one or two instances arranged as corresponding pairs, they all differ more or less in form, and considerably in the details. All of them have a quiet elegance that is very uncommon in buildings of their class. The entrance is rather elaborately adorned with two carved statues of females, holding a lamb and a dove; and there is some pretty carving elsewhere. Mr. Darbishire was the architect of this model village.

The ponds mentioned above are on the estate of the Earl of Mansfield, and lie below Caen Wood, in the fields leading from Highgate Road to Hampstead, between Charles Mathews' house and Traitors' Hill. In the summer season they are the resort of thousands of Londoners, whilst the boys fish in them for tadpoles and sticklebats, or sail miniature boats on their surface. The ponds are very deep, and many a poor fellow has been drowned in them, some by accident, and more, it is to be feared, by suicide. About the year 1869 these ponds were leased to the Hampstead Waterworks Company, which has since become incorporated with the New River Company. These ponds, for a long time, supplied a considerable portion of the parish with water.

Nearly on the brow of the West Hill, a little above the house and grounds of Lady Burdett-Coutts, as we ascend towards the Grove and the town, we notice a roadside inn, of a retired and sequestered aspect, rejoicing in the name of the "Fox and Crown." It bears, however, on its front the royal arms, conspicuously painted, with a notice to the effect that "this coat of arms is a grant from Queen Victoria, for services rendered to Her Majesty when in danger travelling down this hill," and dated a few days after her accession. Some accident, it appears, happened to one of the wheels of the royal carriage, and the landlord had the good luck to stop the horses, and send for a wheelwright to set matters straight, accommodating Her Majesty with a seat in his house whilst the repairs were being executed. The event, if it did not turn the head of Boniface, brought him no luck, for he died heart-broken, the only advantage which he reaped from the adventure being, it is said, the right of setting up the lion and unicorn with the crown.

On West Hill, immediately below the "Fox and Crown," stands a rustic house, at right angles to the road, called West Hill Lodge. This was occupied for many years by William and Mary Howitt, who wrote here many of the books by which their names will be hereafter remembered. Of these we may mention "The Ruined Castles and Abbeys of Great Britain and Ireland," the "Illustrated History of England," "History of the Supernatural in all Ages and Nations," "Visits to Remarkable Places, Old Halls, and Battle Fields;" and last, not least, the "Northern Heights of London." Another residence on West Hill, a little above the entrance to Millfield Lane, was called the Hermitage, of which the Howitts were the last occupants. It stood enclosed by tall trees, and adjoining it was a still smaller tenement, which was said to be the "real and original Hermitage." It is thus described by Mr. Howitt:—"It consisted only of one small low room, with a chamber over it, reached by an outside rustic gallery. The whole of this hermitage was covered with ivy, evidently of a very ancient growth, as shown by the largeness of its stems and boughs, and the prodigality of its foliage. In fact, it looked like one great mass of ivy. What was the origin of the place, or why it acquired the name of the Hermitage, does not appear; but being its last tenant, I found that its succession of inhabitants had been a numerous one, and that it was connected with some curious histories. Some dark tragedies had occurred there. One of its tenants was a Sir Wallis Porter, who was an associate of the Prince Regent. Here the Prince used to come frequently to gamble with Sir Wallis. This hermitage, hidden by the tall surrounding trees, chiefly umbrageous elms, and by the huge ivy growth, seemed a place well concealed for the orgies carried on within it. The ceiling of the room which they used was painted with naked figures in the French style, and there they could both play as deeply and carouse as jovially as they pleased. But the end of Sir Wallis was that of many another gamester and wassailer. Probably his princely companion, and *his* companions, both drained the purse as well as the cellar of Sir Wallis, for he put an end to his existence there, as reported, by shooting himself.

"There was a pleasanter legend of Lord Nelson, when a boy, being once there, and climbing a very tall ash-tree by the roadside, which therefore went by the name of 'Nelson's tree,' till it went the way of all trees—to the timber-yard. It was reported, too, that Fauntleroy, the forger, when the officers of justice were in quest of him, concealed himself for a time at this hermitage." The old Hermitage, however, with its quaint buildings, its secluded lawn, and its towering trees, disappeared about the year 1860, and on its site a terrace of houses has been erected

CHAPTER XXXII.

HIGHGATE (*continued*).

"—— Many to the steep of Highgate hie;
Ask, ye Bœotian shades! the reason why?
'Tis to the worship of the solemn Horn,
Grasped in the holy hand of Mystery,
In whose dread name both men and maids are sworn,
And consecrate the oath with draught and dance till morn." —*Byron.*

Charles Knight—Sir John Wollaston—The Custom of "Swearing on the Horns"—Mr. Mark Boyd's Reminiscence of this Curious Ceremonial—A Poetical Version of the Proceedings—Old Taverns at Highgate—The "Angel Inn"—The Sunday Ordinary—A Touching Story—The Chapel and School of Highgate—Tomb of Coleridge, the Poet—Sir Roger Cholmeley, the Founder of the Grammar School—Southwood Lane—The Almshouses—Park House—St. Michael's Church—Tablet erected to Coleridge—Fitzroy House—Mrs. Caroline Chisholm—Dr. Sacheverel—Dorchester House—Coleridge's Residence—The Grove—Anecdote of Hogarth—Sir John Hawkins' House—A Proclamation in the Time of Henry VIII.—North Hill—The "Bull Inn."

RETURNING once more to the main street of the village—"this romantic rather than picturesque village," as Crabb Robinson calls it in his "Diary"—we resume our perambulation, starting from Arundel House, of which we have given an account in an earlier chapter.*

A small house close by the site of Arundel House was for many years the residence of Mr. Charles Knight, whose name is well known in connection with popular literature.

A little to the north of this house, but standing back from the high road, was the mansion of Sir John Wollaston, the founder of some almshouses in Southwood Lane, which we shall presently notice. Sir John Wollaston, we may here remark, was at one time Lord Mayor of London, and held several appointments of trust in the City. He died in the year 1658, and was buried in the old chapel of Highgate.

The main street of the village, although so near to London, has about it that appearance of quietude and sleepiness which one is accustomed to meet with in villages miles away from the busy metropolis; and like most other villages, the number of its public-houses, as compared with other places of business, is somewhat remarkable. In 1826 there were, in Highgate, no less than nineteen licensed taverns, of which Hone, in his "Every-day Book," gives the signs. In former times a curious old custom prevailed at these public-houses, which has been the means of giving a little gentle merriment to many generations of the citizens of London, but is now only remembered as a thing of the past. It was a sort of burlesque performance, presided over by "mine host," in which the visitor, whoever he might be, was expected to take an oath, which was duly administered to him, and was familiarly called "swearing on the horns." "No one," writes Mr. Samuel Palmer, "ever hears of this hamlet without at once referring to it:—

'It's a custom at Highgate, that all who go through,
Must be sworn on the horns, sir; and so, sir, must you.
Bring the horns, shut the door; now, sir, take off your hat,
When you come here again, don't forget to mind *that*.'

A few years ago it was usual all over the kingdom to ask, 'Have you been sworn at Highgate?' And if any person in conversation laid an emphasis more than usual on the demonstrative pronoun *that*, it was sure to elicit the inquiry. Some sixty years ago upwards of eighty stage-coaches would stop every day at the 'Red Lion' inn, and out of every five passengers three were sworn. So soon as the coach drew up at the inn-door most pressing invitations would be given to the company to alight, and after as many as possible could be collected in the parlour, the landlord would introduce the Highgate oath. A little artifice easily led to the detection of the uninitiated, and as soon as the fact was ascertained the horns were brought in. There were generally sufficient of the initiated to induce compliance with those who had not yet passed through the ordeal. The horns were fixed on a pole five feet in height, and placed upright on the ground before the person who was to be sworn. The neophyte was then required to take off his hat, which all present having also done, the landlord, in a bold voice, began the ceremony. It commenced by the landlord saying—

'Upstanding and uncovered: silence. Take notice what I now say to you, for *that* is the first word of the oath; mind *that!* You must acknowledge me to be your adopted father, I must acknowledge you to be my adopted son. If you do not call me father, you forfeit a bottle of wine; if I do not call you son, I forfeit the same. And now, my good son, if you are travelling through this village of Highgate, and you have no money in your pocket, go call for a bottle of wine at any house you may think proper to enter, and book it to your father's score. If you have any friends with you, you may treat them as well; but if you have money of your own, you must pay for it yourself; for you must not say you

* See *ante*, p. 501.

have no money when you have; neither must you convey your money out of your own pocket into that of your friend's pocket, for I shall search them as well as you, and if I find that you or they have any money, you forfeit a bottle of wine for trying to cheat and cozen your old father. You must not eat brown bread while you can get white, unless you like brown the best; nor must you drink small beer when you can get strong, unless you like small the best; you must not kiss the maid while you can kiss the mistress, unless you like the maid best; but sooner than lose a good chance, you may kiss them both. And now, my good son, I wish you a safe journey through Highgate and this life. I charge you, my good son, that if you know any in this company who have not taken this oath, you must cause them to take it, or make each of them forfeit a bottle of wine; for if you fail to do so, you will forfeit one yourself. So now, my son, God bless you; kiss the horns, or a pretty girl if you see one here, which you like best, and so be free of Highgate.'

If a female were in the room, she was, of course, saluted; if not, the horns were to be kissed, but the option was not allowed formerly. The peculiarity of the oath was in the pronoun *that*, which generally resulted in victimising the strangers of some bottles of wine. So soon as the salutation was over, and the wine drank, the landlord, addressing himself to the newly-made son, said, 'I have now to acquaint you with your privileges as a freeman of Highgate. If at any time you are going through the hamlet, and want to rest yourself, and you see a pig lying in a ditch, you are quite at liberty to kick her out and take her place; but if you see three lying together, you must only kick out the middle one, and lie between the two; so God save the king!'" These last liberties, however, are, according to Mr. Larwood, a later addition to the oath, introduced by a facetious blacksmith, who at one time kept the "Coach and Horses."

THE "OLD CROWN INN," HIGHGATE, IN 1830. (*See page* 418.)

Mr. Mark Boyd describes at length, in his "Social Gleanings," the whole of the process to which it appears that he and his brother were subjected one fine Sunday half a century ago, and to which they submitted with all the less reluctance because they learnt that Lord Bryon and several other distinguished personages had been sworn there before them. He relates the initiatory steps of ordering a bottle of the Boniface's best port, and another of sherry, "which the landlord took care should be excellent in honour of so grave a ceremonial, and for which he did not omit to charge

VIEWS IN HIGHGATE.

accordingly." He goes on to describe how "the landlord and his waiter then retired to prepare for the imposing ceremony, and in ten minutes a thundering knock at the door announced the approach of the officials. In marched, with all solemnity, the swearer-in, dressed in a black gown with bands, and wearing a mask and a wig; his clerk also in a black gown, carrying the horns fixed on a pole in one hand, and in the other a large book, from which the oath was to be read. The landlord then proclaimed, in a loud voice, "Upstanding and uncovered. Take notice what now I say to you, &c.," and so proceeded to administer the oath *verbatim*, as above. "The custom," adds Mr. Boyd, "has now fallen into disuse; but at the 'Gate House Tavern,' some months ago (1875), whilst the waiter was administering to me an excellent luncheon, I mentioned that, were the landlord to revive the custom, many of the present generation would extremely enjoy the fun in which their ancestors had indulged, and none more than our 'American cousins.' 'Moreover,' said I to the waiter, 'where you now make five shillings you would pocket ten; and if your landlord provided as good port and sherry as formerly, he would sell two bottles for one.'" In spite, however, of Mr. Boyd's specious argument, and even the example of Lord Byron, we believe that the landlord has not at present ventured on reviving this absurdity, even in this age of "revivals" of various kinds. In fact, if the truth must be told, he takes no interest in the historic past, and does not care to be questioned about the ceremony.

The following is one version, among several, of an old initiation song which was used on these occasions in one of the Highgate inns, which either "kept a poet," or had a host who was fond of rhyming. We take it from Robert Bell's "Ballads and Songs of the Peasantry of England;" the author states that it was supplied to him by a very old man, who had been an ostler at Highgate. "The old man," adds Mr. Bell, "told him that it was not often used of late years, as 'there was no landlord that could sing, and gentlemen preferred the speech.' He also owned that the lines were not always alike, some saying them one way and some another, some making them long, while others cut them short:"—

Enter Landlord, *dressed in a black gown and bands, and wearing an antique-fashioned wig; followed by the Clerk of the Court, also in appropriate costume, and carrying the register book and the horns.*

Landlord. Do you wish to be sworn at Highgate?
Candidate. I do, father.
Clerk. Amen.

The Landlord then says or sings as follows:

Silence! O yes! you are my son!
Full to your old father turn, sir;
This is an oath you may take as you run,
So lay your hand thus on the horn, sir.

[Here the Candidate places his right hand on the horn.

You shall not spend with cheaters or cozens your life,
Nor waste it on profligate beauty;
And when you are wedded, be kind to your wife,
And true to all petticoat duty.

[The Candidate says "I will," and kisses the horns, in obedience to the Clerk, who exclaims, in a loud and solemn tone, "Kiss the horns, sir."

And while you thus solemnly swear to be kind,
And shield and protect from disaster,
This part of the oath, you must bear it in mind,
That you and not she is the master.

[Clerk: "Kiss the horns again, sir."

You shall pledge no man first when a woman is near,
For 'tis neither proper nor right, sir;
Nor, unless you prefer it, drink small for strong beer,
Nor eat brown bread when you can get white, sir.

[Clerk: "Kiss the horns again, sir."

You shall never drink brandy when wine you can get,
Say when good port or sherry is handy,
Unless that your taste on strong spirit is set,
In which case you may, sir, drink brandy.

[Clerk: "Kiss the horns again, sir."

To kiss the fair maid when the mistress is kind
Remember that you must be loth, sir;
But if the maid's fairest, your oath does not bind,
Or you may, if you like it, kiss both, sir.

[Clerk: "Kiss the horns again, sir."

Should you ever return, take this oath here again,
Like a man of good sense, leal and true, sir;
And be sure to bring with you some more merry men,
That they on the horn may swear too, sir.

Landlord. Now, sir, if you please, sign your name in that book; and if you can't write, then make your mark, and the Clerk of the Court will attest it.

[Here one of the above requests is complied with.

Landlord. You will now please to pay half-a-crown for court fees, and what you please to the Clerk.

The necessary ceremony being thus gone through, the business terminates by the Landlord saying "God bless the King (or Queen) and the Lord of the Manor," to which the Clerk responds, "Amen, amen!" N.B. The court fees are always returned in wine, spirits, or porter, of which the Landlord and the Clerk are invited to partake.

It will now be seen what is the meaning of the old proverb as applied to a knowing fellow:—"He has been sworn at Highgate." The words are applicable to a person who is well acquainted with good things, and who takes care to help himself to the best of all.

Grose speaks of this whimsical ceremony at some length in his "Classical Dictionary of the

Vulgar Tongue," published in 1785, and it is clear from what he says that even in his day the ceremony was very ancient. Hone's "Year Book" contains also a full account of the ceremony, as it was performed in the early part of the present century at the "Fox," or (as it was then styled) "The Fox under the Hill," an inn already mentioned by us. Hone does not throw much light on the origin of the practice, which, doubtless, is as old as the Reformation, and was originally intended as a parody on the admission of neophytes into religious guilds and confraternities by the clergy of the Catholic Church.

Grose, being a shallow antiquary, apparently regarded it as a piece of comparatively modern tomfoolery, got up by some landlord "for the good of the house." A correspondent, however, subsequently points out the antiquity of the custom, and sends a copy of the initiation song, which varies, however, considerably from our version above.

It may be added that Grose was in error on another score, as Mr. Robert Bell observes, when he supposed that the ceremony was confined to the lower orders; for both when he wrote, and in subsequent times, the oath, absurd as it is, has often been taken by persons of rank and education too. An inspection of the register-books, had any still existed, would doubtless have shown that those who have kissed the mystic horn at Highgate have belonged to all ranks of society, and that among them the scholars of Harrow have always been conspicuous—led on, no doubt, like so many sheep, by the example of their bellwether, Lord Byron. When, however, the stage-coaches ceased to pass through Highgate, the custom gradually declined, and appears to have been kept up at only three inns, respectively called "The Original House," the "Old Original House," and the "Real Old Original House." Mr. Bell, writing about the year 1860, says: "Two of the above houses have latterly ceased to hold courts, and the custom is now confined to the 'Fox under the Hill,' where the rite is celebrated with every attention to ancient forms, ceremonies, and costume, and for a fee which, in deference to modern notions of economy, is only one shilling."

The old crier of Highgate is said still to keep a gown and wig ready to swear in any persons who may wish to go through the ceremony; for the swearer-in, whoever he might or may be, generally wore a black gown, mask, and wig, and had with him a person to act as clerk and bearer of the horns.

Of course there was room for a luxuriance of comicality, according to the wit of the imposer of the oath, and the simplicity of the oath-taker; and, as might be expected, the ceremony was not a dry one. Scarcely ever did a stage-coach stop at a Highgate tavern in those days, without a few of the passengers being initiated amidst the laughter of the rest, the landlord usually acting as high priest on the occasion, while a waiter or an ostler would perform the duty of clerk, and sing out "Amen" at all the proper places.

Although some ten or dozen pairs of horns are religiously kept in as many of the chief inns in Highgate, where they pass along with the house in the inventory from one landlord to his successor; yet, singularly enough, none of the register books in which the neophytes were wont to inscribe their names after taking the oath, are now known to exist. Their loss is much to be regretted, as in all probability, as we have above intimated, an inspection of them would have shown that many persons otherwise celebrated for wisdom made fools of themselves at least once in their lives. It appears, however, from an article in the *Penny Magazine*, published in 1832, that even then the ceremony had been abandoned by all respectable members of society.

The origin of this singular custom is variously accounted for. One is that it was devised by a landlord who had lost his licence, and who used it to cover the sale of his liquors. Another, and more probable one, is, that "Highgate being the nearest spot to London where cattle rested on their way from the North to Smithfield for sale, many graziers put up at the 'Gate House' for the night. These men formed a kind of fraternity, and generally endeavoured to secure the inn for their exclusive accommodation on certain days. Finding, however, they had no power to exclude strangers, who, like themselves, were travelling on business, these men formed themselves into a sort of club, and made it imperative on all who wished to join them to take a certain oath, and bringing an ox to the door, compelled them either to kiss its horns, or to quit their company."

The house of greatest dignity and largest accommodation was the "Gate House," so called from the original building having been connected with a gate which here crossed the road, and from which, as we have already stated, the name of the village is understood to have been derived.

The old "Gate House Inn" still stands, though the droll ceremony which we have described has fallen into disuse for more than a quarter of a century. In the hall of the inn, however, are still to be seen a gigantic pair of mounted horns, the same, it is affirmed, which were used in the administration of the Highgate oath.

In Hone's time the principal inn, the "Gate House," had stag-horns, as had also the "Mitre," the "Green Dragon," the "Bell," the "Rose and Crown," the "Bull," the "Wrestlers," the "Lord Nelson," the "Duke of Wellington," the "Crown," and the "Duke's Head." Bullocks' horns were used at the "Red Lion" and "Sun," and rams-horns at the "Coach and Horses," the "Castle," the "Red Lion," the "Coopers' Arms," the "Fox and Hounds," the "Flask," and the "Angel." At each of the above houses the horns were mounted on a stick, to serve in the mock ceremonial when required.

In some cases there was also a pair of mounted horns over the door of the house, as designed to give the chance passengers the assurance that the merry ceremonial was practised there; and Mr. Thorne states that at *one* inn in Highgate the horns are still to be seen on the outside of the house. It is acknowledged that there were great differences in the ceremonial at different houses, some land-lords having much greater command of wit than others.

In the good old days, "when George III. was king," societies and corporations, and groups of workpeople, who were admitting a new member or associate, would come out in a body to High-gate, to have him duly sworn upon the "horns," and to enjoy an afternoon's merrymaking at his expense.

The only historical fact which has been pre-served regarding this singular custom, is that a song embodying the burlesque oath was intro-duced in a pantomime at the Haymarket Theatre in 1742.

If we can put faith in Byron—in the lines quoted as a motto to this chapter—parties of young people, under (it is to be hoped) proper superintendence, would dance away the night after an initiation at the "Horns." It may be added that similar customs prevailed in other places besides High-gate, such as at Ware, at the "Griffin" at Hod-desdon, and other villages.

The "Angel Inn," on the crest of the hill, just opposite the old village forge, is remarkable for its antiquity, dating probably from before the era of the Reformation. It is one of the few hostelries now standing which are built wholly of wood. Doubt-less it was originally the "Salutation" Inn; and when, at the Reformation, the Virgin Mary was struck out of the signboard, the Angel remained, and so became the sign.

Whilst on the subject of taverns and houses of public entertainment, it may not be out of place to speak of the celebrated "Sunday ordinary, at one shilling per head," at one of the Highgate inns, to which in former times the London citizens flocked in great numbers. A curious print, representing some of the characters who frequented this ordi-nary, was published by Harrison and Co., towards the close of the last century. Mr. Palmer, in his "History of St. Pancras," tells the following touching story in connection with this ordinary:—"A constant visitor at this *table d'hôte* was ac-customed to take considerable notice of a very attractive young girl who waited at table, and from passing observations drew her at length to become the partner of his Sunday evening rambles. After some time he made known his passion to the object of his affection, and was accepted. He informed her that his occupation would detain him from her all the week, but that he should dine at home on Sunday, and leave regularly on the Monday morning. He would invest in her own name and for her exclusive use £2,000 in the Three per Cent. Consols on their marriage; but she was not to seek to discover who he was or what he did, for should she once discover it he would never return to her again. Strange as were the terms, she acquiesced, and was married, and everything went on for a long time amicably and comfortably. At length her woman's nature could hold out no longer; she must at all hazards discover her husband's secret. She tried to suppress the desire, for she really loved him; but Eve-like, she could resist no longer; and therefore on his leaving her as usual one Monday morning, she disguised herself as well as she could, and followed him from Highgate to London, when he entered a low coffee-shop, from whence after a while he issued—yes, *her husband*—in the meanest possible dress, and with a broom began to sweep the crossing near Charing Cross. This was more than she could bear; she made herself known, and reviled him for his deceit. After an angry discussion she saw her husband return to the coffee-shop, again dress himself in his gentlemanly attire, and bidding her farewell, depart, no more to return. Grieved and annoyed, she returned to Highgate; his marriage bestowment maintained her in comfort, but it left her solitary and alone."

Close by the old gate, at the summit of the hill, and opposite the tavern now known as the "Gate House," stood, till the year 1833, the chapel and school of Highgate, which dated their origin from the sixteenth century, as the following minute records:—"M^{dum} that the fyrst stone of the Chapell and free Scoole at Higate was leyd the 3rd day of

Julye 1576, and the same Chapell and Scoole was finished in Sept[r] 1578." There had, however, been a chapel on this spot from at least the fourteenth century; for, in the year 1386, Bishop Braybroke gave "to William Lichfield, a poor hermit, oppressed by age and infirmity, the office of keeping our chapel of Highgate, by our park of Haringey, and the house annexed to the said chapel, hitherto accustomed to be kept by other poor hermits." This institution is noticed by Newcourt, in his "Repertorium," but he had met with one other, by which Bishop Stokesley, in 1531, "gave the chapel, then called the chapel of St. Michael, in the parish of Hornesey, to William Forte, with the messuage, garden, and orchard, and their appurtenances, with all tenths, offerings, profits, advantages, and emoluments whatever." "Regarding these hermits," writes Mr. J. Gough Nichols, in the *Gentleman's Magazine*, "we have this further information, or rather tradition, related by the proto-topographer of Middlesex: 'Where now (1596) the Schole standeth was a hermytage, and the hermyte caused to be made the causway* betweene Highgate and Islington, and the gravell was bad from the top of Highgate hill, where is now a standinge ponde of water. There is adjoining unto the schole a chapple for the ease of that part of the countrey, for that they are within the parish of Pancras, which is distant thence neere two miles.'"

Hughson, in his "History of London," tells us that, though the site of the hermitage in ancient times is idealised, little is known about it. Nor is this wonderful, for does not the poet write—

> "Far in a wild, remote from public view,
> From youth to age a reverend hermit grew?"

The chapel itself, for some reason or other, was granted by Bishop Grindal, in 1565, to the newly-founded grammar-school of Sir Roger Cholmeley, together with certain houses, edifices, gardens, and orchards, and also two acres of pasture abutting on the king's highway.

The edifice was a singular, dull, and heavy nondescript sort of building of brick and stone. It consisted of a nave, chancel, two aisles, and galleries, together with a low square embattled tower at the western end, flanked on either side by a porch with a semicircular-headed doorway. Above the lowest window of the tower, between the two doorways, was a stone bearing the following inscription:—

"Sir Roger Cholmeley knt, L[d] chiefe baron of y[e] exchequer, and after that L[d] chiefe justice of the king's bench, did institvte and erect at his own charges this publiqve and free gramer schole; and procvred the same to be established and confirmed by the letters patents of queen Elizabeth, her endowinge the same with yearly maintaynance; which schoole Edwyn Sandys L[d] bishop of London enlarged an[o] D'ni 1565 by the addition of this chapel for divine service and by other endowments of pietie and devotion. Since which the said chappel hath been enlarged by the pietie and bounty of divers hon[ble] and worthy personages. This inscription was renewed anno D'ni 1668 by the governors of the said schoole."

From the above inscription some doubts were raised as to the exact date of the erection of the chapel; and about the year 1822, when the new church was first projected, a warm controversy sprung up respecting it. The main subject of the dispute, however, was the right of property in the chapel, whether it was vested entirely in the governors of the school, or shared by the inhabitants. "The truth appears to have been," writes Mr. Nichols, "that the chapel was actually the property of the charity, as well by grant from the Bishop of London, the ancient patron of the hermitage, as by letters patent from the Crown, and also by transfer from a third party, who had procured a grant of it from the queen as a suppressed religious foundation; that for the first century and a half the inhabitants had been allowed to have seats gratuitously; and that about the year 1723 the pews had been converted into a source of income for the school."

With regard to the association of the name of Bishop Sandys with the date 1565, one error is manifest, for he was not Bishop of London until 1570. Newcourt perceived the incoherency, and in copying the substance of the inscription into his "Repertorium," he altered the year *suo periculo* to 1570. A searching examination which the records of the school have since undergone, has disclosed that the correct date is either 1575 or 1576; for it was in the former year that the rebuilding was projected; and in the latter, when it had not far proceeded, Bishop Sandys was translated to the see of York. The alteration of the date was probably accidentally made when the inscription was re-cut.

One portion of the old chapel had a very extraordinary appearance; for small round windows were placed directly over the round-headed long ones, not unlike the letter *i* and its dot. These round windows originally lighted three rooms belonging to the master's house, which, down to near the close of the last century, stood over the body of the chapel. The edifice had undergone four

* See *ante*, p. 392.

several repairs and enlargements between the years 1616 and 1772, and also, probably, another when the inscription was renewed in 1668. The repairs in 1720 seem to have been important, as they incurred an expense of more than £1,000, of which sum £700 were contributed by Mr. Edward Pauncefort, treasurer to the charity, and the balance by the inhabitants of Highgate. Again, in 1772, the body of the chapel was, in a great measure, rebuilt; and it was then that its ceiling was raised by the removal of the three rooms above mentioned. Within the chapel was a monument to William Platt, Esq. (the founder of some fellowships in St. John's College, Cambridge), who died in 1637; also a monument to the memory of Dr. Lewis Atterbury (brother of the celebrated bishop), who was preacher here. This monument, on the chapel being pulled down for the erection of the present church of St. Michael, was removed to Hornsey Church, of which Dr. Atterbury had been vicar. Sir Francis Pemberton, Chief Justice in the reign of Charles II., who died at his residence in Highgate, was buried in the old chapel; as also was Sir John Wollaston, the founder of the almshouses in Southwood Lane. On the demolition of the chapel, several of the monuments and tablets were removed to the new church. The chapel enjoyed some celebrity and popular favour in the reign of Queen Anne and George I., when it was the only place of worship in a rather extensive neighbourhood, and was consequently a centre of attraction to persons of all classes, who, after service was over, used to promenade the terraced sides of the Green. One of its ministers was the Rev. Henry Felton, D.D., well known as the author of a learned "Dissertation on the Classics," and sometime Principal of St. Edmund's Hall, Oxford.

THE OLD CHAPEL, HIGHGATE, 1830. (*See page* 418.)

Becoming inadequate to the accommodation of the inhabitants of the neighbourhood, and part passing into a state of dilapidation, it was taken down in 1833. The area of the chapel for many years formed the burial-ground for the hamlet; and till 1866 it remained much in its original condition. In it stood, among other tombs, that of Samuel Taylor Coleridge, the poet and philosopher, who during the latter period of his life resided at Highgate, and where he died in 1834. The tomb itself is now to be seen in the resuscitated chapel of the Grammar School.

DORCHESTER HOUSE, 1700. (*See page* 424.)

Sir Roger Cholmeley, the founder of the Grammar School, and the great benefactor of Highgate, was in high favour under Henry VII., who bestowed on him the manor of Hampstead. He held the post of Chief Justice under Mary; but was committed to the Tower for drawing up the will of Edward VI., in which he disinherited his sisters. He spent his declining years in literary retirement at "Hornsey"—probably at no great distance from the school which he had founded—and died in 1565.

We meet with the following description of the school and its situation in Norden's "Speculum Britanniæ:"—"At this place is a free school built of brick, by Sir R. Cholmeley, knight, some time Lord Chief Justice of England, about the year of Christ 1564: the pencion (*sic*) of the master is uncertaine; there is no usher, and the schole is now in the disposition of six governors, or feoffees. Where now the schole standeth was a hermitage, and the hermit made the causeway between Highgate and Islington." From the same authority we learn that Sir Roger Cholmeley "instituted and erected the schole" at his owne charges, obtaining a confirmation by letters patent from Queen Elizabeth, who was always ready to welcome and encourage such improvements, and may be supposed to have taken a personal interest in one which lay so close to her own royal chase and hunting ground. It appears, from Norden, that the chapel was added in order to enlarge the school; but how this addition was calculated to effect such an end does not appear, unless the pew-rents or endowment of the chaplain were added to the salary of the schoolmaster, and this, as we have shown above, really seems to have been the case.

It is perhaps worthy of note that Mr. Carter, who was master of the school during the civil wars, was ejected and treated with great cruelty by the

Puritans. Walker, in his "Sufferings of the Clergy," says that he was "turned out of the house with his family whilst his wife was in labour, and that she was delivered in the church porch." Another fact to be recorded is that Master Nicholas Rowe, the poet and Shakespearian commentator, was a scholar here.

It would appear from the "Account of Public Charities," published in 1828, that the forty boys in the school were then taught no classics, and that, although the "reader" of the chapel was charged with their education, the latter performed his duty by deputy, and that his deputy was the sexton! It is somewhat sarcastically added by the compilers of the "Account," that "this forms the only instance we have met of the conversion of a grammar foundation into a school of English literature!" This school, it may be added, has several scholarships and exhibitions for boys who are proceeding to the universities, and has for some years held a high place among the leading grammar schools of the second class, under Dr. Dyne and his successor. It now numbers upwards of two hundred scholars. The school has attached to it a cricket and football field of about ten acres, on the north side of the road leading to Caen Wood and Hampstead Heath. The ground was in great part paid for by donations of friends of the school, and an annual payment added to the boys' fees. A pavilion also was erected by the donations of "old boys." On this ground the croquet tournament of all England was held in 1869. The original school buildings, as erected by Cholmeley, disappeared many years ago. A new school-house was erected in 1819, but this having at length become inadequate for the wants of the pupils, it was, at the tercentenary of the school which was celebrated in June, 1865, determined to raise new buildings. The old school was accordingly taken down in 1866, and rebuilt from the design of Mr. F. Cockerell. It is now a handsome Gothic structure of red brick, with stone dressings, and has attached to it a handsome chapel in a similar style of architecture, and a spacious library, school-room, and class-rooms. The chapel, built in remembrance of Mr. George Abraham Crawley, a governor of the school, was the gift of his widow and family; the expense incurred in the erection of the library was mostly paid for by funds raised by former scholars.

Southwood Lane is the name of a narrow and irregular road which runs in a south-easterly direction across from the back of Sir R. Cholmeley's school to the "Woodman," and leads thence to Muswell Hill. In this lane, in the year 1658, Sir John Wollaston founded six almshouses, which he devised, with their appurtenances, to the governors of the Free School, "in trust for the use of six poor alms people, men and women, of honest life and conversation, inhabitants of Hornsey and Highgate." In 1722 the almshouses were doubled in number and rebuilt, as a stone over the entrance informs us, at the expense of Mr. Edward Pauncefort, who likewise founded and endowed a charity-school for girls. The school, however, appears, through some neglect, to have lost much of the endowment designed for it by the founder. The Baptist chapel in this lane is one of the oldest buildings in the parish, having been founded as a Presbyterian chapel as far back as 1662. In course of time the Unitarians settled here, when the chapel had among its ministers David Williams, the "High Priest of Nature," and founder of the Literary Fund, of which we have spoken in our notice of Bloomsbury Square.* Dr. Barbauld and Dr. Alexander Crombie were also ministers here. Early in the present century the chapel passed into the hands of the Baptists.

On the north side of the lane stands a large modern brick mansion known as Park House. The Asylum for Idiots was founded here in 1847, by Dr. Andrew Reed; but about eight years later was transplanted to more spacious buildings at Earlswood, near Red Hill, in Surrey. In 1863, Park House was purchased, and converted into the London Diocesan Penitentiary.

The new Church of St. Michael stands at some little distance from the site of the old chapel, on the summit of the hill, overlooking the cemetery on the one side and Highgate Grove on the other; and, as we have stated in the preceding chapter, it occupies the site of the old mansion built by Sir William Ashurst, who was Lord Mayor of London in 1694. It is a poor and ugly sham Gothic structure, though the spire looks well from a distance. It was built from the designs of Mr. Lewis Vulliamy, and was thought to be a wonderful triumph of ecclesiastical art when it was consecrated in 1832. At the end overlooking the cemetery is a magnificent stained-glass window, representing the Saviour and the apostles, the gift of the Rev. C. Mayo, many years preacher in the old chapel. It was executed in Rome. The border contains several coats of arms from the windows of the old chapel. There are a few interesting monuments removed hither from the former edifice; but that which is most worthy of notice is a tablet erected to the memory of Cole-

* See Vol. IV., p. 543.

ridge, of whose tomb we have spoken above. It bears the following inscription :—

Sacred to the memory of
SAMUEL TAYLOR COLERIDGE,
Poet, Philosopher, Theologian.
This truly great and good man resided for
The last nineteen years of his life
In this Hamlet.
He quitted "the body of his death,"
July 25th, 1834,
In the sixty-second year of his age.
Of his profound learning and discursive genius
His literary works are an imperishable record.
To his private worth,
His social and Christian virtues,
JAMES AND ANN GILLMAN,
The friends with whom he resided
During the above period, dedicate this tablet.
Under the pressure of a long
And most painful disease
His disposition was unalterably sweet and angelic.
He was an ever-enduring, ever-loving friend,
The gentlest and kindest teacher,
The most engaging home companion.

"O framed for calmer times and nobler hearts,
O studious poet, eloquent for truth!
Philosopher, contemning wealth and death,
Yet docile, child-like, full of life and love."

Here,
On this monumental stone thy friends inscribe thy worth.

Reader! for the world mourn.
A Light has passed away from the earth!
But for this pious and exalted Christian
"Rejoice, and again I say unto you, Rejoice!"

Ubi
Thesaurus
ibi
Cor.

S. T. C.

Besides the celebrities whose names we have already mentioned, Highgate has been the home of many others. Lord Southampton had a mansion here, called Fitzroy House, which was situated in Fitzroy Park, adjoining Caen Wood. It was built about the year 1780, and is said to have been a handsome square brick building. Lord Southampton was the Lord of the Manor of Tottenhall, or Tottenham Court, in whose family it still remains. In the rooms of the mansion were portraits of Henry, the first Duke of Grafton; George, Earl of Euston; and Charles, Duke of Grafton. The Duke of Buckingham resided at Fitzroy House in 1811. In 1828 the mansion was taken down, and the park sub-divided and improved by the erection of several elegant villas.

Mrs. Caroline Chisholm has lived at Highgate, on the Hill, for some years. A native of Wootton, in Northamptonshire, she was born about the year 1810. Her father, Mr. William Jones, was a man of most philanthropic character, which his daughter inherited from him. The energy of her character was exercised for the benefit of the needy of her own neighbourhood, until her marriage with Captain Alexander Chisholm, of the Indian army, removed her to a more extended sphere of usefulness. The name of Mrs. Chisholm will be best remembered as the champion of the cause of emigration in various social phases, when grievances of any kind required to be redressed. Among her efforts in this direction may be mentioned the consigning of two shiploads of children from various workhouses to their parents in Australia at the expense of the Government. A similar success attended her efforts on behalf of convicts' wives, who had been promised free transmission, in certain cases of meritorious behaviour on the part of their husbands. Her greatest achievement, however, was the establishment of the Female Colonisation Loan Society, for the promotion of female emigration.

In 1724, died at his house in the Grove, Dr. Henry Sacheverel,* the great leader of the Tory party in the factions of 1709. He was a bigoted High Churchman, and his sermons were the brands to set the Established Church on fire. For expressions in his writings he was impeached and brought to the bar of the House; but far from disowning his writings, he gloried in what he had done. His trial lasted three weeks, and excluded all other public business for the time, when his sermons were voted scandalous and seditious libels. The queen was present as a private spectator. His sentence prohibited him from preaching for three years, and his sermons were ordered to be burnt by the common hangman. The following anecdote is recorded:—A portrait of this divine, with the initials S. T. P. attached to his name (signifying *Sanctæ Theologiæ Professor*), was hanging up in a shop window, where some persons looking at it, asked the meaning of the affix, when Thomas Bradbury, the Nonconformist minister, hearing the inquiry, and catching a glimpse of the print in passing, put his head among them, and adroitly said, "Stupid, Troublesome Puppy," and passed on.

Sir Richard Baker, author of the "Chronicles" which bear his name, died at his residence in Highgate at the commencement of the seventeenth century; as also did Sir Thomas Cornwallis, a man who had acquired considerable eminence in the reigns of Edward VI. and Queen Mary. Here lived Sir Henry Blunt, one of the earliest travellers

* See Vol. II., p. 512.

in Turkey, and also Sir John Pettus, a distinguished mineralogist. The great Arbuthnott seems also to have been at one time a resident here, for it appears from a chance expression in one of Dean Swift's letters, that he was obliged to quit Highgate by the *res angusta domi*.

Dorchester House, a large mansion of note here, was formerly the seat of Henry Marquis of Dorchester, and was used in the middle of the last century as a ladies' hospital. Part of Grove Row covers the site of this house, which was devoted by its owner, William Blake, a draper of Covent Garden, to a most excellent charity, the failure of which is deeply to be lamented, as its only fault appears to have been that it was in advance of the selfish age which witnessed its birth. The mansion bore the name of its former owner, the Marquis of Dorchester, from whom Blake purchased it early in the reign of Charles II., for £5,000—all that he possessed—with the intention of establishing it as a school or hospital for forty fatherless boys and girls. "The boys were to be taught the arts of painting, gardening, casting accounts, and navigation, or put out to some good handicraft trade. The girls were to learn to read, write, sew, starch, raise paste, and make dresses, so as to be fitted for any kind of service, thus anticipating the orphan working schools of our own time. When he sunk his money in this purchase, he hoped, and no doubt believed, that the benevolence of the wealthy would furnish the means for its support. But here he was doomed to disappointment." Far from being so fortunate as Franke of Halle, or the Curé d'Ars, or Müller of Bristol, he found charity much colder than he expected. Having exhausted his own resources, he made earnest appeals to the titled personages and city ladies of London, but in vain. For some time, indeed, his generous establishment struggled on. In 1667 there were maintained and educated in it thirty-six poor boys, dressed in a costume of blue and yellow—not unlike that of the boys of Christ's Hospital. It still existed in 1675, but it cannot be traced later than 1688, or about twenty years. In order to describe and recommend the institution which lay so near to his heart, Blake wrote and published a curious book, called "Silver Drops; or, Serious Things." It is written in a most eccentric style. He speaks of the place as meant "at first only for a summer recess from London, which, having that great and noble city, with its numerous childhood, under view, gave first thought to him of such a design." Mr. Howitt infers from the style, which is "almost insane," and from the "nobility of soul struggling through it," the piety and spirituality, the desire to have the boys taught the art of painting, and finally from the name of William Blake, that the "strange and good" founder must have been the grandfather or great-grandfather of the "eccentric but inspired writer-artist" of the same name, whom we have already mentioned more than once in our account of the neighbourhood of Oxford Street, and whose father is known to have been a hosier in Carnaby Market, not far from Covent Garden. A view of the mansion is engraved in Lysons' "Environs," and in the *Gentleman's Magazine*,* and also in William Howitt's "Northern Heights of London."

Part of the site of Dorchester House is now also covered by Pemberton Row, in which, says Mr. Prickett in his "History of Highgate," a part of the materials of the old building seem to have been utilised; for "on examining the elevation of Dorchester House with Pemberton Row, a remarkable similitude will appear in the character and style of the pedimented dormers, cornices, and heavy roofs." Among the early occupants of the houses erected after the removal of Dorchester House, was Sir Francis Pemberton, a distinguished judge of the seventeenth century. Sir Henry Chauncy gives a very high character of him in his "History of Hertfordshire," and there is a portrait of him among the "Council of the Seven Bishops." The row of houses has since borne his name.

Dorchester House itself stood on the west side of the Grove or Green, and the house occupied by Mr. Gillman, the surgeon, who had Coleridge as his inmate, stands on another portion of its site. Charles Lamb and Henry Crabb Robinson were frequent visitors of Coleridge whilst he was living here; in the "Diary" of the latter, under date of July, 1816, we read:—"I walked to Becher's, and he accompanied me to Mr. Gillman's, an apothecary at Highgate, with whom Coleridge is now staying. He seems already to have profited by his abstinence from opium, for I never saw him look so well." Mr. Thorne, in his "Environs of London," describes the house in which Coleridge lived as "the third house in the Grove, facing the church, a roomy, respectable, brick dwelling, with a good garden behind, and a grand look-out Londonwards. In front of the house is a grove of stately elms, beneath which the poet used to pace in meditative mood, discoursing in unmeaning monologue to some earnest listener like Irving or Hare, or an older friend, like Wordsworth or Lamb. The house remains almost unaltered; the elms, too, are there," but, he adds, "some Vandal has deprived

* See *Gentleman's Magazine*, Vol. LXX., Part II., p. 721.

them of their heads." It was in his walks about Highgate that Coleridge one day met Keats. He thus describes him:—"A loose, slack, and not well-dressed youth met me in a lane near Highgate. It was Keats. He was introduced to me, and stayed a minute or so. After he had left us a little way, he ran back and said, 'Let me carry away the memory, Mr. Coleridge, of having pressed your hand.' 'There is death in that hand,' I said, when Keats was gone; yet this was, I believe, before the consumption showed itself distinctly.'"

Coleridge was called by De Quincey "the largest and most spacious intellect, the subtlest and most comprehensive that has yet existed among men;" and Walter Savage Landor admits the truth of the statement with a reserve in favour of only Shakespeare and Milton. Charles Lamb calls him "metaphysician, bard, and magician in one." If he had written nothing but the "Ancient Mariner," his name would have lived as long as English literature itself, though Southey denounces it as "the clumsiest attempted German sublimity that he ever saw." It was after a visit to Coleridge, at Highgate, in all probability, that Shelley thus wrote of him:—

> "You will see Coleridge: him who sits obscure
> In the exceeding lustre, and the pure
> Intense irradiation of a mind
> Which, with its own internal lustre blind,
> Flags wearily through darkness and despair,
> A cloud-encircled meteor of the air,
> A hooded eagle among blinking owls."

Almost everybody knows the general outline of the story of the wasted life of Coleridge. How in early manhood he enlisted into the 15th Light Dragoons, but was released from the uncongenial life he had chosen by friends who accidentally detected his knowledge of Greek and Latin; how even when he had gained a name and a position as an essayist, he refused a handsome salary for regular literary work, declaring that he "would not give up the pleasure of lazily reading old folio columns for a thousand a year," and that "he considered any money beyond three hundred and fifty pounds a year a real evil." But this lazy reading of folios led, in his case, to confirmed idleness, an indolent resolution to gratify the mind and sense, at the cost of duty. "Degenerating into an opium-eater, and a mere purposeless theoriser, Coleridge wasted his time, talents, and health, and came, in his old age, to depend on the charity of others, and at last died; all his friends and many others besides regretted that he had done so little worthy of his genius."

Before he died Coleridge composed for himself the following epitaph, most striking for its simplicity and humility:—

> "Stop, Christian passer-by! stop, child of God!
> And read with gentle breast. Beneath the sod
> A poet lies, or that which once seemed he;
> Oh, lift a thought in prayer for S. T. C.!
> That he who many a year, with toil of breath,
> Found death in life, may here find life in death;
> Mercy for praise—to be forgiven for fame.
> He asked and hoped through Christ. Do thou the same."

Highgate Green, or Grove, is situated on the summit of West Hill, opposite St. Michael's Church. Until within a few years ago, when the Green was completely enclosed with dwarf iron railings, and planted with shrubs by a committee of the inhabitants, aided by the assistance of the vestry of St. Pancras, it was an open space, having several seats placed for the convenience of those who were weary. The green was formerly a favourite resort of the London folk, as it afforded space for recreation or dancing. Almost in the centre of this Green stands the "Flask" Inn, which was formerly one of the head-quarters of revellers at Highgate, as was its namesake at Hampstead.

In a comedy, published in 1601, entitled *Jack Drum's Entertainment*, on the introduction of the Whitsun morris dance, the following song is given in connection with the hostelry:—

> "Skip it, and frisk it nimbly, nimbly!
> Tickle it, tickle it lustily!
> Strike up the tabour,
> For the wenches' favour,
> Tickle it, tickle it lustily!
> Let us be seen on Highgate Green,
> To dance for the honour of Holloway;
> Since we are come hither,
> Let's spare for no leather,
> To dance for the honour of Holloway."

The following story is told connecting Hogarth's name with this Green:—"During his apprenticeship he made an excursion to this favourite spot with three of his companions. The weather being sultry, they went into a public-house on the Green, where they had not been long, before a quarrel arose between two persons in the same room, when, one of the disputants having struck his opponent with a quart pot he had in his hand, and cut him very much, causing him to make a most hideous grin, the humourist could not refrain from taking out his pencil and sketching one of the most ludicrous scenes imaginable, and what rendered it the more valuable was that it exhibited the exact likenesses of all present." The "public-house" here mentioned, no doubt, was the "Flask."

A large part of the Green was formerly a pond, which was fringed on one side, at least, by farm buildings. Once a year, at fair-time, its surface was covered—if tradition speaks the truth—with little sailing vessels, which made the place quite gay with an annual regatta.

It is perhaps worthy of a note, by the way, that this village, or hamlet, was not unrepresented at the "Tournament of Tottenham"—real or imaginary—recorded by Warton, in his "History of Poetry," for we read that among those who repaired to it, either as spectators, or to bear a part in the lists, were

"——all the men of that country—
Of Iseldon (Islington), of Hygate, and of Hakenay."

Church House, on the Green, close by the entrance to Swaine's Lane, was, in the middle of the last century, the abode of Sir John Hawkins, author of a "History of Music," of whom we have spoken in our account of Westminster.* At the time when Sir John Hawkins lived here, the roads were very badly kept; indeed, so difficult was the ascent of Highgate Hill that the worthy knight always rode to the Sessions House, Hicks's Hall, in a carriage drawn by four horses. Pepys tells us how that Lord Brouncker found it necessary to put six horses into his coach in order to climb Highgate Hill. The capacious coach-house and stables belonging to the house now serve as the lecture-hall and offices of the Highgate Literary Institute.

Prior to the construction of the roadway over the hill, the whole of this district was only known as a portion of Hornsey, and was for the greater part covered with the woods of Hornsey and Haringey Park; indeed, it is affirmed that it originally formed part of the Forest of Middlesex, wherein King Henry VIII. indulged in the sports of the chase, as may be seen by the following proclamation issued by him in 1546:—

HORNSEY WOOD HOUSE, 1800. (*See page* 430.)

PROCLAMATION.

Yt noe person interrupt the Kinges game of partridge or pheasant—Rex majori et vicecomitibus London. Vobis mandamus, &c.

Forasmuch as the King's most Royale Majestie is much desirous of having the game of hare, partridge, pheasant, and heron, preserved in and about his manour at Westminster for his disport and pastime; that is to saye, from his said Palace toe our Ladye of Oke, toe Highgate and Hamsted Heathe, to be preserved for his owne pleasure and recreation; his Royale Highnesse doth straightway charge and commandeth all and singular of his subjects, of what estate and condition soev' they be, not toe attempt toe hunte, or hawke, or kill anie of the said games within the precincts of Hamsted, as they tender his favour and wolvde eschewe the imprisonment of theyre bodies and further punishment, at his majestie's will and pleasure.

* See Vol. IV., p. 34.

HORNSEY CHURCH IN 1750. *From a Contemporary Print.* (*See page* 432.)

Teste meipso apud Westm. vij. die Julij anno tercesimo septimo Henrici octavi 1546.

Of Hornsey Wood itself, the chief portion left is Bishop's Wood, extending nearly all the way from Highgate to Hampstead; a smaller fragment, known as Highgate Wood, lies on the north side of Southwood Lane, near the "Woodman" Tavern, but this was much cut up in forming the Highgate and Edgware Railway; another piece, somewhat less encroached upon, lies at the end of Wood Lane.

North Hill, as the broad roadway north of the "Gate House" is called, is cut through what was once part of the Great Park or bishop's land, and joins the main road about half a mile beyond Southwood Lane. The road may be said to form part of the village of Highgate, for its sides are almost wholly occupied by villas and rows of cottages, among which are several public-houses, including the "Red Lion," one of the principal coaching houses of former times, and one where the largest number of persons were "sworn on the horns," as stated above.

The "Bull Inn," on the descent of the Great North Road towards Finchley, is worthy of note as one of the many such residences of the eccentric painter, George Morland, to whom we have frequently alluded. It is recorded that he would stand for hours before this hostelry, with a pipe in his mouth, bandying jests and jokes with the drivers of all the coaches which travelled by this route to Yorkshire and the North.

We may observe, in conclusion, that, in the opinion of many persons, Highgate does not possess the same variety of situations and prospects as Hampstead, nor is it so large and populous a place; but its prospects to the south and east are superior to those in the same direction from Hampstead.

CHAPTER XXXIII.

HORNSEY.

"To vie with all the beaux and belles,
Away they whip to Hornsey Wells."
Spirit of the Public Journals, 1814.

Etymology of Hornsey—Its Situation and Gradual Growth—The Manor of Hornsey—Lodge Hill—The Bishops' Park—Historical Memorabilia—The New River—Hornsey Wood and "Hornsey Wood House"—An Incident in the Life of Crabbe—Finsbury Park—Appearance of this District at the Commencement of the Present Century—Mount Pleasant—Hornsey Church—The Grave of Samuel Rogers, Author of "The Pleasures of Memory"—A Nervous Man—Lalla Rookh Cottage—Thomas Moore—Muswell Hill—The Alexandra Palace and Park—Neighbourhood of Muswell Hill, as seen from its Summit—Noted Residents at Hornsey—Crouch End.

As we have in the preceding chapters been dealing with Highgate—which, by the way, was originally but a hamlet situated within the limits of Hornsey—it is but natural that we should here say something of the mother parish. This once rural, but now suburban village, then, lies about two miles to the north-east from the top of Highgate Hill, whence it is approached either by Hornsey Lane or by Southwood Lane.

The etymology of this locality must be sought for in its more ancient appellation. From the thirteenth to the sixteenth century public records call it "Haringea," "Haringhea," or "Haringey." About Queen Elizabeth's time it was usually called "Harnsey," or, as some will have it, says Norden, "Hornsey." Lysons, indulging in a little pleasantry, observes that "if anything is to be gathered relating to its etymology, it must be sought for in its more ancient appellation, *Har*-ringe, the meadow of hares." In "Crosby's Gazetteer," 1816, Hornsey is described as "a pleasant village situated in a low valley five miles from London, through which the New River flows. This place is a favourite resort of the good citizens of London." Hornsey and London since that time have approached much nearer to each other, and it appears probable that before long it will form a portion of the metropolis. The opening of the Alexandra Park doubtless tended strongly to stretch London considerably in the direction of Hornsey. The citizens of London, instead of making it a place of occasional resort, have made it a place of residence. Crosby continues:—"In its vicinity is a small coppice, known by the name of Hornsey Wood. The Hornsey Wood House is a famous house of entertainment." Both the Wood and the "Wood House" have been swept away, and the sites have been taken into Finsbury Park. In 1818, as we learn from advertisements of the time, "coaches go daily from the 'White Bear,' Aldersgate Street, at eleven in the morning; in the afternoon at seven, in the winter, and at four and eight in the summer." Such, however, have been the changes brought about by the whirligig of time, that now, during the day, there are railway trains to and from London and various parts of Hornsey to the number of upwards of fifty each way.

The Manor of Hornsey has belonged to the Bishops of London from a time antecedent to the Norman Conquest; and in the centuries immediately following that event, those prelates had a residence here long before they owned a palace on the banks of the Thames at Fulham. Mr. Prickett has shown pretty conclusively, in his "History of Highgate," that the site of this residence is to be looked for in the centre of Hornsey Great Park, about half a mile to the north-west of the "High Gate."

Norden, in his "Speculum Britanniæ," thus describes it:—"There is a hill or fort in Hornsey Park, called Lodge Hill, for that thereon stood some time a lodge, when the park was replenished with deer; but it seemeth by the foundation that it was rather a castle than a 'lodge;' for the hill is trenched with two deep ditches, now old and overgrown with bushes; the rubble thereof, as brick, tile, and Cornish slate, are in heaps yet to be seen; the which ruins are of great antiquity, as may appear by the oaks at this day standing, above a hundred years' growth, upon the very foundations of the building." Lysons, writing at the close of the last century, says that "the greater part of it is now covered with a copse, but the remains of a moat or ditch are still to be seen in an adjoining field." Lysons adds a remark to the effect that "Bishop Aylmer's house at Hornsey, the burning of which put him to 200 marks expense, must have been upon another site." When the bishop's lands were sold, the Manor of Hornsey passed into the hands of Sir John Wollaston, of whom we have spoken in the previous chapter; he held it till his death, in 1658, after which his widow enjoyed it till the Restoration. Mr. Prickett adds, that in his time (1842) the form of the moat which surrounded it was still visible, and that it covered seventy yards square. He writes, "The site of the castle is still uneven, and bears the traces of former foundation; it is somewhat higher than the ground outside the trenches. The portion of the moat which still remains consists of a spring constantly running, and is now used as a watering-place for cattle."

It is almost needless to say here that the park of the Bishops of London must have been originally a portion of the great forest of Middlesex, which we have mentioned in our account of Primrose Hill (page 287). It occupied a somewhat irregular triangle, the base of which would extend from Highgate to Hampstead, while its apex reached nearly to Finchley northwards. In fact, a great portion of it still remains as forest-land, though regarded as a part of Caen Wood.

Hornsey Park is not altogether without its scraps of history, for it is said to have been the place where, in the year 1386, the Duke of Gloucester, the Earls of Arundel, Warwick, and other noblemen, assembled in a hostile manner, and marched thence to London to oppose Richard II., and to compel him to dismiss his two favourite ministers—the Earl of Suffolk and Robert Duke of Ireland—from his councils.

As we learn from Stow's "Annals," the Lodge in Hornsey Park, then the residence of the Duke of Gloucester, was, in the reign of Henry VI., the scene of the reputed witchcraft in which Eleanor Duchess of Gloucester was concerned; for here the learned Robert Bolingbroke, an astrologer, and Thomas Southwell, a canon of St. Stephen's, are alleged to have "endeavoured to consume the king's person by necromantic art," Southwell having said masses over the instruments which were to be used for that purpose. Bolingbroke was executed as a traitor at Tyburn; Southwell died in the Tower; whilst the Duchess had to do penance in the public streets, an incident which Shakespeare has rendered familiar to his readers in the second part of the play of *Henry VI.*

Once more, when the ill-fated and short-lived Edward V. was brought to London, after his father's death, under the escort of his uncle, Richard of Gloucester, he was here met by the Lord Mayor and 500 citizens of London. Hall, in his "Chronicles," quaintly tells us that, "When the kynge approached neere the cytee, Edmonde Shawe, goldsmythe, then Mayre of the cytie, with the Aldermenne and shreves [sheriffs] in skarlet, and five hundreth commoners in murraye, receyved his grace reverently at Harnesay Parke, and so conveighed him to the cytie, where he entered the fourth day of May, in the fyrst and last yere of his reigne."

Henry VII., on his return from a victory in Scotland, was likewise here met by the Lord Mayor and citizens of London, and conducted on his progress to the City in like manner.

Miss Jane Porter states, in her "Scottish Chiefs," that "the remains of Wallace were secretly removed and deposited temporarily in the chapel of Hornsey Lodge; and that Robert Bruce was concealed at Lodge Hill, in the garb of a Carmelite, when Gloucester sent him a pair of spurs, as an intimation that he must depart with all speed;" but it should be added that neither Lysons nor Prickett, in his history of the place, mentions these facts, so that possibly they are somewhat apocryphal.

Few villages near London have retained so rural a character down to quite recent times as that of Hornsey; this may perhaps be accounted for by the fact that both the high north road and the thoroughfare leading to Cambridge leave the place untouched. "The surrounding country," writes the author of the "Beauties of England and Wales," "is rendered attractive by soft ranges of hills; and the New River, which winds in a tortuous progress through the parish, is at many points a desirable auxiliary of the picturesque." Hone, in the second volume of his "Every-day Book," gives an engraving of "The New River at Hornsey," the spot represented being the garden of the "Three Compasses" inn. "But," says Mr. Thorne, in his "Environs of London," "the New River would now be sought for there in vain; its course was diverted, and this portion filled up with the vestigia of a London cemetery."

"About a mile nearer to London than Hornsey," observes the *Ambulator*, in 1774, "is a coppice of young trees called Hornsey Wood, at the entrance of which is a public-house, to which great numbers of persons resort from the City."

"Hornsey Wood House," for such was the name of this place of entertainment, stood on the summit of some rising ground on the eastern side of the parish. It was originally a small roadside public-house, with two or three wide-spreading oaks before it, beneath the shade of which the weary wayfarer could rest and refresh himself. The wood itself, immediately contiguous to the house, for some time shared with Chalk Farm the honour of affording a theatre for cockney duellists. The building was just beyond the "Sluice House," so celebrated for its eel-pies in the last generation. Anglers and other visitors could pass to it through an upland meadow along a straight gravel-walk anglewise. It was a good, plain, brown-brick, respectable, modern, London-looking building. Within the entrance, to the left, was a light and spacious room of ample accommodation and dimensions, of which more care seems to have been taken than of its fine leather folding screen in ruins, which Mr. Hone, in his "Every-day Book," speaks of as "an unseemly sight for him who respects old requisites for their former beauty and convenience." "It still bears," he further tells us, "some remains of a spirited painting spread all over its leaves, to represent the amusements and humours of a fair in the low countries. At the top of a pole, which may have been the village May-pole, is a monkey with a cat on his back; then there is a sturdy bear-ward in scarlet, with a wooden leg, exhibiting Mr. Bruin; an old woman telling fortunes to the rustics; a showman's drummer on the stage before a booth beating up for spectators to the performance within, which the show-cloth represents to be a dancer on the tight-rope; a well-set-out stall of toys, with a woman displaying their attractions; besides other really interesting 'bits' of a crowded scene, depicted by no mean hand, especially a group coming from a church in the distance, apparently a wedding procession, the females well looking and well dressed, wearing ribbons and scarfs below their waists in festoons. The destruction of this really interesting screen, by worse than careless keeping, is much to be lamented. This ruin of art is within a ruin of nature. 'Hornsey Tavern' and its grounds have displaced a romantic portion of the wood, the remains of which, however, skirt a large and pleasant piece of water formed at considerable expense. To this water, which is well stored with fish, anglers resort with better prospects of success than to the New River; the walk round it, and the prospect from its banks, are very agreeable."

With advancing years, the old tavern became more and more frequented, and in the end it was altered and enlarged, the grounds laid out as tea-gardens, and the large lake formed, which was much frequented by cockney anglers. For some time previous to the demolition of the house, in 1866, the grounds were used for pigeon-shooting by a gun-club section of the "upper ten thousand;" but it was soon superseded as such by the attractions of the "Welsh Harp" and of "Hurlingham." Hone, in the first volume of his "Every-day Book" (1826), speaks thus of the old house and its successor:—"The *old* 'Hornsey Wood House' well became its situation; it was embowered, and seemed a part of the wood. Two sisters, a Mrs. Lloyd and a Mrs. Collier, kept the house; they were ancient women, large in size, and usually sat before their door on a seat fixed between two venerable oaks, wherein swarms of bees hived themselves. Here the venerable and cheerful dames tasted many a refreshing cup with their good-natured customers, and told tales of bygone days, till, in very old age, one of them passed to her grave, and the other followed in a few months afterwards. Each died regretted by the frequenters of the rural dwelling, which was soon afterwards pulled down, and the oaks felled, to make room for the present roomy and more fashionable building. To those who were acquainted with it in its former rusticity, when it was an unassuming 'calm retreat,' it is, indeed, an altered spot. To produce the alteration, a sum of £10,000 was expended by the present proprietor; and 'Hornsey Wood Tavern' is now a well-frequented house. The pleasantness of its situation is a great attraction in fine weather." The lake was used not merely for fishing, but also for boating, which was largely indulged in during the summer months. Indeed, the attractions of the place seem to have been so great as to inspire the mind of the prosaic antiquary, Mr. Hone, who commemorates it in the following sentimental lines :—

> " A house of entertainment—in a place
> So rural, that it almost doth deface
> The lovely scene ; for like a beauty-spot
> Upon a charming cheek that needs it not,
> So 'Hornsey Tavern' seems to me. And yet,
> Though nature be forgotten, to forget
> The artificial wants of the forgetters
> Is setting up oneself to be their betters.
> This is unwise ; for they are passing wise
> Who have no eyes for scenery, and despise
> Persons like me, who sometimes have sensations
> Through too much sight, and fall in contemplations,
> Which, as cold waters cramp and drown a swimmer,
> Chill and o'erwhelm me. Pleasant is that glimmer
> Whereby trees *seem* but wood. The men who know
> No qualities but forms and axes, go
> Through life for happy people. They are so."

We are told in the "Life of Crabbe," by his son, that Hornsey Wood was one of the favourite haunts of the poet when he first came to London, and that he would often spend whole afternoons here in searching for plants and insects. "On one occasion," writes his son, "he had walked further than usual into the country, and felt himself too much exhausted to return to town. He could not afford to give himself any refreshment at a public-house, and much less to pay for a lodging; so he sheltered himself upon a hay-mow, beguiled the evening with Tibullus, and when he could read no longer, slept there till the morning."

Hornsey Wood House was pulled down in 1866, at which time the tea-gardens and grounds became absorbed in the so-called Finsbury Park, a large triangular space, some 120 acres in extent, laid out with ornamental walks and flower-gardens. It was opened by Sir John Thwaites, under the auspices of the Metropolitan Board of Works, in 1869, as a public recreation-ground and promenade for the working classes. Why the place is called "Finsbury" Park it would be difficult for us to say, seeing that it lies some miles away from Finsbury, the districts of Holloway, Islington, and Hoxton intervening, and that the site has always been known as Hornsey Wood. It ought to be styled, in common honesty, Hornsey Park.

The *Illustrated London News*, in noticing the opening of the park in 1869, says :—"The Act sanctioning the formation of this park was passed so far back as 1857. The site is what was formerly known as Hornsey Wood, which is associated with many interesting events in the history of North London. It commands a view of Wood Green, Highgate, the Green Lanes, and other suburban retreats. The ground has a gentle southern slope, from Highgate on the west and towards Stoke Newington on the east; and is skirted on the south by the Seven Sisters Road and on the east by the Green Lanes. The Great Northern Railway bounds it by a cutting and embankment on the western side, and latterly the London, Edgware, and Highgate Railway has been made with a station adjoining the park. There are several pleasant walks and drives, and in the centre of the park a trench has been cut, into which water will be brought from the New River, and in this way a pretty artificial lake will be added to the other attractions. The cost of the freehold land was about £472 per acre. The funds were principally raised by a loan, in 1864, of £50,000, at 4½ per cent., for thirty years, and £43,000 borrowed on debenture in 1868."

The lake above mentioned is an oblong piece of water surrounded by pleasant walks, and in parts shaded by trees, and in it are one or two islands well covered with young trees, which give to the lake somewhat the appearance of the "ornamental waters" in St. James's Park, a similitude borne out by the number of ducks and other water-fowl disporting themselves on its surface.

The Seven Sisters Road, skirting the south side of Finsbury Park, was constructed in 1832, prior to which time there was no thoroughfare through Holloway and Hornsey to Tottenham.

In a map of the suburbs of London in 1823, "Duval's Lane" is shown as running from Lower Holloway towards Crouch End, with scarcely a house on either side. A small and crooked road, marked Hem Lane, with "Duval's House" at the corner, leads also through fields towards "Hornsey Wood House," and so into the Green Lanes—all being open country. The now populous district of Crouch End appears here as a small group of private residences. Between the "Wood House" and Crouch End is Stroud Green, around which are five or six rustic cottages. On the other side of the "Wood House" is the "Sluice House," where privileged persons and customers of "mine host" went to fish in the New River and to sup upon eels, for which that place was famous, as stated above. Upper Holloway itself figures in this map as a very small collection of houses belonging apparently to private residents.

A pretty walk from Finsbury Park to Hornsey Church in fine dry weather is by the pathway running in a northerly direction over Mount Pleasant, a somewhat steep hill, from which some pleasant views are to be obtained of the surrounding country, embracing Highgate, the Alexandra Palace, Epping Forest, Tottenham Church, and the valley of the river Lea. The summit of Mount Pleasant is upwards of 200 feet above the level of the river; and its eastern end, from its peculiar shape, has been called the Northern Hog's Back.

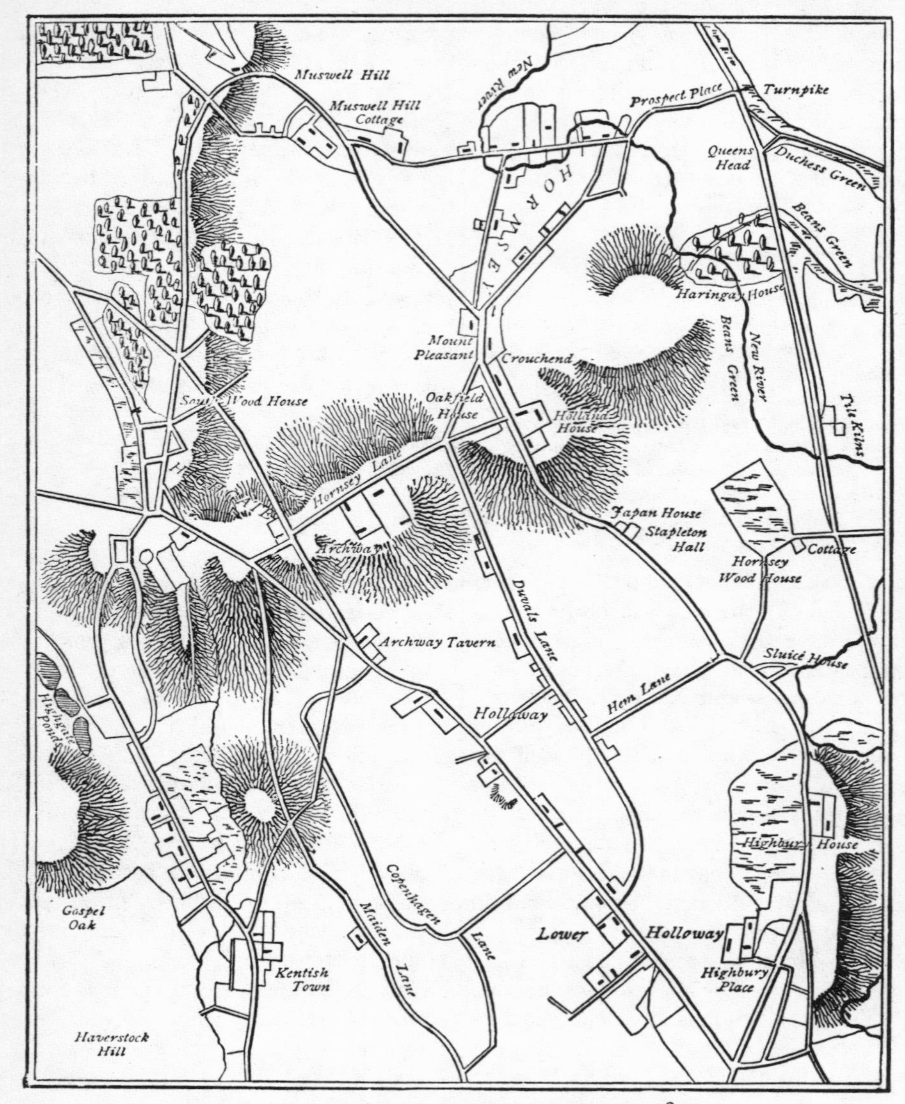

MAP OF HORNSEY AND NEIGHBOURHOOD IN 1819.

The parish church of Hornsey lies, at some little distance from the village, in a valley near the Hornsey Station on the Great Northern Railway, and its tower forms a conspicuous object in the view from the neighbouring uplands. With the exception of the tower, the present fabric is comparatively modern, dating only from about the year 1833; it is built of brick, and is of Gothic architecture. Its predecessor, which was pulled down in 1832, is stated by Norden and Camden to have been built with stones taken from the ruins of the palace of the Bishops of London, about the year 1500. The *Ambulator*, in 1774, describes the church as "a poor, irregular building, said to have been built out of the ruins of an ancient castle." The tower, which is now profusely covered with ivy, is built of a reddish sandstone, and is embattled, with a newel turret rising above the north-west corner. On the western face of the tower are sculptured two winged angels, bearing the arms of Savage and Warham, successively Bishops of London, the former of whom came to the see in 1497. It is probable that both of these prelates were contributors to the fabric. Some of the windows of the present church are filled with stained glass, and among the monuments are a few preserved from the older building. Among these is a large mural slab, on which are engraved the kneeling figures of a man, two females, and a boy; the dress appears to be of the latter part of the sixteenth century, and the monument was erected to the memory of George Rey, of Highgate. A Corinthian column, surmounted with armorial bearings, commemorates Dr. Lewis Atterbury (brother of the celebrated bishop), some time rector of the parish, who died in 1731. This monument was brought hither on the demolition of the old chapel at Highgate, where, as we have stated in a previous chapter, Dr. Atterbury was for many years preacher. Samuel Buckley, the editor of *Thuanus*, who died in 1741, is commemorated by a monument; as also is "Master Richard Candish [Cavendish], of Suffolk, Esq." An inscription in verse upon the latter monument informs us that "this memorial was promised and made by Margaret, Countess of Cōberland, 1601."

THE ALEXANDRA PALACE, 1876. (*See page* 435.)

The churchyard is sheltered by rows of tall elms, which impart to it an air of retirement and seclusion. Here, amongst other tombs, on the northern side of the church, is that of the poet Rogers, of whom we have spoken in our account of St. James's

Place.* It is an altar-tomb, resting on a high base, and surrounded by an iron railing. The following are the inscriptions on the face of the tomb :—"In this vault lie the remains of Henry Rogers, Esq., of Highbury Terrace; died December 25, 1832, aged 58. Also of Sarah Rogers, of the Regent's Park, sister of the above; died January 29, 1855, aged 82. Also of Samuel Rogers, author of the 'Pleasures of Memory,' brother of the above-named Henry and Sarah Rogers; born at Newington Green, July 30, 1763, died at St. James's Place, Westminster, December 18, 1855." Near the south-east corner of the churchyard an upright stone marks the grave of Anne Jane Barbara, the youngest daughter of Thomas Moore, the poet.

Amongst the rectors of Hornsey there have been a few who have become known beyond the circle of the parish. Of these we may mention Thomas Westfield, who resigned the living in 1637, afterwards Bishop of Bristol, and who is described as "the most nervous of men." His biographer says that "he never, though almost fifty years a preacher, went up into the pulpit but he trembled; and never preached before the king but once, and then he fainted." "Yet he was held in such esteem by all parties," writes Mr. Howitt in his "Northern Heights of London," "that on May 13, 1643, the committee for sequestrating the estates of delinquents, being informed that his tenants refused to pay his rents as Bishop of Bristol, speedily compelled them, and granted him a safe conduct for his journey to Bristol with his family, being a man of great learning and merit, and advanced in years. His successor at Hornsey, Thomas Lant, did not meet with quite such agreeable treatment. He was turned out of his living and house with great cruelty by the Puritans, who would not allow him even to procure a place of retirement. Samuel Bendy, rector in 1659, petitioned the committee, setting forth that his income was only £92, out of which he had to pay £16 to the wife and children of the late incumbent. The committee made him recompense." The Rev. William Cole, the Cambridge antiquary, and the friend and correspondent of Horace Walpole, held the rectory for about a year in the middle of the last century.

At the end of the lane running west from the church, and at the foot of Muswell Hill, is Lalla Rookh Cottage, where Moore was residing in 1817 when he wrote, or, at all events, when he published, the poem bearing the title of "Lalla Rookh," for which, as we learn from his "Life," he received £3,000 from Messrs. Longmans, the publishers. In this house his youngest daughter died, as above stated.

A native of Dublin and a son of Roman Catholic parents, Moore came over to England when still young to push his fortunes in the world of literature, and became the poet laureate of Holland House and of the Whig party. During his latter years he occupied Sloperton Cottage, a small house adjoining Lord Lansdowne's park at Bowood, near Calne, in Wiltshire, where he died in 1852, at the age of seventy-three. Lord Russell claims for Moore the first place among our lyric poets, but few will be willing to allow his superiority to Robert Burns, though he was certainly the English Beranger. He was probably the best hand at improvised song-writing on the common topics of every-day life, but he had no real depth of feeling. A refined, voluptuous, and natural character, equally frank and gay, he passed, after all, a somewhat butterfly existence, and has left behind him but little that will last except his "Irish Melodies."

Continuing along the pleasant lane westward from Lalla Rookh Cottage, we come to Muswell Hill, a place which has now become familiar to Londoners—and, probably, to the majority of readers—from the fact that its summit and sides are for the most part occupied by the Alexandra Palace and Park, which covers altogether an area of about five hundred acres. Before venturing to give a description of this place of amusement, or a narrative of its unfortunate career, we may be pardoned for saying a few words about the hill whereon it is situated.

Muswell Hill, then, we may observe, derives its name from a famous well on the top of the hill, where formerly the fraternity of St. John of Jerusalem, in Clerkenwell, had their dairy, with a large farm adjacent. Here they built a chapel for the benefit of some nuns, in which they fixed the image of Our Lady of Muswell. These nuns had the sole management of the dairy; and it is singular that the said well and farm do, at this time, belong to the parish of St. James, Clerkenwell. The water of this spring was then deemed a miraculous cure for scrofulous and cutaneous disorders; and, as tradition says, a king of Scotland—whose name, by the way, does not transpire—being afflicted with a painful malady, made a pilgrimage hither, and was perfectly cured. At any rate, the spring was much resorted to, and became an object of pilgrimage in the Middle Ages; indeed, for some considerable time there was a great throng of pilgrims to the shrine of Our Lady, who came laden with their offerings and buoyed up with their hopes from all parts of the country.

* See Vol. IV., pp. 172—175.

Lysons, writing in 1795, remarks that "the well still remains; but," he somewhat naïvely adds, "it is not famed, as I find, for any extraordinary virtues." Muswell farmhouse, with the site of the chapel, together with the manor of Muswell, was alienated in 1546 by William Cowper to William Goldynge, and, after a few other changes of ownership, passed into the hands of the Rowes, in whose possession it continued at the end of the seventeenth century. It soon afterwards came into the family of Pulteney; and, according to Lysons, on the death of Lady Bath, devolved, under Sir William Pulteney's will, on the Earl of Darlington. Muswell Hill, it may be added, was in former times called also Pinsenhall Hill.

Shortly after the close of the second International Exhibition (that of 1862) at South Kensington, it was resolved to erect on this spot a place of popular entertainment for the working classes of northern London, which should rival the Crystal Palace at Sydenham. To the great mass of people in the north of London the Crystal Palace, except on great occasions and great attractions, is so distant as to be almost inaccessible; and it is reported, as was proved by railway returns, it is mainly the south London population which keeps up the great building "over the water." There seemed no valid reason, therefore, why the north of London, with at least three times the number of inhabitants, should not be able to support a Crystal Palace of its own. It was considered, moreover, that the Alexandra Palace—for such the building was to be named, in honour of the Princess Alexandra—would not be dependent on support from local influences. The rare beauty of its site, which probably has not its equal anywhere round London, together with the special attractions in the building, would be sure to make it a universal favourite with both the north and south of the metropolis.

With regard to the palace itself, it was decided to purchase some portion of the materials of the International Exhibition, and with them to erect the building on the summit of Muswell Hill, in the same manner as the originators of its prototype at Sydenham had purchased for that purpose the materials of the Great Exhibition of 1851. The new palace, therefore, was almost entirely built out of the materials of the Great Exhibition of 1862, but totally altered and improved in their re-construction. It had only one of the noble domes in the centre transept, with two less lofty octagon towers at either end. It had one main nave, exclusive of the entrances, about 900 feet long, and three cross transepts of about 400 feet each. The building was beautifully decorated in the Renaissance style; and round the eight columns which supported the great central dome were ranged groups of statuary surrounded by flowers. Behind this ornamental walk were placed the cases for the exhibitors, mixed, as in the nave itself, with flowers and statuary. Then there were a variety of courts—such as the glass court, china court, furniture court, courts for French goods, courts for American, Indian, Italian—in short, all the courts which we are accustomed to find in a regular exhibition. At the north end of the centre transept was built a splendid organ by Willis, decorated in a style to be in harmony with its surroundings, and in front of this was the orchestra. A large concert-room was in another part of the building. Then there was a theatre capable of holding 2,000 spectators, and having a stage as large as that of Drury Lane Theatre.

During the progress of the building, sundry stoppages and hindrances arose from various causes; and in the grounds great difficulty was at times experienced through the subsidence of the soil; indeed, to use the words of one of the contractor's foremen, the hills round Muswell had during one winter "been slipping about like anything." Strange as such a statement may seem, it is literally true. The hills, it is asserted, had been moving in all sorts of directions. They are mostly of gravel, but resting, at about twenty feet deep, on a two-feet seam of soapy clay, which, when the superincumbent mass was thoroughly penetrated by the constant rain, allowed it to slip. Fortunately, the Alexandra Palace was so deeply moored in its foundations that it never shifted or showed the slightest signs of any subsidence or yielding in any direction; yet a very formidable landslip took place close by it, and in one night between three and four acres slipped quietly down a few feet. Another hill came forward as much as three inches in a single night, but beyond this landslip none of the hills round the palace have moved to any material extent, except where the viaduct for the railway crosses over a small valley just before arriving at the palace.

After a delay of some six or seven years beyond the first appointed time, the palace and grounds being all but completed, the place was opened to the public on the 24th of May, 1873. The proceedings, though not graced by the presence of royalty, were as successful an inauguration of a national institution as could possibly have been expected. The opening was inaugurated by a grand concert, presided over by Sir Michael Costa, in which some of the leading singers of the day took part. But, alas! about mid-day on the 9th of June the whole building fell a prey to the flames, and all that was left was a melancholy and gutted ruin. The fire originated at the base of the great dome, where some workmen had been employed in "repairing the roof," and had, possibly, let some lighted tobacco fall into a crevice. During the brief period the palace was open (fourteen days only) it was visited by as many as 124,124 persons, and its success was no longer doubtful. Thus encouraged, the directors resolved at once to rebuild the palace, and in its re-construction they availed themselves of the experience so dearly purchased, particularly with reference to arrangements for protection from fire.

The new building, which was opened on the 1st of May, 1875, occupies an area of about seven acres, and is constructed in the most substantial manner. It contains the grand hall, capable of seating 12,000 visitors and an orchestra of 2,000; the Italian garden, a spacious court in which are asphalte paths, flower-beds, and a fine fountain; also the concert-room, which has been erected on the best known acoustic principles, and will seat 3,500 visitors. The conservatory is surmounted by a glass dome, and in close proximity are two spacious halls for the exhibition of works of art; also the corridor for displaying ornamental works. The reading-room is a very comfortable apartment, and near thereto are the modern Moorish house and an Egyptian villa. The theatre is of the most perfect kind, and will seat more than 3,000 persons. The exhibition department is divided into two parts, the space occupied being 204 feet by 106 feet. The bazaar department is 213 feet by 140 feet. The frontage of the stalls is upwards of 3,000 feet, and they are so arranged as to give the greatest facility of access to visitors and purchasers. The picture-galleries are on the northern side of the building, and comprise six fine, large, well-lighted rooms. The refreshment department is of the most complete and extensive character, including spacious grill and coffee rooms, two banqueting rooms, drawing, billiard, and smoke rooms, and private rooms for large or small parties, and the grand dining saloon, which will accommodate as many as 1,000 persons at table. For the efficient supply of this vast establishment, the plan of the basement is considered to be the most perfect as well as the most extensive of its kind ever yet seen. Also, within the building, are numerous private offices for manager and clerks, and a spacious board-room.

The park is richly timbered, and of a pleasingly undulated surface, intersected by broad carriage drives, and there are several ornamental lakes of great beauty in connection with the surrounding scenery; a number of Swiss chalets and other rustic buildings, also horticultural gardens, with extensive ranges of glass houses. At the foot of the hill on which the palace stands there is a race-course upwards of a mile in length, and the grand stand is one of the handsomest and most substantial buildings of its kind in this country. There is also a trotting ring on the American principle, and, in connection therewith, an extensive range of stabling for several hundred horses, thus rendering the property well adapted for horse and agricultural shows; and a grand stand and paddock. The cricket-ground is ten acres in extent, with two pavilions, and every convenience for cricketers. There is also a Japanese village, comprising a temple, a residence, and a bazaar. In the bazaar articles of Japanese work were offered for sale. A circus for equestrian performances was likewise erected in the grounds, together with a spacious banqueting hall, an open-air swimming-bath, and other novel features. Besides all these attractions, there is a charming and secluded nook in the grounds, called the Grove, bordering on the Highgate Road. In a house here, Thrale, the brewer, is reported to have lived, and to have had among his guests the great lexicographer of the Georgian era, as is testified to this day by a pathway shaded by trees, called Dr. Johnson's Walk. The Grove has been described by an able writer as "a wild natural garden, clothed with the utmost beauty to which the luxuriance of our northern vegetation can attain. On one side a low, thick hedge of holly, pillared by noble oaks, flanks a great terrace-walk, commanding a noble view over a slope which descends rapidly from the prickly barrier. Very few such oaks are to be found within this island: lofty, sturdy, and well-grown trees, not marked by the hollow boles and distorted limbs of extreme old age, but in the very prime of vegetable manhood. Turning at right angles, at the end of this semi-avenue, the walk skirts a rapid descent, clothed with turf of that silky fineness which denotes long and careful garden culture, and set with a labyrinth of trees, each one of which is a study in itself. A noble cedar of Lebanon rises in a group of spires like a foreshortened Gothic cathedral. A holly, which, from its perfect and unusual symmetry, deceives the eye as to size, and looks like a sapling close at hand, has a bole of some fifteen feet girth, rising for twenty-four feet before it breaks into branches. Farther on, the walk is bordered by laurel hedges, and overlooks a wide sweep of country, undulated, wooded, and studded by many a spiry steeple to the north; and here we meet with an elm, standing alone on the turf, as perfect in its giant symmetry as the holly we have just admired. Then, perhaps, the monarch of all, we come upon a gigantic chestnut, which seems as if, like the trees once in the Garden of Eden, no touch of iron had ever fallen upon its limbs." Notwithstanding all these varied attractions, the Alexandra Palace has never yet answered the expectations of its promoters, and has more than once been offered for sale by auction and withdrawn, the offers falling far short of the value put upon the property by its owners.

The view from the top of the hill on which the palace stands is, perhaps, unrivalled for beauty within many miles of London. At our feet, looking northwards, is Southgate, of which Leigh Hunt wrote that it was a pleasure to be born in so sweet a village, cradled, not only in the lap of Nature, which he loved, but in the midst of the truly English scenery which he loved beyond all other. "Middlesex is," he adds, "a scene of greenery and nestling villages, and Southgate is a prime specimen of Middlesex. It is a place lying out of the way of innovation, and therefore it has the pure sweet air of antiquity about it." And the remark is true, with a few exceptions, of all the towns and villages of this district. Look along the line of railway that branches off at Wood Green, and you will see the Enfield where Keats grew to be a poet, and where Charles Lamb died. Look a little to the left, and there is Colney Hatch Asylum, with its two thousand inmates. A little farther on lies Hadley Wood, a lovely spot for a picnic; and there rises the grey tower of Barnet Church, reminding you of the battle of Barnet, fought but a little farther on. A little on our left is Finchley Common, where they still show us Grimaldi's Cottage and Dick Turpin's Oak. If we look over Wood Green, now a town, but a short time back a wild common, we see in the far distance Tottenham and Edmonton, and what remains of Epping Forest. Hornsey, with its ivy tower, is just beneath; to our right is Highgate; and a little farther on is Hampstead Heath.

Johnson's friend, Topham Beauclerc, it may be added, lived for some time on Muswell Hill; and Sir Robert Walpole, it is asserted, also resided at one time in this locality. Boswell is silent as to the connection of the former with this place, and for the residence of Sir Robert Walpole here we have only a local tradition.

Among its inhabitants during the last century was Lawrence, the "mad" Earl Ferrers, who lodged here for some months previous to committing the murder of his steward, for which he was executed at Tyburn.* His conduct even whilst here was most eccentric, and such as might fairly have consigned him to a lunatic asylum. He mixed with the lowest company, would drink coffee out of the spout of a kettle, mix his porter with mud, and shave one side of his face. He threatened more than once to "do for" his landlady, and on another occasion he violently broke open on a Sunday the stable where his horse was locked up, knocking down with his fist the ostler's wife when she asked him to wait a few minutes while her husband brought the key.

Another resident at Hornsey in former times was the learned John Lightfoot, the commentator, who selected this spot in order that he might have access to the library at Sion College. Lightfoot, who was born at the beginning of the seventeenth century, is stated to have published his first work, entitled "Erubhim; or, Miscellanies Christian and Judaical," in 1629, the next year after settling at Hornsey. He was a strong promoter of the Polyglott Bible, and at the Restoration was appointed one of the assistants at the Savoy Conference. In 1675 he became Vice-Chancellor of the University of Cambridge.

Crouch End, which lies to the south-west of the village, is connected with the Highgate Archway Road by the sloping lands of Hornsey Rise. Stroud Green, of which we have spoken in our account of the manor of Highbury,† is in this district; and although it is fast being encroached upon by the demon of bricks and mortar, it has still some few shady lanes and "bits" of rural scenery left. On rising ground on the south side of Crouch End stands Christ Church, one of the district churches of Hornsey. It was built in 1863, from the designs of Mr. A. W. Blomfield, and is a neat edifice, in the Gothic style of architecture. The church was enlarged about ten years later, when a tower and spire were added. St. Luke's Church, Hornsey Rise, built in 1861, from the designs of Mr. A. D. Gough, is a respectable common-place modern Gothic building; and consists of a nave with side aisles, transepts, and chancel with side chapels.

At the beginning of 1877 a handsome Gothic church was consecrated here; it is dedicated to the Holy Innocents, and stands near the railway station. This church was the third which had been built during the incumbency of Canon Harvey, in which period Hornsey has grown from a mere village into a town of some 10,000 inhabitants.

---

* See *ante*, p. 192.

† See Vol. II., p. 275.

THE VALE OF HEALTH. (*See page* 457.)

CHAPTER XXXIV.

HAMPSTEAD.—CAEN WOOD AND NORTH END.

"When the sweet-breathing spring unfolds the buds,
Love flies the dusty town for shady woods;
Then Tottenham fields with roving beauty swarm,
And Hampstead halls the City virgins warm."—*Gay.*

The Etymology and Early History of Hampstead—"Hot Gospellers"—The Hollow Tree—An Inland Watering-place—Caen Wood Towers—Dufferin Lodge—Origin of the Name of Caen (or Ken) Wood—Thomas Venner and the Fifth Monarchy Men—Caen Wood House and Grounds—Lord Mansfield—The House saved from a Riotous Attack by a Clever Ruse—Visit of William IV.—Highgate and Hampstead Ponds—The Fleet River—Bishop's Wood—The "Spaniards"—New Georgia—Erskine House—The Great Lord Erskine—Heath House—The Firs—North End—Lord Chatham's Gloomy Retirement—Wildwood House—Jackson, the Highwayman—Akenside—William Blake, the Artist and Poet—Coventry Patmore—Miss Meteyard—Sir T. Fowell Buxton—The "Bull and Bush."

In commencing this chapter we may observe that there are two ways by which the pedestrian can reach Hampstead from Highgate—namely, by the road branching off at the "Gate House" and running along the brow of the hill past the "Spaniards," and so on to the Heath; and also by the pleasant footpath which skirts the grounds of Caen Wood on its southern side. This pathway branches off from Millfield Lane, nearly opposite the grounds of Lady Burdett-Coutts, and passing by the well-known Highgate Ponds, winds its course over the gently undulating meadows and uplands which extend westward to the slope of the hill leading up to Hampstead Heath; the pathway itself terminating close by the ponds of Hampstead, of which, together with the charming spot close by, called the Vale of Health, we shall have more to say presently. For our part, we shall take the first-named route; but before setting out on our perambulation, it will be well, perhaps, to say a few words about Hampstead in general.

Starting, then, with the name, we may observe that the etymology of Hampstead is evidently derived from the Saxon "ham" or *home*, and "stede" or *place*. The modern form of the word "homestead" is still in common use for the family residence, or more generally for a farmhouse, surrounded by barns and other out-buildings. "Homestead," too, according to the ingenious Mr. Lysons, is the true etymology of the name. "Hame" is

CAEN WOOD, LORD MANSFIELD'S HOUSE, IN 1785. (*See page* 441.)

the well-known Scotch form for "home;" and the syllable "ham" is preserved in "hamlet," and, as a termination, in innumerable names of places in this country. West Ham, Birming-ham, Old-ham, and many others immediately suggest themselves; and we can easily reckon a dozen Hamptons, in which the first syllable has a similar origin to that of Hampstead; while, under the modern German form, *heim*, we meet with it in Blenheim. There are two Hampsteads in Berkshire, besides Hemel Hempstead in Hertfordshire. The name, then, of the solitary Saxon farm was applied in the course of years to the village or town which gradually surrounded it and at length took its place. Who the hardy Saxon was who first made a clearing in this elevated part of the thick Middlesex forest, we know not; but we have record that this wood afforded pannage or pasturage for a hundred head of swine, which fed on the chestnuts, beech-nuts, and acorns. In 986 King Ethelred granted the manor of Hamstede to the Abbot of Westminster; and this grant was confirmed by Edward the Confessor, with additional privileges. We are told by Mr. Park, in his "History of Hampstead," that in early times it was a little chapelry, dependent on the mother church of Hendon, which was itself an incumbency in the gift of the abbot and monks of the convent of St. Peter in Westminster. To this day the Dean and Chapter of Westminster own a considerable quantity of land in the parish, whence they draw a considerable income, owing to the increased and increasing value of property. Before the Reformation, it is clear that the Rector of Hendon was himself responsible for the cost of the keep of "a separate capellane," or chaplain to serve "the chapell of the Blessed Virgin at Hamsted;" this, however, was not a very heavy cost, for the stipend of an assistant curate at that day was only from six to eight marks a year; and in the reign of Edward VI., the curacy of Hampstead itself, as we learn casually from a Chancery roll, was valued at £10 per annum. It is not at all clear when the benefice of Hampstead was separated from that of Hendon, but the ties of the one must have been separated from those of the other before the year 1598, when the churchwardens of Hampstead were for the first time summoned to the Bishop of London's visitation, a fact which looks like the commencement of a parochial settlement. It is probable that the correct date is 1560, as the register of baptisms, marriages, and burials commences in that year.

In the reign of Edward VI. the manor and advowson of Hampstead were granted by the young king to Sir Thomas Wroth, Knt., from whose family they passed, about seventy years later, by purchase, to Sir Baptist Hickes, afterwards Viscount Campden, whose descendant Baptist, third Earl of Gainsborough, alienated them to Sir W. Langhorne, Bart., in 1707. They passed from the Langhornes by descent through the hands of three females, to the family of the present patron, Sir Spencer Maryon-Wilson, Bart., of Charlton House, Kent.

At the time of the dissolution, Hampstead, it appears, was a very small village, inhabited chiefly by washerwomen, and for the next 150 years its history is almost a blank. In the Puritan times the "Hot Gospellers," as they were nicknamed, often preached under the shade of an enormous elm, which was certainly a great curiosity, its trunk having been occupied by some virtuoso unrecorded in local history, who constructed a winding staircase of forty-two steps within the hollow, and built an octagonal tower on the summit, thirty-four feet in circumference, and capable of holding twenty persons. The height from the ground to the base of the turret was thirty-three feet, and there were sixteen side lights. There is a curious etching, by Hollar, of this "Hollow Tree at Hampstead." The exact locality of this tree is a matter of doubt. The copy of the etching in the royal collection at Windsor forms part of a "broadside" at the foot of which is printed "To be given or sold on the hollow tree at Hampstead." One Robert Codrington, a poetical student, and afterwards a Puritan, inspired by the tree, wrote an elaborate poem, in which he says,

> "In less room, I find,
> With all his trusty knights, King Arthur dined."

Hampstead is now nearly joined to London by rows of villas and terraces; but within the memory of the present generation it was separated from town by a broad belt of pleasant fields. Eighty or a hundred years ago it was a rural village, adorned with many fine mansions, whither retired, in search of health or recreation, some of the most eminent men of the age. The beauty of its fields is celebrated by the author of "Suburban Sonnets" in Hone's "Table Book:"

> "Hampstead, I doubly venerate thy name,"

for it seems it was here that the writer first became imbued with the feeling of love and with the spirit of poetry.

It is the fashion to undervalue the suburbs of London; and several clever writers, proud of their mountains and their lakes, have a smile of contempt ready for us when we talk of our "upland hamlets," our fertile valleys, and our broad river. The fact is that the suburbs of London are beautiful as compared with the suburbs of other great cities. But so long as the breezy heath, and its smooth velvet turf, sloping away to the north and east, remain unbuilt upon, Hampstead will never cease to be the favourite haunt and home of poets, painters, and artists, which it has been for the last century or more. There still attaches to the older part of the town a certain stately air of dignified respectability, in the red-brick spacious mansions; and the parish church, though really not old as churches count age, with its spacious churchyard, bears record of many whose names are familiar to us all.

Hampstead, it has been observed, is in every respect a watering-place—except in there being no sea there. With that important drawback, it possesses all the necessary attributes: it has its donkeys, its bath-chairs, its fashionable esplanade, its sand and sandpits, its chalybeate spring, its "eligible" houses "to be let furnished," its more humble "apartments," its "Vale of Health," where "parties" can be supplied with "hot water for tea," at various prices, from twopence to fourpence per head; its fancy stationers' shop, with the proper supply of dolls, novels, and illustrated note paper; its old church and its new church; its chapel of ease; its flagstaff—ready to "dip" its colours to steamers, which, from the nature of the case, can never appear in the offing; its photographic pavilion, with portraits "in this style" (a style which would effectually prevent any sensible person from entering the place of execution); its country walks and rides; its residents, so exclusive; its troops of visitors; its boys, fishing for tadpoles with crooked pins in the (freshwater) ponds; its tribes of healthy children with their nurses and nursemaids;—in fact, it has all that can make the heart glad, and place Hampstead on the list of sea-bathing places, with the trifling omission mentioned above.

With these remarks, we will once more take up our staff and proceed.

Leaving Highgate by the turning westward close by the "Gate House," and passing by the Grove, we make our way along the high road which connects the village with Hampstead. The old way being narrow, and nearly impassable, a new and more direct road was made, affording a splendid panoramic view of vast extent. In the formation of the new road, too, its course in one or two parts was slightly altered. On the slope of the hill to the left, and standing on ground which originally formed a portion of Fitzroy Park, is Caen Wood Towers, till lately the residence of Mr. Edward Brooke, the patentee of the magenta and other dyes. The building occupies part of the site of Dufferin Lodge, formerly the seat of Lord Dufferin, which was pulled down in 1869. The present house, which was completed in 1872, from the designs of Messrs. Salomons and Jones, is built of red brick with stone dressings; and with its bay windows, gables, and massive towers, stands out prominently amid the surrounding trees.

Pursuing our course along the Hampstead road, we reach the principal entrance to the estate of Caen (or Ken) Wood, the seat of the Earl of Mansfield. Though generally regarded as part and parcel of Hampstead, the estate lies just within the boundary of the parish of St. Pancras, and was part of the manor of Cantelows. It is said by antiquaries to form a part of the remains of the ancient forest of Middlesex. Lysons is of opinion that the wood and the neighbouring hamlet of Kentish Town (anciently Kentestoune) were both named after some very remote possessor. There was, he says, a Dean of St. Paul's named Reginald de "Kentewode," and "the alteration from Kentwode to Kenwood is by no means unlikely to happen." Mr. Howitt looks for the origin of the syllable in the word "Ken," a view. As, however, we have stated in previous chapters,* the word Caen may, perhaps, be an equivalent to "Kaen" or Ken, which lies at the root of *Ken*tish Town, *Ken*sington, &c.

The earliest mention of the place, remarks Mr. Prickett, in his "History of Highgate," appears in Neale's "History of the Puritans," where it is spoken of as affording shelter for a short time to Venner and his associates—the "Fifth monarchy men." In the outbreak of the "Fifth monarchy men," under Thomas Venner, the cooper of Coleman Street, in January, 1661, these fanatics having fought one engagement with the "Train-bands," and expecting another struggle next day, took shelter for a night in Caen Wood, where some of them were taken prisoners next morning, and the rest were dispersed. As probably few or none of them were killed, the spot where the encounter took place cannot now be identified by any discovery of bodies hastily buried, as is commonly the case in the neighbourhood of battle-fields.

From the first volume of "Selected Views in London and its Environs," published in 1804, we glean the following particulars of this demesne:—"Caen Wood, the beautiful seat of the Earl of Mansfield, is situated on a fine eminence between Hampstead and Highgate, and its extensive

* See *ante*, pp. 118, 317.

grounds contribute in no small degree to enrich the neighbouring scenery. These, with the wood which gives name to them, contain about forty acres, and are laid out with great taste. On the right of the garden front of the house (which is a very noble mansion) is a hanging wood of tall spreading trees, mostly beeches; and on the left the rising hills are planted with trees, that produce a pleasing effect. These, with a sweet shrubbery immediately before the front, and a serpentine piece of water, render the whole a very enlivening (*sic*) scene. The enclosed fields adjoining to the pleasure-grounds contain about thirty acres more. Hornsey great woods, held by the Earl of Mansfield under the Bishop of London, join this estate on the north, and have lately been added to the enclosure."

Mr. Howitt, in his "Northern Heights," gives the following interesting particulars about Caen Wood and House:—"Caen House," he writes, "is a large and massive building of yellow stone, impressive from its bulk and its commanding situation, rather than from its architecture, which is that of Robert Adam, who was very fashionable in the early part of the reign of George III. Caen Wood House has two fronts, one facing the north, with projecting wings; the other facing the south, extending along a noble terrace, and has its façade elongated by a one-storeyed wing at each side. The basement storey of the main body of the house is of rustic work, surmounted by a pediment supported by Ionic pilasters, the columns of the wings being of the same order. Within, Adam, as was usual with him, was more successful than without. The rooms are spacious, lofty, and finely proportioned. They contain a few good paintings, among which are some of Claude's; a portrait of Pope, the poet, with whom the first earl was very intimate; and a full-length one of the great law lord himself, as well as a bust of him by Nollekens. The park in front, of fifty acres, is arranged to give a feeling of seclusion in a spot so near to London. The ground descends to some sheets of water forming a continuation of the Highgate Ponds, lying amid trees; and a belt of fine, well-grown wood cuts off the broad open view of the metropolis. Here you have all the sylvan seclusion of a remote country mansion; and charming walks, said to be nearly two miles in extent, conduct you round the park, and through the woods, where stand some trees of huge growth and grandeur, especially cedars of Lebanon and beeches. A good deal of this planting, especially some fine cedars yet near the house, was done under the direction of the first lord himself. A custom is kept up here which smacks of the old feudal times. Every morning, when the night-watchman goes off duty, at six o'clock, he fires a gun, and immediately three long winds are given on a horn to call the servants, gardeners, and labourers to their employment. The horn is blown again at breakfast and dinner hours, and at six in the evening for their dismissal.

"This charming place had been in the hands of a succession of proprietors. In 1661 it was the property of a Mr. John Bill, who married a Lady Pelham, supposed to be the widow of Sir Thomas Pelham, and a daughter of Sir Henry Vane. It must afterwards have belonged to one Dale, an upholsterer, who, as Mackay, in his 'Tour through England,' says, 'had bought it out of the 'Bubbles' —*i.e.*, the South Sea affair. This was in 1720. This Mr. Dale, unlike the majority of speculators, must have been a fortunate one. It then became the property of the Dukes of Argyll; and the great and good Duke John, whom Sir Walter Scott introduces so nobly in the scene with Jeanie Deans and Queen Caroline in 'The Heart of Midlothian,' who had lived in the reigns of Anne and Georges I. and II., and who had fought bravely at Ramillies, Malplaquet, and Oudenarde, and who afterwards beat the rebel Earl of Mar and drove the Pretender from Scotland, resided here when called to London. The property was then devised by the Duke of Argyll to his nephew John, third Earl of Bute, who is only too well remembered in the opening of the reign of George III. for his unpopularity as a minister* of the Crown.

"Lord Bute married the only daughter of the celebrated Lady Mary Wortley Montagu, who, of course, resided much here as Countess of Bute. It is observed that in Lady Mary's letters to her daughter, she always spells the name of the place 'Caen.' The earlier possessors spelt it 'Ken,' and it is curious, too, that though in the patent of the earldom granted to Lord Mansfield it is spelt 'Caen,' Lord Mansfield himself, in his letters, to the end of his life spelt it 'Ken.'

"The Earl of Bute sold Caen Wood, in 1755, to Lord Mansfield, who, on his death, devised it, as an appendage of the title, to his nephew (and successor in the earldom of Mansfield), Lord Stormont, whose descendants now possess it. Lady Mary Wortley Montagu's daughter brought Lord Bute seven sons and six daughters, so at that time the house and grounds of Caen Wood resounded with life enough. It is now very little occupied, its proprietor being much fonder of Scone Palace, his Scotch residence."

* See Vol. IV., p. 88

Among the trees mentioned above are four fine cedars, planted in the reign of George II.; they are now upwards of a hundred feet in height.

Mr. Thorne, in his "Handbook of the Environs of London," says that among the treasures that are preserved here, are "the charred and stained relics saved from the fire made of Lord Mansfield's books, by the Gordon rioters, in 1780."

Coleridge, in one of his letters to Mr. H. C. Robinson, speaks of being "driven in Mr. Gillman's gig to Caen Wood, and its delicious groves and valleys—the finest in England; in fact, a cathedral aisle of giant lime-trees, and Pope's favourite composition walk when staying with the Earl of Mansfield." As, however, Pope died at Twickenham, in 1744, and Lord Mansfield did not come into possession of Caen Wood until ten or eleven years after Pope's death, it is clear that there must be some discrepancy here.

Although born in Scotland, Lord Mansfield seems to have turned his back upon his native country at a very early age; indeed, Dr. Johnson, if we may believe Boswell, "would not allow Scotland to derive any credit from Lord Mansfield, for he was educated in England; much," he would say, "may be made of a Scotchman, if he be caught young."

In our account of Bloomsbury Square,* we have spoken of the burning of Lord Mansfield's house, and of the escape of his lordship and Lady Mansfield. Maddened by this and many other unchecked excesses, the word of command was given "to Ken Wood," the rioters evidently intending that this mansion should share a similar fate. "The routes of the rabble," writes Mr. Prickett, in his work above quoted, "were through Highgate and Hampstead, to the 'Spaniards' Tavern,' kept at the time by a person named Giles Thomas. He quickly learnt their object, and with a coolness and promptitude which did him great credit, persuaded the rioters to refresh themselves thoroughly before commencing the work of devastation; he threw his house open, and even his cellars for their entertainment, but secretly dispatched a messenger to the barracks for a detachment of the Horse Guards, which, arriving through Millfield Farm Lane, intercepted the approach northward, and opportunely presented a bold front to the rebels, who by that time had congregated in the road which then passed within a few paces of the mansion. Whilst some of the rioters were being regaled at the 'Spaniards,' others were liberally supplied with strong ale from the cellars of Ken Wood House, out of tubs placed on the roadside. Mr. William Wetherell, also, who attended the family, happened to be on the spot, and, with great resolution and presence of mind, addressed the mob, and induced many to adjourn to the 'Spaniards' for a short period. The liquors, the excitement, and the infatuation soon overcame the exhausted condition of the rabble, who, in proportion to the time thus gained by the troops, had become doubly disqualified for concerted mischief; for, great as were their numbers, their daring was not equal to the comparatively small display of military, which, the leading rioters felt, would show them no mercy; they instantly abandoned their intentions, and returned to the metropolis in as much disorder as they quitted it."

In 1835, King William IV., accompanied by several members of the royal family, the Duke of Wellington, and many of the leading nobility, paid a visit to Caen Wood. A grand entertainment was given by Lord Mansfield on the occasion, and a triumphal arch was erected on Hampstead Heath, under which the king received an address from his loyal subjects.

In the lower part of Lord Mansfield's grounds are several large ponds, of which we have spoken in our account of Highgate; four of these are within the demesne of Caen Wood, and the other three are in the fields lying in the hollow below Fitzroy Park and Millfield Lane, as we have stated previously. The three outside Caen Wood are known as the Highgate Ponds. The stream which feeds the seven extensive and well-known ponds, and gave its origin to the Hampstead Waterworks, takes its rise in a meadow on the Manor Farm at Highgate, and forms a spacious lake in Caen Wood Park, whence it approaches Hampstead, and so flows on to Camden Town and London. Its waters are of a chalybeate character, as has been ascertained from the circumstance of a large variety of petrifactions having been met with in its channel, more especially in the immediate vicinity of its source. The mineral properties of this streamlet are of a ferruginous nature, its medicinal virtues are of a tonic character, and are said to be efficacious in cases of nervous debility.

In the summer season these ponds are the resort of thousands of Londoners, more especially the possessors of aquariums, for the sake of water-beetles "and other interesting abominations," whilst the boys fish in them for tadpoles and sticklebats, or sail miniature boats on their surface.

Half a mile farther to the south-west are the other large sheets of water, known as the Hampstead Ponds, which form great centres of attraction

* See Vol. IV., p. 539.

to the visitors to the heath. These ponds, we need scarcely add, are familiar to the readers of "Pickwick," the origin of the "tittlebats" or "sticklebacks" in them being among the subjects on which at least one learned paper had been read before the Pickwick Club. It is a matter of interest to record that the originator of these ponds was no other person than Paterson, the founder of the Bank of England.

HIGHGATE PONDS.

The Fleet River, or the River of Wells, of which we have spoken in a previous chapter,* had its rise in this locality. This river, we are told, was the same as the Langbourne, which flowed through London and gave its name to a ward of the City. It was called the Fleet River down to the commencement of the present century.

The authorities of the City of London, remarks Mr. Howitt, in his "Northern Heights," were prohibited by their Act of Henry VIII. from interfering with the spring at the foot of the hill of Hampstead Heath, which, he says, "was closed in with brick for the use and convenience of the inhabitants of Hampstead." At the same time the Bishop of Westminster was authorised to search for springs on the heath, and conveyed water from them to his manor of Hendon. From some cause or other, as Mr. Lysons tells us, the water company and the people of Hampstead fell into disputes about what the Americans call their "water privileges," and the inhabitants amongst themselves even proceeded to law about the year 1700. Park found that the present ponds existed in the seventeenth century, being mentioned amongst the copyholds—the upper pond on the heath stated to contain three roods, thirty perches; the lower pond one acre, one rood, thirty-four perches. The pond in the Vale of Health was added in 1777. "The ponds," he adds, "have been fatal to many incautious bathers, owing to the sudden shelving of their sides." In the Vale of Health are visible, or were till recently, two rows of wooden posts, which, it has been suggested, might be the remains of a bridge either leading across the water, or to some aquatic pleasure-house built upon it.

On the north side of Hampstead Lane, facing the entrance to Caen Wood House, is Bishop's Wood. This wood, with one farther to the north called Mutton Wood, and another to the west

* See *ante*, p. 328.

known as Wild Wood, was, as we have already shown, a portion of the great wood attached to the estate and castle of the Bishop of London, at Highgate.* In 1755 it was purchased by Lord Mansfield, and left as a wild copse; it has since been strictly preserved as a cover for game.

The "Spaniards," a well-known tavern by the roadside, just as it emerges upon Hampstead Heath, stands on the site of a small lodge once occupied by the keeper of the park gate—the toll-gate at the Hampstead entrance to the Bishop of London's lands, of which we have already spoken. It is said by some writers to have derived its name from the fact of its having been once inhabited by a family connected with the Spanish embassy, and by others from its having been taken by a Spaniard, and converted into a house of entertainment. The Spanish Ambassador to King James I. wrote whilst residing here, complaining that he and his suite had not seen very much of the sun in England. Later on, its gardens were "improved and beautifully ornamented" by a Mr. William Staples, who, "out of a wild and thorny wood full of hills, valleys, and sand-pits, hath now made pleasant grass and gravel walks, with a mount, from the elevation whereof the beholder hath a prospect of Hanslope steeple, in Northamptonshire, within eight miles of Northampton; of Langdon Hills, in Essex, full sixty miles east; of Banstead Downs, in Surrey, south; of Shooter's Hill, Kent, south-east; Red Hill, Surrey, south-west; and of Windsor Castle, Berkshire, to the west. These walks and

THE "SPANIARDS," HAMPSTEAD HEATH.

plats this gentleman hath embellished with a great many curious figures, depicted with pebble-stones of various colours." Such is the description of the "Spaniards" in a MS. account of the place, quoted by Park, in "History of Hampstead," and by Prickett, in his "History of Highgate;" but the statement must be received with caution, for certainly no resident of Hampstead, so far as we can learn, has ever been able to descry the steeple of Hanslope, or of any other church, in Northamptonshire. "The 'Spaniards,'" says Mr. Thorne, "still has its garden and its bowling-green; but the curious figures are gone, and so has (is) the mound, and with it the larger part of the prospect, partly, perhaps, owing to the growth of the neighbouring trees, and the erection of two or

* See *ante*, p. 389.

three large houses between it and the Heath." It was the brave landlord of this inn who, as we have said before, saved Caen Wood House from being wrecked by the mob during the Gordon riots. As we have stated above, he detained the mob here by a *ruse* till the military arrived. Curiously enough, the "Spaniards" is not mentioned in Mr. Larwood's otherwise exhaustive "History of Signboards," in connection, at all events, with Hampstead.

Another place of entertainment in this neighbourhood in former times, though now quite forgotten, was a cottage, with gardens attached to it, which rejoiced in the name of New Georgia. It has been identified with Turner's Wood, now enclosed in Lord Mansfield's grounds, opposite the western lodge of Caen Wood. From the same MS. from which the above description of the "Spaniards" was taken, we learn that "here the owner showeth you several little rooms, and numerous contrivances of his own to divert the beholder; and here, the gentleman is put in the pillory, and the ladies are obliged to kiss him, with such other oddities; the building is irregular and low, of wood, and the ground and wilderness is laid out in a romantic taste." Among the "numerous contrivances" was a chair which sank into the ground on a person sitting in it. In 1748, these singular grounds, like "Spring Gardens,"* were interspersed with representations of various reptiles, so connected with mechanism, as to make efforts of attack upon parties who unsuspectingly trod upon a board or spring. It is not improbable that the consequences of those frights to the ladies caused the disuse and decay of New Georgia, for about the year 1770 this species of mechanism seems to have been entirely discontinued.

The house next to the "Spaniards," and close by the entrance of Hampstead Heath, is called Erskine House, as having been the residence of the famous advocate, but less famous chancellor, Thomas Lord Erskine. The building is a plain white house, with a long portico opening upon the roadway. Of the house itself but little is seen from the road, excepting one end; a high wall shuts in what little garden it has on that side, and another high wall shuts out from observation the spacious gardens and grounds formerly belonging to it on the opposite side of the road. The house itself, says Mr. Howitt, is "simply a bald, square mass, shouldered up again by another house at its back. We see, however, the tall windows of its large drawing-room on the second floor, commanding a splendid view over Caen Wood and some part of Highgate. Yet this was the house inhabited by Thomas Lord Erskine, contemporary with both the law lords, his neighbours, Mansfield and Loughborough. Here he converted the place from a spot of no account into a very charming residence, laying out, with great enthusiasm, its grounds, and so planting it with bays and laurels, that he called it Evergreen Hill. He is said also to have planted with his own hand the extraordinary broad holly hedge separating his kitchen-garden from the Heath, opposite to the Fir-tree Avenue." The garden on the opposite side of the road was connected with the house by a subterranean passage. This garden, however, has long been taken into Lord Mansfield's estate.

* See Vol. IV., p. 77.

Lord Erskine's account of his residence, where Edmund Burke was a frequent visitor, is too amusing to be omitted here. It is told by Mr. Rush, in his "Court of London:"—"When we got to Mr. Trotter's, Lord Erskine kept up his sprightly vein at table. 'I believe,' said our host, 'the soil is not the best in that part of Hampstead where your seat is.' 'No; very bad,' he replied, 'for although my grandfather was buried there as an earl near a hundred years ago, what has sprouted up from it since but a mere baron?' He alluded, of course, to his own title. He mentioned, however, a fact which went to show that although the soil yielded no increase in titles of nobility, it did in other things; for in his description he referred to a chestnut-tree upon it, which, when he first went to live there, was bought by his gardener for sixpence, but now yielded him thirty pounds a year."

"Here," says Mr. Howitt, "during the intervals of his arduous professional labour, Lord Erskine was zealously engaged in planning and carrying out his improvements. With his old gardener, John Barnett, he took his spade, and schemed and dug, and planted and transplanted; and no one who has not tried it can tell the immense refreshment derived from such an active diversion of otherwise exhausting trains of thought. To men compelled to spend long days in crowded, ill-ventilated courts, the health and spirits given by such tastes is incalculable. No doubt, from these occupations Erskine returned with tenfold vigour of body and mind to his pleadings, and to his parliamentary conflicts." Lord Erskine, at one time, contemplated cutting down a renowned group of elm-trees, nine in number, which flourished in all their picturesque beauty near his mansion; but the great lawyer thought better of his purpose, and the trees were spared. Cowper commemorated their escape, in a poem, in which we find that the Muses (sympathising, perhaps, with the number nine) interfered :—

> "Erskine (they cried) at our command
> Disarms his sacrilegious hand;
> Whilst yonder castle [Windsor] towers sublime,
> These elms shall brave the threats of Time."

In the same poem the poet of the "Task" refers to another performance of the Muses in the same locality, in relation to another great lawyer, the first Earl of Mansfield :—

> "When Murray deign'd to rove
> Beneath Caen Wood's sequester'd grove,
> They wander'd oft, when all was still,
> With him and Pope, on Hampstead Hill."

Lord Erskine's first rise in his profession, as he himself told Samuel Rogers, was due to an accident—the fact that he was suddenly called upon to defend Captain Baillie, in a matter of contention between himself and the authorities of Greenwich Hospital. His astonishing eloquence and energy, joined to the right being on his side, gained the day; and the all but briefless barrister went home that night with sixty-seven retaining fees in his pocket.

From an account by Sir Samuel Romilly, quoted by Mr. Howitt, we see not only what sort of men frequented his house in those days, but also the nature of Erskine's curious hobbies :—"Here he gave gay parties, of which he was the life, by his good humour and whimsicalities. I dined there one day, at what might be called a great Opposition dinner. The party consisted of the Duke of Norfolk, Lord Grenville, Lord Grey, Lord Holland, Lord Ellenborough, Lord Lauderdale, Lord Henry Petty, Thomas Grenville, Pigot, Adam, Edward Morris, Lord Erskine's son-in-law, and myself. If the most malignant enemies of Erskine had been present, they would have admitted that nothing could be more innocent than the conversation which passed. Politics were hardly mentioned. Amid the light and trifling topics of conversation after dinner, it may be worth while to mention one, as it strongly characterises Lord Erskine. He had always felt and expressed a great sympathy for animals. He has talked for years of a bill he was to bring into Parliament to prevent cruelty to them. He has always had several favourite animals to which he has been much attached, and of whom all his acquaintances have a number of anecdotes to relate. He had a favourite dog, which he used to bring, when he was at the bar, to all his consultations; another favourite dog, which, at the time he was Lord Chancellor, he himself rescued in the street from some boys who were about to kill it, under pretence of its being mad. A favourite goose, which followed him whenever he walked about his grounds; a favourite macaw; and other dumb favourites without number. He told us now, that he had two favourite leeches. He had been blooded by them when he was dangerously ill at Portsmouth; they had saved his life, and he had brought them with him to town—had ever since kept them in a glass—had himself every day given them fresh water, and formed a friendship for them. He said he was sure they knew him, and were grateful to him. He had given them the names of Howe and Clive, the celebrated surgeons, their dispositions being quite different. He went and fetched them for us to see; but without the vivacity, the tones, the details and gestures of Lord Erskine, it would be impossible to give an idea of this singular scene." *Apropos* of Lord Erskine's consideration for dumb animals, Twiss in his "Life of Eldon," tells the following anecdote concerning his lordship :—"On one occasion, in the neighbourhood of Hampstead Heath, a ruffianly driver was pummelling a miserable bare-boned hack horse. Lord Erskine's sympathy provoked him to a smart remonstrance. 'Why,' said the fellow, 'it's my own; mayn't I use it as I please?' and as he spoke, he discharged a fresh shower of blows on the raw back of the beast. Lord Erskine, excessively irritated, laid his walking-stick sharply over the shoulders of the offender, who, crouching and grumbling, asked what business he had to touch him with his stick. 'Why,' replied Erskine, to whom the opportunity of a joke was irresistible, 'it is my own; mayn't I use it as I please?'"

His lordship's witty sallies, indeed, rendered his society particularly enjoyable, and doubtless would have filled a volume of *Punch*. Of those which are on record, we cannot do more than quote one or two.

On one occasion, when Captain Parry remarked that "when frozen up in the Arctic regions they lived much on seals," "Yes," observed the ex-chancellor, "and very good living too, *if you keep them long enough!*" Being invited to attend the ministerial fish dinner at Greenwich when he was chancellor, "To be sure," he replied, "what would your dinner be without the *Great Seal?*"

Mr. Howitt, in his notice of this place, says :—"On the staircase of the house possessed by Lord Erskine, and the copyhold of which he transferred to Lord Mansfield, there is a window of stained glass, in which are emblazoned Lord Erskine's arms, with the baron's coronet, and the motto which he assumed, 'Trial by Jury.' The tunnel under the road, which connected the premises with the pleasure-grounds on the other side, is now built up, Lord Mansfield having resumed the grounds on his side. Baron (Chief Justice) Tindal at one time lived in this house."

Heath House, the residence next to that of Lord Erskine, and overlooking the Heath, was successively the abode of Mr. Edward Cox, the author of some poems, published at the beginning of this century; and of Sir Edward Parry, the Arctic voyager.

The next house, called The Firs, was built by a Mr. Turner, a tobacconist of Fleet Street, who planted the avenue of Scotch firs, which so largely contribute to the beauty of this part of the Heath. Mr. Turner also made the roadway across the Heath, from The Firs to the pleasant hamlet of North End and Golder's Green, on the slope of the hill looking towards Hendon, whither we now proceed.

A large house on the eastern slope of the hill leading from Hampstead to North End and Hendon, is that in which the great Lord Chatham lived for some time in gloomy retirement in 1767. It is now called Wildwood House, but formerly bore the name of North End House. The grounds extend up the hill, as far as the clump of Scotch firs, where the roads divide; and in the highest part of the gardens is a summer-house surmounted by a dome. Recently the house has undergone considerable alteration, having been raised a storey, besides having had other additions made to it; but some part at least of its interior remains unaltered. Mr. Howitt, in his "Northern Heights," says:—"The small room, or rather closet, in which Chatham shut himself up during his singular affliction—on the third storey—still remains in the same condition. Its position from the outside may be known by an oriel window looking towards Finchley. The opening in the wall from the staircase to the room still remains, through which the unhappy man received his meals or anything else conveyed to him. It is an opening of, perhaps, eighteen inches square, having a door on each side of the wall. The door within had a padlock which still hangs upon it. When anything was conveyed to him, a knock was made on the outer door, and the articles placed in the recess. When he heard the outer door again closed, the invalid opened the inner door, took what was there, again closed and locked it. When the dishes or other articles were returned, the same process was observed, so that no one could possibly catch a glimpse of him, nor need there be any exchange of words." It may be added that in making the alterations above mentioned, the condition of the room occupied by Lord Chatham was as little interfered with as possible; and even in the boards of the floor the marks caused by his lordship's wheeled chair are well preserved. In this house, in more recent times, lived Mr. Tagart, the minister of Little Portland Street Unitarian Chapel, and author of "Locke's Writings and Philosophy," "Sketches of the Reformers," &c.

On the opposite side of the road towards Hendon, over against the summer-house mentioned above, an elm-tree marks the spot where formerly stood a gibbet, on which was suspended the body of Jackson, a highwayman, for murdering Henry Miller on or near this spot, in May, 1673. "In 1674 was published," says Park, in his "History of Hampstead," "Jackson's Recantation; or, the Life and Death of the notorious Highwayman now hanging in chains at Hampstead," &c. Park adds that he was told that the post of this gibbet was in his time (1818) remaining as a mantel-tree over the fire-place in the kitchen of the "Castle" public-house on the Heath. One of the two trees between which the gibbet stood was blown down not many years ago. Hampstead, we may add, was a well-known place for highwaymen, who waylaid persons returning from the Wells as they rode or drove down Haverstock Hill, or across the Heath, and towards Finchley. We are told in the "Cabinet of Curiosities," published by Limbird in 1822, that Lord Kenyon referred to a case in which a highwayman had the audacity to file a bill before a Court of Equity to compel his partner to account to him for a half-share of his plunder, in which it was expressly stated that the plaintiff and his partner, one Joseph Williams, continued their joint dealings together in several places—viz., at "Bagshot, in Surrey; at Salisbury, in Wiltshire; at Hampstead, in Middlesex, and elsewhere, to the amount of £2,000 and upwards." It is satisfactory to learn that the insolent plaintiff was afterwards executed, and one of his solicitors transported for being concerned in a robbery.

Golder's Hill, at North End, was the residence of Mark Akenside, the author of "Pleasures of the Imagination." The son of a butcher at Newcastle-on-Tyne, he was born at that place in 1721, and was educated at the grammar-school of that town. He afterwards went to Edinburgh, in order to qualify himself for the ministry; but preferring the study of physic, he took his degree of M.D. in 1744, by royal mandate from the University of Cambridge. In that same year he produced the poem above mentioned, and it was well received. In the following year he published his first collection of odes. His life was uneventful. He practised as a physician with but indifferent success, first at

Northampton, afterwards in Hampstead, and finally in London. At length, just as bright prospects were opening upon him, he was carried off by an attack of fever, in 1770. He was a man of great learning, and of high character and morality; he lies buried, as we have seen,* in the Church of St. James, Piccadilly. His house stood on the site of that now occupied by Sir Spencer Wells.

At a farmhouse close by, just on the edge of the Heath, William Blake, the artist and poet, used to lodge. Linnell, the painter, frequently occupied the house during the summer months. Mr. Coventry Patmore, too, lived for some time at North End; Mrs. Craik, the novelist (formerly Miss Dinah Muloch), likewise formerly resided here, in the house afterwards occupied by Miss Meteyard, the authoress of the "Life of Joshua Wedgwood" and other antiquarian works. Collins' Farm, at North End, has often been painted. It is the subject of a picture by Stuart, exhibited in 1830. The large house on the right of the avenue, descending from the Heath, was for some time the residence of Sir T. Fowell Buxton, whose name became associated with those of Clarkson, Wilberforce, and other kindred spirits, in effecting the abolition of slavery and the emancipation of the slaves throughout the colonial possessions of the British empire.

The "Bull and Bush," a well-known public-house in North End, was, it is said, the frequent resort of Addison and his friends. The house has attached to it some pleasant tea-gardens, in which some of the curiously constructed bowers and arbours are still to be seen.

CHAPTER XXXV.

HAMPSTEAD (*continued*).—THE HEATH AND THE "UPPER FLASK."

"It is a goodly sight through the clear air,
From Hampstead's healthy height, to see at once
England's vast capital in fair expanse—
Towers, belfries, lengthen'd streets, and structures fair.
St. Paul's high dome amidst the vassal bands
Of neighbouring spires a regal chieftain stands;
And over fields of ridgy roofs appear,
With distance softly tinted, side by side
In kindred grace, like twain of sisters dear,
The Towers of Westminster, her Abbey's pride.
Joanna Baillie.

The View from the Heath—Attempted Encroachments by the Lord of the Manor—His Examination before a Committee of the House of Commons—Purchase of the Heath by the Metropolitan Board of Works as a Public Recreation-ground—The Donkeys and Donkey-drivers—Historic Memorabilia—Mr. Hoare's House, and Crabbe's Visits there—The Hampstead Coaches in Former Times—Dickens' Partiality for Hampstead Heath—Jack Straw's Castle—The Race-course—Suicide of John Sadlèir, M.P.—The Vale of Health—John Keats, Leigh Hunt, and Shelley—Hampstead Heath a Favourite Resort for Artists—Judge's Walk, or King's Bench Avenue—The "Upper Flask"—Sir Richard Steele and the Kit-Kat Club—"Clarissa Harlowe."

THE great attractions of Hampstead, as we have endeavoured to show at the commencement of the preceding chapter, are its breezy heath, which has long been a favourite resort not only of cockney holiday folk, but also of artists and poets, and its choice beauties of scenery, to which no mere description can do justice. Standing upon the broad roadway which crosses the Heath, in continuation of the road by the "Spaniards," and leading to the upper part of the town, the visitor will be at a loss whether to admire most the pleasing undulations of the sandy soil, scooped out into a thousand cavities and pits, or the long avenues of limes, or the dark fir-trees and beeches which fringe it on the north—of which we have already spoken—or the gay and careless laughter of the merry crowds who are gambolling on the velvet-like turf, or riding donkeys along the steep ridge which reaches towards Caen Wood. It is probably Hampstead Heath to which Thompson alludes when he writes in his "Seasons:"—

"Or I ascend
Some eminence, Augusta, in thy plains,
And see the country far diffused around,
One boundless bush."

Indeed, few, if any, places in the neighbourhood of the metropolis can compare with its range of scenery, or show an equally "boundless bush." As Richardson puts into the mouth of Clarissa Harlowe: "Now, I own that Hampstead Heath affords very pretty and very extensive prospects; but it is not the wide world neither."

In addition to the charming landscape immediately around us, teeming with varied and picturesque attractions, the view is more extensive, perhaps, than that commanded by any other spot of only

---

* See Vol. IV., p. 256.

equal elevation in the kingdom; for from the broad roadway where we are now standing—which, by the way, seems to be artificially raised along the ridge of the hill—we get a fine view of St. Paul's, with the long line of Surrey Hills in the background extending to Leith Hill, the grand stand on Epsom race-course, and St. Martha's Hill, near Guildford. Standing nearly on a level with the top of its cross, we have the whole of the eastern metropolis spread out at our feet, and the eye follows the line of the river Thames, as it winds its way onwards, nearly down to Gravesend. Dr. Preston, in a lecture on Hampstead, very graphically describes how, throwing himself mentally back five hundred years, he commands from its high ground a distant view of London:—"I am alone in the midst of a wood or forest, and I cannot see around me for the thickness of the wood. Neither roads nor bridle-paths are to be seen; so I climb one of the tallest of the oaks, and survey the landscape at leisure. The City of London rises clear and distinct before me to the south, for I am at least three hundred feet above the level of its river banks, and no coal is burnt within its walls to thicken and blacken the atmosphere. I can just distinguish the Tower, and the walls ranging from Bishopsgate to Cripplegate, Aldersgate, and Ludgate. Outside the City gates, however, all is open country, except a group of cottages round the Priory, at Kilburn." And then he describes how London stands on a group of smaller hills, intersected by brooks and water-courses, as we have already seen in detail.*

JACK STRAW'S CASTLE.

The northern side of the Heath is particularly wild and charming; and the groups of elms and fir-trees, combined with the broken nature of the sandy and gravelly soil, add greatly to the picturesque beauty of the foreground. Looking in this direction, or somewhat to the north-west, the background of the view is formed by the dark sides of Harrow hill; nor is water altogether wanting to lend its aid to the picture, for from certain points the lake at Kingsbury at times gleams out like a sheet of burnished silver in the mid-distance.

From this description it is obvious that a stranger climbing to the top of Hampstead Hill on a bright summer morning, before the air is darkened with the smoke of a single fire, and looking down on the vast expanse of London to his left and to

* See Vol. I., p. 434; Vol. II., p. 416.

HAMPSTEAD HEATH IN 1840. *From a Drawing by Constable.* (*See page* 454.)

his right, stretching away for miles along the bosom of the Thames valley from Greenwich and Woolwich up to Kew and even Richmond, with its towers, spires, and roofs all crowded before him as in a panorama, they, with pride and enthusiasm, may well exclaim, with the essayist, "Yonder is the metropolis of the empire, the abode of the arts and of science, as well as the emporium of trade and commerce; the glory of England, and the wonder of the world."

Turning from poetry to prose, however, we may observe that the Heath, "the region of all suburban ruralities," as it has been called, originally covered a space of ground about five hundred acres in extent; but by the gradual growth of the neighbouring town of Hampstead and of the surrounding hamlets, and also by occasional enclosures which have been made by the lord of the manor, and by the occupiers of villas on its frontiers, it has been shorn of nearly half its dimensions. These encroachments, though unlawful at the time when made, have become legalised by lapse of years. As an "open space" or common for the free use of the Londoners, its fate was for some time very uncertain. About the year 1831 an attempt was made by the lord of the manor, Sir Thomas Wilson, to build on the Heath, near the Vale of Health; but he was forced to desist. A new road and a bridge, and a range of villas was designed and commenced, traces of which are still to be seen on the side of the hill rising from the Vale of Health towards the south front of Lord Mansfield's park. Sir Thomas Wilson made another attempt at enclosing the Heath, near "Jack Straw's Castle," in more recent years, but was forced again to desist by a decree of the Court of Chancery, to which the residents appealed. Indeed, numerous attempts were made by successive lords of the manor to beguile Parliament into sanctioning their natural desire for power of enclosure; but, fortunately, so great was the outcry raised by the general voice of the people, through the press, that all further encroachment was stayed.

How far Sir Thomas Wilson considered himself justified in his attempted enclosures of the Heath, and the consequent shutting out of the holiday folk from their ancient recreation-ground, may be gathered from his answers before the "Select Committee appointed to inquire into the Open Spaces of the Metropolis." The extract is from the Report of the Select Committee; the catechised is Sir Thomas Wilson:—

Are you aware that many thousands of people frequent Hampstead Heath on holidays?—They go there on holidays.

Have you ever treated them as trespassers?—When there are *fêtes*, and people go up there to amuse themselves, they pay an acknowledgment.

Have you not treated pedestrians as trespassers?—No; I do not know that I have. It is unenclosed land, and I could only bring an action for trespass, and should probably get one penny for damages.

You have never treated the public as trespassers?—Some people imagine that they go to Hampstead Heath to play games, but it could not be done. Part of the heath is a bog, and there are cases of horses and cows having been smothered there.

But people go there and amuse themselves?—Just as they do in Greenwich Park, but they have no right in Greenwich Park.

You have never treated people as trespassers?—No. Are they treated as trespassers in Greenwich Park?

Do you claim the right of enclosing the whole of the Heath, leaving no part for public games?—If I were to enclose the whole of it, it would be for those only who are injured to find fault with me.

Would you sell Hampstead Heath?—I have never dreamt of anything of the kind; but if the public chose to prevent me, or to make any bargain that I am not to enclose it, they must pay the value of what they take from me.

Do you consider Hampstead Heath private property?—Yes.

To be paid for at the same rate as private land adjoining?—Yes.

Do you concede that the inhabitants in the neighbourhood have rights on the Heath?—There are presentments in the Court Rolls to show that they have none.

Sir Thomas Wilson valued the Heath at two and a half millions of money for building purposes; and such might, perhaps, have been its market value if actually laid out for building. But the law restricted his rights, and his successor was glad to sell them for less than a twentieth part of the sum.

The Metropolitan Commons Act, procured in 1866 by the Right Hon. William Cowper, then Chief Commissioner of the Board of Works, secured the Heath from further enclosure; and in 1870, the manor having passed to a new lord, the Metropolitan Board of Works were enabled to purchase the manorial rights for the sum of £45,000, and thus to secure the Heath in perpetuity for public use. Prior to this exchange of ownership, the surface of the Heath had for several years been largely denuded of the sand and gravel of which it was composed, the result being that several of the hillocks and lesser elevations had been partially levelled, deep pits had been scooped out, trees in some parts undermined, and their gnarled roots left exposed above the surface of the ground to the action of the wind and rain. But since the Board of Works has taken the Heath under its fostering care, the barren sand has become in many places re-clothed with verdure, and the wild tract of land is again resuming its original appearance, gay and bright with purple heather and golden furze blossom.

Apart from an occasional sham fight on its slopes on a volunteer field day, the Heath is now left to the sole use of the people as a place of common resort and recreation, where they can breathe the fresh air, and indulge in cricket, and in such rural pastimes as may be provided for them by the troops of donkeys and donkey-boys who congregate on these breezy heights. Indeed, "Hampstead," as the modern poet says, "is the place to ruralise;" it is also, it may be added, especially at Whitsuntide, the place to indulge in a sort of equestrian exercise. Decked out with white saddle-cloths, frisking away over the sunny heath, and perhaps occasionally pitching some unlucky rider into a shallow sand-pit, the donkeys, we need hardly say, are, to the juvenile portion of the visitors at least, the chief source of amusement. By the male sex the horse is principally affected; the women and children are content with donkeys. The horse of Hampstead Heath has peculiar marks of his own. His coat is of the roughest, for he knows little about curry-combs, and passes his nights—at any rate, during the summer months—under the canopy of heaven. For his own sake it is to be hoped that he has not often a tender mouth, when we consider the sort of fellows who mount him, and how mercilessly they jerk at the reins. The Hampstead Heath horse is a creature of extremes. He is either to be seen flying at full gallop, urged along by kicks, and shouts, and blows; or if left to himself, he shambles slowly forwards, being usually afflicted in one or more of his legs with some equine infirmity. As for the donkeys, they are much like their brethren everywhere in a country where the donkey is despised and mismanaged. They are much more comfortable to ride when homeward than outward bound. The sullen crawl of the "outward-bound" donkey—his perpetual endeavours to turn round, and his craving after roadside vegetation—are, as may be well imagined, varied at intervals by the onslaughts of the donkey-man, who, with a shower of blows, a string of guttural oaths, and a hoarse "kim up," stimulates the unlucky beast into a spasmodic gallop of two minutes' duration, during which time the equestrian powers of the rider are severely tested. It may be here stated that whatever may have been the torture to which the poor animals were subjected in bygone days, there is at least a possibility of their being more tenderly dealt with hereafter, seeing that the "donkey-boys" are now under the control of the authorities who rule the Heath, and that any undue severity practised by them may end in a suspension or withdrawal of their licence.

We get some little insight into the character and amusements of the company usually brought together here at the commencement of the last century, in a comedy called *Hampstead Heath*, which was produced at Drury Lane Theatre in 1706. The following extract will serve our purpose:—

Act I., Sc. 1. Scene, Hampstead.

Smart. Hampstead for a while assumes the day; the lively season o' the year, the shining crowd assembled at this time, and the noble situation of the place, give us the nearest show of Paradise.

Bloom. London now, indeed, has but a melancholy aspect, and a sweet rural spot seems an adjournment o' the nation where business is laid fast asleep, variety of diversions feast our fickle fancies, and every man wears a face of pleasure. The cards fly, the bowl runs, the dice rattle, some lose their money with ease and negligence, and others are well pleased to pocket it. But what fine ladies does the place afford?

Smart. Assemblies so near the town give us a sample of each degree. We have court ladies that are all air and no dress, city ladies all dress and no air, and country dames with broad brown faces like a Stepney bun; besides an endless number of Fleet Street semptresses that dance minuets in their furbeloe scarfs and cloaths hung as loose about them as their reputations. . . .

Enter *Driver*.

Smart. Mr. Deputy Driver, stock jobber, state botcher, and terror of strolling strumpets, and chief beggar hunter, come to visit Hampstead.

Driver. And d'you think me so very shallow, captain, to leave the good of the nation and getting money to muddle it away here 'mongst fops, fiddlers, and furbeloes, where ev'ry thing's as dear as freeholders' votes, and a greater imposition than a Dutch reckoning? I am come hither, but it is to ferret out a frisking wife o' mine, one o' the giddy multitude that's rambled up to this ridiculous assembly.

That this exhilarating subject has not altogether lost its hold on the play-going public may be inferred when we state that *Happy Hampstead* was the title of a comedy or farce produced at the Royalty Theatre in the year 1877.

On fine Sundays and Mondays, and on Bank Holidays, we need hardly add, the Heath is alive with swarms of visitors; and it is estimated that on a bright and sunny Whit-Monday as many as 50,000 people have been here brought together. Writing on this subject in the "Northern Heights of London," Mr. Howitt observes: "Recent times have seen Sunday dissipation re-asserting itself, by the erection of a monster public-house with a lofty tower and flag, to attract the attention of Sunday strollers on the Heath. Of all places, this raised its Tower of Babel bulk in that formerly quiet and favourite spot, the Vale of Health. That suitable refreshments should be attainable to the numerous visitors of the Heath on Sundays and holidays is quite right and reasonable; but that taps and gin-palaces on a Titanic scale should be licensed, where people resort ostensibly for fresh air, relaxation, and exercise, is the certain mode of turning all such advantages into popular curses, and converting the very bosom of nature into a hotbed of demoralisation and crime. Any one who has witnessed the condition of the enormous crowds who flock to the Heath on summer Sundays, as they return in the evening, needs no argument on the subject."

Hampstead Heath has very few historical associations, like Blackheath; but there is one which, though it savours of poetry and romance, must not be omitted here. Our readers will not have forgotten the lines in Macaulay's ballad of "The Armada," in which are described the beacons which announced to the outlying parts of England the arrival of the Spanish Armada off Plymouth; how

> "High on bleak Hampstead's swarthy moor they started for the North."

It is, of course, quite possible that Hampstead Heath may have been used for telegraphic purposes, but there is no actual record of the fact.

Like Blackheath, however, and, indeed, most of the other bleak and open spaces in the neighbourhood of London, Hampstead Heath has its recollection of highwaymen, of their depredations, and of their executions, as we have mentioned in the previous chapter. In a poem published at the close of the seventeenth century, called "The Triennial Mayor; or, The New Raparees," we read—

> "As often upon Hampstead Heath
> We've seen a felon, long since put to death,
> Hang, crackling in the sun his parchment skin,
> Which to his ear had shrivelled up his chin."

Mr. Howitt, in his "Northern Heights," says that "one of the earliest and most curious facts in history connected with Hampstead Heath is that stated by Matthew of Paris, or rather by Roger of Wendover, from whom he borrows it, that so lately as in the thirteenth century it was the resort of wolves, and was as dangerous to cross on that account at night, as it was for ages afterwards, and, in fact, almost down to our own times, for highwaymen."

Down to the commencement of the last century, when that honour was transferred to Brentford as more central, the elections of knights of the shire for Middlesex were held on Hampstead Heath, as we learn from some notices which appear in the *True Protestant Mercury*, for March 2–5, 1681, the *Flying Post* for October 19–22, 1695, and for November 9–12, of the same year.

The poet Crabbe was a frequent visitor at the hospitable residence of Mr. Samuel Hoare, on the Heath. Campbell writes: "The last time I saw Crabbe was when I dined with him at the house of Mr. Hoare, at Hampstead. He very kindly came to the coach to see me off, and I never pass that spot on the top of Hampstead Heath without thinking of him." The mansion is called "The Hill," and was the seat of Mr. Samuel Hoare, the banker. Here used to congregate the great poets of the age, Rogers, Wordsworth, Coleridge, Campbell, Lucy Aikin, Mrs. Marcet, and Agnes and Joanna Baillie; whilst the centre of the gathering was the poet Crabbe. In the "Life of the Rev. George Crabbe," by his son, we read: "During his first and second visits to London my father spent a good deal of his time beneath the hospitable roof of the late Samuel Hoare, Esq., on Hampstead Heath. He owed his introduction to this respectable family to his friend Mr. Bowles, and the author of the delightful 'Excursions in the West,' Mr. Warner; and though Mr. Hoare was an invalid, and little disposed to form new connections, he was so much gratified with Mr. Crabbe's manners and conversation, that their acquaintance grew into an affectionate and lasting intimacy. Mr. Crabbe, in subsequent years, made Hampstead his head-quarters on his spring visits, and only repaired thence occasionally to the brilliant circles of the metropolis."

At the commencement of the century, if we may trust Mr. Chambers's assertion in his "Book of Days," Hampstead and Highgate could be reached only by "short stages" (*i.e.*, stage-coaches), going twice a day; and a journey thither once or twice in the summer time was the farthest and most ambitious expedition of a cockney's year. Both villages then abounded with inns, with large gardens in their rear, overlooking the pleasant country fields towards Harrow, or the extensive and more open land towards St. Albans or towards the valley of the Thames. The "Spaniards" and "Jack Straw's Castle" still remain as samples of these old "rural delights." The features of the latter place, as they existed more than a century since, have been preserved by Chatelaine in a small engraving executed by him about the year 1745. The formal arrangement of the trees and turf, in humble imitation of the Dutch taste introduced by William III., and exhibited on a larger scale at Hampton Court and Kensington Palace, may be noted in this humbler garden.

To Hampstead Heath, as every reader of his "Life" is aware, Charles Dickens was extremely partial, and he constantly turned his suburban walks in this direction. He writes to Mr. John Forster: "You don't feel disposed, do you, to muffle yourself up, and start off with me for a good brisk walk over Hampstead Heath? I know a good house there where we can have a red-hot chop for dinner and a glass of good wine." "This note," adds Forster, "led to our first experience of 'Jack Straw's Castle,' memorable for many happy meetings in coming years."

Passing into "Jack Straw's Castle," we find the usual number of visitors who have come up in Hansoms to enjoy the view, to dine off its modern fare, and to lounge about its gardens. The inn, or hotel, is not by any means an ancient one, and it would be difficult to find out any connection between the present hostelry and the rebellion which may, or may not, have given to it a name. The following is all that we could glean from an old magazine which lay upon the table at which we sat and dined when we last visited it, and it is to be feared that the statement is not to be taken wholly "for gospel:"—"Jack Straw, who was second in command to Wat Tyler, was probably entrusted with the insurgent division which immortalised itself by burning the Priory of St. John of Jerusalem, thence striking off to Highbury, where they destroyed the house of Sir Robert Hales, and afterwards encamping on Hampstead heights. 'Jack Straw,' whose 'castle' consisted of a mere hovel, or a hole in the hill-side, was to have been king of one of the English counties—probably of Middlesex; and his name alone of all the rioters associated itself with a local habitation, as his celebrated confession showed the rude but still not unorganised intentions of the insurgents to seize the king, and, having him amongst them, to raise the entire country."

This noted hostelry has long been a famous place for public and private dinner-parties and suppers, and its gardens and grounds for alfresco entertainments. In the "Cabinet of Curiosities," published by Limbird in 1822, we find the following lines "on 'Jack Straw's Castle' being repaired:"—

"With best of food—of beer and wines,
Here may you pass a merry day;
So shall mine host, while Phœbus shines,
Instead of straw make good his hay."

The western part of the Heath, behind "Jack Straw's Castle," would appear to have been used in former times as the Hampstead race-course long before the "Derby" or "Ascot" had been established in the popular favour. The races, however, do not appear to have been very highly patronised, if we may judge from the fact that at the September meeting, 1732, one race only was run, and that for the very modest stake of ten guineas. "Three horses started," says the *Daily Courant* of that period; "one was distanced the first heat, and one was drawn; Mr. Bullock's 'Merry Gentleman' won, but was obliged to go the course the second heat alone." We learn from Park's "History of Hampstead" that the races "drew together so much low company, that they were put down on account of the mischief that resulted from them." The very existence of a race-course on Hampstead is now quite forgotten; and the uneven character of the ground, which has been much excavated for gravel and sand, is such as would render a visitor almost disposed to doubt whether such could ever have been the case.

On the greensward behind "Jack Straw's Castle," on Sunday morning, February 17, 1856, was found the dead body of John Sadleir, the fraudulent M.P. for Sligo. The corpse was lying in a hollow on the sloping ground, with the feet very near to a pool of water; beside it was a small phial which had contained essential oil of almonds, and also a silver cream-jug from which he had taken the fatal draught. In his pocket, among other things, was found a piece of paper on which was written "John Sadleir, Gloucester Square, Hyde Park." In 1848, as we learn from his memoir in the *Gentleman's Magazine*, Mr. Sadleir became chairman of the London and County Joint Stock Banking Company, and for several years he presided over that body with great ability. Shortly before his death, he vacated the chair; and though still a director, he ceased to take an active part in its business. He continued to be a principal manager of the affairs of the Tipperary Bank, and he was chairman of the Royal Swedish Railway Company, in which it appeared that, out of 79,925 shares issued, he got into his own possession 48,245; besides which he dishonestly fabricated a large quantity of duplicate shares, of which he had appropriated 19,700. Among other enterprises in which Mr. Sadleir was also actively engaged, were the Grand Junction Railway of France, the Rome and Frascati Railway, a Swiss railway, and the East Kent line. He had dealt largely in the lands sold in the Encumbered Estates Court in Ireland, and in several instances had forged conveyances of such lands, in order to raise money upon them. The catastrophe was brought about by Messrs. Glyn, the London agents of the Tipperary Bank, returning its drafts as "not provided for," a step which was followed a day or two after by the Bank of Ireland. On the day preceding that on which his body was discovered on Hampstead Heath, Sadleir wrote to Mr. Robert Keating, M.P. for Waterford (another director of the Tipperary Bank), a letter, intended to be posthumous, commencing thus:—

"Dear Robert,—To what infamy have I come

step by step—heaping crime upon crime; and now I find myself the author of numberless crimes of a diabolical character, and the cause of ruin, and misery, and disgrace to thousands—aye, tens of thousands! Oh, how I feel for those on whom this ruin must fall! I could bear all punishment, but I could never bear to witness the sufferings of those on whom I have brought this ruin. It must be better that I should not live."

One of the Dublin newspapers—the *Nation*—speaking of this unexampled swindler, thus expresses itself: "He was a man desperate by nature, and in all his designs his character, his objects, his very fate, seemed written in that sallow face, wrinkled with multifarious intrigue—cold, callous, and cunning—instinct with an unscrupulous audacity, and an easy and wily energy. How he contrived and continued to deceive men to the last, and to stave off so securely the evidences of his infamies, until now, that they all seem exploding together over his dead body, is a marvel and a mystery."

"Hampstead," says Mr. Thorne, in his "Environs of London," "is an awkward place for a suicide to select. The lord of the manor possesses very extensive rights, among them being that of deodand, and is, therefore, in the case of a person who commits suicide within the manor, entitled as heir to 'the whole of the goods and chattels of the deceased, of every kind, with the exception of his estate of inheritance, in the event of the jury returning a verdict of *felo de se*.' Sadleir's goods and chattels were already lost or forfeited; but the cream-jug was claimed and received by the lord as an acknowledgment of his right, and then returned." As

THE "UPPER FLASK," ABOUT 1800. (*See page* 459.)

"deodands" have been since abolished by Act of Parliament, such a claim could not arise again.

John Sadleir, we need hardly remind the reader of Charles Dickens's works, figures in "Little Dorritt" as Mr. Merdle. "I shaped Mr. Merdle himself," writes Dickens, "out of that gracious rascality."

In Hardwicke's "Annual Biography" for 1857 we read thus: "Strange as it may sound, there are not wanting those who believe (in spite of the identification of the corpse by the coroner, Mr. Wakley, who had formerly sat in Parliament with him), that, after all, John Sadleir did not commit suicide, but simply played the trick so well known in history and in romance, of a pretended death and a supposititious corpse. These persons believe that he is still alive and in America."

Immediately at our feet, as we look down in the hollow towards the east, from the broad road in front of "Jack Straw's Castle," is the Vale of Health, with its large modern hotel, and its ponds glistening in the sunshine beyond. We wish that it could be added that this hotel forms any ornament to the scene: for down to very recent years this Vale of Health presented a sight at once picturesque and pleasant. "In front of a row of cottages," writes Mr. Howitt, "and under the shade of willows, were set out long tables for tea, where many hundreds, at a trifling cost, partook of a homely and exhilarating refreshment. There families could take their own tea and bread and butter, and have water boiled for them, and table accommodation found for them, for a few pence; but then came this great tavern, with its towers and battlements, and cast them literally and practically into the shade. It was, however, really gratifying to see that the more imposing and dangerous place of entertainment never could compete with the more primitive tea-tables, nor banish the homely and happy groups of families, children, and humble friends."

An "old inhabitant" of Hampstead writes thus in 1876:—"A plot of land lately enclosed in the Vale of Health is classic ground. In a picturesque cottage, with its pretty balcony environed with creepers, and a tall *arbor vitæ* almost overtopping its roof, lived for some time Leigh Hunt. Here Byron and Shelley visited him; and when this cottage from age was obliged to be pulled down, there was still in the parlour window a pane of glass on which Byron had written these lines of Cowper—

> "'Oh for a lodge in some vast wilderness,
> Some boundless contiguity of shade,
> Where rumour of oppression and deceit,
> Of unsuccessful or successful war,
> Shall never reach me more.'"

JOHN KEATS. *Copied by permission from the Sketch taken by Mr. Severn.* (*See page* 458.)

It may be well to note here the fact that on this site South Villa now stands.

Cyrus Redding, in his "Recollections," thus writes, in 1850:—"I visited him (Leigh Hunt) in the Vale of Health at Hampstead, where there was always a heartiness that tempted confidence, and with much imaginativeness, much skimming of literature, and a light culling of its wild flowers, criticism without envy, and opinions free of insincerity. Leigh Hunt yet survives, or I might be tempted to proceed to many details, which would infringe the rule I have made for myself in the mention of but few who are still spared from a day of our literature, the similar of which is hardly likely soon, if ever, to recur again." Leigh Hunt died at the house of a friend at Putney, in 1859.

The "Cockney poets," Keats, Shelley, Leigh

Hunt, and their friends, loved Hampstead. Coleridge, who lived many years at Highgate, was no stranger to "The Spaniards" or the "Vale of Health," with its toy-like cluster of cottages in the little hollow where we are gazing down. Keats (whom the author of "Childe Harold" styled, in his Ravenna letter to the elder Disraeli, "a tadpole of the lakes," but to whom he made the *amende honorable* by a magnificent compliment a year later) was residing in lodgings at Hampstead when he felt the first symptoms of the deadly consumption which shortly afterwards laid the most fervid genius of this century in the Protestant burying-ground at Rome.

The name of John Keats has many associations with Hampstead. At Leigh Hunt's house Keats wrote one of his finest sonnets, and in a beautiful spot between Millfield Lane and Lord Mansfield's house, as we have already narrated, occurred that one short interview between Keats and Coleridge, in which the latter said that death was in the hand of the former after they had parted. These words soon proved true. In a recent volume of the *Gentleman's Magazine* there is a very interesting passage touching the author of "The Eve of St. Agnes." "I see," says Miss Sabilla Novello, "that Sylvanus Urban declares himself an unmeasured admirer of Keats; I therefore enclose for your acceptance the photograph of a sketch made of him, on his death-bed, by his friend Joseph Severn, in whose diary at that epoch are written, under the sketch, these words: '28th January, 3 o'clock, morning—Drawn to keep me awake. A deadly sweat was on him all this night.' I feel you will be interested by the drawing." The sketch is, indeed, a most touching memento of the youth who, having his lot cast in the golden age of modern English poetry, left us some of the finest, and purest, and most perfect poetry in the language, and died at twenty-five. So excellent a work is this little picture, and so accurately does it suggest the conditions under which it was drawn, that no doubt the time will come when it will be regarded as the best personal relic of the author of "Endymion." Severn's portrait of Keats, taken at Hampstead, is in the National Portrait Gallery; and hard by, in the South Kensington Museum, Severn's merits as an artist may be seen in his poetic transcription of Ariel on the bat's back.

Connected with Keats's illness and death may be mentioned two incidents that for the living reader contain a mournful and a striking interest. Among the earliest friends of Keats were Haydon, the painter, and Shelley, the poet. When Keats was first smitten, Haydon visited the sufferer, who had written to his old friend, requesting him to see him before he set out for Italy. Haydon describes in his journal the powerful impression which the visit made upon him—"the very colouring of the scene struck forcibly on the painter's imagination. The white curtains, the white sheets, the white shirt, and the white skin of his friend, all contrasted with the bright hectic flush on his cheek, and heightened the sinister effect; he went away, hardly hoping." And he who hardly hoped for another, what extent of hope had he for himself? From the poet's bed to the painter's studio is but a bound for the curious and eager mind. Keats, pitied and struck down by the hand of disease, lies in paradise compared with the spectacle that comes before us—genius weltering in its blood, self-destroyed because neglected. Pass we to another vision! Amongst the indignant declaimers against the unjust sentence which criticism had passed on Keats, Shelley stood foremost. What added poignancy to indignation was the settled but unfounded conviction that the death of the youth had been mainly occasioned by wanton persecution. Anger found relief in song. "Adonais: an Elegy on the Death of John Keats," is among the most impassioned of Shelley's verses. Give heed to the preface:—"John Keats died at Rome of a consumption in his twenty-fourth year, on the — of ——, 1821, and was buried in the romantic and lovely cemetery of the Protestants in that city, under the pyramid which is the tomb of Cestius, and the massy walls and towers, now mouldering and desolate, which formed the circuit of ancient Rome. The cemetery is an open space among the ruins, covered in winter with violets and daisies. *It might make one in love with death to think that one should be buried in so sweet a place.*" Reader, carry the accents in your ear, and accompany us to Leghorn. A few months only have elapsed. Shelley is on the shore. Keats no longer lives, but you will see that Shelley has not forgotten him. He sets sail for the Gulf of Lerici, where he has his temporary home; he never reaches it. A body is washed ashore at Via Reggio. If the features are not to be recognised, there can be no doubt of the man who carries in his bosom the volume containing "Lamia" and "Hyperion." The body of Shelley is burned, but the remains are carried——whither? You will know by the description, "The cemetery is an open space among the ruins, covered in winter with violets and daisies. *It might make one in love with death to think that one should be buried in so sweet a place.*" There he lies! Keats and he, the mourner and the mourned, almost touch each other!

All the later years of Keats's life, until his departure for Rome, were passed at Hampstead, and here all his finest poetry was written. Leigh Hunt says:—"The poem with which his first volume begins was suggested to him on a delightful summer day, as he stood by the gate which leads from the battery on Hampstead Heath into a field by Caen Wood; and the last poem, the one on 'Sleep and Poetry,' was occasioned by his sleeping in the Vale of Health." There are, perhaps, few spots in the neighbourhood of Hampstead more likely to have suggested the following lines to the sensitive mind of poor Keats than the high ground overlooking the Vale of Health:—

"To one who has been long in city pent
'Tis very sweet to look into the fair
And open space of heaven—to breathe a prayer
Full in the smile of the blue firmament.
Who is more happy when, with heart's content,
Fatigued he sinks into some pleasant lair
Of wavy grass, and reads a debonair
And gentle tale of love and languishment?
Returning home at evening with an ear
Catching the notes of Philomel—an eye
Watching the sailing cloudlets' bright career,
He mourns that day so soon has glided by,
E'en like the passage of an angel's tear,
That falls through the clear ether silently."

No wonder that great painters as well as poets have loved this spot, and made it hallowed ground. Romney, Morland, Haydon, Constable, Collins, Blake, Linnell, Herbert, and Clarkson Stanfield have all in their turn either lived in Hampstead, or, at the least, frequented it, studying, as artists and poets only can, the glorious "sunset effects" and wondrous contrasts of light and shade which are to be seen here far better than anywhere else within five miles of St. Paul's or Charing Cross.

Linnell, the painter of the "Eve of the Deluge" and the "Return of Ulysses," made frequently his abode at a cottage beyond the Heath, between North End and the "Spaniards." To this quiet nook very often resorted, on Sunday afternoons, his friend William Blake, that "dreamer of dreams and seer of visions," and John Varley, artist and astrologer, who were as strange a pair as ever trod this earth.

Goldsmith, who loved to walk here, describes the view from the top of the hill as finer than anything he had seen in his wanderings abroad; and yet he wrote "The Traveller," and had visited the sunny south.

Between the Heath and the western side of the town is a double row of noble lime-trees, the gravel path under which is "still called the Judge's Walk, or King's Bench Avenue." The story is, that when the plague was raging in London, the sittings of the Courts of Law were transferred for a time from Westminster to Hampstead, and that the Heath was tenanted by gentlemen of the wig and gown, who were forced to sleep under canvas, like so many rifle volunteers, because there was no accommodation to be had for love or money in the village. But we do not guarantee the tradition as well founded.

Making our way towards the village of Hampstead, but before actually quitting the Heath, we pass on our left, at the corner of Heath Mount and East Heath Road, the house which marks the spot on which, in former times, stood the "Upper Flask" tavern, celebrated by Richardson, in his novel of "Clarissa Harlowe." A view of the old house, formerly the rendezvous of Pope, Steele, and others, and subsequently the residence of George Steevens, the commentator on Shakespeare, will be found in Mr. Smith's "Historical and Literary Curiosities."

The "Upper Flask" was at one time called the "Upper Bowling-green House," from its possessing a very good bowling-green. We have given an engraving of it on page 456.

When the Kit-Kat Club was in its glory, its members were accustomed to transfer their meetings in the summer time to this tavern, whose walls—if walls have ears—must have listened to some rare and racy conversation. We have already spoken at some length of the doings of this celebrated club in a previous volume.* In 1712, Steele, most genial of wits and most tender of humorists, found it necessary to quit London for a time. As usual, the duns were upon him, and his "darling Prue" had been, we may suppose, a little more unreasonably jealous than usual. He left London in haste, and took the house at Hampstead in which Sir Charles Sedley had recently died. Thither would come Mr. Pope or Dr. Arbuthnot in a coach to carry the eminent moralist off to the cheerful meetings of the Kit-Kat at the "Flask." How Sir Richard returned we are not told, but there is some reason to fear that the coach was even more necessary at the end of the evening than at its beginning. These meetings, however, did not last long. We shall have more to say of Sir Richard Steele when we reach Haverstock Hill.

Mr. Howitt, in his "Northern Heights of London," gives a view of the house as it appeared when that work was published (1869). The author states that the members of the Kit-Kat Club used "to sip their ale under the old mulberry-tree, which

* See Vol. I., p. 70.

still flourishes, though now bound together by iron bands, and showing signs of great age," in the garden adjoining. Sir Richard Blackmore, in his poem, "The Kit-Kats," thus commemorates the summer gatherings of the club at this house :—

> "Or when, Apollo-like, thou'st pleased to lead
> Thy sons to feast on Hampstead's airy head :
> Hampstead, that, towering in superior sky,
> Now with Parnassus does in honour vie."

Since that time the house has been much altered, and additions have been made to it. One Samuel Stanton, a vintner, who came into possession of it near the beginning of the last century, was probably the last person who used it as a tavern. In 1750 it passed from his nephew and successor, "Samuel Stanton, gentleman," to his niece, Lady Charlotte Rich, sister of Mary, Countess of Warwick; a few years later George Steevens, the annotator of Shakespeare, bought the house, and lived there till his death, in 1800.

Steevens is stated to have been a fine classical scholar, and celebrated for his brilliant wit and smart repartee in conversation, in which he was "lively, varied, and eloquent," so that one of his acquaintances said that he regarded him as a speaking Hogarth. He possessed a handsome fortune, which he managed, says his biographer, "with discretion, and was enabled to gratify his wishes, which he did without any regard to expense, in forming his distinguished collections of classical learning, literary antiquity, and the arts connected with it. . . . . He possessed all the grace of exterior accomplishment, acquired when civility and politeness were the characteristics of a gentleman. He received the first part of his education at Kingston-upon-Thames; he went thence to Eton, and was afterwards a fellow-commoner of King's College, Cambridge. He also accepted a commission in the Essex militia, on its first establishment. The latter years of his life he chiefly spent at Hampstead in retirement, and seldom mixed in society except in booksellers' shops, or the Shakespeare Gallery, or the morning conversations of Sir Joseph Banks."

"Steevens," says Cradock, in his "Memoirs," "was the most indefatigable man I had ever met with. He would absolutely set out from his house at Hampstead, with the patrol, and walk to London before daylight, call up his barber in Devereux Court, at whose shop he dressed, and when fully accoutred for the day, generally resorted to the house of his friend Hamilton, the well-known editor and printer of the *Critical Review.*"

Steevens, it is stated, added considerably to the house. It was subsequently occupied for many years by Mr. Thomas Sheppard, M.P. for Frome, and afterwards by Mrs. Raikes, a relative of Mr. Thomas Raikes, to whose "Journal" we have frequently referred in these pages. On her death the house passed into the hands of a Mr. Lister. The old house is still kept in remembrance by a double row of elms in front of it, forming a shady grove.

With the interest attached to the place through the pages of "Clarissa Harlowe," it would be wrong not to make more than a passing allusion to it. We will, therefore, summarise from the work those portions having special reference to the "Upper Flask" and its surroundings :—

Richardson represents the fashionable villain Lovelace as inducing Clarissa—whom he had managed, under promise of marriage, to lure away from her family—to take a drive with him in company with two of the women of the sponging-house into which he had decoyed her. Lovelace, afterwards writing to his friend Belford, says :—"The coach carried us to Hampstead, to Highgate, to Muswell Hill; back to Hampstead, to the 'Upper Flask.' There, in compliment to the nymphs, my beloved consented to alight and take a little repast; then home early by Kentish Town." Clarissa no sooner discovers the nature of the vile place into which Lovelace has brought her, than she at once sets about endeavouring to effect her escape. By one of Lovelace's accomplices she is tracked to a hackney coach, and from her directions to the driver it is at once made clear that Hampstead is her destination. The fellow then disguises himself, and making his way thither, discovers her at the "Upper Flask," which fact he communicates to Lovelace in the following words : —"If your honner come to the 'Upper Flax,' I will be in site (sight) all day about the 'Tapphouse' on the Hethe." Lovelace pursues his victim in all haste, and arrives at the "Upper Flask," but only to find that she had been there, but had since taken up her abode somewhere in the neighbourhood. We next find Lovelace writing from the "Upper Flask :"—"I am now here, and have been this hour and a half. What an industrious spirit have I." But all that he could learn with any certainty respecting the runaway was, that "the Hampstead coach, when the dear fugitive came to it, had but two passengers in it; but she made the fellow go off directly, paying for the vacant places. The two passengers directing the coachman to set them down at the 'Upper Flask,' she bid them set her down there also."

Clarissa has in the meantime taken up her abode in the lodging-house of a Mrs. Moore, as she herself tells us in one of her epistles:—"I am at present at one Mrs. Moore's, at Hampstead. My heart misgave me at coming to this village, because I had been here with him more than once; but the coach hither was such a convenience that I knew not what to do better." She, however, is not allowed to rest quietly here, but is soon surrounded by Lovelace's tools and spies. She attempts to escape, and, making her way to the window, exclaims to the landlady—"'Let me look out! Whither does that path lead to? Is there no probability of getting a coach? Cannot I steal to a neighbouring house, where I may be concealed till I can get quite away? Oh, help me, help me, ladies, or I am ruined!' Then, pausing, she asks—'Is that the way to Hendon? Is Hendon a private place? The Hampstead coach, I am told, will carry passengers thither?'" Richardson writes: "She, indeed, went on towards Hendon, passing by the sign of the 'Castle' on the Heath; then stopping, looked about her, and turned down the valley before her. Then, turning her face towards London, she seemed, by the motion of her handkerchief to her eyes, to weep; repenting (who knows?) the rash step that she had taken, and wishing herself back again. . . . Then, continuing on a few paces, she stopped again, and, as if disliking her road, again seeming to weep, directed her course back towards Hampstead."

Hannah More bears testimony to the fact that, when she was young, "Clarissa" and "Sir Charles Grandison" were the favourite reading in any English household. And her testimony to their excellence is striking. She writes: "Whatever objection may be made to them in certain respects, they contain more maxims of virtue, and more sound moral principle, than half the books called 'moral.'"

At the end of a century, Macaulay tells us that the merits of "Clarissa Harlowe" were still felt and acknowledged. On one occasion he said to Thackeray: "If you have once thoroughly entered on 'Clarissa,' and are infected by it, you can't leave it. When I was in India, I passed one hot season at the hills, and there were the governor-general, and the secretary of the Government, and the commander-in-chief, and their wives. I had 'Clarissa' with me; and as soon as they began to read it, the whole station was in a passion of excitement about Miss Harlowe and the scoundrel Lovelace. The governor's wife seized the book, and the secretary waited for it, and the chief justice could not read it for tears. He acted the whole scene as he paced up and down the Athenæum Library; I daresay he could have spoken pages of the book."

The following is the testimony of R. B. Haydon to the merits of "Clarissa Harlowe" as a work of fiction:—"I was never so moved by a work of genius as by *Othello*, except by 'Clarissa Harlowe.' I read seventeen hours a day at 'Clarissa,' and held up the book so long, leaning on my elbows in an arm-chair, that I stopped the circulation, and could not move. When Lovelace writes, 'Dear Belton, it is all over, and Clarissa lives,' I got up in a fury, and wept like an infant, and cursed Lovelace till I was exhausted. This is the triumph of genius over the imagination and heart of the readers."

Richardson, by all accounts, was one of the vainest of men, and loved to talk of nothing so well as his own writings. It must be owned, however, that he had something to be vain and proud about when he wrote "Clarissa Harlowe," which at once established itself as a classic on the bookshelves of every gentleman and lady throughout England.

"The great author," writes Thackeray, in his "Virginians," "was accustomed to be adored—a gentler wind never puffed mortal vanity; enraptured spinsters flung tea-leaves round him, and incensed him with the coffee-pot. Matrons kissed the slippers they had worked for him. There was a halo of virtue round his nightcap."

So great is the popularity of the author of "Pamela," "Clarissa," and "Sir Charles Grandison," that foreigners of distinction have been known to visit Hampstead, and to inquire with curiosity and wonder for the "Flask Walk," so distinguished as a scene in "Clarissa's" history, just as travellers visit the rocks of Mellerie, in order to view the localities with which they have already been familiarised in Rousseau's tale of passion. The "Lower Flask" tavern, in Flask Walk, is mentioned in "Clarissa Harlowe" as a place where second-rate persons are to be found occasionally in a swinish condition. The "Flask Inn," rebuilt in 1873, is still here, and so is Flask Walk, but both are only ghosts of their former selves!

J Baillie

CHAPTER XXXVI.

HAMPSTEAD (*continued*).—THE TOWN.

"A steeple issuing from a leafy rise,
With balmy fields in front, and sloping green,
Dear Hampstead, is thy southern face serene,
Silently smiling on approaching eyes.
Within, thine ever-shifting looks surprise,
Streets, hills, and dells, trees overhead now seen,
Now down below, with smoking roofs between—
A village revelling in varieties.
Then northward, what a range—with heath and pond,
Nature's own ground; woods that let mansions through,
And cottaged vales, with pillowy fields beyond,
And clumps of darkening pines, and prospects blue,
And that clear path through all, where daily meet
Cool cheeks, and brilliant eyes, and morn-elastic feet."—*Leigh Hunt.*

Description of the Town—Heath Street—The Baptist Chapel—Whitefield's Preaching at Hampstead—The Public Library—Romney, the Painter—The "Hollybush"—The Assembly Rooms—Agnes and Joanna Baillie—The Clock House—Branch Hill Lodge—The Fire Brigade Station—The "Lower Flask Inn"—Flask Walk—Fairs held there—The Militia Barracks—Mrs. Tennyson—Christ Church—The Wells—Concerts and Balls—Irregular Marriages—The Raffling Shops—Well Walk—John Constable—John Keats—Geological Formation of the Northern Heights.

THE town of Hampstead is built on the slope of the hill leading up to the Heath, as Mr. Thorne, in his "Environs" styles it, "in an odd, sidelong, tortuous, irregular, and unconnected fashion. There are," he adds, "the fairly-broad winding High Street, and other good streets and lanes,

THE OLD WELL WALK, HAMPSTEAD, ABOUT 1750. (*See page* 467.)

lined with large old brick houses, within high-walled enclosures, over which lean ancient trees, and alongside them houses small and large, without a scrap of garden, and only a very little dingy yard; narrow and dirty byways, courts, and passages, with steep flights of steps, and mean and crowded tenements; fragments of open green spaces, and again streets and lanes bordered with shady elms and limes. On the whole, however, the pleasanter and sylvan character prevails, especially west of the main street. The trees along the streets and lanes are the most characteristic and redeeming feature of the village. Hampstead was long ago 'the place of groves,' and it retains its early distinction. It is the most sylvan of suburban villages." Besides these avenues or groves, almost every part of "old Hampstead" is distinguished by rows of trees, of either lime or elm, planted along the broad footpaths in true boulevard fashion. Mr. Howitt, in his "Northern Heights," in writing on this subject, says: "Its old narrow roads winding under tall trees, are continually conducting to fresh and secluded places, that seem hidden from the world, and would lead you to suppose yourselves far away from London, and in some especially old-fashioned and old-world part of the country. Extensive old and lofty walls enclose the large old brick houses and grounds of what were once the great merchants' and nobles' of London; and ever and anon you are reminded of people and things which lead your recollection back to the neighbouring capital and its intruding histories."

Like Tunbridge Wells and other fashionable resorts of the same kind, Hampstead was not without its inducements for the "wealthy, the idle, and sickly," who flocked thither; and "houses of entertainment and dissipation started up on all sides." The taverns had their "long-rooms" and assembly-rooms for concerts, balls, and card parties; and attached to them were tea-gardens and bowling-greens. On the Heath races were held, as we have stated in the previous chapter; fairs were held in the Flask Walk, and the Well Walk and Church Row became the fashionable promenades of the place. But to proceed.

Leaving the Lower or East Heath, with its pleasant pathways overlooking the Vale of Health, the "ponds," and the distant slopes of Highgate behind us, we descend Heath Mount and Heath Street, and so make our way into the town. On our left, as we proceed down the hill, we pass the Baptist Chapel which was built for the Rev. William Brock, about the year 1862. It is a good substantial edifice, and its two towers are noticeable features in its architecture. This fabric, or rather its predecessor on the same site, is not without its historical reminiscences. "The Independent congregation at Hampstead," says Mr. Howitt, "is supposed to owe its origin to the preaching of Whitefield there in 1739, who, in his journal of May 17, of that year, says, 'Preached, after several invitations thither, at Hampstead Heath, about five miles from London. The audience was of the politer sort, and I preached very near the horse course, which gave me occasion to speak home to the souls concerning our spiritual race. Most were attentive, but some mocked. Thus the Word of God is either a savour of life unto life, or of death unto death.' The congregation experienced its share of the persecutions of those times. The earliest mention of the chapel is 1775." It was some time leased by Selina, Countess of Huntingdon, who relinquished her right in 1782. The present fabric is called Heath Street Chapel.

In a house on the west side of High Street is the Hampstead Public Library. After undergoing many vicissitudes of fortune, this institution seems to have taken a new lease of life with the commencement of 1880.

On our right, between the High Street and the Heath, lived—from 1797 to 1799, George Romney, the famous painter. He removed hither from his residence in Cavendish Square.* He took great pains in constructing for himself a country house, between the "Hollybush Inn" and the Heath, with a studio adjoining. He did not derive, however, any great pleasure from his investment, for he entered the house when it was still wet, and he never enjoyed a day of good health afterwards. Allan Cunningham, in his "Lives of British Painters," says that Romney had resolved to withdraw to the pure air and retirement of Hampstead "to paint the vast historical conceptions for which all this travail had been undergone, and imagined that a new hour of glory was come;" but after a few months—a little more than a year—finding his health growing worse and worse, he made up his mind to return back to the wife whom more than a quarter of a century before he had deserted, and who nursed him carefully till his death. The great artist's studio was subsequently converted into the Assembly Rooms. These rooms were erected on the principle of a tontine; but all sorts of legal difficulties arose, and no one knows who is now the rightful owner. Here for many years—1820 to 1860—were held, at first every month, and subsequently every quarter of a year, *conversazioni*, to which

* See Vol. IV., p. 446.

the resident artistic and literary celebrities used to lend all sorts of works of art to enliven the winter evenings. The cessation of these pleasant gatherings was much regretted. About 1868 an attempt was made to revive these gatherings by means of a succession of lectures during the winter, but these also came to an end after the second season.

The "Hollybush" is not at all an uncommon sign in England, and as it is generally found near to a church, we may conclude that it points back to the ancient custom—now so generally revived amongst us—of decking our houses with evergreens at Christmas. It is said that this custom is as old as the times of the Druids.

The sisters Agnes and Joanna Baillie lived in the central house of a terrace consisting of three mansions facing the Assembly Rooms at the back of the "Hollybush Inn." The house is now called Bolton House, and is next door but one to Windmill Hill, a name which points to the fact of a windmill having stood there at one time. Joanna Baillie, who is well known for her "Plays on the Passions," enjoyed no small fame as a poetess, and was the author of several plays, which were praised by Sir Walter Scott. *Basil* and *De Montfort*, however, were the only tragedies of Miss Joanna Baillie that were performed on the London stage, though *The Family Secret* was brought out with some success at the Edinburgh Theatre.

In Mr. H. Crabbe Robinson's "Diary," under date of May, 1812, we find the following particulars of this amiable and accomplished lady:—"Joined Wordsworth in the Oxford Road (*i.e.*, Oxford Street); we then got into the fields, and walked to Hampstead. . . . We met Miss Joanna Baillie, and accompanied her home. She is small in figure, and her gait is mean and shuffling; but her manners are those of a well-bred lady. She has none of the unpleasant airs too common to literary ladies. Her conversation is sensible. She possesses apparently considerable information, is prompt without being forward, and has a fixed judgment of her own, without any disposition to force it on others. Wordsworth said of her with warmth, 'If I had to present to a foreigner any one as a model of an English gentlewoman, it would be Joanna Baillie.'"

Indeed, according to the testimony of all those who knew her, Joanna Baillie was a plain, simple, homely, unpretending woman, who made no effort to dazzle others, and was not easily dazzled by others. She loved her home, and she and her sister contrived to make that home for many years a centre of all that was good, as well as intellectual.

"I believe," says Miss Sedgwick, an American lady, "of all my pleasures here, dear J. will most envy me that of seeing Joanna Baillie, and of seeing her repeatedly at her home—the best point of view for all best women. She lives on Hampstead Hill, a few miles from town, in a modest house, with Miss Agnes Baillie, her only sister, a kindly and agreeable person. Miss Baillie—I write this for J., for women always like to know how one another look and dress—Miss Baillie has a well-preserved appearance: her face has nothing of the vexed or sorrowful expression that is often so deeply stamped by a long experience of life. It indicates a strong mind, great sensibility, and the benevolence that, I believe, always proceeds from it if the mental constitution be a sound one, as it eminently is in Miss Baillie's case. She has a pleasing figure, what we call lady-like—that is, delicate, erect, and graceful; not the large-boned, muscular frame of most English women. She wears her own gray hair—a general fashion, by the way, here, which I wish we elderly ladies of America may have the courage and the taste to imitate; and she wears the prettiest of brown silk gowns and bonnets, fitting the *beau-ideal* of an old lady—an ideal she might inspire, if it has no pre-existence. You would, of course, expect her to be free from pedantry and all modes of affectation; but I think you would be surprised to find yourself forgetting, in a domestic and confiding feeling, that you were talking with the woman whose name is best established among the female writers of her country; in short, forgetting everything but that you were in the society of a most charming private gentlewoman."

The *Quarterly Review* also gives her the credit of having borne a most tasteful and effective, though subordinate part, in that entire and wonderful revolution of the public taste in works of imagination and in literature generally, which contrasts this century with the latter half of the last. "Unversed in the ancient languages and literature, and by no means accomplished in those of her own age, or even of her own country, this remarkable woman owed it, partly to the simplicity of her Scottish education, partly to the influence of the better part of Burns's poetry, but chiefly to the spontaneous action of her own powerful genius, that she was able at once, and apparently without effort, to come forth the mistress of a masculine style of thought and diction, which constituted then, as it constitutes now, the characteristic merit of her writings, and which contributed most beneficially to the already commenced reformation of the literary principles of the century."

We learn from Lockhart's "Life," that Sir

Walter Scott, too, on being asked whether among poets born north of the Tweed he preferred Burns or Campbell, gave no direct answer, but said, "If you wish to speak of a real poet, Joanna Baillie is now the highest genius of our country." In fact, Scott was one of her most ardent admirers. Mentioning in a letter at the time his own "House of Aspen," he says, "The 'Plays of the Passions' have put me entirely out of conceit with my Germanised brat." His esteem of the talents of the author led, in Miss Baillie's case, as in that of Miss Edgeworth and others, to Scott's acquaintance and friendship with the woman. The cordial and agreeable intimacy between Miss Baillie and Scott, which ceased but with the life of the latter, dates from his introduction to her at Hampstead, in 1806, by the translator and poet, Sotheby. Joanna Baillie herself, many years afterwards, described the interview to a friend as one of the most remarkable events of her life. She, from that period of their first acquaintance, became a continual correspondent of the mighty minstrel; and some of the most entertaining letters he ever wrote are addressed to her. The author of the "Man of Feeling" was also her friend. The prologue to the play of *The Family Legend* was written by Scott, the epilogue by Mackenzie. Joanna Baillie was honoured also from Lord Byron with the remark that she was the only woman who could write a tragedy.

When her "Plays on the Passions" were first published, they appeared without a name, and great was the speculation of the public as to who the author could be. Mrs. Piozzi stood almost single-handed in maintaining that they were the work of a woman; and she tells us, what is in itself a proof of the faulty taste and judgment of her age, that no sooner was their authorship owned by "an unknown girl" than the work fell so much in value as to become almost unsaleable.

William Howitt, who knew her in her Hampstead home, calls her a "powerful dramatic writer," a "graceful and witty lyrist," and a "sweet and gentle woman." Miss Berry says that her tragedies were highly appreciated by that connoisseur of literature and art, Sir George Beaumont, who sent them to Charles James Fox, and that the latter was in such raptures about them that he wrote a critique of five pages upon the subject.

Miss Lucy Aikin has preserved a few traits of her character, having been acquainted with her through meeting her at Mr. Barbauld's house. She was shy and reserved to a degree, for the "repression of all emotions, even the most gentle and the most honourable to human nature, seems to have been the constant lesson taught by her parents in her Presbyterian home." The first thing which drew upon Joanna the admiring notice of Hampstead society was the devoted assiduity of her attention to her mother, then blind as well as aged, and whom she attended day and night. But this part of her duty came at length to its natural termination; and the secret of her authorship having been at length permitted to transpire, she was no longer privileged to sit in the shade, shuffling off upon others her own fair share of conversation. Latterly her discourse flowed freely enough; but even then it was less on books than on real life and the aspects of rural nature that she loved to talk. "Her genius," writes Miss Aikin, "had shrouded itself under so thick a veil of silent reserve, that its existence seems scarcely to have been ever suspected beyond the domestic circle when the 'Plays on the Passions' burst upon the world. The dedication of the volume to Dr. Baillie gave a hint in what quarter the author was to be sought; but the person chiefly suspected was the accomplished widow of his uncle, John Hunter. Of Joanna, at all events, no one dreamed on this occasion. She and her sister—I well remember the scene—arrived on a morning call at Mr. Barbauld's; my aunt immediately introduced the topic of the anonymous tragedies, and gave utterance to her admiration with that generous delight in the manifestation of kindred genius which always distinguished her. But not even the sudden delight of such praise, so given, would seduce our Scottish damsel into self-betrayal. The faithful sister rushed forward, as we afterwards recollected, to bear the brunt, while the unsuspected author of the 'Plays' lay snugly wrapt up in the asylum of her taciturnity."

Miss Aikin remarks that in spite of her long residence in the neighbourhood of London, Joanna Baillie retained her Scotch predilections to the last. She died in 1851, at the age of ninety, carrying with her to the grave the love, reverence, and regrets of all who had enjoyed her society.

Hard by the house of Joanna Baillie is an old mansion named Fenton House, but generally known as "The Clock House," from a clock which adorned its front, though now superseded by a sundial; the house is chiefly remarkable for its heavy high-pitched roof, not unlike that of many a château in Normandy. It now belongs to a member of Lord Mansfield's family.

The large red-brick house, on the left in ascending from Hollybush Hill towards the Heath, is called Branch Hill Lodge. It was in part rebuilt about the year 1745 for Sir Thomas Clark, Master of the Rolls. The house was afterwards the residence of Lord Chancellor Macclesfield, and subsequently, among others, of Lord Loughborough, before his removal to Rosslyn House, where we shall presently speak of him again. At the close of the last century it was purchased of Colonel Parker, a younger son of Lord Macclesfield, by Sir Thomas Neave, who, as Lysons states in his "Environs of London," here had "a very large and most valuable collection of painted glass, a great part of which was procured from various convents on the Continent, immediately after the French Revolution."

At the junction of Heath and High Street is the Fire Brigade Station, an attractive building of coloured bricks, with a lofty watch tower and clock, erected by public subscription in 1870; it commands a view over a large extent of country. Mr. G. Vulliamy was the architect.

On the east slope of the hill, and covering the ground on our left as we descend Heath Street and the High Street, lies that portion of the town which may fairly lay claim to being called "Old Hampstead." Our approach to this once fashionable quarter is by a narrow passage out of the High Street, which brings us at once to the "Lower Flask Tavern," which we have incidentally mentioned at the close of the previous chapter.

The "Flask" is a very appropriate, and therefore a very common, sign to mark a house devoted to the service of topers. There was a celebrated "Flask" in Pimlico; and the "Upper" and "Lower Flasks" at Hampstead are historical.

Flask Walk, which runs eastward from the tavern, is a long straggling thoroughfare, in part planted with trees along the edge of the broad pavement. In the triangular space near the end—now a pleasant grass-plat—an annual fair was formerly held. It was noted for its riotous character; conducted as it was much on the same principle as the celebrated "Bartlemy Fair" in Smithfield. An advertisement on the cover of the original edition of the *Spectator* is as follows:—"This is to give notice, that Hampstead Fair is to be kept upon the Lower Flask Tavern Walk, on Friday, the first of August, and holds (*i.e.*, lasts) for four days." Formerly the Flask Walk was open to the High Street, and was shaded throughout with fine trees; many of these, however, are now gone, and small houses have taken their place. In Flask Walk were formerly the parish stocks. Not long ago some busy-bodies wanted to change the name of the thoroughfare, but common sense ruled otherwise.

One of the chief sources of the Fleet, as we have already stated, was in Hampstead; it rose in a spring nearly under the walls of Gardnor House, at the east end of Flask Walk, and within a hundred yards westward of the old Wells. At the junction of Flask Walk and Well Walk, and nearly opposite the "Wells Tavern," are the Middlesex Militia Barracks, a spacious brick building, partly formed out of an old mansion, called Burgh House, two projecting wings having been added. The barracks was built in 1863, from the designs of Mr. Henry Pownall.

In a house at the corner of Flask Row, opposite to the Militia Barracks, the mother of the poet Tennyson spent the last years of her life; and here she died about the year 1861. It is almost needless to add that up to that date Alfred Tennyson was a constant visitor at Hampstead, and was frequently to be seen strolling on the Heath wrapped up in thought, though he mixed little with Hampstead society. Mrs. Tennyson lies buried in Highgate Cemetery.

Close by this spot, on the sloping ground leading up to Squire's Mount, is one of the many religious edifices of the town, Christ Church, a large Perpendicular building, with a lofty spire, which serves as a landmark for miles around; this church was built in 1852. In the same neighbourhood is the new workhouse, a large and well-built structure of brick and stone, together with the other parochial offices.

Both Flask Walk and Well Walk have an air of fading gentility about them, and, like many of the other streets and lanes in the village, they are planted with rows of shady limes or elms, which every year, however, are becoming fewer and fewer.

Well Walk (which connects Flask Walk with the lower portion of East Heath) and the "Wells Tavern" still serve to keep in remembrance the famous "wells," which commanded an open view across the green fields towards Highgate.

In the days of the early celebrity of its "waters," Hampstead must have rivalled Tunbridge Wells and Epsom; and its Well Walk in the morning, with all its gay company of gentlemen in laced ruffles and powdered wigs, and of ladies in hoops of monstrous size, must have reminded one of the Mall in St. James's Park, or the gardens of Kensington Palace. At the time when London was surrounded by "spas" and "wells"—when the citizens resorted to Bagnigge Wells in the morning, to Sadlers' Wells and the White Conduit in the evening, and to Tunbridge Wells, Bath, and Cheltenham in the summer and autumn—the springs of Hampstead were in great repute, and they were, no doubt, exceedingly beneficial to people whose principal complaints were those of idleness, dissipation, and frivolity. A local physician wrote a long account of these valuable waters, describing them in terms of extravagant hyperbole, and lauding their virtues to the skies. The analysis which he publishes is, however, a curious practical comment on his rapturous enthusiasm. As a matter of fact, the water was and is simply exceedingly pure spring water, with a faint trace of earthy salts such as those of iron, magnesia, and lime. The total amount of solid matter is but seven grains to the gallon—about as much as is to be found in the water of the Kent Company, and about a fourth of the quantity held in solution by the water of the companies which derive their supply from the Thames. Other physicians were to be found who were as ready as he of Hampstead to trumpet the merits of the spa. Says one of them, "It is a stimulant diuretic, very beneficial in chronic diseases arising from languor of the circulation, general debility of the system, or laxity of the solids, or in all cases where tonics and gentle stimulants are required, and in cutaneous affections. The season for drinking it is from April to the end of October."

THE OLD CLOCK HOUSE, 1780. (*See page* 466.)

The "Wells," we need hardly say, formed one of the leading features of Hampstead in its palmy days. As far back as the year 1698 they are spoken of by the name of "The Wells;" and two years later it is ordered by the authorities of the Manor Court, "that the spring lyeing by the purging wells be forthwith brot to the toune of Hamsted, at the parish charge, and y^{t} ye money profitts arising thereout be applied tow^{rds} easing the Poor Rates hereafter to be made." It was not long before they came into fashion and general use. The *Postman* of April, 1700, announces that "the chalybeate waters of Hampstead, being of the same nature, and equal in virtue, with Tunbridge Wells, are sold by Mr. R. Philps, apothecary, at the "Eagle and Child," in Fleet Street, every morning, at threepence per flask, and conveyed to persons at their own houses for one penny more. [N.B.—The flask to be returned daily.]"

Early in the eighteenth century we meet with advertisements to the effect that the mineral waters from the wells at Hampstead might be obtained from the "lessee," who lived "at the 'Black Posts,' in King Street, near Guildhall." They are also to be had at ten or twelve other houses in London, including "Sam's Coffee-house, near Ludgate, and the 'Sugar Loaf,' at Charing Cross."

In 1734, Mr. John Soame, M.D., published some directions for drinking the Hampstead waters, which he designated the "Inexhaustible Fountain of Health." In this work the worthy doctor placed on record some "experiments of the

KEATS' SEAT, OLD WELL WALK.

Hampstead waters, and histories of cures." Hampstead has long been celebrated for the choice medicinal herbs growing abundantly in its fields and hedgerows; and Dr. Soame in his pamphlet tells us how that "the Apothecaries Company very seldom miss coming to Hampstead every spring, and here have their herbalising feast. I have heard them say," he adds, "that they have found a greater variety of curious and useful plants near and about Hampstead than in any other place."

For the first ten or twelve years of the last century the Wells seem to have been in full favour, for at that time dancing and music were added to the attractions of the place. In the *Postman*, of August 14-16, 1701, it is announced that "At Hampstead Wells, on Monday next, being the 18th of this instant August, will be performed a Consort (*sic*) of both vocal and instrumental musick, with some particular performance of both kinds, by the best masters, to begin at 10 o'clock precisely. Tickets will be delivered at the said Wells for 1s. per ticket; and Dancing in the afternoon for 6d. per ticket, to be delivered as before." In September the following advertisement appeared:—"In the Great Room at Hampstead Wells, on Monday next, being the 15th instant, exactly at 11 o'clock forenoon, will be performed a Consort of vocal and instrumental musick, by the best masters; and, at the request of several gentlemen, Jemmy Bowen will perform several songs, and particular performances on the violin by 2 several masters. Tickets to be had at the Wells, and at Stephen's Coffeehouse in King Street, Bloomsbury, at 1s. each ticket. There will be Dancing in the afternoon, as usual." In 1702, the *London Post*, for May 5, has this advertisement:—"Hampstead Consort. In the Great Room of Hampstead Wells, on Monday next, the 11th instant, will be performed a Consort of vocal and instrumental musick by the best masters, with particular entertainments on the violin by Mr. Dean, beginning exactly at 11 o'clock, rain or fair. To continue every Monday, at the same place and time, during the season of drinking the waters. Tickets to be had at Stephen's Coffeehouse, in Bloomsbury, and at the Wells (by reason the room is very large) at one shilling each ticket. There will be dancing in the afternoon as usual." The *Postboy*, of May 8-10, 1707, informs "all persons that have occasion to drink the Hampstead mineral waters, that the Wells will be open on Monday next, with very good music for dancing all day long, and to continue every Monday during the season;" and it further adds that "there is all needful accommodation for water-drinkers of both sex (*sic*), and all other entertainments for good eating and drinking, and a very pleasant bowling-green, with convenience of coach-horses; and very good stables for fine horses, with good attendance; and a farther accommodation of a stage-coach and chariot from the Wells at any time in the evening or morning." No. 201 of the *Tatler*, July 22, 1710, contains the following announcement:—"A Consort of Musick will be performed in the Great Room at Hampstead this present Saturday, the 22nd instant, at the desire of the gentlemen and ladies living in and near Hampstead, by the best masters. Several of the Opera songs by a girl of nine years, a scholar of Mr. Tenoe's, who never performed in public but once at York Buildings with very good success. To begin exactly at five, for the conveniency of gentlemen's returning. Tickets to be had only at the Wells, at 2s. and 6d. each. For the benefit of Mr. Tenoe."

Gay, author of the "Fables" and the *Beggar's Opera*, drank of the waters and rambled about the Heath in 1727, and was cured of the colic; but his friend, Dr. Arbuthnot, had less success a few years afterwards, perhaps from medical want of faith. While he was staying there, Pope used to visit him; and then it probably was that the worthy doctor enjoyed those meetings with Pope's friend, Murray, which Cowper celebrated.

In more than one novel, written about the middle of the last century, we are treated with some remarks upon the visitors to the Wells at Hampstead, where we get a glimpse of the vulgar cockneyism which had succeeded to the witty flirtations of the fine ladies and gentlemen of fifty years previously. One author tells us how Madame Duval, rouged and decked in all the colours of the rainbow, danced a minuet; how "Beau Smith" pestered the pensive Evelina, who was thinking only of the accomplished and uncomfortably perfect Lord Orville, and much annoyed at the vulgar impertinence of the young men who begged the favour of "hopping a dance with her." Of the Long Room our author says: "The room seems very well named, for I believe it would be difficult to find any other epithet which might with propriety distinguish it, as it is without ornament, elegance, or any sort of singularity, and merely to be marked by its length." This building was used for many years previous to 1850 as a chapel of ease to the parish church; and a few years later was fitted up as the drill-room for the Hampstead (3rd Middlesex) Volunteers.

Nor is this all that we have to say about the Wells. From an advertisement in the *Postboy*, April 18, 1710, it appears that Hampstead rivalled for a time Mayfair* and the Fleet† in the practice of performing "irregular" marriages, and that the "Wells" even enjoyed sufficient popularity to have a chapel of their own.

"As there are many weddings at Zion Chapel, Hampstead," we read, "five shillings only is required for all the church fees of any couple that are married there, provided they bring with them a licence or certificate according to the Act of Parliament. Two sermons are continued to be preached in the said chapel every Sunday; and the place will be given to any clergyman that is willing to accept of it, if he is approved of."

The lessee at this time was one Howell, who was commonly spoken of as "the Welsh ambassador," and under his management irregular marriages were frequently celebrated. The advertisements of the period show pretty plainly what was the nature of the proceedings here. One notice which appeared in 1711 announced that those who go to be married must carry with them licences or dispensations, a formality which we may readily imagine was not unfrequently dispensed with. In *Read's Weekly Journal*, September 8,

* See Vol. IV., p. 347. † See Vol. II., p. 411.

1716, it is announced that "Sion Chapel, at Hampstead, being a private and pleasure place, many persons of the best fashion have lately been married there. Now, as a minister is obliged constantly to attend, this is to give notice that all persons upon bringing a licence, and who shall have their wedding dinner in the gardens, may be married in that said chapel without giving any fee or reward whatsoever; and such as do not keep their wedding dinner at the gardens, only five shillings will be demanded of them for all fees."

The exact site of this chapel is no longer known, but in all probability it adjoined the Wells, and belonged to the keeper of the adjoining tavern. There can be little doubt that it was a capital speculation before the trade in such matters was spoiled, a century or so ago, by the introduction of the "Private Marriage Act," so cruelly introduced by Lord Hardwicke.

This being the condition of the place, we need not be surprised to learn that its popularity with certain classes was unbounded. In fact, so much was Hampstead the rage at the beginning of the last century, that in the comedy of *Hampstead Heath* above referred to we find one of the characters, "Arabella," the wife of a citizen, thus telling us what she thinks of the place:—

"Well, this Hampstead 's a charming place, to dance all night at the Wells, and be treated at Mother Huff's; to have presents made one at the raffling shops, and then take a walk in Caen Wood with a man of wit. But to be five or six miles from one's husband!—marriage were a happy state could one be always five or six miles from one's husband."

This, we need scarcely remark, is a sentiment very congenial with the morals—or rather want of morals—which marked the age. The "Mother Huff" referred to so admiringly by the lady, was better known in the gossiping literature of the time by the even less euphonious name of "Mother Damnable." As we have seen in a previous chapter,* she appears to have been a person of accommodating disposition, who fixed her modest abode near the junction of the roads leading to Hampstead and through Kentish Town to Highgate, and made herself useful and agreeable to such modish ladies as Arabella and her witty friend.

The "raffling shops," also alluded to, are mentioned in the *Tatler*, in which Mr. Isaac Bickerstaffe, otherwise Sir Richard Steele, the "Christian hero," thought fit, as censor of public morals, to call attention to them. Writing in August, 1709, he says:—"I am diverted from my train of discourse by letters from Hampstead, which give me an account there is a late institution there under the name of a Raffling Shop, which is (it seems) secretly supported by a person who is a deep practitioner in the law, and out of tenderness of conscience has, under the name of his maid Sisly, set up this easier way of conveyancing and alienating estates from one family to another."

The Wells continued to be more or less a place of resort for invalids, real and imaginary, down to the early part of the present century, when their fame was revived for a time by Mr. Thomas Goodwin, a medical practitioner of the place, who had made the discovery that the Hampstead waters were possessed of two kinds of saline qualities, answering to the springs of Cheltenham and Harrogate; but the tide of popular favour seems to have flowed in another direction, after the visit of George III. and his Court to Cheltenham, and Hampstead soon became deserted by its fashionable loungers, notwithstanding the efforts of the doctors, who missed their guineas, and those of the proprietors of the ball-rooms and the raffling-shops, to resuscitate its fame. Dr. Soame complained that the royal family visited the wells at Islington, then achieving a temporary popularity, and neglected Hampstead; and he also seized the opportunity of levelling his shafts at the habit of tea-drinking, then a comparatively modern innovation. "I hope," he says, "that the inordinate drinking of tea will be retrenched, which, if continued, must bring a thousand ills upon us, and generations after us—the next generation may be in stature more like pigmies than men and women." What would Dr. Soame have said could he have lived to see the members of the Middlesex Rifle Volunteers, every fine fellow of which corps drinks tea every day, performing feats of prowess and agility while skirmishing among the furze-bushes and gravel-pits of his beloved Hampstead?

But no amount of appeal or puff direct could make Hampstead what it was in its aristocratic days. The wells and ball-rooms remained, and were well attended, but by another class. Their prestige was gone, and the world of fashion resigned them to the London aborigines dwelling east of Temple Bar. The waters of Hampstead are no longer taken medicinally, and their former celebrity is now only remembered in the name of the charming little grove called Well Walk, which leads from Flask Walk towards the eastern side of the Heath, and where there has been set up, as though in mockery of the past, a modern drinking-fountain.

Well Walk was in former times the fashionable

* See *ante*, p. 310.

morning lounge for the visitor to the "Wells;" and here the gallants of the period could enjoy the fresh air in the shade of the tall lime-trees, which still remain along the edge of the raised pathway. In Well Walk, between the "Long Room" and the "Wells Tavern," lived and died John Constable, the painter. Like Gainsborough and Crome, Constable always proved himself a heartfelt lover of an English homestead. "I love," he said, "every stile, and stump, and lane in the village; as long as I am able to hold a brush I shall never cease to paint them." "The Cornfield or Country Lane" and "The Valley Farm," both in the National Gallery, may have suggested to Leslie the following passage:—"There is a place," says this most sympathetic of critics on simply English art, "among our painters which Turner left unoccupied, and which neither Wilson, Gainsborough, Cozens, nor Girtin so completely filled as Constable. He was the most genuine painter of English cultivated scenery, leaving untouched its mountains and its lakes." His tomb in the old churchyard records that he was "many years an inhabitant of this parish." He died in 1837. Mrs. Barbauld, too, at one time, lived in Well Walk, where she was visited, not only by literary folks, but by men of high scientific attainments, such as Josiah Wedgwood. She afterwards lived at the foot of Rosslyn Hill, where we shall presently have more to say concerning her.

It was in Well Walk that John Keats wrote both his "Endymion" and his "Eve of St. Agnes;" and it was probably after hearing the nightingale in the adjoining gardens that he wrote those well-known stanzas, in which he apostrophises "The light-winged Dryad of the trees."

Hone, in his "Table Book," writes of this place: "Winding south from the Lower Heath, there is a charming little grove in Well Walk, with a bench at the end, whereon I last saw poor Keats, the poet of the 'Pot of Basil,' sitting and sobbing his dying breath into a handkerchief—glancing parting looks towards the quiet landscape he had delighted in so much—musing as in his 'Ode to a Nightingale.'"

Samuel Taylor Coleridge would sometimes come over across the green fields, by way of Millfield Lane, from Highgate, to have a chat with Keats on his seat at the end of Well Walk; and when he last shook hands with him here, he turned to Leigh Hunt, and whispered, "There is death in that hand." And such was too truly the case; for John Keats was in a consumption; and he went abroad very soon afterwards, to die beneath the sunny skies of Italy.

"And wilt thou ponder on the silent grave
  Of broken-hearted Keats, whom still we love
To image sleeping where the willows wave
  By Memory's fount, deep in the Muses' grove;
Shaded, enshrouded, where no steps intrude,
  But peace is granted him; his dearest boon;
And while he sleeps, with night-time tears bedew'd,
  'Endymion' still is watched by his enamoured moon."

The copyhold property in the rear of Well Walk belongs to the trustees of the Wells Charity, who are bound to devote its proceeds to apprenticing children, natives of Hampstead, under a scheme lately approved by the Court of Chancery.

Although it has not been attempted in these columns to enter into details respecting the geological structure of the localities which we have described, yet we ought not to omit to mention, with respect to Highgate and Hampstead, a few facts of interest to those who have the least taste for that branch of science.

It is well known to most readers that the whole of London lies on a substratum of chalk formation, which is covered by a higher stratum of a stiff bluish clay. On this again, there is every reason to believe, there once lay a covering of gravel and sand, which in the course of long ages has been washed away by the action of water, at a time when, probably, the whole valley of the Thames was an arm of the sea.

The "Northern Heights" of Highgate and Hampstead, if their formation is considered in detail, throw considerable light on this statement. Their summits exhibit a top coating or "cap" of gravel and sand, which, by some chance or other, has not been so swept away, but has maintained its position unchanged. This gravel and sand rest on an undersoil of a soft and spongy nature, from which issue springs of water, which appear to be squeezed out of the sides of the hills by the weight of the superincumbent mass.

These spongy soils gradually die away into a blue clay from thirty to five hundred feet in depth, in which, both at Hampstead and at Highgate, a variety of fossils have been found, proving the existence here of plants, trees, and animals akin to, but still differing from, those of our own age and latitude; some of these are of a marine and estuarine aquatic nature, showing that a sea must at one time have washed the sides of the heights that we have been climbing. As an instance in point, it may be mentioned that, in 1876, in boring a well through the clay at the brewery in High Street, the workmen came upon a fine specimen of the nautilus. Other marine shells of a smaller kind have been constantly dug up in the same stratum about these parts.

CHAPTER XXXVII.

HAMPSTEAD (*continued*).—ITS LITERARY ASSOCIATIONS, &c.

"Well, this Hampstead 's a charming place."—*Old Play.*

Church Row—Fashionable Frequenters of "the Row" in the Last Century—Dr. Sherlock—Dr. John Arbuthnot—Dr. Anthony Askew—Dr. George Sewell—The Rev. Rochmont Barbauld—Mr. J. Park—Miss Lucy Aikin—Reformatory Schools—John Rogers Herbert—Henry Fuseli—Hannah Lightfoot—Charles Dickens—Charles Knight—An Artistic Gift rejected by Hampstead—The Parish Church—Repairs and Alterations in the Building—Eminent Incumbents—The Graves of Joanna Baillie, Sir James Mackintosh, John Constable, Lord Erskine, and Others—St. Mary's Roman Catholic Chapel—Grove Lodge and Montagu Grove—The Old Workhouse.

RETRACING our steps to the High Street, and passing up a narrow lane on the west side, called Church Lane, we find ourselves in Church Row. Here, and almost only here, the hand of the "improver" and "restorer" has not been at work; the projecting hooded doorways of the days of Queen Anne still frown over the entrances of the red-bricked houses on our right and left, just as they did in the days "when George III. was king;" and the whole street has an air of quiet, homely, and venerable respectability which we can scarcely see elsewhere. Long may it remain in *statu quo*, this venerable relic of the days when the fashionable crowd—the "quality"—gentlemen with powdered wigs and gold-headed canes, and ladies in farthingales and "hoops of wondrous size"—used to make "the Row" their evening parade, after drinking the waters at the chalybeate spring, which, as we have just seen, still flows so invitingly on the other side of the High Street. Like Flask Walk and Well Walk, and some other thoroughfares which we have mentioned, Church Row—and, indeed, the High Street also—could in former times boast of its row of lime-trees growing down the centre of the roadway. Those in the High Street, save one, disappeared long ago; and of those in Church Row one solitary lime remains as a memento of the past. It may not be out of place to add here that the sedan-chairs continued in use in Hampstead longer than in any other part of London; indeed, it was no farther back than the early part of the present century that they were superseded by the donkey-carriages, which may still be seen driven along the quiet thoroughfares. Till comparatively recent times, too, the link-extinguishers of former days remained *in situ* by the doors of most of the houses in Church Row, although their use had been long ago set aside by the introduction of gas.

Among the frequenters of Church Row at the beginning of the last century doubtless might have been seen Dr. William Sherlock, Dean of St. Paul's and Master of the Temple, and also Dr. Arbuthnot, the witty physician, and friend of Swift, Gay, and Pope. The former, at all events, died at Hampstead, in June, 1707, at the age of sixty-six. He was induced by his wife, somewhat reluctantly, to submit to William and Mary. Walking with his spouse, he was pointed at by a bookseller, who said, "There goes Dr. Sherlock with his reasons for taking the oaths on his arm." Dr. Sherlock was the author of a "Practical Treatise on Death." He was buried in St. Paul's Cathedral.

Dr. John Arbuthnot, of whom we have already spoken in our account of Dover Street, Piccadilly,* was for some time a resident at Hampstead. He was eminent as a wit and man of letters, even among the choice spirits of the reign of Queen Anne. Soon after coming to England from Scotland, the place of his birth, he went to practise as a physician at Dorchester, but the salubrity of the air was unfriendly to his success, and he took horse for London. A neighbour, meeting him on full gallop, asked him where he was going. "To leave your confounded place, where I can neither live nor die." His wit and pleasantry sometimes assisted his prescriptions, and in some cases superseded the necessity of prescribing. Queen Anne and her consort appointed him their physician; the Royal Society elected him a member, and the College of Physicians followed. "He gained the admiration of Swift, Pope, and Gay," writes Hone in his "Year Book," "and with them he wrote and laughed. No man had more friends, or fewer enemies; yet he did not want energy of character; he diverged from the laughter-loving mood to tear away the mask from the infamous 'Charitable Corporation.' He could do all things well but walk. His health declined, while his mind remained sound to the last. He long wished for death to release him from a complication of disorders, and declared himself tired with 'keeping so much bad company.' A few weeks before his decease he wrote, 'I am as well as a man can be who is gasping for breath, and has a house full of men and women unprovided for.' . . . Dr. Arbuthnot was a man of great humanity and benevolence. Swift said to Pope, 'Oh that the world had but a

* See Vol. IV., p. 292.

dozen Arbuthnots in it; if so, I would burn my travels.' Pope no less passionately lamented him, and said of him, 'He was a man of humour, whose mind seemed to be always pregnant with comic ideas.' Arbuthnot was, indeed, seldom serious, except in his attacks upon great enormities, and then his pen was masterly. The condemnation of the play of *Three Hours after Marriage*, written by him, Pope, and Gay, was published by Wilkes, in his prologue to the *Sultaness*:—

> 'Such were the wags who boldly did adventure
> To club a farce by tripartite indenture;
> But let them share their dividend of praise,
> And wear their own fool's cap instead of bays.'

Arbuthnot simply retorted, in 'Gulliver Decyphered.' Satire was his chief weapon, but the wound he inflicted on folly soon healed; he was always playful, unless he added weight to keenness for the chastisement of crime."

OLD HOUSES IN CHURCH ROW.

To the above names of the frequenters of Church Row may be added that of Dr. Johnson, during his sojourn at Frognal, just round by the western end of the church, whose "ivy-mantled tower" forms a pleasing termination to the bottom of Church Row.

Another distinguished physician who resided for some time at Hampstead, and who, doubtless, might have been seen mixing with the fashionable throng in Church Row, was Dr. Anthony Askew, who died here in 1774. He practised originally at

CHURCH ROW, HAMPSTEAD, IN 1750.

Cambridge, but seems to have been introduced to London, and zealously recommended there, by the celebrated Dr. Mead. Dr. Askew was chiefly noted for his collection of classical works, which were sold at his death. Nichols says that his collection of Greek and Latin works was "one of the best, rarest, and most valuable ever sold in Great Britain."

Dr. George Sewell, an intimate friend of Pope and Arbuthnot, had lodgings in Hampstead, where he died in 1725. He contributed largely to the supplemental volumes of the *Tatler* and *Spectator*, and wrote the principal part of a translation of Ovid's "Metamorphoses." His principal work, however, was the tragedy of *Sir Walter Raleigh*, which was produced at the Duke's Theatre, in Lincoln's Inn Fields.

John Wylde, Lord Chief Baron of the Exchequer during the civil war, spent the last few years of his life in retirement at Hampstead, and died about ten years after the Restoration.

The Rev. Rochmont Barbauld—a well-known Unitarian minister at Hampstead at the close of the last century—resided in Church Row, where he had a few pupils. Hampstead at that time was deemed almost inaccessible. In a diary kept by Mr. Barbauld, he frequently speaks of being prevented from going to town by the state of the roads. Mrs. Barbauld resided in Hampstead long after her husband's death, but chiefly on Rosslyn Hill; we shall have more to say of her on reaching that place.

Mr. J. Park, the author of the "History of Hampstead," most excellent as a man and as an antiquary, lived in Church Row; he died in June, 1833. The work associated with his name was published before Mr. Park came of age, and in closing the preface, which is dated November 30, 1813, Mr. Park remarked, "The severer studies of an arduous profession now call upon me to bid a final adieu to those literary blandishments which have beguiled my youthful days." To this resolution he firmly adhered; but afterwards committed to the care of Mr. Nichols, the well-known antiquary, to whom we have frequently had occasion to refer, some additional documents, which were printed as an appendix, in 1818. Mr. Park became a barrister-at-law of Lincoln's Inn, and two years before his death he was appointed Professor of Law and Jurisprudence at King's College, London.

Another literary name, long associated with Hampstead, is that of Miss Lucy Aikin, niece of Mrs. Barbauld, and the author of "Memories of the Court of Queen Elizabeth," &c. On the death of her father, Dr. Aikin, which happened at Stoke Newington, in December, 1822, she took up her abode in Church Row, to be near her aunt, Mrs. Barbauld. Her mother accompanied her, and spent here her declining years, and died here in 1830. She had been brought up among the descendants of the old Puritans, and afterwards lived much among the disciples and fellow-workers of Price and Priestley and Dr. Enfield—all Unitarians, or men of the broadest views in that direction. Her only, or at all events her chief, publication whilst living here was her "Memoir of Addison," which appeared in 1843. She quitted Hampstead in the next year, to reside first in London and afterwards at Wimbledon, but returned to it some seven or eight years later, and spent the last twelve years of her life in the house of Mr. P. H. Le Breton, who had married her niece. Late in life she wrote in one of her letters, "I am all but a prisoner to my house and little garden." She died here in January, 1864, in her eighty-third year, and her grave in the old churchyard is next to that of her great friend, Joanna Baillie. "To Hampstead," writes Mr. Le Breton, in his preface to her "Memoirs," "Lucy Aikin was much attached, and her return to it gave her much pleasure, as many dear relatives and friends lived there. The vicinity of Hampstead to the metropolis afforded, at the same time, the opportunity of intercourse with a more varied society. She enjoyed with a keen relish, and thoroughly appreciated, the company of literary men and of eminent politicians and lawyers, with whom she delighted to discuss questions of interest. With almost every distinguished writer of this period she was acquainted, and of many of them notices will be found in her correspondence." Miss Harriet Martineau was among her numerous friends and visitors here.

The Hampstead of 1830–40 is thus portrayed by Miss Lucy Aikin, in one of her charming letters to Dr. Channing:—"Several circumstances render society here peculiarly easy and pleasant; in many respects the place unites the advantages and escapes the evils both of London and provincial towns. It is near enough (to London) to allow its inhabitants to partake in the society, the amusements, and the accommodations of the capital as freely as ever the dissipated could desire; whilst it affords pure air, lovely scenery, and retired and beautiful walks. Because every one here is supposed to have a London set of friends, neighbours do not think it necessary, as in the provinces, to force their acquaintance upon you; of local society you may have much, little, or none, as you please; and with a little, which is very good, you may associate on the easiest terms. Then the summer brings an influx of Londoners, who are often genteel and agreeable people, and pleasingly vary the scene. Such is Hampstead." And such, to a certain extent, it may be added, is Hampstead in the present day; for as yet it is quite distinct from the great metropolis, and has quite a character of its own.

The Hampstead Reformatory School for Girls, founded in 1857, occupied a large-sized house in Church Row, down to the close of 1876, when the establishment was removed to Heathfield House, near "Jack Straw's Castle." This institution is certified under the Reformatory Schools Act of 1866; and the inmates, numbering on an average about a hundred, receive an excellent education. Their former home is still devoted to reformatory purposes, being occupied by girls from the Field Lane Refuge on Saffron Hill. The large old-fashioned house at the corner of Church Row and Church Lane is devoted to a similar purpose, though its inmates are somewhat older.

This quarter of Hampstead, in fact, seems to have had particular attractions for authors and artists. Here, or close at hand, lived Henry Fuseli, R.A., of whom we quote the following extract from the "Mitchell Manuscripts" in the British Museum. The letter is from Mr. Murdock, of Hampstead, to a friend at Berlin, dated Hampstead, 12th June, 1764:—"I like Fuseli very much; he comes out to see us at times, and is just now gone from this with your letter to A. Ramsay, and another from me. He is of himself disposed to all possible economy; but to be decently lodged and fed, in a decent family, cannot be for less than three shillings a day, which he pays. He might, according to Miller's wish, live a little cheaper; but then he must have been lodged in some garret, where nobody could have found their way, and must have been thrown into ale-houses and eating-houses, with company every way unsuitable, or, indeed, insupportable to a stranger of any taste, especially as the common people are of late brutalised. Some time hence, I hope, he may do something for himself; his talent at grouping figures and his faculty of execution being really surprising."

Another eminent artist, in more recent times an inhabitant of Church Row, was John Rogers Herbert. He was for some years head-master of the School of Design at Somerset House, and in 1846 was selected to paint one of the frescoes in the vestibule of the Houses of Parliament. He was afterwards commissioned to paint a series of nine subjects, illustrating "Human Justice," for the peers' robing-room. Mr. Herbert was elected a Royal Academician in 1846. His works since 1840, when he embraced the Roman Catholic faith, have assumed a character in accordance with his religious convictions. Of these we may mention his "Introduction of Christianity into Great Britain," "Sir Thomas More and his Daughter observing from their Prison Window the Monks going to Execution," "St. John the Baptist reproving Herod," and "The Virgin Mary." This last-mentioned picture was painted for the Queen in 1860. Sundry other Royal Academicians and artists have likewise been residents here, besides the artists whose names we have enumerated.

Among the residents at Hampstead, in the middle of the last century, was Hannah Lightfoot, the fair Quakeress who is said to have captivated the heart of George III.;* and here she made her will in 1767–8, signing it "Hannah Regina," recommending "my two sons and daughter to the kind protection of their royal father, my husband, His Majesty George III."

Another resident here was Mr. Hamond, one of the literary friends of Mr. H. Crabbe Robinson. The latter writes in his "Diary," under date August, 1812: "A delightful day. The pleasantest walk by far I have had this summer. The very rising from one's bed at Hamond's house is enjoyment worth going to Hampstead over night to partake of. The morning scene from his back rooms is extremely beautiful." And then he describes his walk past the "Spaniards," and down some fields opposite Ken Wood, and so across Finchley to Colney Hatch and Southgate.

Mr. J. Forster, in his "Life of Charles Dickens," speaks several times of his almost daily "foregatherings" here, in the early period of his literary life, with Maclise, Stanfield, David Roberts, and other literary friends.

At Hampstead the elder Mr. Dickens resided during part of the time whilst his son was at school in Mornington Place, but the exact house is not known. Charles Knight, the well-known author and publisher, was a resident at Hampstead from 1865 to 1871. Mr. Knight died at Addlestone, in Surrey, in 1873, aged eighty-one. The whole of his long and honourable career was devoted to the cause of popular literature, of which he was one of the earliest and most accomplished advocates. We have already mentioned him as living at Highgate. Among the numerous works which he published or edited were the "Penny Magazine," the "Library of Entertaining Knowledge," the "Pictorial History of England," "London Pictorially Illustrated," the "Land we Live in," the "English

* See Vol. IV., p. 207.

Cyclopædia," and the "Popular History of England." At Hampstead his venerable, but genial and pleasant, face and snow-white locks were familiar to rich and poor, old and young. Here, surrounded by his books and a small but attached circle of literary friends, he spent his declining years, busying himself chiefly with two genial retrospective works—his "Shadows of the Old Booksellers," and "Passages of a Working Life," as he modestly termed his autobiography, and occasionally contributing a stray paper or two to the literature of the day.

We have mentioned Hampstead as a place which for many a long year has been a favourite home and resort of artists. As a proof of this fact, it may be mentioned that the survivor of the brothers Chalon, the eminent painters, about the year 1860 proposed to bestow on Hampstead the whole of his own and his brother's drawings on condition of the inhabitants building a gallery for their reception, and paying the salary of a custodian until his own decease. The lord of the manor, in order to forward the arrangement, offered to give a freehold site upon the Heath, just opposite to the "Upper Flask;" but there was not enough public spirit or taste in the residents to raise the sum required to meet the benefaction; the gift consequently lapsed, and the arrangement fell through.

The old parish church of Hampstead, as we have stated above, stands at the bottom of Church Row, and its green coating of ivy contrasts pleasingly with the red brick and tiled houses on either hand as we approach it. The building seems to have exercised a strange fascination over the artistic mind of the day, for a proposal to pull it down and rebuild it was received a short time ago with a perfect shout of disapproval. It is true that the church is most picturesquely situated, and that the distant view of the spire as it peeps from the mass of variegated foliage which adorns the churchyard is exceedingly pretty; but there is no reason why another church built on the same site should not be even more pleasing. The body of the church is ugly, awkward, and inconvenient in no common degree; the tower is mean, and the spire a shabby minaret, without grace or beauty of any kind. Nor has the structure the merit of antiquity. It dates only from 1747, when church architecture was at its lowest ebb, and it was designed with a wilful disregard of all true principles. The soil being sandy, and the position the side of a steep hill, it was necessary to lay the walls upon timber. In process of time the timber—it is hardly necessary to say—rotted away, and there has been a series of somewhat alarming settlements. The church had hardly been finished a dozen years when it was found necessary to pull down and rebuild the tower and spire. As a reason, we are told that the mason had proved a rogue, and had used Purbeck instead of Portland stone. The fact probably was that the foundations had given way, as it appears has been the case on more than one occasion since. In 1772 the church was subjected to a general repair and ornamentation after the usual churchwarden's fashion, but it has always been insecure and uncomfortable.

As we have stated in a previous chapter, Hampstead, before the Reformation, was only a chapelry in, and dependent on, the mother church of Hendon, and it was only after the dissolution of the monasteries that it came to be formed into a separate parish, the advowson of the living being appended to the lordship of the manor.

In 1549 the lord of the manor presented to the living for the first time; but it was not till a much later date that the vicar and churchwardens of Hampstead put in an appearance at the bishop's visitation; and, indeed, it was only in the year 1588 that the incumbent acknowledged himself as bound to apply to the bishop for his licence in order to officiate. The old chapel of St. Mary, which in the pre-Reformation times had been "served" on Sundays and other holy days by the monks from Westminster, or by a chaplain from Hendon, was a quaint and unpretending edifice, consisting of a nave and low side-aisles, surmounted by a wooden belfry. There is a very scarce print of it by Hollar, which was republished by Park in his "History of Hampstead," now a rare and valuable book. Park tells us that in the early part of the eighteenth century, having been "patched up as long as it would last, and being at length quite worn out," as well as too small to accommodate the inhabitants of Hampstead, the former church was taken down in 1745, and that the present edifice was finished two years later. It is a mistake, therefore, to speak of it as dating from the reign of Queen Anne, for it has nothing about it older than the second George. Before undertaking the work of rebuilding their church, the good people of Hampstead applied to Parliament for aid, but apparently without success, for shortly afterwards they raised by subscription the sum of £3,000 for the purpose; and this not being sufficient, they had recourse to a measure of very doubtful legality, in order to "raise the wind;" for they entered into a sort of joint-stock combination, by which it was agreed that several persons who contributed £20 and upwards should be elected trustees, and that those who subscribed £50 and upwards should have the first choice of seats and pews, which should become heirlooms in their families, though not to be alienated by purchase, but should be distributed to other benefactors of the church by the lord of the manor, the vicar, and the trustees; and in the main this principle still holds good, in spite of all efforts to put an end to such arrangements. It then contained pew-room for 550 persons, exclusive of benches; but further accommodation has since been made on several occasions by the addition of transepts and by other expedients. The church is described by Park as "a neat but ill-designed brick building, in the common style of modern churches, except that, contrary to all custom, the belfry and tower are at the east end, behind the chancel." No doubt the motive for this arrangement was economy, as the ground slopes down abruptly at the west end, and had the tower been placed there it would have been necessary to lay deeper foundations; and another inducement, no doubt, was the wish to create an imposing effect as the parishioners approached their church by the road from the High Street. The total cost of this unsightly structure—for such it really is externally—was between four and five thousand pounds, to which nearly half as much more must be added for repairing the ravages of the dry rot five years later, and for pulling down and rebuilding in 1759 the greater part of the steeple, owing to the knavery of the mason, who, as stated above, had used Purbeck instead of Portland stone as agreed by the contract. The present insignificant copper spire was added in 1784.

Park, who wrote at the commencement of this century, observed, in words which are as true now as then, that "considerable settlements are appearing at the east end, owing to the weight of the tower." The church, we may add, is still under the management of a body of local trustees, who direct the repairs and alterations, and receive and administer the pew rents for the benefit of the incumbent. In 1874-5 the parishioners of Hampstead were engaged in a keen controversy as to whether the church should be "rebuilt" or "restored," mainly through the threatened subsidence of the tower; and matters even went so far that the trustees appointed Mr. F. P. Cockerell as their architect, and that he supplied designs for the twofold purpose; but here the matter seems to have rested for a time, when it was finally decided that the church should be enlarged by the addition of a chancel at the western end, sundry alterations being made in the interior arrangements at the same time, and the tower being underpinned and strengthened.

And yet it must be owned that the church itself looks well, and even imposing, when seen from a distance, especially from the south. The following interesting sketch of the parish church appears in the *Sunday at Home* for July, 1876:—"From Primrose Hill a full view is obtained of the outline of the fine ridge to the north on which rest the suburbs of Highgate and Hampstead. The steeples of Highgate Church and of Christ's Church, Hampstead, are conspicuous marks in the landscape, while St. John's Church, or, as it is commonly called, old Hampstead Church, may be dimly descried amid a clustering group of trees. Proceeding by the Finchley Road to the old church, and taking the ascending pathway through the fields, a stranger would confront before he was aware the object of his quest, which he would find to be a brick-built and substantial, though a plain and unpretentious building in the Italian style. The belfry and tower are placed in the east end, behind the chancel, contrary to the usual method of church architecture. The advantage, however, is gained, that the handsomest part of the building is brought prominently into view and faces the village, while the clinging ivy covering almost the whole front removes to some extent the prosaic character of the brickwork, and lends an air of antiquity and a certain poetic charm to the sacred edifice, much in keeping with the beauty of the situation and with the decayed memorials of the surrounding burying-ground. The still older church—smaller but more picturesque—occupied the site of the existing building. It had been patched up as long as it would last; but becoming at length quite worn out from inevitable decay, and besides being too small to accommodate the increased population, it was pulled down. The new building was finished in 1747, at a cost of between £4,000 and £5,000, and was consecrated by Dr. Gilbert, Bishop of Llandaff, by commission from the Bishop of London, on the 8th of October of that year; it was dedicated to St. John."

Of the various clergymen who have held the incumbency of Hampstead, since the living passed into the hands of the lord of the manor, there have been some few whose names have become known beyond the circle of their parishioners. Of these we may mention the Rev. Robert Warren, D.D., who was an able, learned, and pious minister, and a man of mark among the clergy of his day. He preached repeatedly before the Lord Mayor of London, and was the author of several works of practical devotion, which in their time were popular, and ran through numerous editions. The general pious character of Dr. Warren's writings may be learned from the title of one of his most successful books, originally published in the year 1720, "The Daily Self-Examinant, or an Earnest Perswasion to the duty of Self-Examination; with Devout Prayers, Meditations, Directions, and Ejaculations for a Holy Life and Happy Death." Dr. Warren broke a lance with Bishop Hoadley on the nature of the sacrament, and, in his "Impartial Churchman," published an earnest and affectionate address to Protestant dissenters. He died in 1740; his son, Langhorne, was nominated his successor. Unlike to the father, the son does not appear to have been addicted to authorship; his only publication is a sermon on a text from the Book of Proverbs. During the incumbency of Langhorne Warren, the celebrated Dr. Butler, Bishop of Durham, resided at Hampstead, in the house built, and for a time occupied, by Sir Harry Vane—the house, indeed, from which the latter was taken to the Tower, where he was executed in 1662.

One of the witnesses to the bishop's will is the Rev. Langhorne Warren; the will was made at Hampstead, and bears date 25th of April, 1752. The following is one of the directions contained in it:—"It is my positive and express will that all my sermons, letters, and papers whatever, which are now in a deal box directed to Dr. Forester (his chaplain), and now standing in my library at Hampstead, be burnt, without being read by any, as soon as may be after my decease."

Samuel Butler and Dr. Secker, afterwards Archbishop of Canterbury, were both the sons of Dissenters, and were schoolfellows together at the Dissenting academy of Mr. Jones, at Tewkesbury, where, in the impressible days of their boyhood, was contracted that warm friendship which lasted through life between these eminent men. Secker, when in residence as Dean of St. Paul's, was constantly in the society of the author of the "Analogy" at Hampstead, and, it is said, dined with him every day. "A friend of mine, since deceased, told me," says the Rev. John Newton, "that when he was a young man he once dined with the late Dr. Butler, at that time Bishop of Durham, and though the guest was a man of fortune, and the interview by appointment, the provision was no more than a joint of meat and a pudding. The bishop apologised for his plain fare by saying that it was his way of living; that he had been long

VANE HOUSE, IN 1800.

disgusted with the fashionable expense of time and money in entertainments, and was determined that it should receive no countenance from his example."

When his health was fast failing, Dr. Butler left Hampstead for Clifton. Afterwards he went to Bath, to try the effect of the waters of that place. Dr. Forester thus writes from Bath to Secker, then Bishop of Oxford, on the 4th of June, 1752:—"My lord, I have barely strength and spirits to inform your lordship that my good lord was brought hither, in a very weak state, yesterday, in hopes of receiving some benefit from the waters." On the 16th of the same month Dr. Butler died. He was buried in the cathedral of Bristol, where two monuments have been erected to his memory.

ROSSLYN HOUSE. (*See page* 488.)

Ten years after the death of the great bishop, died his friend Langhorne Warren, curate of Hampstead, who, in his turn, was succeeded by his son Erasmus. This gentleman lived until 1806; so that for nearly a century the perpetual curacy of Hampstead was held by the Warren family. Mr. Warren's two assistant curates, the Rev. Charles Grant, and the Rev. Samuel White, in turn succeeded to the incumbency. Dr. White dying in 1841, was succeeded by the Rev. Thomas Ainger, under whose incumbency the parish was subdivided into ecclesiastical districts, for which five new churches were erected. Mr. Ainger was succeeded by the Rev. Charlton Lane, one of the professors in Gresham College; and he by the Rev. Sherard Burnaby.

Able and zealous clergymen connected with the churches which have sprung up of late years efficiently sustain the cause of the Church of England in Hampstead. Of these we would mention the name of the Rev. E. H. Bickersteth, the vicar of Christ Church. Mr. Bickersteth is besides favourably known in the world of letters, both as a poet and an essayist.

The amiable and accomplished Joanna Baillie, of whom we have already spoken, was scrupulously regular in her attendance on divine service in the parish church. She died on the 23rd of February, 1851; her grave may readily be found among the other memorials of the dead in the burying-ground adjoining the edifice. One other grave there will specially attract the visitor—it is that of Sir James Mackintosh, the brilliant lawyer and historian, who died in May, 1832. Mackintosh was a man of great powers and intellectual ability, and was President of the Board of Control under Earl Grey.

In a previous chapter (page 149) we have mentioned Sir Thomas Fowell Buxton in the midst of his benevolent labours residing at North End. In his "Memoirs" we find a letter from him to Sir James Mackintosh, whose mind was then engaged on the questions of the criminal law and colonial reform, inviting him to lend a full, hearty, and unreserved co-operation in the cause of the West Indian slaves. The death of Sir James Mackintosh, after a long illness, was really occasioned by a piece of chicken sticking in his throat when at dinner. He was nearly strangled, and though the meat was dislodged at the time, his health suffered ever afterwards.

Sir James Mackintosh is praised by all his cotemporaries for his wonderful stores of information, his philanthropy, his amiability, and great powers of conversation. Lord Russell tells us that he was "the ablest, the most brilliant, and the best-informed" of all those whose conversational talents are mentioned by Tommy Moore, who often came from Muswell Hill to meet him at the hospitable table of the Longmans on the Green Hill. He is thus portrayed in the "New Whig Guide:"—

"—— Mackintosh strives to unite
The grave and the gay, the profound and polite,
And piques himself much that the ladies should say
How well Scottish strength softens down in Bombay!
He frequents the assembly, the supper, the ball,
The *philosophe beau* of unlovable Staël;
Affects to talk French in his hoarse Highland note,
And gurgles Italian half-way down his throat.
His gait is a shuffle, his smile is a leer,
His converse is quaint, his civility queer;
In short, to all grace and deportment a rebel,
At best he is but a half-polished Scotch pebble."

This beautiful churchyard, perhaps one of the loveliest in England, and one of which it may be said with truth that "it would make one in love with death to think that he should be buried in so sweet a spot," is crowded with other tombs which bear distinguished names. Among them are those of John Constable, the artist; of Lord Erskine; of Harrison, who discovered the mode of ascertaining the longitude; and of the sweet-voiced Incledon, "the most wonderful nature-taught singer this country has ever produced." Not the least interesting of the graves is that of an old lady from St. Giles's parish, who was the solitary victim in Hampstead to the visitation of the cholera in 1849. The story is extant, and written in very choice English in the reports of the medical officer of the Privy Council. She had, it seems, lived in the parish of St. Giles, and having drank of the water from the church pump, fondly imagined that no other could be so good. When, therefore, her husband died, and she retired upon a modest competency to the northern suburb, she arranged with the conductor of an omnibus to bring her a jar of it daily. She drank of it and of it only, and never tired of praising its excellences: The sparkle which she found so attractive was, however, but a form of death; the water was literally loaded with sewage gas and with the phosphates which had filtered through the earth from the churchyard close by. It was, as it were, a matter of course that she should die, but she did not die in vain. The history of her case has been of a value to medical science which few can over-estimate. Had the old lady known much of local history, she would, perhaps, have pinned her faith to the waters of Hampstead, and perhaps have been living at the present time. Among other notabilities preserved in local memories as resting here is Miss West, better known as "Jenny Diver," the most accomplished lady pickpocket of her age, who died here in 1783, leaving £3,000, the fruits of her industry, to her two children, one of whom was born in Bridewell. This desultory gossip leads us to curious associations; but the grave, like misery, makes us acquainted with strange bedfellows; and the ashes of poor Jenny lie peacefully enough with those of better people.

The old churchyard covers about three acres, and lies chiefly on the south of the church. A little higher up on the slope of the hill is the new or upper churchyard, one end of which abuts upon Church Row. It is not quite so large as the other, and was consecrated in 1812.

At the northern extremity of this churchyard stands the little Roman Catholic chapel of St. Mary's, its western front conspicuously decorated with a handsome statue of the Virgin and the Divine Child in a niche. It was built in 1815–16 by the exertions of the Abbé Morel, one of those French *emigrés* whom the waves of the first French Revolution threw upon our shores. For many years the abbé lived in Hampstead, teaching his native language; his gains he laid by in order to found the mission and chapel, in which he rests beneath a handsome altar-tomb. Before the consecration of the chapel by the "Vicar Apostolic" of the London district in 1816, the abbé used to say mass over a stable in Rosslyn Park, and afterwards at Oriel House, at the upper end of Church Row. He died in 1851. In the interior of the chapel are some fine sacred pictures.

Grove Lodge and Montagu Grove, near here, are places worthy of mention, the former as having been at one time the residence of Sir Gilbert Scott, the architect; and the latter as the residence of Mr. Edward Montagu, the first patron of the Hampstead Sunday School. Concerning this gentleman, the *European Magazine* for June, 1788, tells the following anecdote:—"June 10. This morning Lord Mansfield sent a servant from Caen Lodge, to Mr. Montagu, the Master in Chancery, Frognal Grove, near Hampstead, requesting that gentleman's company to dinner. The answer returned was that 'Mr. Montagu had come home the preceding evening from London ill, and remained then indisposed.' The messenger returned back, pressing Mr. Montagu's attendance on his lordship, who had some material business to communicate, upon which Mr. Montagu replied, 'He would wait on the earl in the afternoon.' At five the master went to Caen Wood Lodge, where he was introduced to Earl Mansfield, who was alone. 'I sent for you, sir,' said his lordship, 'to receive, as well officially as my acquaintance and friend, the resignation of my office; and, in order to save trouble, I have caused the instrument to be prepared, as you here see.' He then introduced the paper, which, after Mr. Montagu had perused, and found proper, the earl signed. The master underwrote it, and afterwards dispatched it to the Lord Chancellor's house, who laid it before the king." Montagu Grove was afterwards the residence of Chief Baron Richards.

Opposite Montagu Grove, on some sloping ground leading towards Mount Vernon, and now occupied as a garden, it is said that the workhouse of Hampstead formerly stood. The old house, as depicted in Park's "Hampstead," was a picturesque building, with projecting wings, gabled roof, and bay windows. Here, before it became the parish poorhouse, Colley Cibber used to meet his friends, Booth and Wilkes, the actors, to concert plans for their dramatic campaigns.

CHAPTER XXXVIII.

HAMPSTEAD (*continued*).—ROSSLYN HILL, &c.

"Hæ latebræ dulces, et jam, si credis, amœnæ."—*Horace.*

Sailors' Orphan Girls' School and Home—Clarkson Stanfield—The Residence of the Longmans—Vane House, now the Soldiers' Daughters' Home—Bishop Butler—The "Red Lion" Inn—The Chicken House—Queen Elizabeth's House—Carlisle House—The Presbyterian Chapel—Mr. and Mrs. Barbauld—Rosslyn House—Lord Loughborough—Belsize Lane—Downshire Hill—Hampstead Green—Sir Rowland Hill—Sir Francis Palgrave—Kenmore House and the Rev. Edward Irving—St. Stephen's Church—The "George" Inn—The Hampstead Waterworks—Pond Street—The New Spa—The Small-pox Hospital—The Hampstead Town Hall—The "Load of Hay"—Sir Richard Steele's Cottage—Nancy Dawson—Moll King's House—Tunnels made under Rosslyn and Haverstock Hills.

RETRACING our steps through Church Row on our way towards Rosslyn Hill—which is a continuation of the High Street towards London—we notice on our right, at the corner of Greenhill Road and Church Lane, a large and handsome brick building, with slightly projecting wings, gables, and a cupola turret. This is the Sailors' Orphan Girls' School and Home, which was originally established in 1829, in Frognal House, on the west side of the parish church. The present building was erected in 1869, from the designs of Mr. Ellis. The objects of the institution are the "maintenance, clothing, and education of orphan daughters of sailors and marines, and the providing of a home for them after leaving, when out of situations." The number of inmates is about one hundred, and the children look healthy and cheerful. Its annual income averages about £2,000. This institution was opened by Prince Arthur, now Duke of Connaught, in whose honour the road between it and the Greenhill is named Prince Arthur's Road.

On the Greenhill, close by the Wesleyan chapel, and where Prince Arthur's Road opens into the High Street, stands a venerable house, once the home of Clarkson Stanfield, the artist, till lately used as a branch of the Consumptive Hospital. It is now a school, and named Stanfield House. A native of Sunderland, and born about the end of the last century, Clarkson Stanfield, as we have stated in a previous chapter,* commenced life as a sailor. He, however, soon abandoned the sea for the more congenial pursuit of a scene-painter, having accepted an engagement at an east-end theatre, whence he soon after migrated to Drury Lane. His familiarity with the mysteries of the deep enabled him to surpass most other painters of sea-pieces. Among his early works, not already mentioned by us, were his "View near Chalons-sur-Saône," and "Mount St. Michael," painted for the Senior United Service Club. Among his more

* See *ante*, p. 306.

important later works we may mention his "Castle of Ischia," the "Day after the Wreck," "French Troops crossing the Magra," "Wind against Tide," and "The *Victory* towed into Gibraltar after the Battle of Trafalgar. Great as was Mr. Stanfield's knowledge of the sea, he comparatively seldom painted it in a storm. Throughout his industry was almost as remarkable as his genius. As a scene-painter he had the means of doing much towards advancing the taste of the English public for landscape art. For many years he taught the public from the stage—the pit and the gallery to admire landscape art, and the boxes to become connoisseurs; and he decorated the theatre with works so beautiful, that we can but regret the frail material of which they were constructed, and the necessity for "new and gorgeous effects," and "magnificent novelties," which caused the artist's works to be carried away. It was not the public only whom Stanfield delighted, and awakened, and educated into admiration—the members of his own profession were as enthusiastic as the rest of the world in recognising and applauding his magnificent imagination and skill. Mr. J. T. Smith, in his "Book for a Rainy Day," says, "Mr. Stanfield's easel pictures adorn the cabinets of some of our first collectors, and are, like those of Callcott, Constable, Turner, Collins, and Arnold, much admired by the now numerous publishers of little works, who unquestionably produce specimens of the powers of England's engravers, which immeasurably out-distance the efforts of all other countries." Clarkson Stanfield died in 1867 at his residence in Belsize Park, a few months after removing from his long-cherished home.

Another large old red-brick house, just below that formerly occupied by Clarkson Stanfield, for many years the home of the Longmans, and the place of reunion for the Moores, Scotts, Russells, and other clients and friends of that firm, has been swept away to make room for the chapel mentioned above. The cedars which stood on the lawn are still left, and so also are some of the ornamental evergreens; the rookery and grounds adjoining are appropriated to sundry new Italian villas. The rooks, who for successive generations had built their nests in these grounds for the best part of a century, frightened at the operations of the builders, flew away a few years since, and, strangely, migrated to a small grove half a mile nearer to London, at the corner of Belsize Lane.

A little below the Greenhill, on the same side of the High Street, is Vane House; this edifice stands a short distance back from the road, with a gravelled court in front of it. Though almost wholly rebuilt of late years, it is still called by the name of its predecessor, and it is occupied as the Soldiers' Daughters' Home. Vane House was originally a large square building, standing in its own ample grounds. In Park's time—that is, at the beginning of the present century—the house had been considerably modernised in some parts, but it still retained enough of the antique hue to make it a very interesting object. The entrance at the back, with the carved staircase, remained in their original condition. In the upper storey one very large room had been divided into a number of smaller apartments, running along the whole back front of the house. The old mansion, when inhabited by Sir Harry Vane, probably received and welcomed within its walls such men as Cromwell, Milton, Pym, Fairfax, Hampden, and Algernon Sidney; and from its doors its master was carried off by order of Charles II. to the executioner's block on Tower Hill. The house was afterwards owned and occupied by Bishop Butler, who is said to have written here some portions of his masterly work, "The Analogy between Natural and Revealed Religion." The Soldiers' Daughters' Home was instituted in 1855, in connection with the Central Association for the Relief of the Wives and Children of Soldiers on Service in the Crimea, and, as the report tells us, "for the maintenance, clothing, and education of the daughters of soldiers, whether orphans or not." This "Home" is one of the most popular among the various charitable institutions in the metropolis. The present buildings, which are spacious, substantial, and well adapted to their purpose, were erected in 1858, from the designs of Mr. Munt, and they have since been enlarged. The "Home" was inaugurated under the auspices of the late Prince Consort, and has ever since been under the patronage of royalty, including Her Majesty, the Prince of Wales, the Duke of Cambridge, and others. The annual *fête* on behalf of the institution, held in the charming grounds of the "Home," is attended by the *élite* of fashion, and has always been quite a gala day at Hampstead. In 1874 the committee of the institution unanimously resolved to add three girls to the number of admissions into the Home by election, to be called the "Gold Coast Scholars," one from each of the regiments serving in the African war, as a tribute to the gallantry and self-sacrifice displayed by the troops employed under Sir Garnet Wolseley during the campaign in Ashantee. A fourth scholar from the Royal Marines has since been added. The Regimental Scholarships' Fund, established in 1864, was then very liberally responded to, but the contributions have since fluctuated greatly. These contributions are all funded; and when they accumulate to a sufficient sum, according to the age of the girl, and to the scale of payment in force, enable regiments to nominate a scholar for direct admission into the Home independently of election. The average number of girls in the institution is about 150, but there is accommodation for 200 when the income is sufficient for their maintenance.

Still on our right, half way down the steep descent of Rosslyn Hill, on the site now occupied by the police-station, stood formerly the "Red Lion Inn," a wooden house of great antiquity, probably dating from the fourteenth century. The "Red Lion" is so common a sign as to need no other remark except that it probably was put up in allusion to the marriage of John of Gaunt, Duke of Lancaster, with Constance, daughter of Don Pedro, King of Leon and Castile. But this house is worthy of special note, as it was held on lease from the Dean and Chapter of Westminster, on condition of its "Boniface" supplying a truss of hay for the horse of the "mass- priest," who came up from the Abbey to celebrate divine service at Hampstead on Sundays and the greater saints' days, in the Chapel of St. Mary, on the site of which now stands the parish church. Although the inn is gone, its name remains in "Red Lion Hill," as Rosslyn Hill is usually called among the working classes.

On the opposite side of the road, but a trifle lower down the hill, may be seen what little now remains of a noted old building, called the Chicken House, which Mr. Park, in his "History of Hampstead," says that local tradition designates as "an appendage to royalty." In this work it is stated that there was nothing remarkable in the interior of the house, except some painted glass, well executed, representing Our Saviour in the arms of Simeon, and (in another window) small portraits of King James and the Duke of Buckingham, under the former of which was the following inscription: "Icy dans cette chambre coucha nostre Roy Iaques, premier le nom. Le 25 Aoust, 1619." This glass afterwards formed part of the collection of Sir Thomas Neave, at Branch Hill Lodge, which we have already mentioned. Originally it was a low brick building in the farmhouse style, and of ordinary appearance. The side which abutted upon the roadway is now hid by houses and small shops; the only view of the building, therefore, is obtained by passing up a narrow passage from the street. The old building is now cut up into small tenements, inhabited by several families.

Gale, the antiquary, died at the Chicken House in 1754; he lies buried in the churchyard. In the Chicken House Lord Mansfield is stated to have lodged before he purchased Caen Wood. "But at that time, no doubt," says Mr. Howitt in his "Northern Heights," "the Chicken House had an ample garden, and overlooked the open country, for it is described as being at the entrance of Hampstead." In 1766, not many years after Lord Mansfield and his legal friends had ceased to resort hither for the purposes of "relaxation from the fatigues of their profession," the place seems to have sadly degenerated, for we are told that it had become a rendezvous of thieves and vagabonds.

Near to the Chicken House there used to stand another building, commonly known as "Queen Elizabeth's House;" its architecture, however, was of too late a date to warrant such a name, though the tradition was current that the "Virgin Queen" once spent a night there. It was subsequently occupied by some nuns, who changed its name to "St. Elizabeth's Home."

Close by the Chicken House stood, till 1875–6, a fine mansion in its own grounds, known as Carlisle House. It was the property of, or at all events occupied by, a gallant admiral, at the close of the last century; and it is a tradition in Hampstead that Lord Nelson, when in the zenith of his fame, was often a guest within its walls. The house has been pulled down, and the site utilised for building purposes.

Adjoining is the site of the Presbyterian chapel. This edifice was constructed as the successor of another chapel which is supposed to have been established in the reign of Charles II., by one of the ejected ministers whose lives are recorded by Dr. Calamy. The first Presbyterian minister was Mr. Thomas Woodcock, son of a learned divine of the same name, who had been ejected, and cousin to Milton's second wife. Zechariah Merrell, who was minister in the reign of Queen Anne, wrote the exposition of the First Epistle of Peter, in continuation of Matthew Henry's "Commentary." He died in 1732. The Rev. Mr. Barbauld, of whom we have spoken above, in our account of Church Row, was a minister here. On his leaving the congregation it ceased to be Presbyterian. The cause of Presbyterianism has, however, within the last twenty-five years been resuscitated at Hampstead. For about ten years, and until his failing health compelled him to desist, the Rev. James D. Burns preached at Hampstead to the congregation known as English Presbyterians. He was the author of "The Vision of Prophecy," and other poems. The original Presbyterian chapel is supposed to have been removed in 1736, and the chapel which superseded it was rebuilt in 1828. This, in turn, gave way to the present building, which was completed in 1862, and is one of the ugliest of modern ecclesiastical structures.

Mr. Barbauld officiated in the old Presbyterian chapel from 1785 till the commencement of this century, when he removed to Newington Green. He was a native of Germany, and died in the year 1808. His widow, who resided for many years in a house on the west side of Rosslyn Hill, was the celebrated Mrs. Anna Letitia Barbauld, and sister of Dr. John Aikin, the distinguished author and physician. The eldest child and only daughter of Dr. John Aikin, and of Jane, his wife, daughter of the Rev. John Jennings, she was born at the village of Kibworth Harcourt, in Leicestershire. Shortly after their marriage, Mr. and Mrs. Barbauld settled at Palgrave, in Suffolk, where Mr. Barbauld was a Dissenting minister, and kept a school. At first all seemed prosperous. In addition to Lord Denman, Sir William Gell, Dr. Sayers, and William Taylor, of Norwich, were amongst the pupils of the Palgrave school. Here also Mrs. Barbauld wrote her "Early Lessons" and "Hymns in Prose." Their winter vacation was always spent in London, where they had the *entrée* into good society. After eleven years of teaching, Mrs. Barbauld and her husband left Palgrave, and ultimately planted themselves in Hampstead. Here Mrs. Barbauld found many excellent friends—Miss Joanna Baillie and others. One of Mrs. Barbauld's occasional guests at Hampstead was Samuel Rogers, the poet. Mr. H. Crabb Robinson's "Diary" contains several interesting entries concerning this lady. "In 1805, at Hackney," writes Crabb Robinson, "I saw repeatedly Miss Wakefield, a charming girl. And one day, at a party, when Mrs. Barbauld had been the subject of conversation, and I had spoken of her in enthusiastic terms, Miss Wakefield came to me and said, 'Would you like to know Mrs. Barbauld?' I exclaimed, 'You might as well

SIR RICHARD STEELE. (*See page* 491.)

VIEW FROM "MOLL KING'S HOUSE," HAMPSTEAD, IN 1760.

ask me whether I should like to know the angel Gabriel!' Said she, 'Mrs. Barbauld is much more accessible. I will introduce you to her nephew.' She then called to Charles Aikin, whom she soon after married. And he said, 'I dine every Sunday with my uncle and aunt at Stoke Newington, and I am expected always to bring a friend with me. Two knives and forks are laid for me. Will you go with me next Sunday?' Gladly acceding to the proposal, I had the good fortune to make myself agreeable, and soon became intimate in the house.

"Mr. Barbauld had a slim figure, a weazen face, and a shrill voice. He talked a great deal, and was fond of dwelling on controversial points of religion. He was by no means destitute of ability, though the afflictive disease was lurking in him which in a few years broke out, and, as is well known, caused a sad termination to his life.

"Mrs. Barbauld bore the remains of great personal beauty. She had a brilliant complexion, light hair, blue eyes, a small elegant figure, and her manners were very agreeable, with something of the generation then departing. Mrs. Barbauld is so well known by her prose writings, that it is needless for me to attempt to characterise her here. Her excellence lay in the soundness and acuteness of her understanding, and in the perfection of her taste. In the estimation of Wordsworth she was the first of our literary women, and he was not bribed to this judgment by any especial congeniality of feeling, or by concurrence in speculative opinions."

Wordsworth, like Rogers, greatly admired Mrs. Barbauld's "Address to Life," written in extreme old age. "Repeat me that stanza by Mrs. Barbauld," he said to Robinson, one day at Rydal; the latter did so, and Wordsworth made him repeat it again. "And," as Robinson tells us, "so he learned it by heart. He was at the time walking in his sitting-room, with his hands behind him; and I heard him mutter to himself, 'I am not in the habit of grudging people their good things, but I wish I had written those lines:—

> 'Life! we've been long together,
> Through pleasant and through cloudy weather:
> 'Tis hard to part when friends are dear,
> Perhaps 'twill cost a sigh, a tear:
> Then steal away, give little warning;
> Choose thine own time;
> Say not good night, but in some brighter clime
> Bid me good morning.'"

Mrs. Barbauld incurred great reproach by writing a poem entitled "1811." It is in heroic rhyme, and prophesies that on some future day a traveller from the antipodes will, from a broken arch of Blackfriars Bridge, contemplate the ruins of St. Paul's! "This," remarks Mr. Robinson, "was written more in sorrow than in anger; but there was a disheartening and even gloomy tone, which even I, with all my love for her, could not quite excuse. It provoked a very coarse review in the *Quarterly*, which many years afterwards Murray told me he was more ashamed of than any other article that had appeared in the *Review*." Mrs. Barbauld spent the last few years of her life at Stoke Newington, where we shall again have occasion to speak of her.

A little lower down the hill, and on the same side of the way, stands Rosslyn House, formerly the property of Alexander Wedderburn, first Earl of Rosslyn, better known, perhaps, by his former title of Lord Loughborough, which he took on being appointed Lord Chancellor in the year 1795. Before purchasing this mansion, Lord Loughborough, as we have stated in a previous chapter, resided at Branch Hill Lodge, higher up in the town, on the verge of the Heath. Rosslyn House—or as it was originally called, Shelford Lodge—at that time, and long after, stood alone amidst the green fields, commanding an extensive view over the distant country. It was surrounded by its gardens, groves, and fields, with no house nearer to it than the village of Hampstead above and Belsize House below.

Lysons states that the mansion was for many years "in the occupation of the Cary family," and that it was held under the Church of Westminster. It has been supposed that it was built by a family of the name of Shelford, who, being Catholics, planted the great avenue leading to it in the form of a cross, the head being towards the east, and leading direct to the high road. "But," says Mr. Howitt, "this is very doubtful. The celebrated Lord Chesterfield," he adds, "is said to have lived here some years, when he held the lease of the manor of Belsize, of which it was a part; and more probably his ancestors gave it the name from Shelford Manor, their seat in Nottinghamshire;" for the Earls of Chesterfield held the estate of Belsize from 1683 down to early in the present century, when the land was cut up in lots, and sold for building purposes. Mr. Howitt tells us that "when Lord Rosslyn purchased the place, he added a large oval room, thirty-four feet long, on the west side, with a spacious room over it. These rooms, of a form then much in vogue, whilst they contributed greatly to the pleasantness of the house, disguised the original design of it, which was on the plan of what the French call a *maison* or *château à quatre tourelles*, four-square, with a high mansard roof in the centre, and a square turret at each corner, with pyramidal roof. Notwithstanding various other alterations by Lord Rosslyn and his successors, part of this original structure is still visible, including two at least of the turrets."

Here Lord Loughborough used to entertain the Prince of Wales and the leaders of the Whig party, including Fox, Sheridan, and Burke, with other distinguished personages of opposite politics, such as Pitt, Windham, and the Duke of Portland. "Junius" was not among his friends, as may be guessed from the fact of his describing him as "Wedderburn the wary, who has something about him which even treachery cannot trust."

Whilst holding a subordinate legal office, he fomented the war against America by furiously attacking the colonists to such an extent that Benjamin Franklin swore that he would never forgive the insults that he heaped upon his countrymen. Lord Loughborough was much disliked, and, to speak the honest truth, despised also, by Lord Thurlow. The fact is that he was rather a turncoat, and played fast and loose with both parties.

"Lord Loughborough," says Mr. Howitt in his "Northern Heights of London," "was one of that group of great lawyers who, about the same time, planted themselves on the heights of Hampstead, but with very different characters and aims—Mansfield, Loughborough, and Erskine. Lord Loughborough was, in simple fact, a legal adventurer of consummate powers, which he unscrupulously and unblushingly employed for the purposes of his own soaring and successful ambition." From the time of his promotion to the Lord Chancellorship—the grand aim of his ambition—he seems to have given way fully to his unbounded love of making a great figure on the public stage. "His style of living," says Lord Campbell, "was most splendid. Ever indifferent about money, instead of showing mean contrivances to save a shilling, he spent the whole of his official income in official splendour. Though himself very temperate, his banquets were princely; he maintained an immense retinue of servants, and, not dreaming that his successor would walk through the mud to Westminster, sending the Great Seal thither in a hackney coach, he never stirred about without his two splendid carriages, exactly alike, drawn by the most beautiful horses, one for himself, and another for his attendants. Though of low stature and slender frame, his features were well chiselled, his countenance was marked by strong lines of intelligence, his eye was piercing, his appearance was dignified, and his manners were noble."

In 1801 the Great Seal passed from his hands to those of Lord Eldon. "After this," writes Mr. Howitt, "his influence wholly declined. He seemed to retain only the ambition of being about the person of the king, and he hired a villa at Baylis, near Slough, to be near the Court; yet so little confidence had he inspired in George III., with all his assiduous attentions, that when the news of his death was brought to the monarch, who had seen him the day before—for he went off in a fit of gout in the stomach—the king cautiously asked if the news were really true; and being answered that it was, said, as if with a sense of relief, 'Then he has not left a greater knave behind him in my dominions!'"

Lord Brougham, in his "Historical Sketches," gives his own estimate of Lord Rosslyn's character, which is equally severe. He describes him as a "man of shining but superficial talents, supported by no fixed principles, embellished by no feat of patriotism, nor made memorable by any monuments of national utility; whose life being at length closed in the disappointment of mean and unworthy desires, and amidst universal neglect, left behind it no claim to the respect or gratitude of mankind, though it may have excited the admiration or envy of the contemporary vulgar."

After Lord Rosslyn's death the house passed through several hands. It was first of all inhabited by Mr. Robert Milligan, the projector of the West India Docks, and afterwards successively by Sir Francis Freeling, secretary of the General Post Office, by Admiral Sir Moore Disney, and by the Earl of Galloway. The place subsequently fell into the hands of a speculative builder, who, happily, failed before the old mansion was destroyed or all the old trees were cut down, though it was shorn of much of its beauty. The house still stands, though much altered externally and internally, and deprived of most of its grounds. The estate was cut up for building purposes about 1860–5, and is intersected by roads named after Lords Thurlow, Mansfield, Lyndhurst, Eldon, and other great legal luminaries. For some four years before the above-mentioned period the house had been used as a cradle for the Soldiers' Daughters' Home. In 1860 Prince Albert led the children up the hill to their new home, which, as we have already stated, occupies the site of old Vane House. In 1861 the mansion was purchased by Mr. Charles H. L. Woodd, a descendant of John Evelyn, and of Dr. Basil Woodd, Chancellor of Rochester, who fought under Charles I. at the battle of Edge Hill. In the course of alterations and repairs, which this gentleman has had effected, several coins of Elizabeth, Charles II., and William III. were found under the flooring. "Upon the old panellings, when the canvas covering was removed," Mr. Howitt tells us, "were seen the words written, 'To-morrow last day of Holidays!!! 1769.' At first it was supposed that Lord Chesterfield's son, to whom the 'Letters' were addressed, might have inscribed this pathetic sentence; but the date shuts out the possibility. Lord Chesterfield died in 1773, and this his only son five years before him."

The main body of the avenue still exists, and amongst its trees are some very fine Spanish chestnuts; they are supposed to have been planted about the close of the reign of Queen Elizabeth.

On the south side of Rosslyn House there is a narrow thoroughfare called Belsize Lane, which, down to about the year 1860, had a truly rural appearance, its sides being in part bordered by hedge-rows, and overhung by tall and flourishing trees. Part of these trees and hedgerows still remain. In it, too, was a turnpike gate, which stood close to the farm-house which still stands about the centre. The Queen was driving up this lane on one occasion to look at Rosslyn House, with the idea of taking it as a nursery for the royal children. A little girl, left in charge of the gate, refused to allow Her Majesty to pass. The Queen turned back, according to one account; according to another, she was much amused, and one of her equerries advanced the money necessary to satisfy the toll; but however that may have been, Her Majesty did not become the owner or the tenant of Rosslyn House.

At the foot of Rosslyn Hill, on the left, next to Pilgrim's Lane, is Downshire Hill, so called after one of the ministers in Lord North's cabinet, Lord Hillsborough, afterwards first Marquis of Downshire. At the foot of Downshire Hill, where John Street branches off, stands a plain heavy structure, which has long served as a chapel of ease to Hampstead, and known as St. John's Chapel.

Hampstead Green, as the triangular spot at the junction of Belsize Lane and Haverstock Hill was called till it was appropriated as the site for St. Stephen's new church, has many literary associations. In one of the largest houses at the southern end, now called Bartram's, Sir Rowland Hill, the philanthropic deviser of our penny post system, spent the declining years of his useful and valuable life. Born of yeoman parents, at Kidderminster, in December, 1796, in early life he became a schoolmaster, and, together with his brothers, he established the large private school which for more than half a century has flourished at Bruce Castle, Tottenham. It was he who showed forcibly the abuses and wastefulness of the old system of high-priced postage, and it is to him that the middle classes of this country mainly owe the introduction of the penny post, which superseded that system in 1840, as well as the improvements of the Money-Order Office, and the use of postage-stamps. His next public benefit was the establishment of cheap excursion trains on our railways on Saturdays, Sundays, and Mondays, an experiment first made when Sir Rowland Hill was chairman of the Brighton Railway Company. In 1854 he was recalled to assist in the Control of the General Post Office, first as Assistant Joint-Secretary, and afterwards as Chief Secretary. He was rewarded for his great public services by a knighthood, with the Order of the Bath, Civil Division, coupled with a pension on his retirement. But the reward which he valued the most was the sum of £13,000 which was presented to him, and which was largely contributed from the pence of the poor. In 1876, when he was upwards of eighty, it was resolved to erect in his honour a public statue at Kidderminster, where he was born. The veteran philanthropist was a man who never spared himself from hard work, and as a schoolmaster, as a postal reformer, as an officer of "my Lords of the Treasury," as a railway reformer, and as a social reformer, he did good work in his day. He died here in 1879.

Next door to Sir Rowland Hill lived Sir Francis Palgrave, the historian of the Norman Conquest, &c. He was of Jewish extraction, and at an early age became connected with the Office of Public Records, of which he became the Deputy Keeper in 1838. His name is well known as the author of the "History of the Norman Conquest," "Calendars of the Treasury of the Exchequer," and of many antiquarian essays, and also of a work of a lighter character, the "Merchant and the Friar." Two of his sons, who spent their childhood here, have since attained to eminence—Mr. Francis T. Palgrave, of the Privy Council Educational Department, as a poet and art-critic; and Mr. William Gifford Palgrave, as an Eastern traveller, and the author of the best work that has been published of late years on Arabia.

Kenmore House, a little lower down, has attached to it a large room originally built for the Rev. Edward Irving, who would here occasionally manifest to his followers the proofs of his power of speaking in the "unknown tongues."

St. Stephen's Church, mentioned above, was built in 1870, from the designs of Mr. S. S. Teulon. It is of the early semi-French style of architecture, of very irregular outline, and unusually rich in external ornament. Altogether, the church has a very handsome and picturesque appearance. In the lofty campanile tower there is a beautiful peal of bells and a magnificent carillon, the gift of an inhabitant of the place.

The "George" Inn, on Hampstead Green, once a quaint old roadside public-house, is now resplendent with gas-lamps, and all the other accessories of a modern hotel. Close by this hotel is the church belonging to the religious community known as the Sisters of Providence; their house, formerly Bartram's Park, was the residence of Lord S. G. Osborne.

Hampstead Green, at the lower or eastern end, gradually dies away, and is lost in Pond Street, which leads to the bottom of the five or six ponds on the Lower Heath. Pond Street has been, at various times, the temporary home and haunt of many a painter and poet. Leigh Hunt at one time lived in lodgings here; John Keats occupied, at the same date, a house near the bottom of John Street, immediately in the rear, almost facing the ponds. Among the more recent residents of Pond Street may be enumerated Mr. George Clarkson Stanfield, who inherits much of his father's talent, and Mr. Charles E. Mudie, the founder of the great lending library in New Oxford Street.

Near one of the lower ponds on the East Heath, nearly opposite the bottom of Downshire Hill and John Street, is a singular octagonal dome-crowned building, built about the reign of Queen Anne; it is connected with the Hampstead Water-works, and forms a picturesque object to the stranger as he approaches Hampstead from Fleet Road and Gospel Oak.

At the commencement of the present century another mineral spring was discovered on the clay soil, between the bottom of Pond Street and the lower end of the Heath. It was called the "New Spa," and is so marked on a map which appears in a small work published in 1804 by a local practitioner, Thomas Goodwin, M.D., and a Fellow of the College of Surgeons, under the title of "An Account of the Neutral Saline Waters lately discovered at Hampstead." The work includes an essay on the importance of bathing in general, and an analysis of the newly-found waters; but the New Spa never displaced or superseded the older "Wells" near Flask Walk; and its memory and all traces of its site have perished, though, no doubt, its existence caused the erection of so many modern houses at the foot of the slope of Pond Street.

Close to Hampstead Green, on the eastern slope looking down upon Fleet Road and Gospel Oak, is an irregular structure, which at the first view resembles barracks hastily thrown up, or a camp of wooden huts. This structure was first raised under the authority of the Metropolitan Asylums Board, as a temporary Fever Hospital, about the year 1867; it has since been used for the accommodation of pauper lunatics; and in 1876–7 it was appropriated to patients suffering from an outbreak of small-pox, very much to the discomfort and annoyance of the residents of Hampstead, who petitioned Parliament for its removal, but in vain. Its location here, in the midst of a population like that of Hampstead, and close to two thoroughfares which during the summer are crowded by pleasure-seekers, cannot be too strongly censured, as tending sadly to depreciate the value of property around the entire neighbourhood.

On the right of Haverstock Hill the visitor can scarcely fail to remark a fine old avenue of elms, which, as we shall see presently, once formed the approach to Belsize House. At the corner of this avenue is a drinking-fountain, most conveniently placed for the weary foot-passenger as he ascends the hill; and close by it stands a handsome Town Hall, in red brick and stone, in the Italian style, erected in 1876–7, at the cost of £10,000. It is used for the meetings of the Hampstead Liberal Club, and of the Hampstead Parliament.

Lower down the road, on the opposite side of the way, and just by the top of the somewhat sharp hill, is the "Load of Hay," which occupies the place of a much older inn, bearing witness to the once rural character of the place. Its tea-garden used to be a favourite resort of visitors on their way to Hampstead Heath, who wished to break the long and tedious walk. The entrance to the gardens was guarded by two painted grenadiers—flat boards cut into shape and painted—the customary custodians of the suburban tea-gardens of former times. The house itself was a picturesque wooden structure until about the year 1870, when, shorn of most of its garden, and built closely round with villas, it degenerated into a mere suburban gin-palace.

On the opposite side of the road were the poplars that stood before the gate of Sir Richard Steele's cottage, over the site of which Londoners now drive in cabs and carriages along Steele's Road. A view of Sir Richard Steele's cottage on Haverstock Hill, standing in the midst of green fields, and apparently without even a road in front of it, from a drawing taken in 1809, is to be found in Smith's "Historical and Literary Curiosities," and it is also shown in our illustration above, on p. 295. It may be interesting to know that it was much the same in outward appearance until its demolition, about the year 1869, though close in front of it ran the road to Hampstead, from which it was sheltered by the row of tall poplars alluded to above.

Sir Richard Steele was living on Haverstock Hill in June, 1712, as shown by the date of a letter republished in *fac-simile* in Smith's "Historical and Literary Curiosities." "I am at a solitude," he writes, "an house between Hampstead and London, where Sir Charles Sedley died. This circumstance set me thinking and ruminating upon the employment in which men of wit exercise themselves. It was said of Sir Charles, who breathed his last in a room in this house—

> 'Sedley had that prevailing, gentle art
> Which can with a resistless charm impart
> The loosest wishes to the chastest heart:
> Raise such a conflict, kindle such a fire,
> Between declining virtue and desire,
> Till the poor vanquished maid dissolves away
> In dreams all night, in sighs and tears all day.'

This was a happy talent to a man about town, but I dare say, without presuming to make uncharitable conjectures on the author's present condition, he would rather have had it said of him that he prayed—

> 'O thou my voice inspire
> Who touched Isaiah's hallowed lips with fire.'"

Nichols somewhat unkindly suggests that there "were too many pecuniary reasons for the temporary solitude" in which Steele resided here.

We have already spoken at some length of Sir Richard Steele in our account of Bury Street, St. James's,* but still something remains to be told about him. "The life of Steele," writes his biographer, "was not that of a retired scholar; hence his moral character becomes all the more instructive. He was one of those whose hearts are the dupes of their imaginations, and who are hurried through life by the most despotic volition. He always preferred his caprices to his interests; or, according to his own notion, very ingenious, but not a little absurd, 'he was always of the humour of preferring the state of his mind to that of his fortune.' The result of this principle of moral conduct was, that a man of the most admirable qualities was perpetually acting like a fool, and,

BELSIZE HOUSE IN 1800.

* See Vol. IV., p. 202.

with a warm attachment to virtue, was the frailest of human beings." The editor of the "Biographia Dramatica" says: "Sir Richard retired to a small house on Haverstock Hill, on the road to Hampstead. . . . Here Mr. Pope, and other members of the Kit-Cat Club, which during the summer was held at the 'Upper Flask,' on Hampstead Heath, used to call on him, and take him in their carriages to the place of rendezvous." Dr. Garth, too, was a frequent visitor here. He was a member of the Kit-Cat Club, and notorious for his indolence. One night, when sitting at the "Upper Flask," he accidentally betrayed the fact that he had half-a-dozen patients waiting to see him, and Steele, who sat next him, asked him, in a tone of banter, why he did not get up at once and visit them. "Oh, it's no great matter," replied Garth; "for one-half of them have got such bad constitutions that all the doctors in the world can't save them, and the others such good ones that all the doctors could not possibly kill them."

SHEPHERD'S WELL IN 1820. (*See page* 500.)

Here Steele spent the summer days of 1712, in the company of many of his "Spectators," returning generally to town at night, and to the society of his wife, who, as we have stated, at that time had lodgings in Bury Street. Fortune seems to have smiled on Steele for a time, and we next hear of him as having taken a house in Bloomsbury Square, where Lady Steele set up that coach which landed its master in so many difficulties. No mention, apparently, is to be found of Steele's residence at Haverstock Hill in Mr. Montgomery's work on "Sir Richard Steele and his Contemporaries." In the *Monthly Magazine*, Sir Richard Phillips tells us that in his time Steele's house had been "converted into two small ornamental cottages for citizens' sleeping boxes. . . . Opposite to it," he adds, "the famous 'Mother' or 'Moll' King built three substantial houses; and in a small villa behind them resided her favourite pupil, Nancy Dawson. An apartment in the cottage was called the Philosopher's Room, probably the same in which Steele used to write. In Hogarth's 'March to Finchley' this cottage and Mother King's house are seen in the distance . . . Coeval with the *Spectator* and *Tatler*, this cottage must have been a delightful retreat, as at that time there were not a score of buildings between it and Oxford Street and Montagu and Bloomsbury Houses. Now continuous rows of streets extend from London to this spot."

Steele's cottage was a low plain building, and

the only ornament was a scroll over the central window. It was pulled down in 1867. The site of the house and its garden is marked by a row of houses, called Steele's Terrace, and the "Sir Richard Steele" tavern. A house, very near to Steele's, was tenanted by an author and a wit of not dissimilar character. When Gay, who had lost his entire fortune in the South Sea Bubble, showed symptoms of insanity, he was placed by his friends in retirement here. The kindly attentions of sundry physicians, who visited him without fee or reward, sufficed to restore his mental equilibrium even without the aid of the famous Hampstead waters.

Nancy Dawson died at her residence here in May, 1767. Of this memorable character Mr. John Timbs writes thus in his "Romance of London:"—"Nancy Dawson, the famous hornpipe dancer of Covent Garden Theatre, in the last century, when a girl, set up the skittles at a tavern in High Street, Marylebone. She next, according to Sir William Musgrove's 'Adversaria,' in the British Museum, became the wife of a publican near Kelso, on the borders of Scotland. She became so popular a dancer that every verse of a song in praise of her declared the poet to be dying in love for Nancy Dawson, and its tune is as lively as that of 'Sir Roger de Coverley.' In 1760 she transferred her services from Covent Garden Theatre to the other house. On the 23rd of September, in that year, the *Beggar's Opera* was performed at Drury Lane, when the play-bill thus announced her: 'In Act 3, a hornpipe by Miss Dawson, her first appearance here.' It seems that she was engaged to oppose Mrs. Vernon in the same exhibition at the rival house; and there is a full-length print of her in that character. There is also a portrait of her in the Garrick Club collection." She lies buried behind the Foundling Hospital, in the ground belonging to St. George the Martyr, where there is a tomb-stone to her memory, simply stating, "Here lies Nancy Dawson."

Both Rosslyn and Haverstock Hills, it may here be stated, have had tunnels carried through them at a very heavy cost, owing to the fact that the soil hereabouts is a stiff and wet clay. The northernmost tunnel connects the Hampstead Heath station with the Finchley Road station on the branch of the North London Railway which leads to Kew and Richmond. The other tunnel, which is one mile long, with four lines of rails, passes nearly under the Fever Hospital, and was made by the Midland Railway in 1862–3.

CHAPTER XXXIX.

HAMPSTEAD (*continued*).—BELSIZE AND FROGNAL.

> "Estates are landscapes gazed upon awhile,
> Then advertised, and auctioneered away."

Grant of the Manor of Belsize to Westminster Abbey—Belsize Avenue—Old Belsize House—The Family of Waad—Lord Wotton—Pepys' Account of the Gardens of Belsize—The House attacked by Highway Robbers—A Zealous Protestant—Belsize converted into a Place of Public Amusement, and becomes an "Academy" for Dissipation and Lewdness—The House again becomes a Private Residence—The Right Hon. Spencer Perceval—Demolition of the House—The Murder of Mr. James Delarue—St. Peter's Church—Belsize Square—New College—The Shepherds' or Conduit Fields—Shepherds' Well—Leigh Hunt, Shelley, and Keats—Fitzjohn's Avenue—Finchley Road—Frognal Priory and Memory-Corner Thompson—Dr. Johnson and other Residents at Frognal—Oak Hill Park—Upper Terrace—West End—Rural Festivities—The Cemetery—Child's Hill—Concluding Remarks on Hampstead.

On our right, as we descend Haverstock Hill, lies the now populous district of South Hampstead, or Belsize Park. It is approached on the eastern side through the beautiful avenue of elms mentioned at the close of the preceding chapter; on the west it nearly joins the "Swiss Cottage," which, as we have seen, stands at the farthest point of St. John's Wood.

It is traditionally stated that the manor of Belsize had belonged to the Dean and Chapter of Westminster from the reign of King Edgar, nearly a century before the Conquest; but it is on actual record that in the reign of Edward II. the Crown made a formal grant to Westminster Abbey of the manor of Belsize, then described as consisting of a house and 284 acres of land, on condition of the monks finding a chaplain to celebrate mass daily for the repose of the souls of Edmund, Earl of Lancaster, and of Blanche, his wife. This earl was a grandson of Henry III.; he had taken up arms against Edward, but was captured and beheaded. His name survives still in Lancaster Road.

About 1870 the Dean and Chapter of Westminster gave up the fine avenue above-mentioned, called Belsize Avenue, to the parish of Hampstead, on condition of the vestry planting new trees as the old ones failed. A row of villas is now built on the north side, and at the south-east corner, as stated above, a new town-hall for Hampstead was erected in 1876–7.

At the lower end of the avenue stood, till very recently, a house which, a century ago, enjoyed a celebrity akin to that of the Vauxhall of our own time, but which at an earlier period had a history of its own. An engraving of the house soon after this date will be found in Lysons' "Environs of London," from which it is reproduced in Charles Knight's "Pictorial History of England." It stood near the site of what is now St. Peter's Church, facing the avenue above mentioned, at right angles.

Upon the dissolution of the monasteries one Armigel Wade, or Waad, who had been clerk to the Council under Henry VIII. and Edward VI., and who is known as the British Columbus, obtained a lease of "Old Belsize"—for so this house was called—for a term of two lives. He thereupon retired to Belsize House, where he ended his days in 1568. There was a monument erected to his memory in the old parish church of Hampstead. His son, Sir William Waad, made Lieutenant of the Tower, and knighted by James I., also lived at Belsize and died in 1623. Sir William had married, as his second wife, a daughter of Sir Thomas Wotton, who, surviving as his widow, got the lease of the house and estate renewed to her for two more lives, at a yearly rental of £19 2s. 10d., exclusive of ten loads of hay and five quarters of oats payable to Westminster. She left Belsize to her son, Charles Henry de Kirkhaven, by her first husband; and he, on account of his mother's lineage, was created a peer of the realm, as Lord Wotton, by Charles II., and made this place his residence.

That old gossip, Pepys, thus speaks of it in his "Diary," under date August 17, 1668: "To Hampstead, to speak with the attorney-general, whom we met in the fields, by his old rout and house. And after a little talk about our business, went and saw the Lord Wotton's house and garden, which is wonderful fine: too good for the house the gardens are, being, indeed, the most noble that ever I saw, and such brave orange and lemon trees."

The gardens, indeed, were quite fine enough to offer temptations to thieves and robbers, for soon after this date we find that an attack was made upon the place. In the *True Protestant Mercury* of October 15—19, 1681, we read—"London, October 18. Last night, eleven or twelve highway robbers came on horseback to the house of Lord Wotton, at Hampstead, and attempted to enter therein, breaking down part of the wall and the gate; but there being four or five within the house, they very courageously fired several musquets and a blunderbuss upon the thieves, which gave the alarm to one of the lord's tenants, a farmer, that dwelt not far off, who thereupon went immediately into the town and raised the inhabitants, who, going towards the house, which was about half a mile off, it is thought the robbers hearing thereof, and withal finding the business difficult, they all made their escape. It is judged they had notice of my lord's absence from his house, and likewise of a great booty which was therein, which put them upon this desperate attempt."

On Lord Wotton's death the Belsize estate fell to the hands of his half-brother, Lord Chesterfield. The latter, however, did not care to live there, but sold his interest in the place, and the house remained for some time unoccupied. In the reign of George I., however, we find Belsize in the hands of a retired "sea-coal" merchant, named Povey, to whom the then French ambassador, the Duc d'Aumont, offered the (at that time) immense rental of £1,000 a year on a repairing lease. It transpired that the duke wanted the place because it contained or had attached to it a private chapel. On this the coal-merchant refused to carry out the bargain, on the ground that he "would not have his chapel desecrated by Popery." For this piece of Protestant zeal he hoped that he would have been applauded by the magistrates; his surprise, therefore, must have been great when, instead of praise, he received from the Privy Council a reprimand, as being an "enemy to the king." It is recorded that when the Prince of Wales (afterwards George II.) came soon afterwards to see the house, Povey addressed to him a letter, informing his royal highness of these particulars, but the prince never condescended to vouchsafe him a reply. Povey, we may add, made himself notorious in his day by the publication of sundry pamphlets exposing the evil practices of Government agencies. He also took to himself great credit as a patriot for having refused to let his mansion to the French ambassador, and modestly put in a claim for some reimbursement from the nation, for having "kept the Romish host" from being offered in Hampstead, at a cost to himself of one thousand pounds. Our readers will hardly need to be told that Mr. Povey got no thanks for his pains, any more than he did shortly afterwards for his equally disinterested offer of his house and chapel for the use of his Royal Highness the Prince of Wales, "for a place of recess or constant residence." Not obtaining an answer to his impertinent intrusion, he seems to have turned Belsize to good account pecuniarily, and perhaps, at the same time, to have "paid out" his neighbours for their coolness to him, by allowing it to be opened as a place of fashionable amusement.

For a period of about forty years—in fact, during the reigns of George I. and George II.—Belsize ceased to be occupied as a private residence, being opened by a Welshman of the name of Howell as a place of public amusement, and sank apparently down into a second-rate house of refreshments and gambling. In the park, which was said to be a mile in circumference, were exhibited foot-races, athletic sports, and sometimes deer-hunts and fox-hunts: and it is said that one diversion occasionally was a race between men and women in wooden shoes. Upon the whole, it is to be feared that Belsize was not as respectably conducted as it might have been and ought to have been; the consequence was that its customers fell off, and in the end it was shut up.

The newspapers of the period announce that the house was opened as a place of public entertainment "with an uncommon solemnity of music and dancing." It is somewhat amusing to note that the advertisements wind up with an assurance that for the benefit of visitors timid about highwaymen "twelve stout fellows completely armed patrol between Belsize and London." Notwithstanding that the house had been the residence of the lord of the manor, better company (we are told) came to it in its fallen estate than before. A year or two after it was opened to the public grievous complaints were made by the people of Hampstead of the multitude of coaches which invaded their rural solitude. The numbers were often as many as two or three hundred in a single night. We glean from Park's "History of Hampstead" the following particulars concerning Belsize House as a place of amusement:—"Of Belsize House, as the mansion of a manorial district in the parish of Hampstead, I have already spoken; it is introduced again here as a place formerly of considerable notoriety for public diversions. The following extracts will give some idea of the nature and character of these amusements, and indicate that it was the prototype of Vauxhall, Ranelagh, and many other more modern establishments:—'Whereas that the ancient and noble house near Hampstead, commonly called Bellasis-house, is now taken and fitted up for the entertainment of gentlemen and ladies during the whole summer season, the same will be opened with an uncommon solemnity of music and dancing. This undertaking will exceed all of the kind that has hitherto been known near London, commencing every day at six in the morning, and continuing till eight at night, all persons being privileged to admittance without necessity of expense,' &c., &c.—*Mist's Journal*, April 16, 1720.

"A hand-bill of the amusements at Belsize (formerly in the possession of Dr. Combe), which has a print of the old mansion-house prefixed, announces Belsize to be open for the season (no date), 'the park, wilderness, and garden being wonderfully improved and filled with variety of birds, which compose a most melodious and delightful harmony. Persons inclined to walk and divert themselves, may breakfast on tea and coffee as cheap as at their own chambers. Twelve stout fellows, completely armed, to patrole between Belsize and London,' &c., &c. 'Last Saturday their Royal Highnesses the Prince and Princess of Wales dined at Belsize-house, near Hampstead, attended by several persons of quality, where they were entertained with the diversion of hunting, and such other as the place afforded, with which they seemed well pleased, and at their departure were very liberal to the servants.'—*Read's Journal*, July 15, 1721.

"In the same journal, September 9, 1721, is an account of his Excellency the Welsh ambassador giving a plate of six guineas to be run for by eleven footmen. The Welsh ambassador appears to have been the nickname of one Howell, who kept the house.

"'The Court of Justices, at the general quarter sessions at Hickes's-hall, have ordered the high-constable of Holborn division to issue his precepts to the petty constables and headboroughs of the parish of Hampstead, to prevent all unlawful gaming, riots, &c., at Belsize-house and the Great Room at Hampstead.'—*St. James's Journal*, May 24, 1722.

"'On Monday last the appearance of nobility and gentry at Belsize was so great that they reckoned between three and four hundred coaches, at which time a wild deer was hunted down and killed in the park before the company, which gave near three hours' diversion.'—*Ibid.*, June 7, 1722."

In 1722 was published, in an octavo volume, "'Belsize House,' a satire, exposing, 1. The Fops and Beaux who daily frequent that academy. 2. The characters of the women who make this an exchange for assignations. 3. The buffoonery of the Welsh ambassador. 4. The humours of his customers in their several apartments, &c. By a Serious Person of Quality." The volume, however, is of little real value, except as a somewhat coarse sketch of the manners of the age.

According to this poetical sarcasm, Belsize was an *academy* for dissipation and lewdness, to a degree that would scarcely be tolerated in the present times, and that would be a scandal in any; but some allowance must probably be made for the jaundiced vision of the caustic writer. We find in it the following brief description of the house :—

> "This house, which is a nuisance to the land,
> Doth near a park and handsome garden stand,
> Fronting the road, betwixt a range of trees,
> Which is perfumed with a Hampstead breeze;
> And on each side the gate 's a grenadier,
> Howe'er, they cannot speak, think, see, nor hear;
> But why they 're posted there no mortal knows,
> Unless it be to fright jackdaws and crows;
> For rooks they cannot scare, who there resort,
> To make of most unthoughtful bubbles sport."

The grounds and gardens of Belsize continued open as late as the year 1745, when foot-races were advertised there. In the course of the next generation, however, a great change would seem to have come over the place; at all events, in the "Ambulator," (1774), we read: "Belsize is situated on the south-west side of Hampstead Hill, Middlesex, and was a fine seat belonging to the Lord Wotton, and afterwards to the Earl of Chesterfield; but in the year 1720 it was converted into a place of polite entertainment, particularly for music, dancing, and play, when it was much frequented, on account of its neighbourhood to London, but since that time it has been suffered to run to ruin."

After the lapse of many years, during which little or nothing is recorded of its history, Belsize came again to be occupied as a private residence, and among its other tenants was the Right Hon. Spencer Perceval, afterwards Prime Minister, who lived here for about ten years before taking office as Chancellor of the Exchequer, namely, from 1798 to 1807. Mr. Perceval was the second son of the Earl of Egmont. Having first applied himself to the study of the law, he entered Parliament, in 1796, as member for Northampton, and under Mr. Addington's administration, in 1801, was appointed Solicitor-General. Next year he became Attorney-General, attaining also great distinction as a Parliamentary debater. On the fall of the Duke of Portland's Administration, in 1809, Mr. Perceval was appointed First Lord of the Treasury and Chancellor of the Exchequer, and he was still in office when he was assassinated by Bellingham, in the lobby of the House of Commons, in 1812.* A portrait of Mr. Perceval, painted by Joseph, from a mask taken after death by Nollekens, is to be seen in the National Portrait Gallery.

In more recent times Belsize House was occupied by a Roman Catholic family named Wright, who were bankers in London. The old house, originally a large but plain Elizabethan mansion, with central tower and slightly projecting wings, was remodelled during the reign of Charles II., and subsequently again considerably altered. Its park, less than a century ago, was a real park, somewhat like that which encompasses Holland House, at Kensington. It was surrounded by a solid wall, which skirted the south side of a lane leading from the wood of the Knights of St. John towards Hampstead.

Belsize seems, on the whole, to have been rather an unlucky place. The mansion was pulled down about the year 1852, and the bricks of the house and of the park wall were used to make the roads which now traverse the estate, and to form the site of the handsome villa residences which now form Belsize Park; and at the present time all that is left to remind the visitor of the past glories of the spot is the noble avenue of elms which, as we have stated, once formed its principal approach.

On the 21st of February, 1845, Mr. James Delarue, a teacher of music, was murdered by a young man named Hocker, close by the corner of Belsize Park, in the narrow lane leading from Chalk Farm to Hampstead. The lane, at that time, as may be imagined, was very solitary, seeing that, with the exception of Belsize House, there were no houses near the spot. The crime was perpetrated about seven o'clock in the evening. Cries of "murder" were heard by a person who happened to be passing at the time, and on an alarm being given, the body of the murdered man was quickly discovered. Hocker, it seems, had in the meanwhile gone to the "Swiss Tavern," and there called for brandy and water; but on the arrival of the police and others, Hocker too appeared on the spot, inquired what was amiss, and, taking the dead man's hand, felt his pulse and pronounced him dead, and gave some bystanders money to help carry the corpse away. Mr. Howitt, in noticing this tragedy in his "Northern Heights," says, "The murder was afterwards clearly traced to Hocker, the cause of it being jealousy and revenge, so far as it appeared, for his being supplanted by Delarue in the affections of a young woman of Hampstead. On the trial Hocker read a paper endeavouring to throw the charge of the murder on a friend, whose name, of course, he did not disclose, and added an improbable story of the manner in which his clothes had become stained with blood. The reading of this paper only impressed the court and the crowd of spectators with an idea of Hocker's excessive hypocrisy and cold-bloodedness. He was convicted and executed." Miss Lucy Aikin alludes to

* See Vol. III., p. 530.

this murder of Delarue in one of her letters to a friend: "I rather congratulate myself on not being in Church Row during the delightful excitement of this murder and the inquest, which appear to have had so many charms for the million. . . . . But I think the event will give me a kind of a dislike to Belsize Lane, which hitherto I used to think the pleasantest way from us to you."

We have stated above that the manor of Belsize belongs to the Dean and Chapter of Westminster; we may add here that "Buckland" Crescent and "Stanley" Gardens, which now form part of the estate, are named after deans of that collegiate establishment, and that St. Peter's Church is so dedicated after St. Peter's Abbey itself. It is a neat cruciform building, in the Decorated style of architecture, with side aisle and tower, and was erected in 1860.

In Belsize Square lived for some time, and there died in 1875, Henry Malden, M.A., formerly Fellow of Trinity College, Cambridge, and for forty-five years Professor of Greek in University College, London. The son of a surgeon at Putney, he was born in the year 1800, and was educated at Trinity College, Cambridge, where he was elected to a Craven Scholarship, together with the late Lord Macaulay. Whilst at Cambridge, he contributed to *Knight's Quarterly Magazine*, and wrote a poem entitled "Evening," which was published in a volume of poems edited by Joanna Baillie. In 1834 he published a small work on the "Origin of Universities and Academical Degrees," which was written as an introduction to the Report of the Argument before the Privy Council in support of the application of the University of London for a charter empowering it to grant degrees.

FROGNAL PRIORY. (*See page* 501.)

On the western side of the Belsize estate, at the angle of the Finchley and Belsize Roads, stands New College, a substantial-looking stone-built edifice, erected about the year 1853, as a place of training for young men for the ministry of the Independent persuasion. Not far from it, at the top of Avenue Road, is a handsome Gothic Chapel belonging also to the Nonconformists, and known as New College Chapel.

Down till very recently, Hampstead was separated from Belsize Park, Kilburn, Portland Town, &c., by a broad belt of green meadows, known as the Shepherds' or Conduit Fields, across which ran

POND STREET, HAMPSTEAD, IN 1750.

a pleasant pathway sloping up to the south-western corner of the village, and terminating near Church Row. On the eastern side of these fields is an old well or conduit, called the Shepherd's Well, where visitors in former times used to be supplied with a glass of the clearest and purest water. This conduit is probably of very ancient date. The spring formerly served not only visitors but also the dwellers in Hampstead with water, and poor people used to fetch it and sell it by the bucket. There used to be an arch over the conduit, and rails stood round it; but since Hampstead has been supplied by the New River Company the conduit has become neglected, and the spring is covered over.

Towards the close of the last century, Lord Loughborough, who, as we have seen, was then living close by, desired to stop the inhabitants from obtaining the water, by enclosing the well, or otherwise cutting off all communication with it; but so great was the popular indignation, that an appeal was made to the Courts of Law, when a decision was very wisely given in the people's favour, and so the well remained in constant use till our own times. In this we are reminded of

> "Some village Hampden that, with dauntless breast,
> The little tyrant of the fields withstood;"

but who the "village Hampden" was on this occasion is not recorded by local tradition.

From Hone's "Table Book" (1827) we glean the following particulars concerning this well:—"The arch, embedded above and around by the green turf, forms a conduit-head to a beautiful spring; the specific gravity of the fluid, which yields several tons a day, is little more than that of distilled water. Hampstead abounds in other springs, but they are mostly impregnated with mineral substances. The water of 'Shepherd's Well,' therefore, is in continual request; and those who cannot otherwise obtain it are supplied through a few of the villagers, who make a scanty living by carrying it to houses for a penny a pailful. There is no carriage-way to the spot, and these poor things have much hard work for a very little money. . . . The water of Shepherd's Well is remarkable for not being subject to freeze. There is another spring sometimes resorted to near Kilburn; but this and the ponds in the Vale of Health are the ordinary sources of public supply to Hampstead. The chief inconvenience of habitations in this delightful village is the inadequate distribution of good water. Occasional visitants, for the sake of health, frequently sustain considerable injury by the insalubrity of private springs, and charge upon the fluid they breathe the mischief they derive from the fluid they drink. The localities of the place afford almost every variety of aspect and temperature that invalids require; and a constant sufficiency of wholesome water might be easily obtained by a few simple arrangements." It may be well to add, however, that the want of good water is not among the requirements of Hampstead at the present day; and also that what Lord Loughborough was unable to effect in the way of stopping the supply of water from this spring, was partially accomplished about the years 1860–70, through the excavation of tunnels under the hill on the side of which it stands, when the spring became almost dried up.

The fields which we have now before us are those over which Leigh Hunt so much delighted to ramble, and which, no doubt, he found far more pleasant than the interior of Newgate, in which he had been immured for calling the Prince of Wales "a fat Adonis." In these fields Hunt would often meet with the genial company of his fellow-poets. Shelley would walk hither from his lodgings in Pond Street, and Keats would turn up from Well Walk. Here the three friends once frightened an old lady terribly: they thought themselves quite alone, and Shelley, throwing himself into attitude, began to spout the lines—

> "Come, brothers, let us sit upon the ground,
> And tell sad stories of the deaths of kings."

The old lady made off as quick as her feet could carry her, and told her friends that she had met in the fields three dangerous characters, who, she was quite sure, were either madmen, or republicans, or actors! It was the view of Hampstead from these fields that suggested to the mind of Leigh Hunt the following lines, descriptive of their beauties, and which are well worthy to appear among his various poems on the scenery of this neighbourhood:—

> "A turret looking o'er a leafy vine,
> With hedgerow styles in front, and sloping green,
> Sweet Hampstead, is thy southward look serene;
> And such thou welcomest approaching eyes.
> To me a double charm is in thy skies
> From her meek spirit, oft in fancy seen
> Blessing the twilight with her placid mien."

In 1874–5 it was proposed by some of the inhabitants of Hampstead to purchase a portion of these grassy slopes, and to devote them to public use, in the shape of a "park" for the working classes of the neighbourhood; but the plan was brought to an abrupt termination by some speculative builders, by whom the greater part of the ground was bought and laid out for building purposes, a broad roadway, called Fitzjohn's Avenue, being made at the same time across their centre, thus connecting the town of Hampstead with St. John's Wood, Kilburn, and the west end of London. It is not a little singular that just a hundred years previously—namely, in 1776—the construction of a new road was proposed from Portman Square to Alsopp's Farm, across the fields, and on through a part of Belsize, to the foot of Hampstead Town.

In these fields and in those lying between the southern terrace of the churchyard and the lower portions of Frognal, rise two or three springs, which form the sources of the brook which we have already seen trickling through Kilburn, and by Westbourne Green down to Bayswater, where it forms the head of the Serpentine river.

Leaving the Conduit Fields and Fitzjohn's Avenue on our right, and making our way down College Lane by some neat school-buildings, which have been lately erected there, we emerge upon the Finchley Road, close by the "North Star" tavern, whence a short walk along the road, with pleasant fields and hedgerows on either hand, brings us to the western part of the village of Hampstead. On our way along the Finchley Road we pass, on our right, the large, new, and handsome church of the Holy Trinity; and on our left, the Finchley Road stations on the Midland and North London Railways, which here again emerge into daylight, after passing through tunnels, as already stated, under the Belsize and Rosslyn estates. A footpath, cut diagonally across a sloping meadow, between some venerable oaks, takes us from the main road, behind Frognal Priory, to West End Lane, a narrow carriage-way connecting the Finchley Road with the village of Hampstead. This lane is still in parts overhung at the sides by elms and quickset hedges, and has about it some of that quiet air of rusticity which Constable so delighted in painting.

Frognal, as the neighbourhood of the western slope of Hampstead is called, is still, happily, a "beautiful and suburban village," just as it is described by the Rev. J. Richardson in his amusing "Recollections." He writes: "The view from the upper part of this locality is one of the finest in England [he should have said in the neighbourhood of London]. The late Dr. White, who held some years back the living of Hampstead, and also that of Nettlebed, in Oxfordshire, used to affirm that on a clear day, with the aid of a good telescope, he could discern the windmill at Nettlebed from his garden at Frognal, the distance between the two places being about thirty-five miles in a direct line."

This neighbourhood is full of gentlemen's seats and villas, standing in their own grounds. On our right, as we ascend the hill, we pass the site on which, from the close of the last century down to the year 1876, stood a curious building—an absurd specimen of modern antiquity—in the gingerbread Gothic style, a not very successful imitation of Horace Walpole's Strawberry Hill, pretentiously styled Frognal Priory. Mr. Howitt, in his "Northern Heights," published in 1869, gives the following particulars of the eccentric house, and its still more eccentric owner:—"This house, now hastening fast to ruin, was built by a Mr. Thompson, best known by the name of 'Memory Thompson,' or, as stated by others, as 'Memory-Corner Thompson.' This Mr. Thompson built the house on a lease of twenty years, subject to a fine to the lord of the manor. He appears to have been an auctioneer and public-house broker, who grew rich, and, having a peculiar taste in architecture and old furniture, built this house in an old English style, approaching the Elizabethan. That the house, though now ruinous, is of modern date, is also witnessed by the trees around it being common poplar, evidently planted to run up quickly. Thompson is said to have belonged to a club of auctioneers or brokers, which met once a week; and at one of these meetings, boasting that he had a better memory than any man living, he offered to prove it by stating the name and business of every person who kept a corner shop in the City, or, as others have it, the name, number, and business of every person who kept a shop in Cheapside. The former statement is the one most received, and is the more probable, because Thompson, being a public-house broker, was no doubt familiar with all these corner-haunting drink-houses. Having maintained his boast, he was thence called 'Memory,' or 'Memory-Corner Thompson;' but his general cognomen was the first. Thompson not only asserted that he built his house on the site of an ancient priory, continuing down to the Dissolution, and inhabited as a suburban house by Cardinal Wolsey, but, as an auctioneer, he had the opportunity of collecting old furniture, pieces of carving in wood, ebony, ivory, &c. With these he filled his house, dignifying his furniture (some of which had been made up from fragments) as having belonged to Cardinal Wolsey, to Queen Elizabeth, the Queen of Scots, and other historical magnates. On the marriage of Queen Victoria, he offered for sale a huge old bedstead, as Queen Elizabeth's, with chairs to match, to Her Majesty, but the queen declined it. It is said, however, to have been purchased by Government, and to be somewhere in one of the palaces. This bedstead, and the chairs possibly, had some authentic character, as he built a wing of his house especially for their reception. Thompson had an ostensibly magnificent library, containing, to all appearance, most valuable works of all kinds; but, on examination, they proved to be only pasteboard bound up and labelled as books. The windows of the chief room were of stained glass, casting 'a dim, religious light.' And this great warehouse of articles of furniture, of real and manufactured antiquity, of coins, china, and articles of *virtu*, became so great a show place, that people flocked far and near to see it. This greatly flattered Thompson, who excluded no one of tolerable appearance, nor restricted visitors to stated hours. It is said that, in his ostentation, he used to leave five-guinea gold pieces about on the window seats." But this last statement is mythical. The best, and indeed the only good portion of the house, was the porch, a handsome and massive structure, in the ornamented Jacobean style, and which had formed the entrance of some one of the many timber mansions still to be found in Cheshire and in other remote counties, and which Thompson had "picked up" as a bargain in one of his business tours. It was surmounted with the armorial bearings of the family to whom it had belonged, and was often sketched by artists. After his death, at the age of eighty years, a sale of his goods and chattels took place; but the principal part of his wealth descended to his niece, who married Barnard Gregory, the proprietor of the notorious *Satirist*. Gregory, it seems, on the death of his wife, did not pay the customary fine to the lord of the manor, and Sir Thomas Wilson recovered possession by an injunction, intending to remove the offices of the manor thither. From a fear, however, of the appearance of some heir of Thompson after he had repaired it, which was at one time a possibility, Sir Thomas left it *in statu quo ante;* and the house having gone rapidly to decay and ruin, was, in the end, wholly demolished. A few trees, forming a sort of grove, and the remains of a small lodge-house, now profusely overgrown with ivy, are all that is left to mark the site of the singular edifice heretofore known as Frognal Priory.

In a cottage close by the entrance to the Priory, as we have stated in a previous chapter, Dr. Johnson stayed for a time as a visitor; and here Boswell tells us that he wrote his "Town," and busied himself during a summer with his essay on the "Vanity of Human Riches." It is not a little singular, however, that neither of these poems bear much trace of the inspiration of the Hampstead Muses. The fact is that the burly doctor preferred society to scenery, and with the winter returned to Fleet Street, and presented himself once more amongst his friends, in whose company he felt, we may be sure, much more at home than amidst the breezes of Hampstead, and whose conversation gave him more gratification than the songs of her nightingales. Park says the house at which Dr. Johnson used to lodge was "the last in Frognal southward, occupied in his (Park's) time by Benjamin Charles Stephenson, Esq., F.S.A." The house has been rebuilt, or, at all events, remodelled since that date.

At Frognal lived also Mr. Thomas William Carr, some time solicitor of the Excise, whose house was the centre of literary *réunions*. Here, Crabb Robinson tells us in his "Diary," he met Wordsworth, Sir Humphrey Davy, Joanna Baillie, and some other persons of note. One of Mr. Carr's daughters married Sir Robert M. Rolfe, afterwards Lord Chancellor Cranworth.

Frognal Hall, standing close to the western end of the church, was formerly the residence of Mr. Isaac Ware,* the architect, and author of "A Complete Body of Architecture," and of a translation of "Palladio on the Fine Arts," &c. Although Mr. Ware found a patron in the great Lord Burlington, he is stated to have died at his house near Kensington Gravel Pits in "depressed circumstances." A French family, named Guyons, occupied the hall after Ware quitted it; and it was subsequently the residence of Lord Alvanley, Master of the Rolls, and some time Chief Justice of the Court of Common Pleas. After passing through one or two other hands, Frognal Hall became the residence of Mr. Julius Talbot Airey. It has now been turned into a Roman Catholic boarding-school. The adjoining seat, that of Miss Sulivan, is known as Frognal Mansion, and was originally the manor house of this district. A part of the manorial rights attached to this property consists of a private road leading past the north side of the parish church, with a private toll-gate, which even royalty cannot pass without payment of the customary toll. It is nearly the only toll-gate now remaining in all the suburbs of London.

It was probably in the upper part of Frognal that Cyrus Redding for some time resided; at all events, it was in a lodging on the western slope of the hill, as he tells us himself, that he began in 1858 his "Fifty Years' Recollections, Literary and

* See *ante*, p. 214.

Personal." His windows commanded a charming and extensive view. He writes picturesquely:—"Before me palatial Windsor is seen rising proudly in the distance. The spire of Harrow, like a burial obelisk, ascending in another direction, brings before the glass of memory eminent names with which it is associated—Parr, Byron, Peel, and others, no longer of the quick, but the dead. The hills of Surrey southward blend their faint grey outline with the remoter heaven. The middle landscape slumbers in beauty; clouds roll heavily and sluggishly along, with here and there a break permitting the glory of the superior region to shine obliquely through, in strong contrast to the shadowy face of things beneath."

To the west of Frognal there is some rising ground, which the late Mr. Sheffield Neave laid out for the erection of about twelve handsome houses, called Oak Hill Park. One of these has been frequently occupied during the summer months by Miss Florence Nightingale. Near the entrance of this park is a house which was occupied for many years as the Sailors' Orphan Girls' Home, before the transfer of that institution to its new buildings between Church Row and Greenhill, and Prince Arthur's Road. To the north of Frognal is the Upper Terrace, which screens this portion of Hampstead from the bleak winds that blow across the Heath. In this terrace a house known as the "Priory" was the residence of the eminent sculptor and Royal Academician, Mr. J. H. Foley. In another house in this terrace lived Mr. Magrath, one of the founders, and during its earlier years the secretary, of the Athenæum Club.

Half a mile westward, beyond Frognal, lies West End, a group of houses surrounding an open space which is still a village green. This used to be the scene of a fair held annually in July; but the fair was suppressed about the year 1820 on account of the disorderly conduct of its frequenters. There is extant in the British Museum a curious handbill, dated 1708, and entitled "The Hampstead Fair Rambler; or, The World's Going quite Mad. To the tune of 'Brother Soldier, dost hear of the News?' London, printed for J. Bland, near Holborn, 1708." From this it is clear that, like most rural and suburban fairs, it was remarkable chiefly for its swings, roundabouts, penny trumpets, spiced gingerbread, and halfpenny rattles. Occasionally, however, its proceedings were varied; under date July 2, 1744, we read: "This is to give notice that the Fair will be kept on Wednesday, Thursday, and Friday next, in a pleasant, shady walk, in the middle of the town. On Wednesday a pig will be turned loose, and he that takes it up by the tail and throws it over his head shall have it. To pay twopence entrance, and no less than twelve to enter. On Thursday, a match will be run by two men, a hundred yards, in two sacks, for a large sum. And to encourage the sport, the landlord of the inn will give a pair of gloves, to be run for by six men, the winner to have them. And on Friday, a hat, value ten shillings, will be run for by men twelve times round the green; to pay one shilling entrance; no less than four to start. As many as will may enter, and the second man to have all the money above four."

This, doubtless, was the *locale* of the scenes mentioned in the public prints of June, 1786:—"On Whit Tuesday was celebrated, near Hendon, in Middlesex, a burlesque imitation of the Olympic Games. One prize was a gold-laced hat, to be grinned for by six candidates, who were placed on a platform with horses' collars to grin through. Over their heads was written '*detur tetriori*'—'The ugliest grinner shall be the winner.' Each party had to grin for five minutes by himself, and then all the other candidates joined in a grand chorus of distortion. The prize was carried by a porter to a vinegar-merchant, though he was accused by his competitors of foul play, for rinsing his mouth with verjuice. The sports were concluded by a hog with his tail shaved and soaped being let loose among some ten or twelve peasants, any one of whom that could seize him by the *queue* and throw him across his own shoulders was to keep him as a prize. The animal, after running for some miles about the neighbourhood of the Heath, so tired his pursuers, that they at last gave up the chase in despair. We are told that on this occasion a prodigious concourse of people attended, among whom were the Tripoline Ambassador, and several other persons of distinction and quality."

The Rev. Mr. Richardson, in his amusing "Recollections," states that as lately as 1819 the fair was attended by about two hundred "roughs" from London, who assaulted the men and the women with brutal violence, cutting their clothes from their backs. The Hampstead magistrates were obliged to call the aid of special constables in order to suppress the riot. This riot, however, had one good effect, as it helped to pave the way for the introduction of the new police by Sir Robert Peel. There is a tradition that the last Maypole in the neighbourhood stood on this green. A good sketch of a dance round a country Maypole will be found in Hone's "Every-Day Book," under "May-day."

West End, for the most part, lies low, and the houses are but poor second and third-rate cottages; and there is a public-house bearing the sign of the "Cock and Hoop." Here is a small Gothic structure, forming at once a village school and a chapel of ease for the parish.

A new cemetery for the parish of Hampstead was formed on the north of West End in 1876; it covers twenty acres of ground, and is picturesquely laid out; and close by is a reservoir belonging to the Grand Junction Waterworks Company.

A little farther on the road to Hendon is an outlying district of Hampstead parish, known as Child's Hill, consisting almost wholly of cottages, dotted irregularly around two or three cross-roads. Here a small district church was erected about the year 1850; it is a Gothic edifice, consisting of a nave and chancel, with a small bell-turret. The road, here branching off to the right, will take the tourist through a pleasant lane to the north-west corner of the Heath, where the gorse and furze bloom in all their native beauty. Following this road, and leaving on his right Telegraph Hill—the site of a semaphore half a century ago—he will find himself once more at the back of "Jack Straw's Castle," whence a short walk will take him back into the centre of Hampstead.

Having thus far made our survey of the parish of Hampstead, little remains to be said. The place, as we have endeavoured to show, has long been considered healthy and salubrious, and, therefore, has been the frequent resort of invalids for the benefit of the air. From the formal reports of the medical officer of health for Hampstead, issued yearly, we learn that the death-rate of late years has varied from 14 to 16 in a thousand —a very low rate of mortality, it must be owned, though not quite so low as it stood in the year 1875, when Dr. Lord gave to the parish, in allusion to its lofty and salubrious situation, the name of *Mons Salutis*.

The parish extends over upwards of 2,000 acres of land, of which, as we have stated, between 200 and 300 are waste. In 1801 there were 691 inhabited houses in the parish, and the number of families occupying them was 953; and the total number of the inhabitants was 4,343. In 1851 the population had grown to 12,000. Ten years later it had increased to 19,000; in 1865 it had reached 22,000; and at the present time (1884) its numbers may be estimated at nearly 50,000.

On more than one occasion, when silly prophets and astrologers have alarmed the inhabitants of London by rumours of approaching earthquakes, and tides that should swallow up its citizens, the high ground of Hampstead and Highgate has afforded to the crowds in their alarm a place of refuge and safety. An amusing description of, at all events, two such instances will be found in Dr. Mackay's "Memoirs of Extraordinary Popular Delusions," in the chapter devoted to the subject of "Modern Prophecies." It may sound not a little strange when we tell our readers that one of these unreasoning panics occurred so lately as the first year of the reign of George III. It is only fair to add that a slight shock of an earthquake had been felt in London a month before, but so slight, that it did no harm, beyond throwing down one or two tottering stacks of chimneys.

Apropos of the gradual extension of the limits of the metropolis, of which we have already more than once had occasion to speak, we cannot do better, in concluding this part of our perambulations, than to quote the following lines of Mr. Thomas Miller, in his "Picturesque Sketches of London." "Twelve miles," he writes, "would scarcely exceed the almost unbroken line of buildings which extends from Blackwall to far beyond Chelsea, where street still joins to street in apparently endless succession. And yet all around this vast city lie miles of the most beautiful rural scenery. Highgate, Hornsey, and Hampstead, on the Middlesex side, hilly, wooded, and watered; and facing these, the vast range called the Hog's Back, which hems in the far-distant Surrey side from beyond Norwood; . . . . whilst the valleys on both sides of the river are filled with pleasant fields, parks, and green, winding lanes. Were London to extend five miles farther every way, it would still be hemmed in with some of the most beautiful country scenery in England; and the lowness of the fares, together with the rapidity of railway travelling, would render as nothing this extent of streets."

COLUMBIA MARKET, HACKNEY. (*See page* 506.)

CHAPTER XL.

THE NORTH-EASTERN SUBURBS.—HAGGERSTON, HACKNEY, &c.

"Oppidum rure commistum."—*Tacitus.*

Appearance of Haggerston in the Last Century—Cambridge Heath—Nova Scotia Gardens—Columbia Buildings—Columbia Market—The "New" Burial-ground of St. Leonard's, Shoreditch—Halley, the Astronomer—Nichols Square—St. Chad's Church—St. Mary's Church—Brunswick Square Almshouses—Mutton Lane—The "Cat and Mutton" Tavern—London Fields—The Hackney Bun-house—Goldsmiths' Row—The Goldsmiths' Almshouses—The North-Eastern Hospital for Sick Children—The Orphan Asylum, Bonner's Road—City of London Hospital for Diseases of the Chest—Bonner's Hall—Bishop Bonner's Fields—Botany Bay—Victoria Park—The East-enders' Fondness for Flowers—Amateur Yachting—The Jews' Burial-ground—The French Hospital—The Church of St. John of Jerusalem—The Etymology of "Hackney."

HAVING in the preceding chapters devoted our attention to the north-western part of London, we now take up fresh ground, and begin anew with the north-eastern districts, which, although not so extensive as the ground over which we have travelled since starting from Belgravia and Pimlico, will doubtless be found to contain much that may prove interesting to the general reader.

Taking our stand close by the north-easternmost point described in the previous parts of this work—namely, by St. Leonard's Church, Shoreditch*—we have on our left the districts of Hoxton and Islington, and on our right that of Bethnal Green. Stretching away in an easterly direction is the Hackney Road, which divides these last-named districts from that of Haggerston.

In Rocque's map of Hackney, published in 1745, the Hackney Road appears entirely unbuilt upon, with the exception of a couple of houses at the corner of the roadway leading to the hamlet of Agostone (now Haggerston), and a small cluster of dwellings and a roadside public-house called the "Nag's Head," at the bottom of a narrow thoroughfare called Mutton Lane, which passes through the fields in the north, by the front of the Goldsmiths' Almshouses, of which we shall have more to say presently. The greater part of the lane itself is now called Goldsmiths' Row. At the eastern end of the Hackney Road, Cambridge Heath is marked as a large triangular space, the apex of

* See Vol. II., p. 195.

which terminates close by Coats's Lane, Bethnal Green. From Cambridge Heath the roadway trends to the north by Mare (or Meare) Street, on the east side of London Fields, forming the principal roadway through the town of Hackney.

At a short distance eastward of Shoreditch Church, on our right hand as we pass along the Hackney Road, and therefore within the limits of the parish of Bethnal Green, the eye is struck by Columbia Square and Market, the tall roofs of which rise against the sky, reminding us of the Houses of Parliament, though on a smaller scale. They were erected in 1869, from the designs of Mr. H. A. Darbishire. On the site now occupied by the market and a few of the surrounding buildings existed till very recently a foul colony of squalor and misery, consisting of wretched low tenements—or, more correctly speaking, hovels—and still more wretched inhabitants; the locality bore the name of Nova Scotia Gardens, and it abounded in pestilential drains and dust heaps. Nova Scotia Gardens and its surroundings, in fact, were formerly one of the most poverty-stricken quarters of the whole East-end, and, doubtless, one of those spots to which Charles Dickens refers in his "Uncommercial Traveller," when he draws attention to the fact that while the poor rate in St. George's, Hanover Square, stands at sevenpence in the pound, there are districts in these eastern slums where it stands at five shillings and sixpence. By the benevolence of Lady Burdett-Coutts, whose charity and will to benefit the poor of London we have already had occasion to remark upon in our account of Highgate,* the whole of this seat of foulness and disease was cleared away, and in its place four large blocks of model lodging-houses, forming a square called Columbia Buildings, have been erected, and are occupied by an orderly and well-behaved section of the working-class population of the district. Contiguous to the square stands the Market, which was also established by the same benevolent lady for the convenience of the neighbourhood. The market covers about two acres of ground, and the buildings, which are principally constructed of brick, with stone dressings, are very elaborately ornamented with carved work, in the shape of medallions and armorial bearings. The market-place forms three sides of a square, having an arcade opening on the central area through Gothic arches. Tables for the various commodities which may be brought to the market for sale, occupy the centre of the quadrangular space, and are partly covered in by a light roof. The chief feature of the building, which occupies the whole of the eastern side of the quadrangle, is a large and lofty Gothic hall. The exterior of this edifice is particularly rich in ornamentation. The basement is lighted by a range of small pointed windows, above which is an ornamental string-course. The hall itself, which is reached by a short flight of steps, is lighted by seven large pointed windows on each side, with others still larger at either end; the buttresses between the windows terminate in elaborate pinnacles; in fact, the whole building, including the louvre in the centre of the roof, and the tall clock-tower, bristles with crocketed pinnacles and foliated finials.

Whether the building is too ornate, or whatever may be the cause, it is not for us to say; but, at all events, as a place of business in the way designed by its noble founder, Columbia Market for many years proved a comparative failure. Scarcely any of the shops which open upon the arcades were occupied; indeed, very little in the way of business was ever carried on there. In 1877, it was re-opened as a market for American meat, but the attempt proved ineffectual. It afterwards, however, became established as a fish depôt, to which, in January, 1884, a vegetable market was added.

On the opposite side of the Hackney Road, facing the entrance to Columbia Square, is the "new" burial-ground belonging to St. Leonard's, Shoreditch. This has been long disused, and within the last few years the grave-mounds have been levelled, the place being made to serve as a recreation-ground for the children in the neighbourhood.

Haggerston, on our left, at one time an outlying hamlet in the parish of St. Leonard's, Shoreditch, is mentioned in "Domesday Book" under the name of Hergotestane. It is now an extensive district, stretching away from the north side of the Hackney Road to Dalston, and from the Kingsland Road on the west to London Fields, and is crowded with factories and with the residences of the artisan class. In the seventeenth century the hamlet contained only a few houses, designed for country retirement. The celebrated astronomer, Halley, was born and resided here, though the house which he occupied is not known. He died in 1741, and lies buried in the churchyard of Lee, Kent.

Nichols Square, which we pass on our left, keeps in remembrance the name of Mr. John Nichols, F.S.A., the well-known antiquary, and "the Dugdale of the present age." Mr. Nichols was the author of "Literary Anecdotes of the Eighteenth

* See *ante*, p. 411.

Century," the "History of the County of Leicester," "Progresses and Processions of Queen Elizabeth," &c., and was many years editor of the *Gentleman's Magazine* in its palmy days. He was a native of the adjoining parish of Islington, where he chiefly resided. He died in 1826, and was succeeded in his property in this neighbourhood by his son, Mr. John Bowyer Nichols, who shortly afterwards became proprietor of the *Gentleman's Magazine*. This gentleman died at Ealing in 1863. The Messrs. Nichols have been for many years printers to the two Houses of Parliament.

In the north-east corner of Nichols Square stands St. Chad's Church. It is a large red-brick edifice, with an apsidal eastern end, and comprises nave and aisles, transepts, and chancel, with a dwarf spire at the intersection. The transepts are lighted by large wheel windows, and the body of the fabric by narrow Gothic pointed windows. The church was built about 1865. It is noted for its "High Church" or ritualistic services.

St. Mary's Church, in Brunswick Square, close by, was built in 1830, but considerably altered in 1862. It is of Gothic architecture, and, externally, is chiefly remarkable for the lofty tower at the western end. The organ, which was originally in St. George's Chapel, Windsor, was built by Father Smith. It has been within the last few years much enlarged by Willis.

The parish of Haggerston contains a Church Association, of which all the communicants are members, and each member is required to do some work for the cause of the Established Church.

On the west side of Brunswick Square is a row of almshouses, of neat and picturesque appearance. These almshouses, belonging to the parish of Shoreditch, were founded in 1836, and stood originally on the south side of the Hackney Road, but were rebuilt on this site on the demolition of the houses, in order to make room for the approaches to Columbia Square, &c.

Passing eastward, by the Imperial Gas-works, we arrive at Goldsmiths' Row, which, as stated above, was formerly known as Mutton Lane, a name still given to that part of the thoroughfare bordering upon the southern extremity of London Fields, where stands a noted public-house, rejoicing in the sign of the "Cat and Mutton." Affixed to the house are two sign-boards, which are rather curious; they have upon them the following doggrel lines:—

> "Pray, Puss, do not tare,
> Because the mutton is so rare."
>
> "Pray, Puss, do not claw,
> Because the Mutton is so raw."

The open space in front, known as London Fields, and extending over several acres, has within the last few years been taken in hand by the Board of Works, and has had its surface levelled, and, where necessary, sown with fresh grass; it is crossed by numerous paths, and in part planted with trees. The spot has been for ages the resort of the dwellers in the neighbourhood for the purposes of recreation, and from the neighbouring tavern and its associations had in process of time become better known as the "Cat and Mutton" fields.

Strype tells us that the Bishop of London held demesnes in Hackney as far back as the time of Edward I., in the nineteenth year of whose reign (A.D. 1290) the right of free warren in this parish was granted to Richard de Gravesend, who then held the see; and from an "inquisition" in the same reign, it is clear that a yeoman named Duckett held lands here under the bishop, who in his turn held them from the king as his superior. There are, or were, several manors within the parish of Hackney; the principal of these is termed the "Lord's-hold," and was attached to the bishopric of London until the year 1550, when it was surrendered to the Crown by Bishop Ridley, whose memory is kept up in connection with this locality by the name of Ridley, given to a roadway on the north side of Dalston Lane.

In the short thoroughfare connecting the London Fields with Goldsmiths' Row there is a shop which in bygone times was almost as much noted for its "Hackney Buns" as the well-known Bun-house at Chelsea was for that particular kind of pastry about which we have already spoken.*

Goldsmiths' Row extends from the canal bridge, near the south-west corner of London Fields, to the Hackney Road. The thoroughfare is very narrow, and in parts consists of very inferior shops and tenements. On the west side, about half way down, stand a row of almshouses belonging to the Goldsmiths' Company. They were founded in 1703, by a Mr. Morrell, for six poor almsmen belonging to the above-mentioned company, each of whom has a pension of £21 per annum. On the opposite side, near the corner of the Hackney Road, are some new buildings in connection with the North-Eastern Hospital for Sick Children, which was founded in 1867, in the Hackney Road. The new buildings were inaugurated a few years ago by the Princess Louise. The institution was established, as its name implies, for the purpose of affording medical relief to sick children; and about

* See *ante*, p. 69.

10,000 patients are annually relieved here. Patients are admitted free, on the production of a subscriber's ticket; otherwise a small fee is paid by out-patients and in-patients.

At the eastern end of Hackney Road formerly stood the Cambridge Heath turnpike gate, which was removed a few years ago, when tolls upon the metropolitan highways were abolished; its site is now marked by an obelisk set up in the centre of the roadway. From this point, Mare Street, of which we shall have more to say presently, branches off to the left; Cambridge Road, on our right, leads past the Bethnal Green Museum, and so on to the Whitechapel Road and Mile End. Prospect Place, which extends eastward from the Hackney Road, and its continuation, Bishop's Road, leads direct to the principal entrance to Victoria Park.

On the east side of Bonner's Road, which here branches off to the right, leading to Old Ford Road, stands an Orphan Asylum, or Home for outcast children; and also the City of London Hospital for Diseases of the Chest. The latter edifice is a large and well-proportioned building of red brick, consisting of a centre and wings, in the Queen Anne style, and was constructed from the designs of Mr. Ordish. It has a central campanile, and a small Gothic chapel on the north side, connected with the main building by a covered corridor. The hospital, which was opened by Prince Albert in 1848, for "the relief of indigent persons afflicted with consumption and other diseases of the chest," was first of all located in Liverpool Street, Finsbury, and by the end of the year 1849 about 900 patients were relieved. Since its removal to the neighbourhood of Victoria Park its accommodation has vastly increased, so that in the year 1883 about 800 in-patients and 15,000 out-patients had experienced the benefits of this most excellent charity. The hospital stands upon a large triangular plot of ground, surrounded by a light iron railing; and the grounds are laid out in grass plats, and flower-beds, and are well planted with shrubs and trees. Some of the latter are the remains of an avenue formerly extending from the Old Ford Lane to the principal entrance of Bonner's Hall, which stood on the east side of where the hospital now stands. The old building is traditionally said to have been the residence of Bishop Bonner, and certainly to have been his property. The surrounding land down to a comparatively recent date was known as Bishop Bonner's Fields, names which are now preserved in the two roads above mentioned. The site of Bishop Bonner's Hall was occupied by some private buildings in the early part of the present century; and Bishop Bonner's Hall Farm, a curious old-fashioned structure of plaster and brickwork, stood near what is now the western entrance to Victoria Park down to about the year 1850.

In this neighbourhood, at the time of the formation of Victoria Park, was swept away a wretched village of hovels, formerly known as "Botany Bay," from so many of its inhabitants being sent to "another place" bearing that name.

By the side of the park gates is a picturesque lodge-house of the Elizabethan character, built from the designs of Mr. Pennethorne; it is constructed chiefly of red bricks, and has a lofty tower and porch. The ground now forming Victoria Park was purchased by the Government with the proceeds of the sale of York (now Stafford) House,* St. James's, in pursuance of an Act of Parliament passed in 1840 for that purpose. It is bounded on the south-east by Sir George Duckett's Canal—a branch cut from the Regent's Canal, near Bonner's Hall Farm, crossing the Grove Road, and communicating with the river Lea, near Old Ford; on the north-east by Old Ford Lane, or Wick Lane; on the north-west by Grove Street and lands belonging to Sir John Cass's charity and to St. Thomas's Hospital; and on the west by the Regent's Canal.

Victoria Park is nearly 300 acres in extent, with avenues which one day with an ampler growth will be really superb, a lake, or chain of lakes, on which adventurous spirits daily learn to "tug the labouring oar," and such a pleasant arrangement of walks, shrubberies, green turf, gay flowers, and shady trees, that if the place were situated in the western suburbs, it would, perhaps, become the resort of the *élite* of fashion. On an island upon one of the lakes is a two-storeyed Chinese pagoda, which, with the trees and foliage surrounding it, has a pretty effect. Here, as in the West-end parks, floriculture has been greatly extended of late; and through the summer months, its variegated parterres are aglow with flowers of every hue, making altogether a glorious show. Among the large foliage plants which have found their way here, may be remarked, on one sheltered slope, a group of *Ficus elastica*, the india-rubber tree, and close by is a specimen of the *Yucca gloriosa*, which has the more popular name of "Adam's needle," the tradition probably being that one of its pointed leaves helped to make the fig-leaf apron. Tropical plants of different varieties are to be found in the snug nooks and recesses which abound here. As to the flowering plants, such as the geranium, calceolaria, verbena, lobelia, &c., reliance is placed

* See Vol. IV., p. 122.

chiefly upon masses of colour instead of the narrow bands adopted in the other parks. In the Regent's Park, as we have already seen,* great skill has been shown in grouping and composition; there is an attempt in landscape-gardening at something of the effects of landscape painting, using Nature's own colours, with the ground for canvas. In Hyde Park the red line of geraniums between Stanhope Gate and Grosvenor Gate is as well known among gardeners as the "thin red line" at Balaclava among soldiers. But in Victoria Park the old gardening tactics prevail; for the most part, masses of colour are brought to bear upon the eye in oval, round, and square; and with a wide area of turf in which to manœuvre our floral forces, these tactics are probably the most effective that could be adopted. More ingenious designs, however, are not wanting. Near the ornamental water, a pretty effect is produced by scrolls of purple verbena enclosed by the white-leaved *Cerastium tomentosum*, looking like amethysts set in silver. In another part of the park this design is reversed, and the blue lobelia is made a frame for a central pattern of the same delicate silvery foliage plant, lit up by an occasional patch of scarlet, with a background of dahlias and evergreens. Elsewhere we come upon a fanciful figure which, after some study, resolves itself into an outstretched butterfly of enormous size, with wings as vividly coloured as those of any that fly in the sun. For borderings the *Amaranthus melancholicus* and the usual foliage plants of small growth are employed.

In fine weather, when the band plays, over 100,000 persons are frequently collected in this park. The people are orderly, most of them being of the humbler class, and their appreciation of the flowers is quite as keen as that of the frequenters of the West-end parks. Some of the dwellers in the East-end have a great fondness for flowers, and contrive somehow or other, in the most unlikely places, to rear very choice varieties. In small, wretched-looking yards, where little air and only the mid-day sun can penetrate, may be seen patches of garden, evidently tended with uncommon care, and yielding to their cultivators a fair reward in fragrance and in blossom. In some places may be descried bits of broken glass and a framework which just holds together, doing duty as a greenhouse; and in this triumph of patience and ingenuity the poor artisan spends much of his leisure, happy when he can make up a birthday bouquet for some friend or relation. The flowers in the neighbouring park, with their novel grouping and striking contrasts of colour, are, of course, a continual source of pleasure for these struggling artisans, and gladden many a moment when, perhaps, work is not too plentiful, and home thoughts are not very happy. In Victoria Park the plants and flowers are labelled in letters which he who walks may read without need of getting over fence or bordering. This is not always the case in the other parks, where the labels, from dirt or the smallness of the characters, are often practically illegible. One of the lakes is devoted to miniature yacht sailing. This amusement seems almost confined to East London; and here on a summer evening, when a capful of wind is to be had, the surface of the lake is whitened by some forty or fifty toy boats and yachts, of all rigs and sizes, while here and there a miniature steamboat is puffing and panting. There is even a yacht-club, whose members compete with their toy-yachts for silver cups and other prizes. The expense of keeping up a yacht here is not considerable, and the whole squadron may be laid up until wanted in a boat-house provided for the purpose. But the matches and trials of these tiny crafts are a special attraction of the park, and draw together every evening hundreds of people. Bathing, too, is largely indulged in during the summer. Ample space is available for cricket, and in the two gymnasia candidates for swinging, jumping, and climbing appear to be never wanting.

In one open part of the grounds stands a very handsome drinking-fountain, surrounded by parterres of flowers. It was erected by Lady Burdett-Coutts, whose care for the social welfare of the poor of London, and particularly in the East-end districts, we have already had occasion to mention. In the part devoted to cricket and such like sports, some of the semi-octagonal recesses, which afforded shelter for foot-passengers on old Westminster Bridge,† have been re-erected, and serve as alcoves.

On the north side of Victoria Park is a large plot of ground, which since the end of the last century has been used as a burial-place for the Jewish community, belonging to the Hamburg synagogue.

Making our way through Grove Street, we reach the south-west corner of Hackney Common. Close by this point stands the French Hospital, a large and ornamental building of dark red brick, with stone dressings, which presents a pleasing contrast to the foliage of the trees which surround it. The institution was established as far back as 1708, for

* See *ante*, p. 266.

† See Vol. III., p. 299.

the "support of poor French Protestants and their descendants."

A short walk through Lammas Road and Groombridge Road, which skirt the western side of the Common, brings us to Grove Street, by the end of King Edward Road, where stands the large and handsome church of St. John of Jerusalem, the parish church of the recently-formed district of South Hackney. The church, which is built of Kentish rag-stone, is in the best Pointed style of the thirteenth and fourteenth centuries, and was erected in 1846 from the designs of Mr. E. C. Hakewell, to supersede a church erected in Well Street early in the present century. The plan of the edifice is cruciform, with a tower and spire of equal height, together rising nearly 200 feet; the latter has graceful lights and broaches, and the four Evangelists beneath canopies at the four angles. The nave has side aisles, with flying buttresses to the clerestory; each transept is lit by a magnificent window, about thirty feet high, and the choir has an apse with seven lancet windows. The principal entrance, at the western end, is through a screen of open arches. The roof, of open work, is very lofty, and has massive arched and foliated ribs; the chancel has a stone roof, and the walls of the apse are painted and diapered—red with fleur-de-lis, and blue powdered with stars. All the windows are filled with painted, stained, or richly-diapered glass. The tower has a fine peal of eight bells.

HACKNEY, LOOKING TOWARDS THE CHURCH, 1840.

Before proceeding with a description of the old town of Hackney, upon which we are now entering, we may remark that it has been suggested, and with considerable probability, that the name of the place is derived from "Hacon's ey," or the island which some Danish chief named Hacon had, in the mild method prevalent among the warriors of fifteen hundred years ago, appropriated to himself. But authentic history is silent upon the point; and, indeed, almost the earliest record we find of the place is that the Knights Templars held the manor, which afterwards became the property of their rivals, the Knights of St. John of Jerusalem. Of late years the parish has been styled by the name of St. John at Hackney, as though it belonged to the fraternity of the Knights of St. John of Jerusalem, who had, as it is said, a mansion and other possessions in the parish; but from ancient records preserved in the Tower

BITS OF OLD HACKNEY.
1 Brook House, 1765. 2 Barber's Barn, 1750. 3. Shore Place, 1736.

of London it is found to be written, *Ecclesia Parochialis S. Augustini de Hackney*. The Temple Mills, in Hackney Marshes, even now preserve the memory of the priestly warriors of the Templar order.

In the reign of Henry III., when the first mention of the place occurs as a village, it is called Hackenaye, and Hacquenye; and in a patent of Edward IV., granting the manors of Stepney and Hackney to Thomas Lord Wentworth, it is styled Hackeney, otherwise Hackney. "The parish, no doubt," says Dr. Robinson, "derived its appellation from circumstances of no common nature, but what they were it is at this time difficult to conjecture; and no one will venture to assert that it received its name from the Teutonic or Welsh language, as some have supposed."

We may conclude this chapter by remarking that Dr. Robinson, in his "History and Antiquities of Hackney," describes it as an ancient, extensive, and populous village, "situated on the west side of the river Lea, about two miles and a half from the City of London, within the division of the Tower Hamlets, in the hundred of Ossulston, in the county of Middlesex." "In former times," he adds, "many noblemen, gentlemen, and others, of the first rank and consequence, had their country seats in this village, on account of its pleasant and healthy situation." In the parish of Hackney are comprised the nominal hamlets of Clapton (Upper and Lower), Homerton, Dalston, Shacklewell, the greater part of Kingsland, and that part of Stoke Newington which lies on the eastern side of the high road to Tottenham; but modern Hackney, considered as an assemblage of dwellings, is quite united to Homerton and Lower Clapton, on the east and north, and also by rows of buildings on the west to the parish of St. Leonard, Shoreditch.

CHAPTER XLI.

THE NORTH-EASTERN SUBURBS.—HACKNEY (*continued*).

"I had a parcel of as honest religious girls about me as ever pious matron had under her tuition at a Hackney boarding-school."
Tom Brown: Madam Cresswell to Moll Quarles.

Hackney in the Last Century—Its Gradual Growth—Well Street—Hackney College—Monger's Almshouses—The Residence of Dr. Frampton—St. John's Priory—St. John's Church—Mare Street—Hackney a Great Centre of Nonconformity—The Roman Catholic Church of St. John the Baptist—The "Flying Horse" Tavern—Elizabeth Fry's Refuge—Dr. Spurstowe's Almshouses—Hackney Town Hall—The New Line of the Great Eastern Railway—John Milton's Visits to Hackney—Barber's Barn—Loddidge's Nursery—Watercress-beds—The Gravel-pit Meeting House—The Church House—The Parish Church—The "Three Cranes"—The Old Church Tower—The Churchyard—The New Church of St. John—The Black and White House—Boarding Schools for Young Ladies—Sutton Place—The "Mermaid" Tavern—"Ward's Corner"—The Templars' House—Brooke House—Noted Residents at Hackney—Homerton—The City of London Union—Lower Clapton—John Howard, the Prison Reformer—The London Orphan Asylum—Salvation Army Barracks and Congress Hall—The Asylum for Deaf and Dumb Females—Concluding Remarks on Hackney.

In treating of this parish we have no Pepys or Boswell to guide or interest us, and to gossip with us over this neighbourhood, and to furnish us with stores of anecdote; but, fortunately, we have the assistance of Strype, who, in his edition of Stow's "London," includes Hackney in his "Circuit Walk on the North of London." He styles it a "pleasant and healthful town, where divers nobles in former times had their country seats," enumerating among its residents an Earl of Northumberland, a Countess of Warwick, and a Lord Brooke. Still, the houses and their walks, for the most part, have no stories connected with them, *carent quia vate sacro*, and the whole district supplies us but scanty materials, historical, topographical, and biographical, as compared with St. Pancras or Hampstead.

Hackney is described in the "Ambulator," in 1774, as "a very large and populous village, on the north of London, inhabited by such numbers of merchants and wealthy persons, that it is said there are near a hundred gentlemen's coaches kept." The writer enumerates its several hamlets, viz., "Clapton on the north, Dorleston [Dalston] and Shacklewell on the west; and on the east, Homerton, leading to Hackney Marshes."

There is still an old-fashioned air about Hackney itself; but Dalston has thrown out lines of commonplace villas across the fields and orchards on the south-west; Clapton has developed itself on the north; Victoria Park has initiated a new town on the south; a busy railway station stands near the tower of the old church, of which we shall speak presently; and down in the Marshes are now large hives of manufacturing industry.

The town (if considered independently of its hamlets), down to a comparatively recent date, consisted chiefly of four streets, termed Church Street, Mare (or Meare) Street, Grove Street, and Well Street; but such has been the growth of the place during the past half century that large numbers of other streets and terraces have sprung up in all directions, on land which hitherto had served as the gardens attached to the mansions of the nobility and City merchants, or as nursery grounds, market gardens, and even watercress-beds. The population of Hackney, too, which at the commencement of this century was about equal to that of a good-sized country village, had, according to the census returns for 1881, reached something like 400,000; and the place, since 1868, has enjoyed the privilege of Parliamentary representation.

From Grove Street, incidentally mentioned near the close of the preceding chapter, we pass into Well Street, which winds somewhat circuitously to the west, where it unites with Mare Street. Hackney College, which we notice on our left immediately on entering Well Street, was founded in 1803 with the object of preparing students for the Congregational ministry, and of granting votes in support of chapels. The average number of students in the college is about twenty, and the annual receipts about £1,500. At the close of the last century there was a college for Dissenters established at Lower Clapton, to which Dr. Rees, Dr. Priestley, and his scarcely less renowned Unitarian coadjutor, Mr. Belsham, and Gilbert Wakefield were attached; but it was broken up in 1797, owing to the bad conduct of some of the students. The well-known college at Homerton was established about the latter part of the seventeenth century. Dr. Pye Smith, the great geologist, whose conclusions anticipated some of the views of Mr. Goodwin in his "Mosaic Cosmogony," was for many years the principal of the seminary; and many eminent ministers of the Nonconformist bodies there received their education.

In Well Street are almshouses for six aged and poor men, founded by Henry Monger in 1669.

Farther on, on the right, a large old-fashioned mansion may be observed, although it is now cut up into tenements, and the lower part converted into shops. This was once the residence of the celebrated Dr. Frampton, whose memory is preserved in the locality in the name of Frampton Park Road.

The residence of the Knights of St. John existed till a very recent period, under the name of the Priory, in Well Street. In 1352 the Prior of St. John disposed of the mansion, then called Beaulieu, to John Blaunch and Nicholas Shordych. In Stow's time it bore the name of Shoreditch Place,* since shortened into Shore Place and Shore Road. The Priory, within the memory of the present generation, was a strange-looking brick building, divided into small tenements, and inhabited by chimney-sweeps and others of kindred calling.

A chapel of ease, dedicated to St. John, in this street, was consecrated in 1810 by Bishop Randolph, and endowed as a district parish church for South Hackney. In 1846 it was superseded by the new parish church, which we have already described.

Mare Street, as we have already stated, commences at the eastern end of the Hackney Road, and forms the main thoroughfare through the centre of the town. Throughout its entire length it is well sprinkled with the remains of dwellings of the wealthy classes of society, who formerly inhabited this now unfashionable quarter of London. Here, too, the number of religious edifices, of all denominations, is somewhat remarkable, and in some cases the buildings are fine specimens of ecclesiastical architecture.

Hackney has altogether upwards of twenty places of worship for Dissenters; it has, in fact, long been renowned as a great centre of Nonconformity, and some eminent Dissenting divines have preached there. Dr. Bates, the learned author of the "Harmony of the Divine Attributes," died there in 1679. Matthew Henry, the compiler of the well-known "Commentary" on the Bible, preached at Hackney between 1710 and 1714. Robert Fleming, the author of "The Rise and Fall of the Papacy," died at Hackney on the 24th of May, 1716. His prophecies were believed to have been fulfilled in 1794; and in 1848, when a second revolution occurred in Paris, Fleming's book was eagerly sought for, and reprinted, and read by thousands.

The Presbyterian Dissenters' Chapel was established in this street early in the seventeenth century. Here Philip Nye and Adoniram Byfield, two eminent Puritan divines, preached in 1636. The old meeting-house has been taken down, and a new one built on the opposite side of the street, and occupied by Independents.

On the east side of Mare Street, near King Edward Road, stands the Roman Catholic Church of St. John the Baptist, which was built about the year 1848, from the designs of Mr. Wardell. It is built in the decorated Gothic style, and comprises nave, chancel, aisles, and sacristy. The rood-screen and altar are elaborately carved, and some of the windows are filled with painted glass. In 1856 a brass plate was placed in the chancel, over the grave of the founder and first rector, the Rev. J. Leucona, who died in 1855. Mr. Leucona was a Spanish Catholic missionary, and the author of a

* See Vol. II., p. 194.

few published works, among them a pamphlet in reply to some of the writings of Dr. Pusey.

On the west side of this street, near the narrow lane leading into London Fields, stands a very old public-house, bearing the sign of the "Flying Horse." It is a large, rambling house, of two storeys, and consists of a centre and two wings. It is traditionally said to have been one of the old posting-houses of the time of "Queen Bess," on the old road to Cambridge and Newmarket.

Farther to the north, one of a row of old mansions with small gardens before them, has a large board displayed upon its front inscribed with the words "Elizabeth Fry's Refuge." This institution was founded in the year 1849, for the purpose of providing temporary homes for female criminals on their release from prison.

Hackney has always been remarkable for the number of its charitable institutions: besides those which we have already mentioned, and others which we have still to notice, are some almshouses for widows near Mare Street, founded by Dr. Spurstowe, who died in the reign of Charles II.

The Town Hall, which stands in The Grove, is a modern structure, having been erected only a few years ago to supersede an older and less commodious building farther on, near the old parish church. The edifice, with its noble portico, and its ample supply of windows—for, like Hardwick Hall, it might almost be said to have "more windows than wall"—presents a striking contrast to many of the quaint old buildings which surround it. Notwithstanding the grand appearance of the building externally, and the thousands of pounds spent in its erection, the interior does not seem to have given that satisfaction to the parishioners which they were led to expect, and the accommodation, or rather, the want of accommodation in some of the rooms which the edifice affords, was such as to serve as a bone of contention among them for some considerable time after its erection.

Running parallel with Mare Street, on the west side, and overlooking the London Fields, is the new line of the Great Eastern Railway, from which, at the Hackney Downs station, a line branches off on the left to Enfield. In the construction of this railway several old houses were swept away, among them an ancient mansion which had long been used as a private lunatic asylum, and another which, with its gardens, covered a large space of ground, and was formerly used as a hospital by the Honourable East India Company.

To the Tower House, at the corner of London Lane, which connects Mare Street with London Fields and the railway station, often came an illustrious Parliamentarian, no other than John Milton; for there he wooed his second wife, the daughter of Captain Woodcock, who lived here.

On the east side of Mare Street, and covering the ground now occupied by St. Thomas's Place, once stood an ancient edifice known as Barber's Barn, or Barbour Berns, which dated from about the end of the sixteenth century. It was in the Elizabethan style of architecture, with pediments, bay-windows, and an entrance porch, and contained numerous rooms. It is said to have been the residence of John Okey, the regicide. He is reported to have been originally a drayman and stoker in a brewery at Islington, but having entered the Parliamentary army, to have risen to become one of Cromwell's generals. He sat in judgment on Charles I., and was the sixth who signed the warrant for the king's execution. About the middle of the last century Barber's Barn, with its grounds and some adjoining land, passed into the possession of one John Busch, who formed a large nursery ground on the estate. Mr. Loudon, in his *Gardeners' Magazine*, says that Catharine II., Empress of Russia, "finding that she could have nothing done to her mind, determined to have a person from England to lay out her garden." Busch was the person engaged to go out to Russia for this purpose. In 1771 he disposed of his nursery at Hackney to Messrs. Loddige, who ranked with the most eminent florists and nurserymen of their time. Indeed, the name of the Loddige family has been known for nearly a century in the horticultural and botanical world; and few persons who take an interest in gardening and flowers can fail to recognise the names of Conrad Loddige and his sons, of Hackney, as the authors of the "Botanical Cabinet," published in twenty large quarto volumes during the Regency and the subsequent reign of George IV. They had here extensive greenhouses, and also hothouses which were heated by steam. The ancient house having become the property of Mr. Conrad Loddige, was taken down many years ago, and Loddige's Terrace, together with some residences called St. Thomas's Place, were built on its site. A few houses in Well Street occupy the other portion of the former gardens.

In 1787 Mr. Loddige removed from what was called Busch's Nursery, and formed another nursery on some grounds which he purchased from the governors of St. Thomas's Hospital; these grounds had until then been open fields, and he enclosed them towards the north with a brick wall. The last vestiges of Loddige's gardens disappeared about the year 1860, when some of the plants were transferred to the Crystal Palace at Sydenham.

Hackney, it may be added, was celebrated till a comparatively recent date for its market gardens, and even for its watercress beds. A large water-cress garden was in existence until 1860, and perhaps even more recently, only a few yards to the south of the North London Railway Station.

In Paradise Place, at the end of Paragon Road, stands the New Gravel-pit Meeting House, "Sacred to One God the Father." The chapel was built on what was formerly Paradise Fields. The old Gravel-pit Meeting House, where Dr. Price and Dr. Priestley were formerly ministers, and which dates its erection from the early part of the last century, stands at a short distance to the east. Dr. Priestley preached his farewell sermon in the old chapel in 1794, previous to his departure for America.

At a short distance northward from the new Town Hall, Mare Street is spanned by the North London Railway. Near this spot, on the east side of the street, and close by the entrance to the churchyard, was standing, in Lysons' time or at the end of the last century, an ancient building, thus described in the chantry-roll at the Augmentation Office, which bears date the first year of the reign of Edward I.:—"A tenement buylded by the parishioners, called the Churche Howse, that they might mete together and comen of matters as well for the kyng's business as for the churche and parishe, worth 20s. per an." It appeared by an inscription, remaining on the front towards the street, that it was built in the year 1520, when Christopher Urswick was rector. The house was for many years, in the last century, used as a free school, but in its latter years it seems to have reverted again to its original purpose. The site was afterwards occupied by a more modern Town Hall, which is still standing, but which, as we have already seen, has since been superseded by the new building in Mare Street.

If we may follow the statements of Stow and Strype, Hackney was, as far back as the close of the thirteenth century, a distinct parish, with a rector and also a vicar, and a church dedicated to St. Augustine; but the Knights of St. John of Jerusalem having obtained possession of a mill and other possessions in the parish formerly held by the Knights Templars, the appellation of the church came to be changed from St. Augustine to St. John. In the reign of Edward III. this church, in lieu of that of Bishop's Stortford, in Hertfordshire, was annexed to the precentorship of St. Paul's Cathedral. In confirmation of the assertion that the church was dedicated to St. Augustine, it may be added that a statue of that saint, erected in it as lately as the reign of Henry VIII., is mentioned in the will of Christopher Urswick, rector, and also Dean of Windsor.

This old church, then, of which the tower alone now remains, though dedicated to St. Augustine, has for many years been known as St. John's Church. Newport, in his "Repertorium," speaking of Hackney Church, says:—"The church has of late years gone by the name of St. John of Jerusalem at Hackney, as if dedicated to St. John, which I take to be a mistake; because I find that Arthur Wood, in December, 1509, instituted to the vicarage of St. Augustin at Hackney—to which saint, I rather believe, that church had been dedicated—no presentation having been made by the name of St. John of Jerusalem at Hackney till after the restoration of King Charles II. One — Heron, Esq., is taken by some to be the founder of it, by his arms engraven upon every pillar, which is a *chevron ermine between three herons;* but I rather think that he was a very great benefactor to the new building or repairing of the church, for which reason his arms (are) upon every pillar; and in the north aisle thereof, in a tomb of white free-stone, without any inscription, his body lies."

In the Cottonian Library there is a volume relating to the Knights Templars, in which mention is made of St. Augustine's at Hackney, and of the lands and rents there which belonged to that order, including a mill which was known as Temple Mill. It appears that these, after the suppression of the Templar order, passed into the hands of the Knights of St. John, whose influence in and upon the parish was so great, that the very dedication of the church to St. Augustine was forgotten.

There is in the Tower records a patent or licence to one Henry Sharp, the "parson" of St. Augustine's at Hackney, to erect in his church a "Guild of the Holy Trinity and of the Glorious Virgin Mary;" in whose honour, therefore, doubtless a light was kept constantly burning before an altar in an aisle or side chapel. This guild, or "perpetual fraternity," was to consist of "two guardians or brethren, and sisters, of the same parish, and of others who, from their devotion, will be of the same fraternity."

It is impossible to fix the date of erection of the *first* church of St. Augustine at Hackney. It appears to have been taken down and rebuilt in the early part of the sixteenth century; and "it is probable," says Dr. Robinson, in his "History of Hackney," "that Sir Thomas Heron, who was master of the jewel house to King Henry VIII., and Christopher Urswick (then rector) were the principal benefactors to its re-erection; for besides the arms above-mentioned, the same arms occurred on one side of the chancel window, and on the other side the arms of Urswick." The conjecture that some member of the Heron family had at least something to do with the rebuilding of the fabric, receives a certain amount of support or confirmation from a tradition that the house called the "Three Cranes," nearly opposite, was the first public-house in the parish, and that it was built for the accommodation of the workmen whilst they were erecting the church: it is said to have had originally the sign of "The Herons." The ancient church of St. Augustine was taken down towards the close of the last century, except the old tower, which, as we have stated, still remains. It is of Gothic architecture, and contains a peal of eight bells. From an account of the old church printed in the *Gentleman's Magazine* for April, 1796, we learn that its exterior, in its latter days, was "an incomprehensible jumble of dissonant repairs, without a trace of the original building remaining, except the windows of part of it." There were two side aisles, and the pillars, twelve in number, are described as being "remarkably strong, good, and well-proportioned, and the arches pointed." The galleries, of which there were several, seem to have been erected at different periods, and did not reach, as is usual, from one end to the other of the church, nor extend to the pillars which divided the aisles; and one of the galleries appeared as if it "were hung to the roof by iron hooks." Along the frieze of the organ gallery there was an inscription, setting forth that the church was repaired in 1720; and above, in the panels, were three pictures, "drawn with much taste and freedom in black and white, though very slight;" the subjects were, the Miraculous Draught of Fishes, Christ in the Storm at Sea, and Elijah fed by Ravens.

HACKNEY CHURCH, 1750.

A view of the old church, taken in 1806, shortly before its removal, will be found in a work on the suburbs of London, entitled, "Ecclesiastical Topography," published in 1811, anonymously. The writer describes it as having been a large irregular building, with few traces remaining of the original structure, except the windows; and, to do the writer justice, it must be owned that never was a fine mediæval church more ruthlessly and tastelessly perverted into a chaos of confusion. "The nave and the tower," he adds, "may probably be referred to the middle of the fourteenth century. The sepulchral inscriptions were extremely numerous, but fortunately most of these are preserved in Strype's additions to Stow, and others in Weever's 'Funeral Monuments,' and in Lysons' 'Environs of London.'"

The parish of Hackney in former times had among its vicars many men who attained some eminence in the ecclesiastical world. Among them were Cardinal Gauselinus, who flourished about 1320; David Doulben, afterwards Bishop of Bangor; Gilbert Sheldon, afterwards Archbishop of Canterbury; and William Spurstowe, a well-known divine among the Nonconformists, and mentioned in the well-known definition of the name "Smectymnus."

"If any are ignorant who this Smectymnus is,
*S*tephen *M*arshall,
*E*dmund *C*alamy,
*T*homas *Y*oung, } can tell you."
*M*atthew *N*ewcomen,
*W*illiam *S*purstowe,

The old church, before its demolition, was extremely rich in monuments and brasses, most of which have now altogether disappeared, whilst some few have been preserved and fixed against the new church of St. John. Among many other members of the nobility buried here were Henry Lord Percy, Earl of Northumberland, who died in this town in 1537, and of whom we shall have more to say presently. The funeral service over his remains was performed by the Bishop of St. Asaph and the Abbot of Stratford.

Alice Ryder, who died in 1517, was commemorated by her "portraiture in brass, with a milk-pail upon her head." She appears to have been a milkwoman, who, having obtained great wealth by selling milk in the City, was a great benefactress to the church. The following was her epitaph:—

"For the Sowl of Alice Ryder, of your Charite,
Say a Pater-noster, and an Ave . . . 1517."

THE BLACK AND WHITE HOUSE, 1800. (*See page* 519.)

Besides the tower mentioned above, the Rowe Chapel, which was built in the reign of James I., and attached to the south side of the church, also remained after the demolition of the body of the fabric, and is still standing. This chapel or mausoleum was founded by Sir Henry Rowe, of Shacklewell, as a place of interment for his family. The Rowes possessed some property at Muswell Hill, in the parish of Hornsey, and the family became extinct in the male line in the person of Anthony Rowe, of Muswell Hill, who was buried here in 1704. He left some daughters, co-heirs, one of whom married an ancestor of the Marquis of Downshire, in the possession of whose descendants the Rowe Chapel has continued. Among the freeholders of Hackney, the Marquis of Downshire is mentioned as possessing "a freehold, fifteen feet square, in the old church yard;" this refers, of course, to the above-mentioned burial-place of the Rowes, and it is added that it "descended to the marquis as an heir-loom." A monument against the interior south wall of the mausoleum is inscribed with the following quaint epitaph:—

"Here (under fine of Adam's first defection)
Rests in hope of happie resurrection,
Sir Henry Rowe (sonne of Sir Thomas Rowe,
And of Dame Mary, his deare yoke-fellowe,
Knight and right worthy), as his father late
Lord Maior of London, with his vertuous Mate
Dame Susan (his twice fifteen yeres and seeven),
Their issue five (surviving of eleven),
Four named here, in these four names forepast,
The fifth is found, if eccho sound the last,
Sad Orphanes all, but most their heir (most debtor)
Who built them this, but in his heart a better.
Quam pie obiit Anno Salutis 1612
die Novembris 12, Ætatis 68."

It is worthy of mention that John Strype, the antiquary, to whom we owe so much of the retrospective portions of this work, was lecturer at this church for thirty-six years, and died in 1737, at the great age of ninety-four.

The reason why the tower of the old church was permitted to remain was that the eight bells were believed to be too heavy for the tower of the new building; and as the parishioners were unwilling to lose their peal, it was decided that they should retain their original position, but some years later they were moved to the new church, where they still remain. So there stand the weather-beaten old tower and the little Rowe Chapel, a few paces farther to the east, amidst the graves of the ancient inhabitants of Hackney, among which a winding path leads to the more modern church, in which are preserved some of the tombs and carved work of the older edifice. It is recorded that on the 27th of September, 1731, a sailor slid down on a rope from the top of the church steeple, with a streamer in each hand.

The old burial-ground has many walks through it, most of which are public thoroughfares, and occupied by the hurrying and thoughtless passengers. "Its numerous paths, all concentrating towards the sacred edifice," says Dr. Robinson, writing about forty years ago, "are lined with lofty trees, and in the summer season the vastly peopled city of the dead seems one beautiful verdant canopy stretching over the peaceful ashes of the 'forefathers of the hamlet.' Great taste has been displayed in planting Hackney churchyard with so many fine trees, but amongst them the yew-tree, with its sombre foliage, is nowhere to be found. Every visitor to this burial-ground must be struck with the curious and solitary appearance of the old square grey tower, rearing its lofty walls, a singular relic of the ancient church of which nothing but this building now remains. We can only guess at the edifice, which must, in times long since passed away, have extended its aisles and raised its sacred oriel for the devotions of our ancestors. The marble tombs which once must have filled the edifice with 'hoar antiquity,' and the 'storied urn and animated bust,' which once told of the honoured dead, seem all swept away by the hand of oblivion—obscuring the humble and the great—yet Time, as if willing to spare us some resemblance of the older days, left only this old grey tower, as a conspicuous monument, which, by its lonely desolation, tells so forcibly of the terrible power which, by one fell swoop, has eradicated all besides. The bells whose music once cheered or soothed the ears of those who have now for some centuries slept the sleep of death around its enduring walls, still remain and retain their vigorous tones in the same elevated chamber where they have swung from the time of our Edwards and Henries. This tower must have sent forth its loud clamorous notes in the passing of many a royal progress, when banners and knights and ladies gay, 'in purple and pall,' have circled past, or when the proud and mitred abbot, with princely train, passed to and fro from his princely abbey."

The new church of St. John, which stands at a short distance to the north-east of the old tower, was built at the close of the last century, and is constructed chiefly of brick, in the "late classical" style of architecture. The plan, though pretending to be cruciform, is really an unsightly square; the projecting face of the elevation of each front is finished by a triangular pediment, the cornice of which receives and terminates the covering of the roof. There are five entrances, each of which opens to a spacious vestibule, like that of a theatre or a town-hall. The principal entrance is on the north, and is protected by a semi-circular Ionic portico of Portland stone. The interior of the church is plain and utterly unecclesiastical, and is surmounted by a vaulted and stuccoed ceiling—certainly no improvement on the structure which it was built to supersede. Some of the windows are enriched with coloured glass, and that over the communion-table is painted with a design illustrative of the Scriptural verse, "Let there be light," &c.

Near the church, on the west side, formerly stood an ancient mansion called the "Black and White House." It appears to have been built in the year 1578 by a citizen of London, whose arms, with those of the Merchant Adventurers and the Russian Company, appeared over the chimney in one of the principal rooms, and also in the windows of the great parlour; other armorial bearings also occurred in some of the windows. In the seventeenth century the house was the residence of the Vyner family, and the building was enlarged and considerably repaired in 1662 by Sir Thomas Vyner. At the close of the last century, when it was pulled down, it had been for many years used as a boarding-school for girls.

Hackney in former times seems to have been noted for its boarding-schools for young ladies. In the *Tatler*, No. 83, there is this reference to them:—"For the publication of this discourse, I wait only for subscriptions from the undergraduates of each university, and the young ladies in the boarding-schools at Hackney." Again, "Don Diego," in Wycherly's *Gentleman's Dancing Master*, makes this remark:—"If she be not married to-morrow (which I am to consider of), she will dance a corant in twice or thrice teaching more; will she not? for 'tis but a twelvemonth since she came from Hackney School." Shadwell also, in *The Humourists*, makes "Striker" (a haberdasher's wife) give vent to the following ejaculation:—"Good, Mistress Gig-em-bob! your breeding! ha! I am sure my husband married me from Hackney School, where there was a number of substantial citizens' daughters. Your breeding!" These three quotations we owe to Mr. Peter Cunningham.

At Hackney Downs are large Middle Class Schools founded by the Grocer's Company under the sanction of the Charity Commissioners.

Sutton Place, on the south-east side of the churchyard, reminds us of a great and good man, whose latter days were passed at Hackney; for at his house here died, on the 12th of December, 1611, Thomas Sutton, the worthy and benevolent founder of the hospital and school of the Charterhouse, of whom we have already spoken at some length in a previous part of this work.*

Close by the "Three Cranes," in Mare Street, stood, till recently, another ancient hostelry, called the "Mermaid," which in its time was noted for its tea-gardens and its assembly-room. Modern shops have now taken the place of the old tavern, and its gardens have been covered with rows of private houses.

* See Vol. II., p. 383—8.

At the upper end of Mare Street, close by Dalston Lane, in a large house which remained standing till comparatively recently, and known as "Ward's Corner," lived in the last century a man who was noted for his great wealth and insatiable avarice—the famous and infamous John Ward, member of Parliament, pilloried to all posterity in two stinging lines by Pope, who linked him with the infamous Colonel Francis Chartres, and a kindred worthy, Waters:—

> "Given to the fool, the mad, the vain, the evil,
> To Ward, to Waters, Chartres, and the devil."

John Ward was prosecuted by the Duchess of Buckingham for forgery, and being convicted, expelled the House of Commons, and stood in the pillory in March, 1727. He was suspected of joining in a conveyance with Sir John Blunt to secrete £50,000 of that director's estate, forfeited to the South Sea Company by Act of Parliament. The company recovered the £50,000 against Ward; but he set up prior conveyances of his real estate to his brother and son, and concealed all his personal, which was computed to be £150,000. These conveyances being also set aside by a bill in Chancery, Ward was imprisoned, and amused himself in confinement by giving poison to cats and dogs, in order that he might watch their dying agonies. To sum up the worth of this gentleman at the several eras of his life: at his standing in the pillory he was worth above £200,000; at his commitment to prison he was worth £150,000; but has been so far diminished in his reputation as to be thought a worse man by fifty or sixty thousand. After his death, a most characteristic prayer was found among his papers. The old sinner did not pray for forgiveness of his sins, but in this fashion:—"O Lord, Thou knowest I have nine estates in the City of London, and likewise that I have lately purchased an estate in fee-simple in the county of Essex. I beseech Thee to preserve the two counties of Middlesex and Essex from fire and earthquake; and as I have a mortgage in Hertfordshire, I beg of Thee likewise to have an eye of compassion on that county; and for the rest of the counties Thou mayest deal with them as Thou art pleased." He then prays for the bank, that his debtors may be all good men; and for the death of a profligate young man, whose reversion he had bought—"as Thou hast said the days of the wicked are but short"—against thieves, and for honest servants.

Tradition says that an old building close by the spot, nearly opposite Dalston Lane, which was not completely pulled down till 1825, was the Templars' House. It may have occupied the site, but could scarcely have been the identical edifice; for it was built with projecting bays, in what is called the Renaissance style. About the middle of the last century it was a public-house, the "Blue Posts;" afterwards it was known as "Bob's Hall," and the road between the churchyard and Clapton Square was styled Bob's Hall Lane.

On the south side of the road to Clapton formerly stood a mansion called "Brooke House," and at one time the "King's House," the manor-house of the manor termed King's Hold. It is said to have belonged originally to the Knights Templars; and after the dissolution of the order to have been granted, in common with other possessions, to the monastery of St. John of Jerusalem. On the dissolution of the latter order the estate appears to have been granted to Henry, Earl of Northumberland, who possibly died here, since he was buried, as we have seen, at Hackney. This earl was the person employed, in conjunction with Sir Walter Walsh, to arrest Cardinal Wolsey at his house at Cawood. He had, as every reader of English history knows, been, in his youthful days, a lover of Anne Boleyn (then one of the maids of honour to Queen Catherine), but withdrew his suit in consequence of the interference of his father, who had been purposely made acquainted with the king's partiality to that lady. When the inconstant monarch's affection for Anne Boleyn (then his queen) began to decline, a supposed pre-contract with the Earl of Northumberland was made the pretence for a divorce, though the earl, in a letter to Secretary Cromwell (dated Newington Green, May 13th, 1537), denied the existence of any such contract in the most solemn manner. "Henry, Earl of Northumberland, died," says the account of his funeral in the Heralds' College, "at his manor of Hackney, now the King's House, between two and three in the morning, on the 29th of June, 1537; 29 Hen. VIII." The earl, as we have stated above, was buried in the old church close by. The estate afterwards reverted to the Crown, and was granted by Edward VI., in 1547, to William Herbert, Earl of Pembroke. The house occupied by Lord Pembroke is described in the particulars for the grant of the manor, as "a fayre house, all of brick, with a fayre hall and parlour, a large gallery, a proper chapel, and a proper gallery to laye books in," &c. It is also stated to be "situated near the London road," and to be "enclosed on the back side with a great and broad ditch."

A few years later it was purchased by Sir Henry Carey, Lord Hunsdon, who again conveyed it, in 1583, to Sir Rowland Hayward. It was subsequently possessed by Fulke Greville (afterwards Lord Brooke) and by Sir George Vyner. Under date of May 8, 1654, John Evelyn, in his "Diary," gives us the following note of a visit he paid to this place:—"I went to Hackney," he writes, "to see my Lady Brooke's garden, which was one of the neatest and most celebrated in England; the house well furnish'd, but a despicable building."

At the end of the seventeenth century this manor became part of the Tyssen property, of which we shall have occasion to speak more fully hereafter.

When Lord Brooke sold the manor of King's Hold, he reserved the mansion, which, it is stated, continued vested in his family, and at the commencement of this century was the property of the Earl of Warwick. The author of the "Beauties of England and Wales," writing in 1816, says: "This house has experienced considerable alterations, but large portions of the ancient edifice have been preserved. These consist principally of a quadrangle, with internal galleries, those on the north and south sides being 174 feet in length. On the ceiling of the south gallery are the arms of Lord Hunsdon, with those of his lady, and the crests of both families frequently repeated. The arms of Lord Hunsdon are likewise remaining on the ceiling of a room connected with this gallery. It is therefore probable that the greater part of the house was rebuilt by this nobleman during the short period for which he held the manor, a term of no longer duration than from 1578 to 1583. The other divisions of this extensive building are of various but more modern dates." At the time when the above description was written, the house seems to have been occupied as a private lunatic asylum.

Several of the nobility and wealthy gentry, indeed, appear to have chosen Hackney for a residence. There is a record of a visit to Hackney by Queen Elizabeth, but to whom is not certain, in 1591. The son and daughter of her dancing chancellor, Sir Christopher Hatton, were both married in Hackney Church, so that he, too, probably lived here. Vere, Earl of Oxford, the soldier and poet, who accompanied Leicester on his expedition to Holland, who supplied ships to oppose the Armada, and sat on the trials of Mary Queen of Scots and the Earls of Arundel, Essex, and Southampton, was, in his latter days, a resident of Hackney. It is also said that Rose Herbert, a lady of noble family, and one of the nuns who at the Reformation were turned adrift upon the world from the Convent of Godstow, near Oxford, died here towards the end of Elizabeth's reign, in a state of destitution, at the age of ninety-six.

Early in the seventeenth century, George Lord Zouch, a noted man in his day, and Lord Warden of the Cinque Ports, had a house at Hackney, where he amused himself with experimental gardening. He died there, and was buried in a small chapel adjoining his house. Ben Jonson, who was his intimate friend, discovered that there was a hole in the wall affording communication between the last resting-place of Lord Zouch and the wine-cellar, and thereupon vented this impromptu :—

" Wherever I die, let this be my fate,
To lye by my good Lord Zouch,
That when I am dry, to the tap I may hye,
And so back again to my couch."

Owen Rowe, one of those who sat as "judges" at the trial of King Charles, died and was buried at Hackney, in 1660.

Another memorable inhabitant of Hackney at this time was Susanna Prewick, or Perwick, a young musical phenomenon, whose death, at the age of twenty-five, in 1661, was celebrated in some lengthy poems, chiefly commendatory of her personal graces. We have no means of judging of her musical powers, which created an extraordinary sensation at the time ; but it is gratifying to know that—

"All vain, conceited affectation
Was unto her abomination.
With body she ne'er sat ascue,
Or mouth awry, as others do."

Dr. Thomas Wood, Bishop of Lichfield, who died in 1692, was a native of Hackney.

Defoe, who at one time lived at Stoke Newington, in all probability also was a resident here ; for in 1701 his daughter Sophia was baptised in Hackney Church ; and in 1724, an infant son, named Daniel, after his distinguished father, was buried in the same church.

Eastward of Hackney churchyard lies Homerton, which, together with Lower Clapton, may be said to form part of the town of itself. Hackney Union is here situated in High Street.

In 1843 a college was founded close by, for the purpose of giving unsectarian religious training to young men and women who wish to become teachers in Government-aided schools.

Homerton was noted in the last and early part of the present century for its academy for the education of young men designed for Dissenting ministers. The late Dr. John Pye Smith was some time divinity tutor here.

A row of almshouses in the village, termed the Widows' Retreat, has upon the front of a small chapel in the centre, the following inscription :— "For the Glory of God, and the comfort of twelve widows of Dissenting Ministers, this retreat was erected and endowed by Samuel Robinson, A.D. 1812."

Homerton High Street leads direct to Hackney Marsh, where, says the "Ambulator" of 1774, "there have been discovered within the last few years the remains of a great causeway of stone, which, by the Roman coins found there, would appear to have been one of the famous highways made by the Romans." The Marsh Road, too, leads straight on to Temple Mills, of which we have already had occasion to make mention.

The City of London Union covers a large space of ground to the north-east of Hackney churchyard, abutting upon Templar Road. Northward lies the rapidly extending hamlet of Lower Clapton. Here, in a curious old house, which was pulled down many years ago, was born, in the year 1727, John Howard, the future prison reformer and philanthropist. The house had been the "country residence" of John Howard's father, who was an upholsterer in London ; and it descended to the son, who sold it in 1785. In an article in the *Mirror* in 1826, this house, so interesting to humanity, is said to have been "taken down some years ago." Much of Howard's early life seems to have been passed here ; and his education, which was rather imperfect, was gained among one of the Dissenting sects, of which his father was a member. On the death of his father he was apprenticed to a wholesale grocer in the City. On quitting business he indulged in a tour through France and Italy. He subsequently, for the benefit of his health, took lodgings at Stoke Newington. We shall have more to say about him on reaching that place. The old house at Clapton where Howard was born is said to have been built in the early part of the last century ; it had large bay-windows, a pedimented roof, numerous and well-proportioned rooms, and a large garden. The site of the house was afterwards covered by Laura Place, and its memory is now kept up by the name of Howard Villas, which has been given to some houses lately erected on the opposite side of the road. A view of the house in which Howard was born will be found in "Smith's Historical and Literary Curiosities," and also in the seventh volume of the *Mirror*.

At no great distance from the site of Howard's old house, but on the west side of the road, was a school, known by the name of Hackney School, which had flourished for upwards of a century on the same spot. This academy was long under the direction of the Newcome family. "It was celebrated," says Mr. Lysons, "for the excellence of the dramatic performances exhibited every third year by the scholars. In these dramas Dr. Benjamin Hoadly, author of the *Suspicious Husband*, and his brother, Dr. John Hoadly, a dramatic writer also, who were both educated at this school, formerly distinguished themselves."

In 1813, the London Orphan Asylum was instituted at Lower Clapton; but about the year 1870 its inmates were removed to new buildings erected at Watford, in Hertfordshire. The building here, which consisted of a centre, with a spacious portico and wings, together with the outlying grounds, was bought in 1882, for about £23,000, by the Salvation Army, and converted into a "Barrack and Congress Hall." What was once an extensive lawn in front of the building is now covered with houses.

HOWARD'S HOUSE, AT CLAPTON, ABOUT 1800. (*See page* 521.)

Dr. Robinson, in his "History of Hackney," says that on the west side of the road, nearly opposite the Congress Hall, stood an old house, which many years ago was known by a very vulgar appellation, from the circumstance of the person who built it having made a considerable fortune by manufacturing and selling sundry articles of bed-room ware adorned with the head of Dr. Sacheverell. "The date of its erection is not exactly known; but it probably was after the year 1710, because the trial of Sacheverell did not take place till the February or March of that year. . . There are at the present time (1842)," he adds, "two urns with flowers, surmounting the gate-piers at the entrance." The building was subsequently converted into an Asylum for Deaf and Dumb Females.

Among the historical characters connected with this place whom we have not already named, was Major André, hanged by Washington as a spy; he was born at Clapton. He was originally intended for a merchant; but being disappointed in love for Honora Sneyd (the friend of Anna Seward), who became afterwards the mother-in-law of Miss Maria Edgeworth, he entered the army, and ultimately met with the fate above mentioned.

To go back a little into the reign of antiquity, we may remark that, though far removed from the crowded city, and generally considered a salubrious spot, Hackney suffered much from visitations of the plague, which in 1593 carried off 42 persons; in

VIEWS IN KINGSLAND.

1 Kingsland Chapel, 1780. 2. Lock Hospital, 1780. 3. Shacklewell House, 1700.

1603, 269; in 1625, 170; and in the terrible year 1665, as many as 225.

In the early part of the eighteenth century Hackney was much infested by robbers, which rendered travelling after dark very insecure. The roads between London and this rural suburb were then lonely and unprotected; and it was not until January, 1756, that lamps were placed between Shoreditch and Hackney, and patrols, armed with guns and bayonets, placed on the road. In the Marshes towards Hackney Wick were low public-houses, the haunt of highwaymen and their Dulcineas. Dick Turpin was a constant guest at the "White House," or "Tyler's Ferry," near Joe Sowter's cock-pit, at Temple Mills; and few police-officers were bold enough to approach the spot.

Maitland, in his "History of London," says, "The village of Hackney being anciently celebrated for the numerous seats of the nobility and gentry, occasioned a mighty resort thither of persons of all conditions from the City of London, whereby so great a number of horses were daily hired in the City on that account, that at length all horses to be let received the common appellation of 'Hackney horses;' which denomination has since communicated itself both to public coaches and chairs; and though this place at present be deserted by the nobility, yet it so greatly abounds with merchants and persons of distinction, that it excels all other villages in the kingdom, and probably on earth, in the riches and opulence of its inhabitants, as may be judged from the great number of persons who keep coaches there." But it is to be feared that in this matter Maitland is not to be trusted; for though it has often been supposed, and occasionally assumed even by well-informed writers, that as Sedan-chairs and Bath-chairs were named from the places where they were first respectively used, so the village of Hackney has had the honour of giving the name to those hackney carriages which were the immediate forerunners of the London cabriolet, it is simply a fact that the word "hackney" may be traced to the Dutch, French, Spanish, and Italian languages. In our own tongue it is at least as old as Chaucer and Froissart, who borrowed it from the French *haquenée*, a slow-paced nag. At all events, in Chaucer's "Romaunt of the Rose," we find the phrase thus used :—

> "Dame Richesse on her hand gan lede
> A yonge man full of semely hede,
> That she best loved of any thing,
> His lust was much in householdyng;
> In clothyng was he full fetyse,
> And loved wel to have horse of prise;
> He wende to have reproved be
> Of thrifte or murdre, if that be
> Had in his stable an *hackenay*."

Froissart, in one of his Chronicles, says, "The knights are well horsed, and the common people and others on litell *hakeneys* and geldyngs." The word subsequently acquired the meaning of "let for hire," and was soon applied to other matters than horses. In *Love's Labour's Lost* Shakespeare says, "Your love, perhaps, is a hacknie." In "Hudibras" we meet with "a broom, the nag and hackney of a Lapland hag." Pope calls himself "a hackney scribbler." Addison and Steele, in the *Spectator* and *Tatler*, speak of "driving in a hack," and our readers surely remember the hackney coach in which Sir Roger de Coverley went to Westminster Abbey. Hogarth gave the expressive name of "Kate Hackabout" to the poor harlot whose progress he depicted. Cowper, in the "Task," uses "hackneyed" as a passive verb; and Churchill employs it as an adjective. So there are authorities enough for the meaning of "hackney;" and the pleasant village, now the centre of a suburban town, must, we fear, be deprived of the honour of having invented hackney coaches.

CHAPTER XLII.

HOXTON, KINGSLAND, DALSTON, &c.

"Dalston, or Shacklewell, or some other suburban retreat northerly."—*C. Lamb, "Essays of Elia."*

Kingsland Road—Harmer's Almshouses—Gefferey's Almshouses—The Almshouses of the Framework Knitters—Shoreditch Workhouse—St. Columba's Church—Hoxton—"Pimlico"—Discovery of a Medicinal Spring—Charles Square—Aske's Hospital—Balmes, or Baumes House—The Practising Ground of the Artillery Company—De Beauvoir Town—The Tyssen Family—St. Peter's Church, De Beauvoir Square—The Roman Catholic Church of Our Lady and St. Joseph—Ball's Pond—Kingsland—A Hospital for Lepers—Dalston—The Refuge for Destitute Females—The German Hospital—Shacklewell.

HERE, it is true, we have no historian or old annalist to guide our steps, for the district had no entity of its own till quite a recent date, and it is not old enough to have a history. Its records are the annals of a "quiet neighbourhood." Beyond an occasional remark, too, we can glean nothing of interest about the neighbourhood from the pages of Strype, Maitland, or honest John Stow;

"The quaint and antique Stow, whose words alone
Seem letter'd records graven upon stone."

These close-lying suburbs—which we scarcely know whether to reckon as parts and parcels of the great metropolis or not—have been wittily defined by Mr. G. O. Trevelyan, in his "Life of Lord Macaulay," as "places which, as regards the company and the way of living, are little else than sections of London removed into a purer air." And so rapidly is London growing year by year that even Mr. Trevelyan's words will soon prove out of date, so far as regards purity of air.

This district is approached from the City by Bishopsgate Street and the broad and open thoroughfare called Kingsland Road, which runs northward from the end of Old Street Road, diverging at Shoreditch Church from the road by which we have travelled towards Hackney.

On the east side of the road we pass several almshouses. The first of these belong to the Drapers' Company, and are known as Harmer's Almshouses. The buildings, which were erected in 1713, have a somewhat picturesque appearance, and afford homes for twelve single men and women. Gefferey's Almshouses and Charity, in the gift of the Ironmongers' Company, are situated close to the above; these were founded in 1703, for the purpose of providing homes and pensions for a certain number of poor persons. Next we have the almshouses belonging to the Framework Knitters' Company. These were established in the early part of the last century as homes, &c., for twelve poor freemen and widows of the above-mentioned company.

The only buildings worthy of mention in the Kingsland Road, which we pass on the west side on our way northward, are the Workhouse of the parish of Shoreditch, and St. Columba's Church. The latter building, a large and lofty red-brick edifice, with a clergy house adjoining, was built about the year 1868 from the designs of Mr. P. Brooks; and the services in the church are conducted on "Ritualistic" principles.

Hoxton, which lies on the west side of the Kingsland Road, and north of Old Street Road, now included in Shoreditch parish, was formerly, as we have stated in the previous chapter, reckoned as part of Hackney. The locality in bygone times acquired a certain celebrity from a noted tavern or ale-house, called "Pimlico," which existed there; it is referred to by Ben Jonson, Dodsley, and others in plays of the seventeenth century. The name of "Pimlico" is kept in remembrance by Pimlico Walk, near the junction of the New North Road and Pitfield Street. The origin of the name of Hoxton is somewhat involved in obscurity. The place was formerly sometimes called Hogsdon, as we have already seen;* and Hog Lane, in Norton Folgate, close by, would lead to the inference that it was so named in consequence of the number of hogs that might have been reared there; but this seems doubtful, for in the "Domesday" record we find the name of the place entered as Hocheston, and in a lease of the time of Edward III. it is mentioned as Hoggeston. Stow, in 1598, describes the place as "a large street with houses on both sides;" but it has long since lost all pretensions to a rural or retired character. A medicinal spring was discovered at Hoxton in the seventeenth century, on digging the cellar for a house near Charles Square; but it does not appear to have attained any eminence or reputation. In Charles Square lived the Rev. John Newton, Cowper's friend and correspondent, many years rector of St. Mary Woolnoth, in Lombard Street, and who died in 1807. Peter Cunningham, in his "Handbook of London" (1850), speaks of the house of Oliver, third Lord St. John of Bletsoe, who died in 1618, as still standing.

Hoxton has long been noted for the number of its charitable institutions, among which Aske's Hospital, at the upper end of Pitfield Street, held a prominent place. It consisted of some almshouses and schools, founded by Robert Aske, an alderman of London, and a member of the Haberdashers' Company, in 1688, as homes for twenty poor freemen of that company, and for the education of 220 sons of freemen. The buildings were extensive, and had in front a piazza upwards of 300 feet in length. The chapel was consecrated by Archbishop Tillotson in 1695. In 1875-6 the almshouses were removed, and a large middle-class school, called Aske's Haberdashers' School, now occupies the site.

Hoxton in former times boasted of at least one mansion of some importance; this was Balmes House—termed in old writings Bawmes, or Baulmes. In the early part of the seventeenth century the old house was rebuilt on a scale of great magnificence by Sir George Whitmore, who was Lord Mayor of London, and a considerable sufferer for his loyalty to Charles I. The mansion was purchased about fifty years afterwards by Richard de Beauvoir, a Guernsey gentleman, who lived there in great style. Foreigners visited the

* See *ante*, p. 39.

mansion as one of the sights of London; and it was noticed as a memorable show place in French and German works on architecture and landscape gardening. At the end of the last century it was surrounded by a moat spanned by drawbridges, and there were beautiful gardens, watered by streams from Canonbury Fields. But Time worked strange changes in Baumes; and in the end the "old house at Hoxton"—a melancholy high-roofed dingy building, enclosed by high walls—came to be a private lunatic asylum, of which Charles Lamb was once, and his sister Mary more than once, an inmate. Some few years ago the building was pulled down; but Whitmore Bridge preserves the memory of the hospitable alderman of the Stuart days, and the smart De Beauvoir Town, near at hand, is a handsome memorial of his successor in the splendour of Baumes.

The fields near the old building appear to have been formerly used by the Artillery Company as a place of exercise; and the "Baumes March" is said to have been "a favourite exercise at arms." A melancholy interest attaches to the fields hereabouts, from the fact that it was in one of them that Ben Jonson killed in a duel Gabriel Spenser, the player.*

Nearly all the land round this part belongs to the Tyssen and De Beauvoir families, after whom and their connections and alliances, streets, squares, and terraces are named in almost endless succession. One district, indeed, is collectively named De Beauvoir Town.

The Tyssens were formerly merchants at Flushing, in Holland, but about the reign of James II. they settled in London and became naturalised subjects. Like many other City merchants at that time, they seem to have fixed their abode at Hackney and Shacklewell, and several of them were buried in Hackney Church. Francis Tyssen, of Shacklewell, married Rachel, the youngest daughter of Richard de Beauvoir, of Guernsey, and subsequently of Baumes, as mentioned above; and on his death, in 1717, he was buried at Hackney "with great funeral pomp" by his brother merchants, who had resolved to do honour to his memory. His body lay in state in Goldsmiths' Hall (from which we may infer that he was very rich indeed), surrounded by a magnificent display of plate, gold and silver sconces and trophies. Then the corpse was borne to Hackney Church with a great procession of horse and footmen, and such an abundant following, that the Earl of Suffolk, deputy Earl-Marshal, became alarmed for the funeral privileges of people of quality, and published a notice in the *Gazette* to the effect that the display "far exceeded the quality of the deceased, being only a private gentleman," and that "funerals of ignoble persons should not be set forth with such trophies of honour as belong only to the peers and gentles of the realm." The funeral must really have been a grand affair, for it cost £2,000, a large sum in those days. Three days after Tyssen was laid in the grave with so much pomp, his widow was confined of a son, the heir to the large property. This his only son, Francis John Tyssen, lord of the manor of Hackney, died in 1781, leaving a daughter, who subsequently conveyed the property by marriage to the Amhursts, of Rochester. At the close of the last century, through failure of male heirs, the property passed, by marriage of an heiress, to Mr. William George Daniel, of Foley House, Kent, and Westbrook, Dorset, who thereupon assumed, by royal sign-manual, the surname and arms of Tyssen. His eldest son, who inherited the manor of Hackney, took the additional name of Amhurst, a name given to one of the principal thoroughfares connecting the main street of Hackney with the high road at Stoke Newington.

De Beauvoir Town is that part of this neighbourhood lying on the north side of Hoxton, stretching away from the Regent's Canal on the south to Ball's Pond Road on the north, and from Kingsland Road on the east to the New North Road and Canonbury on the west. Its centre is formed by De Beauvoir Square, which is surrounded by a number of small streets and terraces. St. Peter's Church, in the south-west corner of the square, is a pseudo-Gothic edifice, and was erected about the year 1830.

In Tottenham Road, near the Kingsland main road, is the Roman Catholic church of Our Lady and St. Joseph, which was solemnly opened in the year 1856 by the late Cardinal Wiseman. The presbytery, which adjoins the church, fronts the Culford Road. The church is a spacious brick edifice. It was originally built for manufacturing purposes, but was converted to its present use under the direction of Mr. Wardell. Externally, the building has not much pretensions to beauty or ecclesiastical architecture. It is, however, spacious, and will accommodate about six hundred worshippers. The division of the chancel from the body of the church is formed by a flight of steps of considerable elevation, and on each side is a screened enclosure—the one used for the organ-chamber and choir, and the other for the sacristy. At the western ends of these enclosures are the side altars. The high altar is arranged with

* See Vol. II., p. 195

baldachino, reredos, and frontal; and the roof of the chancel is divided into panels of a blue ground, relieved with sacred monograms. Underneath the church are spacious and convenient schools.

The north end of the De Beauvoir and Culford Roads is crossed at right angles by Ball's Pond Road, which connects Kingsland Road and Dalston Lane with Essex Road, Islington.

Ball's Pond was originally a small hamlet belonging to the parish of Islington, and abutting upon the Newington Road. It consisted of only a few houses and gardens, and received its name from one John Ball, whose memory is preserved on a penny token, as the keeper of a house of entertainment called the "Salutation," or more commonly the "Boarded House," at this place about the middle of the seventeenth century. The inscription on the token is as follows: "John Ball, at the Boarded House, neere Newington Green: his Penny;" and the sign is depicted upon the coin by the representation of two gentlemen saluting each other. The place was formerly famous for the exercise of bull-baiting and other brutal sports, and was much resorted to by the lower orders of society from all parts of the metropolis. There was, near this spot, a large pond, which by the frequenters of the place became coupled with the name of "mine host." This pond was used, doubtless, like that which we have mentioned in our account of May Fair,* for duck-hunting and other such cruel and unmanly sports.

When the citizens of London used to take lodgings for the summer at Islington for the sake of its pure and healthy air, the district all around us must have consisted of open fields, and nothing met the eye between Hoxton and Stoke Newington. The fields were doubtless used by the Finsbury archers when Hoxton got too hot, or rather too populous, to hold them; and probably within this present century a stray toxophilite may have been seen hereabouts stringing his bow, and dreaming of the days that were past.

In passing through Ball's Pond we have the New River on our left, not, however, any longer, as it used to be, open to the view, and reflecting the sky as in a mirror, but stealing along, like the mole, underground, being arched over in order to keep its stream clean and pure, and free from the smuts and other impurities from which it would be difficult to purify it by all the filtration in the world.

Kingsland lies to the north of the Regent's Canal, which, after leaving the Regent's Park and Camden Town, is carried by a tunnel under the high ground of Islington, and passes hence through Hackney to Mile End, and so into the Thames at Limehouse. It probably derived its name from the royal residence on Stoke Newington Green, of which we shall have more to say presently. The fields adjoining being occupied by royalty for the chase, came conventionally to be styled the "King's lands"—hence Kingsland.

We get a glimpse of the pastoral scenery that at one time lay between London and Kingsland in the "Diary" of the inimitable Pepys. Under date of May 12th, 1667, he writes:—"Walked over the fields to Kingsland and back again; a walk, I think, I have not taken these twenty years; but puts me in mind of my boy's time, when I boarded at Kingsland, and used to shoot with my bow and arrow in these fields."

This, and the whole neighbourhood with which we are now concerned, must at one time have been part and parcel of the great northern forest of Middlesex, if there be truth in what Lord Lyttelton tells us on the authority of an old chronicler of the reign of Henry II., that the citizens of London once had a chace or forest which extended from Hounsditch nearly twelve miles north. The last part of this large forest was Enfield Chace, the farthest portion from town; and if it all once belonged to the people, it would be interesting to find out how it passed into the hands of the sovereign.

Kingsland is a chapelry partly in Hackney and partly in Islington parish. It is described by the "Ambulator," in 1774, as a hamlet of the parish of Islington, lying between Hoxton and Clapton. It consists chiefly of rows of houses, extending in a somewhat monotonous series along the road from London to Stamford Hill.

Lewis, in his "Topographical Dictionary" (1835), writes: "Here are brick-fields, and some part of the ground is occupied by nurserymen and market-gardens. Previously to the middle of the fifteenth century there was at Kingsland a hospital for lepers, which, after the Reformation, became annexed to St. Bartholomew's Hospital, and was used as a sort of out-ward to that institution."

This hospital appears to have been established at a very early period; for, as we learn from Strype's "Survey of London," as far back as the year 1437, "John Pope, citizen and barber, gave by will to the Masters and Governors of the House of Lepers, called *Le Lokes*, at Kingeslond without London, an annual rent of 6s. 8d. issuing out of certain shops, situate in Shirborne Lane, toward the sustentation of the said House at

* See Vol. IV., p. 352.

Kingeslond, for ever." It appears from the records of St. Bartholomew's Hospital, that soon after the establishment of that charity in the reign of Henry VIII., certain Lock, or Lazar, Hospitals were opened in situations remote from the City, for the reception of peculiar patients; and the ancient house for lepers at Kingsland was converted into one of these receptacles. It was afterwards rebuilt on a larger and more commodious plan. A substantial edifice of brick, formerly appropriated to the use of the diseased, having over the door the arms of St. Bartholomew's Hospital, remained standing here down to the commencement of the present century.

BALMES HOUSE IN 1750. (*See page* 525.)

This hospital was anciently called the "Loke," or "Lock."* The greater part of the building was burnt down in the middle of the last century, but was subsequently rebuilt. The structure joined a little old chapel, which escaped the fire.

A writer in *Notes and Queries* states that "a sundial on the premises formerly bore this inscription, significant of sin and sorrow: 'Post voluptatem misericordia.'" Prior to its alienation from the mother hospital, the house had a communication with the chapel, so contrived that the patients might take part in the service without seeing or being seen by the congregation. It may be mentioned here that there was a similar arrangement in the Lock Chapel, Grosvenor Place. In 1761 the patients were removed from Kingsland, and the site of the establishment was let out on building leases, though the chapel itself was suffered to stand, and to be used as a proprietary chapel. It was a small edifice in the Early English style of Gothic architecture, with pointed windows and a bell turret. It was in the patronage of the Governors of St. Bartholomew's Hospital, and the endowment was very insignificant. The chapel, it should be added, was removed in the reign of William IV., in order to make room for building private residences. The chapel adjoined the turnpike at the south-eastern corner of the road leading to Ball's Pond, and was, perhaps, coeval with the first establishment of the house for lepers on this spot. The lower part of the structure, in its latter years, was so much hidden by the accumulation of earth on the outside, that the floor of the area was full three feet below the surface of the highway.

* See *ante*, pp. 214 and 215.

Dalston, or Dorlston, as it was spelt formerly, is usually regarded as a hamlet of Hackney parish; it properly designates the houses on either side of the road leading from Kingsland and Ball's Pond to Hackney, called Dalston Lane; but has gradually come to be applied to the whole neighbouring locality.

The district, which is still styled Dorlston, is curtly described in the "Amulator" (1774) as "a small but pleasant village near Hackney, to which parish it belongs;" and it is spoken of by Lambert, in his "History and Survey of London and its Environs," published in 1806, as "a small hamlet adjoining Hackney, which has nothing remarkable but its nursery grounds." Some of these grounds were still cultivated as lately as 1860; but now the "demon of bricks and mortar" has fairly possessed the neighbourhood, and a crowded railway junction, with constant trains, covers the once rural spot; indeed, Dalston has lately become an important suburb, on account of its railway junction. Of late years, too, large numbers of streets and terraces have sprung up in this neighbourhood; even the small open space known as Kingsland Green is now (January, 1884,) doomed to become a "thing of the past," so that the place is now one of the most populous districts in the suburbs of London.

The old manor-house at Dalston is now used as the Refuge for Destitute Females, which was instituted in 1805, with the view of reforming female criminals, and training them for domestic service. The Refuge was founded under the auspices of Zachary Macaulay, William Wilberforce, Stephen Lushington, Samuel Hoare, Thomas Fowell Buxton, and other leading philanthropists of that day. The sight of a poor destitute boy sitting on a door-step, just discharged from prison homeless and friendless, first kindled the spark of compassion which resulted in the foundation of this time-honoured charity, which was first opened in the month of June, 1805, at Cupar's Bridge, Lambeth. In 1811 the establishment was removed to the Hackney Road. The male branch, in 1815, was transferred to Hoxton, although the females continued in the former locality. The institution for boys was discontinued altogether in 1849, ten years after the incorporation of the society (1 & 2 Vic., cap. 71), on account of Government retrenchments, and about the same time the females were removed to the present commodious and desirable premises at

THE MANOR-HOUSE, DALSTON.

the Manor House, Dalston. Another charitable institution, in Dalston Lane, is the German Hospital, which was erected in 1845. It is a handsome building of red brick, capable of affording relief to a considerable number of patients. It was established for the benefit of Germans suffering from disease, and also of English in cases of accidents. The total number of persons annually relieved is about 12,000. There are in London, principally at the East-end, about 30,000 Germans, chiefly of the working classes, and occupied as sugar-bakers, skin-dressers, and skin-dyers.

Shacklewell, on the north side of Dalston Lane, is said to have been named after some springs or wells which were of high repute in former days, but the very site of which is now forgotten. It is a hamlet to the parish of Hackney lying on the east side of the Stoke Newington Road, and covering a triangular plot of ground, the north-east side of which is bounded by Amhurst Road and Hackney Downs. The old manor-house originally belonged to the family of Heron, and is worthy of mention, as having been the abode of Cecilia, the daughter of the great Sir Thomas More, who married George Heron, "of Shacklewell." Her husband becoming involved in the ruin of his father-in-law, and her only son dying in infancy, the family became extinct. The estate then passed into other hands, and in 1700 was sold to Mr. Francis Tyssen, by its then owner, a gentleman named Rowe, who, it is said, late in life was forced to apply for relief to the parish in which he had once owned a manor.

CHAPTER XLIII.

STOKE NEWINGTON.

"I like the neighbourhood, too, the ancient places
That bring back the past ages to the eye,
Filling the gap of centuries—the traces
Mouldering beneath your head that lie!"
Adam and Eve, a Margate Story.

Stoke Newington in the Last Century—The Old Roman Road, called Ermine Street—Beaumont and Fletcher's Reference to May-day Doings at Newington In the Olden Times—Mildmay Park—The Village Green—Mildmay House—Remains of the King's House—King Henry's Walk—St. Jude's Church and the Conference Hall—Bishop's Place—The Residence of Samuel Rogers, the Poet—James Burgh's Academy—Mary Wollstonecraft Godwin—St. Matthias' Church—The New and Old Parish Churches—Sir John Hartopp and his Family—Queen Elizabeth's Walk—The Old Rectory House—The Green Lanes—Church Street—The House of Isaac D'Israeli—The School of Edgar Allan Poe—John Howard, the Prison Reformer—Sandford House—Defoe Street—Defoe's House—The Mansion of the Old Earls of Essex—The Manor House—Fleetwood Road—The Old "Rose and Crown"—The Residence of Dr. John Aikin and Mrs. Barbauld—The "Three Crowns"—The Reservoirs of the New River Company—Remarks on the Gradual Extension of London.

We are now about to traverse another of the northern suburbs of London, but one which it would not be possible to include among the "northern heights" of the great metropolis. We shall find ourselves in far less romantic scenery than that which we have so lately seen at Highgate and Hampstead, but still the neighbourhood now before us is not deficient in interest; at all events, to those who in their youth have strolled along the banks of the Lea, rod in hand, or mused in its meadows over the pleasant pages of Izaak Walton; or to those who remember the legend of Johnny Gilpin and his ride to Edmonton, as told by Cowper; or who rejoice in the "Essays of Elia" and the other desultory writings of Charles Lamb. To such persons, and doubtless they may be counted by millions, even the full straight level road which leads from Dalston and Kingsland, through Stoke Newington, and Stamford Hill, and Tottenham, to Edmonton, can scarcely be wholly devoid of interest and of pleasant reminiscences. There is also another section of the community to whom this part of the northern suburbs of London will always be a welcome subject; we mean the Nonconformist portion of the religious world, in whose eyes the cemetery of Abney Park is scarcely less sacred than that of Bunhill Fields.

Stoke Newington is described in the "Ambulator" (1774) as "a pleasant village near Islington, where a great number of the citizens of London have built houses, and rendered it extremely populous, more like a large flourishing town than a village. The church," adds the writer, "is a small low Gothic building, belonging to the Dean and Chapter of St. Paul's. . . . . Behind the church is a pleasant grove of tall trees, where the inhabitants resort for the benefit of shade and a wholesome air."

"Our village," writes the Rev. Thomas Jackson, the rector, "was once called Neweton Canonicorum, in order to distinguish it from all other Stokes, Newtowns, and Newingtowns in the world, and especially from its rival on the south of the Thames, Newington Butts; and it was so called doubtless because the manor was given by Athelstan or by Edward the Confessor to the canons of St. Paul's."

The name of the village carries us back to the Saxon times, denoting the new village or town built on the borders of a wood. We may remind the reader that our land is full of Stokes, and that wherever there is a Stoke we may be sure that there was once a wood. Newington, indeed, appears formerly to have been situated in a wood, which was part of the great Middlesex forest already mentioned by us. At the time when King Charles was beheaded there were still seventy-seven acres of woodland in the parish. The timber of Stoke Newington probably helped to build again that London which had perished in the Great Fire of 1666, and possibly at an earlier date it furnished fagots for the fires lit at Smithfield alternately by the Protestants and the Catholics.

The old Roman road, known as the Ermine or Irmin Street, ran northwards through Stoke Newington to Enfield, though its exact route is a subject of debate. Mr. Jackson, in his "Lecture on Stoke Newington," says:—"One boundary of our Saxon manor is the Irmin Street, one of the central highways which our forefathers dedicated to the Hero-god, the illustrious War-man, or Man of Hosts, as his name literally means—that Herman or Arminius, the mighty Cheruscan, who fought the fight of Winfield on the Weser, who turned back the tide of Roman invasion, routing Varus and his legions, and delivering Germany from Italian despotism—a hero truly national, the benefactor and relative of us all. Coming a little down the stream of time, I find Newington Manor among the first of religious endowments in this country. . . . I find the rents and profits of our lands, the fruits of the fields that we daily tread, supporting the men who chanted at the funeral of Edward the Confessor, and assisted at the coronation of William the Norman."

We read of Stoke Newington in the plays of the seventeenth century as a place of pleasant conviviality. Thus Beaumont and Fletcher, in the *Knight of the Burning Pestle*, first published in 1613, introduce Ralph, dressed as a king of the May, who thus speaks:—

"London, to thee I do present this merry month of May;
Let each true subject be content to hear me what I say.
* * * * * * *
March out and show your willing minds by twenty and by twenty,
To Hogsdon (Hoxton) or to Newington, where ale and cakes are plenty."

Soon afterwards Stoke Newington appears, by the testimony of some historians, to have become conspicuous for its Puritanism, through the influence, probably, of the Pophams and the Fleetwoods, and afterwards through the worthy family of Abney, who had purchased the manor.

The parish is described in Lewis's "Topographical Dictionary" (1835), as consisting principally of one long street, extending from Kingsland Road to Stamford Hill, on the high road from London to Cambridge, and containing at that time a population of nearly 3,500 souls. The eastern side of this street is actually in the parish of Hackney, and from the western side, near the centre of it, branches off a street, called Church Street, leading to the parish church and the Green Lanes.

From the western end of Ball's Pond Road, a thoroughfare called Mildmay Park—a good roadway lined on either side by private residences—leads direct to Newington Green. This place, says the "Ambulator" just a century ago, "consists of a handsome square of considerable extent, surrounded by houses which are in general well built; before each side is a row of trees, and an extensive grass-plat in the middle." The green is still adorned with lofty elms, has an old-world appearance, and forms really a handsome, though somewhat irregular square. It is situated partly in the parish of Newington, and partly in that of Islington, and is principally inhabited by merchants and private families.

In the "Beauties of England and Wales" (1816), we read of an old dwelling situated here, called Mildmay House, then a boarding-school for young ladies. It is said to have been, in the reign of Charles I., the property of Sir Henry Mildmay, who had acquired the estate by marriage with the daughter and heiress of William Halliday, an alderman of London. On one of the chimney-pieces appeared the arms of Halliday; and the ceilings contained the arms of England, with the initials of King James, and medallions of Hector, Alexander, &c. Mildmay Park Road, mentioned above, was so named from this house.

On the southern side of the green is an old mansion, now divided into two, which is traditionally said to have been at one time a residence of Henry VIII., when his Majesty wished to divert himself with the pleasures of the chase, which about three centuries ago extended northerly hence to Haringay and Enfield. On the ceiling of the principal room in the house are to be seen the armorial bearings and royal monogram of James I. This room contains a very fine and lofty carved mantelpiece of the "Jacobean" style, not unlike that in the Governor's Room at the

Charterhouse. Most of the rooms have also their walls handsomely panelled in oak. It is probable that this residence caused the adjoining fields to the south to be called the King's Land—now abridged into Kingsland.

At the north-west corner of the green there formerly stood a large building, called Bishop's Place; it is said to have been the residence of Percy, Earl of Northumberland, when he wrote the memorable letter disclaiming any matrimonial contract between himself and Queen Anne Boleyn, referred to in our account of Hackney Church, and which was dated from Newington Green the 13th of May, in the 28th year of Henry VIII. "This house," writes the author of the "Beauties of England and Wales," "was popularly reported to have been occupied by Henry VIII. for the convenience of his irregular amours. The tradition is supported chiefly by the circumstance of a pleasant winding path, which leads to the turnpike road by Ball's Pond, bearing the name of 'King Henry's Walk.'" Mr. Jackson, in his "Lecture on Stoke Newington," thus muses on this old mansion in connection with Bluff King Hal:—"Let us imagine that we see him, blunt, big, and sturdy, with his feet wide apart, and his chin already doubling, sallying forth with a crowd of obsequious attendants from the house afterwards called Mildmay House, or from that just mentioned, to disport himself in the woodlands of Newington. Is Catharine of Arragon his queen, or the hapless Anne, of the swan-like neck, or Jane Seymour, who died so young? Is he plotting the death of a wife, or of his chancellor? Look at him as represented in the portraits of Holbein. His eye good-natured; his mouth indicative of an iron and unscrupulous will; his brow strong in intellectual vigour; his whole physiognomy sensual and selfish. Can you not suppose that you meet him in some of our by-lanes wondering at the changes which have passed upon the London of the sixteenth century, or musing on the suspicions which he entertained respecting a contract of marriage presumed to have been made between the Earl of Northumberland and Anne Boleyn previous to her marriage with the king. Poor earl! he writes to Lord Cromwell from his house on Newington Green a letter of such abject earnestness, that one would imagine his neck already felt the halter, or his eye caught the cold gleam of the executioner's axe, while he denies with the greatest solemnity the fact of any such contract."

In King Henry's Walk, at the corner of Queen Margaret's Grove, and near the North London Railway, stands St. Jude's Church, a large edifice of the "late Decorated" style of architecture, built in 1855 from the designs of Mr. A. D. Gough. It was enlarged, and indeed almost reconstructed, in 1871. In connection with this church, but situated in Mildmay Park, near Newington Green, is a large building known as the Conference Hall.

Dr. Robinson, in his "History of Stoke Newington," describes Bishop's Place as having been a quadrangular building of wood and plaster, and as having had a square court in the centre, with communications to the various apartments all round by means of small doors opening from one room into another. The house, prior to its demolition, had been for many years divided into a number of small tenements, occupied by poor people. When the house was taken down, some parts of the old wainscot were found to be richly gilt, and ornamented with paintings, but well-nigh obliterated from the effects of time.

Newington Green, in its time, seems to have had among its residents many members of the nobility and of the world of letters. An old house on the western side, not far from that above described, was for many years the residence of Samuel Rogers, the poet. The building, which was considerably altered in appearance by its subsequent owners, was pulled down about 1879 to make room for shops. The hall, mentioned by Rogers in his "Pleasures of Memory," and the little room on the first floor in which he used to sit and write, together with the three rooms on the ground floor, facing the south and the sunny garden, remained unchanged. But the hall became lined with modern canvas, spread over the old panelling, and had lost its venerable appearance. The plane-tree, under which the poet would sit and entertain his friends in summer evenings, also flourished; but the greater part of the little paddock in the rear had disappeared, and a new street was carried across the poet's garden, destroying a part of the mushroom-beds which he cultivated with such care and pride. Though nearly a quarter of a century had passed since Samuel Rogers was its master, the house bore to the end tokens of his former presence; and it required no great stretch of imagination to picture the venerable face and figure of the author of "The Pleasures of Memory" seated in his arm-chair here among his books and his friends.

Although the poem is stated by the author to refer to "an obscure village," there can be little doubt in the minds of those who read the "Pleasures of Memory" with attention, that many of the opening lines reflect the old house at Stoke Newington:—

"Mark yon old mansion frowning through the trees.
* * * * * * * *
As jars the hinge what sullen echoes call!
Oh! haste, unfold the hospitable hall!
That hall where once in antiquated state
The chair of justice held the grave debate;
Now stained with dews, with cobwebs darkly hung,
Oft has its roof with peals of rapture rung,
When round yon ample board in one degree
We sweetened every meal with social glee.
* * * * * * * *
Ye household deities, whose guardian eye
Marked each pure thought, ere registered on high,
Still, still ye walk the consecrated ground,
And breathe the soul of Inspiration round.
* * * * * * * *
As o'er the dusky furniture I bend,
Each chair awakes the feelings of a friend.
The storied arras, source of fond delight,
With old achievement charms the wildered sight.
* * * * * * * *
That massive beam, with curious carvings wrought,
Whence the caged linnet soothed my pensive thought;
Those muskets, cased with venerable rust,
Those once-loved forms, still breathing through their dust;
Still from the frame, in mould gigantic cast,
Starting to life—all whisper of the past.
As through the garden's desert paths I rove,
What fond illusions swarm in every grove.
* * * * * * * *
Childhood's lov'd group revisits every scene,
The tangled wood-walk and the tufted green;
Indulgent memory wakes, and lo! they live,
Clothed with far softer hues than light can give."

A writer in the *Mirror* (1824), in giving his "Recollections of Newington Green," says that it is memorable for having been the residence of persons of distinguished talents. An academy, which was some years since pulled down, formerly (1747) belonged to the celebrated James Burgh, which he supported with great reputation to himself and benefit to his scholars for nineteen years. He was the author of "The Dignity of Human Nature," "Thoughts on Education," "A Warning to Dram-drinkers," &c. Its last master was Dr. James Lindsay, who suddenly expired at Dr. Williams's Library, Red Cross Street, whilst advocating the cause of public education. He was long pastor of the Dissenting meeting-house upon the green, whose pulpit had been occupied by Dr. Price, Dr. Towers, &c. On this spot, too, at one time, resided Mary Wollstonecraft Godwin, of whom we have already spoken in our account of St. Pancras.*

The handsome church of St. Matthias, so noted for its "ritualistic" services, is situated at the end of Howard Road, between the green and the main road. It was consecrated about the year 1854. It is a large Gothic edifice, and was built from the designs of Mr. W. Butterfield.

From Newington Green a short walk by way of Albion Road brings us near to the western end of Church Street, mentioned above, where stands the new parish church, dedicated to St. Mary. It is a very spacious and handsome structure, consisting of nave, side aisles, chancel, choir, and transepts, in the Early Decorated style, and was built from the designs of Sir G. Gilbert Scott. The interior is enriched with an elaborate reredos, representing the "Last Supper;" and the capitals of the pillars of the nave are sculptured with varieties of English foliage in bold relief. Some of the windows are filled with painted glass, and the organ and the pulpit are both much admired. The church was consecrated in 1858, and is complete except the tower and spire.

It stands on the south of the road directly facing the former parish church, which is still allowed to remain as hitherto, though practically reduced to the second rank of a chapel of ease to the daughter edifice. The old parish church is a low-roofed structure. It was erected, in the place of a still older edifice, by William Patten, the lessee of the manor in 1563, which date appears over the south doorway. The building has since been repeatedly enlarged, and a spire added. It is small and unattractive, especially in its interior, where are to be seen a variety of specimens of the square family pews, now almost obsolete. It was enlarged and "beautified" about the year 1829 by Sir Charles Barry, and was one of his first and poorest attempts in the Gothic style. The only part of the structure that can boast of antiquity is the south aisle, which contains the manorial pew, where it is said that the Princess Elizabeth was an occasional worshipper during the reign of her sister Mary, during the stolen visits which she paid to Newington from Hatfield House.

In the chancel is a fine mural monument to Mrs. Sutton, who was married first to a Mr. Dudley, and whose second husband was Thomas Sutton, the founder of Charterhouse School and Hospital.† It was restored some years ago by a subscription among the gentlemen who had been educated at the Charterhouse. The Rev. Dr. Gaskin, a former rector, lies in a vault on the north side of the church. Fearing that his body might be removed from its grave after his death, he was buried, by his own desire, not here, but in St. Gabriel's, Fenchurch Street. When that church was taken down in order to carry out improve-

* See *ante*, p. 335.

† See Vol. II., p. 383.

ments in the City, his coffin was removed hither by the care of his successor in the rectory, the Rev. Thomas Jackson, and consigned to what it may be hoped will prove his last resting-place.

The churchyard, which is planted with evergreens, is full of family tombs; few of them, however, possess any antiquarian interest. Near the southern entrance, where once probably stood a "lych-gate," a square tomb covers the remains of whom we have already mentioned† as having endeavoured to improve the Strand on the west side of Temple Bar. His son and his daughter also are recorded on his monument. The former was killed in India, and the latter was burnt to death whilst performing some filial attention by her father's sick bed. Bridget, the daughter of Oliver Cromwell, and wife of General Fleetwood, lies buried beneath the church.

STOKE NEWINGTON CHURCH, 1750.

Mrs. Barbauld and of her brother, Dr. Aikin, whom we have already mentioned in our account of Hampstead.* At the extreme south-west corner is the grave of some of the Wilberforces, members of the family of the eminent philanthropist † who lies in Westminster Abbey. Had not a public funeral been voted to him, in all probability, he would himself have been laid to rest in this quiet and peaceful spot. On the south of the chancel is the family grave of Wilberforce's friend and fellow-worker in the cause of the slave, Mr. James Stephen, a Master in Chancery, the father of the late Right Honourable Sir James Stephen.

In the churchyard lies buried Alderman Pickett,

The parish church has many monuments and memorials of the family of Sir John Hartopp, who were at one time residents at Stoke Newington. Among the rest is this curious entry in the register, relative to the wife of Sir John:—"1711, Dame Elizabeth Hartopp was buried in woollen the 26th day of November, according to an Act of Parliament made on that behalf: attested before Mr. Gostling, minor canon of St. Paul's, London." And again, relative to another member of the family:—"My lady Hartopp was buried in a velvet coffin, September 22, 1730, in the church." The dame Elizabeth, who was buried in woollen, was the daughter of General Fleetwood, who married

† See Vol. III., p. 10.

* See *ante*, p. 476. † See *ante*, p. 95.

VIEWS IN STOKE NEWINGTON.

1. Rogers' House, 1877. 2. Fleetwood House, 1750. 3. St. Mary's Rectory. 4. St. Mary's New Church. 5. New River at Stoke Newington. 6. Queen Elizabeth's Walk, 1800. 7. Old Gateway.

Bridget, one of Oliver Cromwell's children; and the education of her son was entrusted to the learned and pious Dr. Watts, of whom we shall have more to say presently. The Rev. Dr. Stoughton, in his "Shades and Echoes of Old London," says:—"Dame Hartopp has been sometimes regarded as the offspring of Bridget, and consequently as the Protector's granddaughter; and if that view of her lineage were correct, then the youth to whom Watts became tutor would be no other than a great-grandson of the strong-willed man who, without a crown, swayed a sceptre over three old kingdoms." But Noble, in his "Memoirs of the Protectoral House," shows, as we think satisfactorily, that Elizabeth, who was married to Sir John Hartopp, was a daughter of Fleetwood by his first wife, Frances Smith. Still, as the Hartopps would be intimately connected with the Cromwells, the family traditions of the latter would be familiar to the former, and stories of Oliver and his son-in-law would often be told in the dining-hall and the gardens of Sir John at Newington.

Near the old church, on the northern side of it, is a walk between trees, still called Queen Elizabeth's Walk; and as some justification of the name, it may be added that Newington was the abode of her Majesty's favourite, Robert Dudley, Earl of Leicester, and of his contemporary, Edward Vere, Earl of Oxford.

On the south side of the road, between the two churches, stood formerly a picturesque old rectory-house, mostly built of wood, with a curious gable projecting into the street, over the pavement. The south and west sides of the house and its garden were bounded by a moat, which is now filled up, the present rectory being built upon its site. The ribs and back-bone of the old rectory-house were evidently part and parcel of large forest trees; and where oak was not used in its construction, its place was supplied by other hard and vigorous timber, equally heavy and durable.

On the western side of the parish there is a large but rather winding road, running northwards, popularly known as the "Green Lanes," and leading, by way of Wood Green and Winchmore Hill, to Enfield. This is rather a sporting neighbourhood, and the road is largely used for trotting matches by farmers, butchers, and other tradesfolk, a fact which does not contribute to the quiet or comfort of the residents. The Green Lanes dispute with Stoke Newington Road the claim to be considered the old Saxon Ermine Street mentioned above. At this point commences a narrow and slightly-winding thoroughfare, called Church Street, which, passing eastward, leads us into the straight and wide road from Dalston to Stamford Hill. It was evidently once a rural lane, and was probably used more by farmers' wagons than by gentlemen's carriages. It is fringed, however, on both sides with a long series of private dwelling-houses, most of them red-bricked mansions of the date of Queen Anne and George I., with projecting summits to the doorways, and screened from the street by iron railings of varied and handsome designs, not unlike those still to be seen in the older parts of Kensington, Chelsea, Hampstead, and Highgate. One of the first houses on the northern side of the way, now a ladies' school, was the home of Mr. Isaac D'Israeli, the author of the "Curiosities of Literature," before he settled down in Bloomsbury Square. A large white house near it was the scene of the school-days of the eccentric and gifted poet, Edgar Allan Poe, who in his writings ascribes much of the romantic element in his character to the fact of having been sent as a boy to a place so abounding in old associations. Edgar Poe (born at Baltimore in January, 1811) was adopted as a child by a Mr. Allan, a rich gentleman who had no children of his own. Mr. Allan brought him to England, and placed the spoiled child, then a witty, and beautiful, and precocious boy, at school in Church Street. He remained here five years, but returned to the United States in 1822.

A tall red house on the same side of the way, now embodied in Church Row, was the house where John Howard lodged when he married the widow lady who kept it, as we have mentioned in our account of Lower Clapton.* Here he studied his first essays in philanthropy. "The delicate state of his health required better and more attentive nursing than he found where he first lodged, so he removed into apartments under the roof of one Mrs. Sarah Lowne, a widow possessed of a little property, residing in Church Street, who devoted her time to the care and comfort of the young invalid, who was only twenty-five, while she was fifty-two. From being his nurse, she became his wife. She died in 1755, and lies buried in St. Mary's, Whitechapel." It is on record that Mr. Howard was a constant worshipper in the old Independent chapel here. After the death of the nurse whom he thus strangely endeavoured to reward, Mr. Howard married into a respectable family of Cambridgeshire. His second wife, however, died soon after she had given birth to a son. In the course of a voyage to Lisbon Mr. Howard had the misfortune to be captured, and was lodged in France as a prisoner of war. The sufferings

* See *ante*, p. 521.

which he was now compelled to witness are supposed to have operated with such force on his mind as to lead to those indefatigable exertions for the redress of abuses in prisons which speedily produced such important effects throughout the greater part of Europe. Mr. Howard died, in the year 1790, at one of the Russian settlements on the Black Sea, the victim of a malignant fever, which he had caught in visiting some prisoners. A monument to his memory was erected in 1876 at Kherson.

On the south side of the street, a similar house, with lofty windows and a handsome entrance doorway, was the home of the eccentric Thomas Day, the author of "Sandford and Merton." It is now styled Sandford House.

A few yards farther to the east, on the same side of the way, we come to Defoe Street. This was formed in 1875, by the demolition of the house in which Defoe resided, and in which he is reputed to have written "Robinson Crusoe." It is said to have been remarkable for the number of its doors, and for the massive locks and bolts with which they were secured. The house itself was a gloomy and irregular pile of red brick, apparently of the reign of Queen Anne. It had thick walls and deep window seats, with curious panelling and cupboards in the recesses. Here, besides writing that matchless story with which his name is associated, Defoe plotted as a politician; and here he set in order the materials on which were founded the union between England and Scotland. Hence he was carried a prisoner to Newgate in 1713. A native of Cripplegate, he had been educated at an academy on Newington Green, kept by Charles Morton. "Robinson Crusoe" was published in April, 1719, in which year the rolls of the manor of Stoke Newington mention Defoe as a resident in Church Street.

Close by, and on the same side of the street, stands a portion, though only a fragment, of the mansion of the old Earls of Essex, dating perhaps from the reign of Elizabeth. On the same side of the street, but considerably more to the east, stood a house which at the beginning of the last century was a large hotel or tavern, with gardens and pleasure-grounds, which formed a favourite resort for newly-married couples to spend their honeymoon, in the days when there were no railways to whirl them off on the wings of steam to Brighton, Hastings, or the Isle of Wight. It was afterwards converted into two private houses, one of which contained a spacious apartment that had formerly been the assembly-room of the tavern.

On the opposite, or northern, side of Church Street, is a dwelling called, though incorrectly, the Manor House, in the grounds of which is a curious archway of brick, which must formerly have been the entrance to a large and important residence. It is probably of the fifteenth or sixteenth century. It is now filled up with modern bricks; but the hinges on which its huge doors once swung are still to be seen *in situ*. Little or nothing appears to be known about its history. Mr. Lewis, in his "Dictionary" quoted above, says that "the ancient manor-house is particularly worthy of notice; but," curiously enough, he adds, "a brick gateway, with a pointed arch on the northern side of Church Street, is the only part now standing of the buildings belonging to the old manor-house."

The same ancient tradition which connects Henry VIII. with the southern portion of Stoke Newington, tells us that Queen Elizabeth visited the manor-house in Church Street; and a pleasant grove of elms, close by the old church, as mentioned above, once the "mall" of the parish, still retains the name of "Queen Elizabeth's Walk." But when did the "maiden" queen make Stoke Newington her abode? Was it in her childhood, her girlhood, or her early womanhood? We know that a branch of the Dudleys, Earls of Essex, lived here after Elizabeth had come to the throne, but there is no proof of their having been here at an earlier date. Mr. Jackson tells us that the story current in the village in the last century was that, some time in Mary's reign, "probably when the house of the French Ambassador Noailles was the rendezvous of the discontented of every description, and when the princess herself was the hope of the Protestants, exasperated by persecution, she was brought by her friends to the secluded manor-house, embosomed in trees, as to a secure asylum, where she might communicate with her friends, and be ready for any political emergency. They tell us that an ancient brick tower stood in the early part of the last century near the mansion, and that a staircase was remembered leading to the identical spot where the princess was concealed." But even Mr. Jackson, with all his poetic antiquarianism, is unable to confirm the tradition. Church Row, we may add, stands on the site of the old manor-house and grounds.

Fleetwood Road, a little to the east of this, still commemorates the residence of Fleetwood, the Parliamentarian general.

About a hundred yards farther to the east we come to some handsome and lofty iron gates, behind which are some fine cedars of Lebanon and other tall evergreens. These were the front entrance of Sir Thomas Abney's mansion, of which we shall have more to say presently, as well as of its owners.

The old "Rose and Crown" tavern stood at the corner of a road leading out of Church Street in a southward direction. The old tavern retained its ancient appearance until early in the present century, when it was pulled down, and a new house erected on its site, which was enlarged and brought forward in a line with the adjoining houses; previous to which the old house stood back some feet from the footpath. Robinson, in his history of the parish, gives an illustration of the tavern as it appeared in 1806. Upon the sign-post is shown a pair of horns, similar to those which we have described in our account of Highgate.*

Near the middle of Church Street are two houses, nearly opposite to one another, which have had some distinguished residents; that on the north side was Dr. John Aikin's; his sister, Mrs. Barbauld, lived on the south, in a small private residence, now converted into a jeweller's shop. In Dr. Aikin's house the "Winter Evening Conversations" were written. Dr. Aikin died in December, 1822. Crabb Robinson writes of him that "he had for some years sunk into imbecility after a youth and middle age of great activity. He was in his better days a man of talent of the highest personal worth—in fact, one of the 'salt of the earth.'" Mrs. Barbauld was a resident here both before and after her living at Hampstead. She is frequently mentioned in H. Crabb Robinson's "Diary," from which we cull the following characteristic entries :—

"1816—*11th Feb.*—I walked to Newington, and dined with Mrs. Barbauld. As usual, we were very comfortable. Mrs. Barbauld can keep up a lively argumentative conversation as well as any one I know; and at her advanced age (she is turned of seventy), she is certainly the best specimen of female Presbyterian society in the country. N.B.—Anthony Robinson requested me to inquire whether she thought the doctrine of Universal Restoration scriptural. She said she thought we must bring to the interpretation of the Scriptures a very liberal notion of the beneficence of the Deity to find the doctrine there."

Here is a picture of her five years afterwards :—"1821—*21st Jan.*—Went to Mrs. Barbauld's. She was in good spirits, but she is now the confirmed old lady. Independently of her fine understanding and literary reputation, she would be interesting. Her white locks, fair and unwrinkled skin, brilliant starched linen, and rich silk gown, make her a fit object for a painter. Her conversation is lively, her remarks judicious and always pertinent."

About four years subsequently Robinson writes :—"1824—*4th Nov.*—Walked to Newington. Mrs. Barbauld was going out, but she stayed a short time with me. The old lady is much shrunk in appearance, and is declining in strength. She is but the shade of her former self, but a venerable shade. She is eighty-one years of age, but she retains her cheerfulness, and seems not afraid of death. She has a serene hope and quiet faith—delightful qualities at all times, and in old age peculiarly enviable."

Four months afterwards, on the 9th of March, 1825, she died, after a few days' serious illness. At the end of the same year we find Robinson making this entry:—"*27th Dec.*—At Royston. This morning I read to the young folks Mrs. Barbauld's 'Legacy.' This delightful book has in it some of the sweetest things I ever read. 'The King in his Castle' and 'True Magicians' are perfect allegories, in her best style. Some didactic pieces are also delightful."

Among other distinguished residents and personages connected with Stoke Newington, whose names we have not already mentioned, were Adam Anderson, author of the "History of Commerce," and Archbishop Tillotson.

The "Three Crowns," at the junction of Church Street and the main road, commemorates the spot where James I.—in whom the three crowns were first united—stayed to bait his horses, after meeting the Lord Mayor and aldermen at the top of Stamford Hill.

The western side of the High Road, as far as Stamford Hill, formed, till recently, part of the original parish of Hackney; but the latter has been sub-divided, and West Hackney and Stamford Hill have been made independent ecclesiastical districts. The latter was formerly a private and proprietary chapel of ease, but it was purchased by a subscription among the residents, enlarged, and consecrated.

About half a mile to the north, between Stoke Newington and the Seven Sisters' Road, at the entrance of the Green Lanes, are the large reservoirs in which the New River Company filter their water before it is brought into London. We have already sketched the history of this river in our account of Islington,† but for the following particulars, which ought to have a place here, we are indebted to the "Life of Sir Hugh Middleton," in Mr. Charles

* See *ante*, p. 418.

† See Vol. II., pp. 266, 267.

Knight's *Penny Cyclopædia*:—"The fall of the New River is three feet per mile, which gives a velocity of about two miles an hour. The average width is about twenty-one feet, and the average depth about four feet in the centre; so that, taking it at about half that depth, there is a section of forty-two square feet of water flowing into London at the rate of two miles an hour. At the sluice, near Highbury, the river is dammed back to the height of twenty inches, and at Enfield to two feet four inches; and there are three or four more such interruptions for the purpose of checking the current. . . . The New River is occasionally rendered dirty, especially in winter, by drainage from the land and villages along its course; and the company has been at a great expense in order to purify the water before it is delivered to the inhabitants of London. For this purpose two large settling reservoirs were formed in 1832 at Stoke Newington, under the direction of Mr. Mylne, the company's engineer. The water here covers an area of thirty-eight acres, more than twenty feet deep in some parts, and twelve feet on an average throughout. The water of the New River can be turned into the upper reservoir, where it settles, and it is then drawn off by a steam-engine, and poured into the lower reservoir, where another settlement takes place, and the water is then turned again once more into the channel of the river. Bathing in the New River is entirely prohibited; and men called 'walksmen' mow the bed of the river every week in order to keep down the growth of weeds, which are stopped by gratings placed at intervals, where the weeds are regularly removed."

We may conclude this chapter with an apt quotation from the Rev. T. Jackson's "Lecture on Stoke Newington:"—"It is said that in North America the line of civilisation stretches farther and farther into the west at the rate of about fifteen miles a year. The modest backwoodsman who now stands on the frontier of civilised life, finds himself a twelvemonth hence within its boundary. The progress of London—the Babylon and Nineveh of modern times—is scarcely less remarkable, if less rapid. There are persons yet living (1855) who remember the erection of Finsbury Square, upon what was then the northern limit of the great town. Others have heard their fathers speak of the wall in front of Old Bedlam, and of the cherry-trees that grew in Broad Street and London Wall. Now the south of Stoke Newington may be regarded as within the capital. The meadows and cornfields of Kingsland are no more; they are covered with lines of busy and well-inhabited streets. The tide of population is scarcely arrested by the uplands of Highbury Hill, once the seat of a Roman summer camp, and threatens to invade the quiet hill-top of Crouch End. When will our green fields be finally absorbed? when will Lordship Road be covered with villas, to be, as time rolls on, gradually deteriorated, till they are joined by intervening houses and broken into shops?"

CHAPTER XLIV.

STOKE NEWINGTON (*continued*), AND STAMFORD HILL.

"Si monumenta quæris, circumspice."

Abney House—Sir Thomas and Lady Abney—The Visit of Dr. Isaac Watts to Abney House—His Library and Study—The Death of Dr. Watts—Sale of Abney Park, and the Formation of the Cemetery—Abney House converted into a School—Monument of Isaac Watts—The Mound and Grotto in the Cemetery—Distinguished Personages buried here—Stamford Hill—Meeting of King James and the Lord Mayor at Stamford Hill—The River Lea—Izaak Walton and the "Complete Angler."

In the foregoing chapter we have briefly referred to the mansion of Sir Thomas Abney, the entrance to which was on the north side of Church Street. It was a large square substantial red-brick building with stone quoins, and dated its erection from the close of the seventeenth century. The roof was flat, with a balustrade around it; and it had a central turret, which commanded an extensive prospect of the surrounding country. The iron entrance-gates, which still remain, are richly ornamented with carved work of fruit and flowers. The principal rooms of the house were all large and stately, and the walls were lined with oak wainscoting. On the first floor an apartment termed the "painted chamber" was finished in a costly manner, and might be considered an interesting specimen of the taste of the age in which it was arranged. The mouldings were gilt, and the whole of the panels on the sides were painted with subjects taken from the works of Ovid. On the window-shutters were some pictorial decorations—strangely contrasting with the above heathenish embellishments—in the form of emblems of grief and death, and mingled with the arms of Gunston and Abney, and intended, doubtless, to honour their memory; these were supposed to have been added by the pencil of Dr. Isaac Watts himself, who was an artist as well as poet and divine, and who, as we shall presently see, found in this mansion an asylum for upwards of six-and-thirty years.

THE OLD RECTORY, STOKE NEWINGTON, IN 1858. (*See page* 536.)

The building, with its "old brick front, its old brick wall, and its old iron gate, all redolent of the times of William III. and Queen Anne," was commenced about the year 1690, by a Mr. Gunston, who at that time had purchased considerable property at Stoke Newington. He died, however, before the house was completely finished; an event which drew forth a funeral poem from the pen of Dr. Watts, in which, not content with the calling on "the buildings to weep," he writes—

"Mourn, ye young gardens, ye *unfinished gates!*"

The mansion now became the property and residence of Sir Thomas and Lady Abney, who, with their family, of which Dr. Watts may be considered a member, took up their abode here.

Sir Thomas Abney was a member of the Fishmongers' Company, and a distinguished Nonconformist. He was knighted by William III., and served the office of Lord Mayor in 1700. He is celebrated for the costliness of his procession on the occasion of entering on the mayoralty, as may be seen in detail in Mr. J. G. Nichols' "London Pageants." We are told how that "a person rode before the cavalcade in armour, with a dagger in his hand, representing Sir William Walworth, the head of the rebel Wat Tyler being carried on a pole before him." "Sir Thomas," as John Timbs informs us, "was not more distinguished by his hospitality than by his personal piety. Neither business nor pleasure ever interrupted his observance of public and private domestic worship. Upon the evening of the day that he entered on the office of Lord Mayor, without any notice he withdrew from the public assembly at Guildhall after supper, went back to his house, there performed his devotions, and then returned back to his company."

Isaac Watts began to preach at the age of twenty-three, while living under the roof of Sir John and Lady Hartopp at Stoke Newington, where, as we have seen in the preceding chapter, he was engaged as tutor. He was soon afterwards invited to assist Dr. Chauncey, of whose congregation in Mark Lane Sir John Hartopp was a member; subsequently, on the retirement of the old pastor, Watts was induced—though somewhat reluctantly, owing to ill health—to undertake the charge, in March, 1702. Ten years later, a nervous disease had so grown upon him that he was compelled to suspend his public labours, and abandon the exercise of his ministry. In the meantime the congregation had removed from Mark Lane to a chapel in Bury Street, where Sir Thomas Abney and his amiable lady were members. They had become devoted friends to the poet and divine. "Watts, being lonely—a bachelor in the midst of his sad affliction—the Abneys invited him to come and stay with them for a few weeks' change. He did so. One day, long afterwards, the Countess of Huntingdon called upon the invalid. 'Madam,' said he, 'your ladyship is come to see me on a very remarkable day.' 'Why so remarkable?' she asked. 'This day thirty years I came hither to the house of my good friend Sir Thomas Abney, intending to spend but one single week under his friendly roof, and I have extended my visit to the length of exactly thirty years.' 'Sir,' added Lady Abney, in words which contained infinitely more than mere compliment, 'what you have termed a long thirty years' visit, I consider as the shortest visit my family ever received.'"

ABNEY HOUSE, 1845.

Stoke Newington thus became Dr. Watts's home; and here, and at Theobalds, where Sir Thomas Abney had a favourite summer retreat, he wrote most of those "Divine and Moral Songs" with which his name is so closely associated. Old Sir Thomas Abney died in 1722, upwards of fourscore years old; but Watts continued to reside at Abney Park with Lady Abney and her daughter until his own death. "Here," writes Dr. Stoughton, "he enjoyed the uninterrupted demonstrations of the truest friendship. Here, without any care of his own, he had everything which could contribute to the enjoyment of life, and favour the unwearied pursuit of his studies. Here he dwelt in a family which, for piety, order, harmony, and every virtue, was a house of God. Here he had the privilege of a country recess—the fragrant bower, the spreading lawn, the flowery garden, and other advantages—to soothe his mind and aid his restoration to health, to yield him, whenever he chose them, the most grateful intervals from his laborious studies, and enable him to return to them with redoubled vigour and delight."

Watts was chaplain to the household of the good old knight; and morning and evening he led the devotions, and on Sunday night preached to the family. The doctor's study in Lady Abney's house at Stoke Newington was the local centre of his existence. From it he at times diverged only to return to it again with a deeper feeling of home attachment. Mrs. S. Carter Hall, in her "Pilgrimages to English Shrines," describing her visit to this mansion, after speaking of the library, says, "We followed our conductor to the top of the house, where, in a turret upon the roof, many of Dr. Watts's literary and religious works were composed. We sat upon the seamed bench, rough and worn, the very bench upon which he sat by daylight and moonlight—poet, logician, and Christian teacher. The chamber upon whose walls hung the parting breath of this benevolent man might well be an object of the deepest interest to all who follow, however humbly, the faith of Jesus. We were told of a little child who, knowing every hymn he had written, was taken into his room, having some vague but happy idea that she should meet him there. Learning, as she eagerly looked round, that the author of 'Watts's Hymns' was dead, she burst into bitter tears, which did not cease while she remained in the house. Many of his works are said to have been produced in this room, which, though small, was lofty and pleasant."

Here is a picture of the doctor's study and its learned occupant, as drawn by Dr. Stoughton, in his "Shades and Echoes of Old London:"—"Here are some lines from Horace, hung up in a frame outside the door, denouncing the faithless friend. Within, the shelves are loaded with a goodly array of books—poetical, philosophical, historical, theological, and critical. Where there are no shelves, there are prints of noted persons, chiefly divines. A lofty panel covers the fireplace, with inscriptions from Horace on either side: the one, where the portraits are numerous, indicating that the space is filled up by shades of the departed; the other, where they are fewer, soliciting additions to the illustrious group. The classical fancifulness of all this indicates the scholar and the poet; but the avocations of the worthy occupant of this literary retreat indicate those noble purposes, those high Christian aims, of which all else in his character and habits were ornamental adjuncts. There he sits at his writing table, enveloped in a scholarly robe, small in figure, and sickly in complexion; the forehead not so broad and high as we might expect, limited somewhat by the wig that crowns and borders it; the features large and marked, the eyes clear and burning."

"Isaac Watts," observes the Rev. T. Jackson, in his lecture on Stoke Newington, "adopted substantially the fatal errors of Arius." This accusation may or may not be true; but as Dr. Stoughton remarks, "without trimming, without temporising, he was quiet and without bustle; without boasting or parade, he did his own business—the work that God had given him. And now no church repudiates him; Nonconformity cannot monopolise him. His eulogium is pronounced by Samuel Johnson and Robert Southey, as well as by Josiah Conder; and whilst his monument looks down on Dissenting graves in Abney Park, his effigy reposes beneath the consecrated roof of Westminster Abbey." Dr. Watts died at Abney Park, surrounded by his friends, on the 24th of November, 1748; and his remains were interred in Bunhill Fields.

Miss Abney, the daughter of Sir Thomas Abney, ordered by her will that on her death the estate of Abney Park should be sold and the proceeds given to the poor, and distributed among charities. It was accordingly sold, and the purchase money of the new owner, whose name was Eade, was devoted to the execution of her intentions.

The mansion, after having been for many years used as a college for the instruction of youths of the Wesleyan Society, was pulled down in 1845, the park and garden-grounds having, four or five years previously, been converted into a cemetery. Many of the fine old cedars and yews that adorn the cemetery flourished here during the lifetime of Dr. Watts, who, it is said, wrote much of his poetry beneath their shade, and upon the mound consecrated by his name, and which, a vague tradition tells us, covers the ashes of no less a personage than Oliver Cromwell. We have already had occasion, more than once, to record some of the traditions concerning Cromwell's supposed resting-place.* That his body received but a mock funeral at Westminster, and was really peaceably reposing elsewhere, is said to have been a favourite belief with his partisans; and General Fleetwood's residence at Stoke Newington, the circumstance of his marriage with Bridget, the eldest daughter of the "Lord High Protector," and widow of General Ireton, and the fact that he was a very distinguished character during the Protectorate of his father-in-law—may easily have led to the tradition above mentioned, however unfounded. A large portion of Abney Park, ranging from the magnificent

* See Vol. III., pp. 437, 539; Vol. IV., p. 546.

cedar of Lebanon, in the part of the grounds once called the Wilderness, and stretching away to the north extremity, where the mound is placed, and all the land eastward of that line, extending as far as the principal entrance to the cemetery, was, during the Commonwealth, and after the Restoration, the property of General Fleetwood, of whose house we have spoken in the previous chapter.

Abney Park Cemetery covers in all about thirty acres of ground, and was opened in 1840. It is full of monuments of men whom time will not let die. A cenotaph monument and statue to the memory of Dr. Isaac Watts rises conspicuously above other mementoes of the departed, connecting the place with his name, and exciting the visitor to some recollections of his works and virtues. Mrs. S. C. Hall, writing in 1850, says:—"The trees and the avenues, preserved with a most delicate respect to the memory of the poet, are so well kept, there is such an air of solemnity and peace and positive 'beauty' in the arrangement of the whole, that if spirits were permitted to visit the earth, we might hope to meet his shade amid his once favourite haunts. There is nothing to offend us in such receptacles for the perishing dust of humanity, but everything to soothe and harmonise the feelings of the past and present. A statue in pure and simple character of this high-priest of charity stands (we are told) upon the 'exact spot' where the house stood; but we think it has been placed rather farther back than was the dwelling." The inscription upon the pedestal of the statue, which was executed by Mr. E. H. Baily, R.A., and "erected by public subscription, September, 1845," is as follows:—

"In memory of Isaac Watts, D.D., and in testimony of the high and lasting esteem in which his character and writings are held in the great Christian community by whom the English language is spoken. Of his Psalms and Hymns, it may be predicted in his own words:—

'Ages unborn will make his songs
The joy and labour of their tongues.'

He was born at Southampton, July 17th, 1674, and died November 24th, 1748, after a residence of thirty-six years in the mansion of Sir Thomas Abney, Bart., then standing in these grounds."

Dr. Johnson wrote of him:—"Few men have left behind such purity of character, or such monuments of laborious piety; he has provided instruction for all ages, from those who are lisping their first lessons to the enlightened readers of Malebranche and Locke. He has left neither corporeal nor spiritual nature unexamined; he has taught the Art of Reasoning and the Science of the Stars; such he was, as every Christian Church would rejoice to have adopted."

The "mound," too, which we have mentioned above, whence the poet loved to overlook the green and fertile country—for London at that time had not escaped from Shoreditch—is walled in, fenced round, and guarded as a sanctuary. It is in the north-east corner of the grounds.

As a cemetery, Abney Park has some natural features of great beauty and interest. It is remarkable for its fine old trees, amongst which there is a splendid cedar of Lebanon of two centuries' growth. It contains also a beautiful arboretum, formed with great taste. The buildings are bold and effective, though of limited extent; and what is wanting in costliness has been more than compensated by the skill of the architect, Mr. W. Hosking, who has here shown how much may be effected by "that true simplicity which results from a few carefully-studied and well-finished features." Near the centre of the grounds stands a neat brick-built chapel, of Gothic architecture, the tower of which is surmounted by a tapering spire. The ground is (using the words of the proprietors) "a General Cemetery for the City of London, and its eastern and north-eastern suburbs, which shall be open to all classes of the community, and to all denominations of Christians, without restraint in forms." There is, therefore, no separating line in this cemetery between the parts appropriated to members of the Church of England and to Dissenters. The greater part of the ground is thickly studded with tombs and monuments, most of which are remarkable for simplicity, and many of the graves are enriched with flowers or other touching emblems of the grief of sorrowing friends of the departed. Unlike Kensal Green and other cemeteries which we have visited in the course of our perambulation round London, Abney Park cannot boast of containing the ashes of many who have distinguished themselves "by flood and field;" but a large number of those who achieved distinction in more peaceable walks of life have here found a resting-place. Among them we may mention the Rev. Dr. Fletcher, of Finsbury, "the Children's Friend;" the Rev. Andrew Reed, D.D., the philanthropic founder of many orphan asylums and other public charities, who died in 1862; the Rev. Dr. Fletcher, of Stepney; Dr. John Campbell; the Rev. Thomas Binney, one of the most prominent leaders of the Independent connexion, and for many years minister at the Weigh-house Chapel, Fish Street Hill; the Rev. Dr. Pye Smith; Dr. Archer; and last, not least, Mr. Braidwood, who was many years chief of the London Fire Brigade, and who lost his life during the great fire in Tooley Street, in June, 1861.

Passing northward, after leaving the cemetery gates, we soon arrive at Stamford Hill, a gentle eminence on the main road. The old Cambridge Road, which we have mentioned as passing through Hackney by way of Mare Street, after continuing its course through Lower and Upper Clapton, joins the new road, by which we are now proceeding, at the summit of the hill. Both sides of the road, as we pass up the hill, are occupied by rows of houses and detached villas, many of them of an elegant character, that almost force upon the recollection the lines of Cowper—

> "Suburban villas, highway side retreats,
> That dread th' encroachment of our growing streets.
> Tight boxes, neatly sashed, and in a blaze
> With all a July's sun's collected rays,
> Delight the citizen, who, gasping there,
> Breathes clouds of dust and calls it country air."

So much may the neighbourhood now be considered part of London, that the road itself is traversed by tram-cars, which run between the City and the top of Stamford Hill. On our right we pass a new Congregational Chapel, a large Gothic structure, the tall spire of which forms a prominent object for some distance round.

On reaching the summit of the hill, where the two roads meet as above mentioned, an entirely different scene presents itself, and we begin to feel that we have reached almost the limits of our journey in this direction. Green fields, trees, and hedge-rows now burst upon the view; and winding away to the north-east the road leads on towards the village of Tottenham, whither we will presently direct our steps. Before proceeding thither, however, we will give a glance back over the ground we have wandered; and conjure up to our imagination the sweeping change which must have taken place within the last three or four centuries, when London was walled in on every side, and all away to the north was fields—"Moor Felde," "Smeeth Felde," and the like—and forest land, through which passed the lonely road, called "Hermen [or Ermine] Strete," of which we have spoken in the previous chapter, after emerging from "Creple Gate," on its way by Stoke Newington, to St. Albans and the north. The swampy nature of the ground, too, in some parts is still indicated by the name of Finsbury (*Fensbury*); but all this, as we have seen, has long been built upon, and "Moorfields are fields no more."

As Mr. Matthew Browne writes in "Chaucer's England," we must "either be at a great distance from London or must possess a very lively imagination to conceive of the English capital as a place of gardens, such as it was in the time of the Plantagenets. Within my own memory, the area within which roses will not grow in the metropolis has been widening and widening in the most odious manner, and in every direction. The great brick-giant marches out towards the fields, and the roses fly before him; and you have to go nearly out of the sound of 'Big Ben' to see gardens no sweeter and gayer than lay under the shadow of St. Paul's and the Savoy Palace in the days of John of Gaunt."

In the reign of King James, Stamford Hill was crowned with a grove of trees, and its eastern declivity was overgrown with brushwood. The whole country on the Essex side was marshy as far as Epping Forest, some three miles distant. Through a swampy vale on the right the river Lea, so dear to the angler, took its slow and silent course, while through a green valley on the left flowed the New River.

In Mr. Harrison Ainsworth's romance of the "Star Chamber" is a graphic and spirited, though somewhat sensational, sketch of the view looking towards London from this elevated spot at the above period:—"Arrived at the summit of the hill commanding such extensively charming views, Jocelyn halted and looked back with wonder at the vast and populous city he had just quitted, now spread out before him in all its splendour and beauty. In his eyes it seemed already overgrown, though it had not attained a tithe of its present proportions; but he could only judge according to his opportunity, and was unable to foresee its future magnitude. But if London has waxed in size, wealth, and population during the last two centuries and a half, it has lost nearly all the peculiar features of beauty which distinguished it up to that time, and made it so attractive to Jocelyn's eyes. The diversified and picturesque architecture of its ancient habitations, as yet undisturbed by the innovations of the Italian and Dutch schools, and brought to full perfection in the latter part of the reign of Elizabeth, gave the whole city a characteristic and fanciful appearance. Old towers, old belfries, old crosses, slender spires innumerable, rose up amid a world of quaint gables and angular roofs. Storey above storey sprang those curious dwellings, irregular, yet homogeneous; dear to the painter's and the poet's eye; elaborate in ornament, grotesque in design, well suited to the climate, and admirably adapted to the wants and comforts of the inhabitants; picturesque like the age itself, like its costume, its manners, its literature. . . . Another advantage in those days must not be forgotten. The canopy of smoke overhanging the vast modern Babel, and oftentimes obscuring even the light of the sun itself, did not dim the beauties of the ancient city—sea-coal being but little used in comparison with wood, of which there was then abundance, as at this time in the capital of France. Thus the atmosphere was clearer and lighter, and served as a finer medium to reveal objects which would now be lost at a quarter the distance.

"Fair, sparkling, and clearly defined, then rose up Old London before Jocelyn's gaze. Girded round with grey walls, defended by battlements, and approached by lofty gates, four of which—to wit, Cripplegate, Moorgate, Bishopsgate, and Aldgate—were visible from where he stood; it riveted attention from its immense congregation of roofs, spires, pinnacles, and vanes, all glittering in the sunshine; while in the midst of all, and preeminent above all, towered one gigantic pile—the glorious Gothic cathedral. Far on the east, and beyond the city walls, though surrounded by its own mural defences, was seen the frowning Tower of London—part fortress and part prison—a structure never viewed in those days without terror, being the scene of so many passing tragedies. Looking westward, and rapidly surveying the gardens and pleasant suburban villages lying on the north of the Strand, the young man's gaze settled for a moment on Charing Cross—the elaborately-carved memorial to his queen Eleanor, erected by Edward I., and then ranging over the palace of Whitehall and its two gates, Westminster Abbey—more beautiful without its towers than with them—it became fixed upon Westminster Hall; for there, in one of its chambers, the ceiling of which was adorned with gilded stars, were held the councils of that terrible tribunal which had robbed him of his inheritance, and now threatened him with deprivation of liberty and mutilation of person. A shudder crossed him as he thought of the Star-Chamber, and he turned his gaze elsewhere, trying to bring the whole glorious city within his ken.

"A splendid view, indeed! Well might King James himself exclaim, when standing, not many years previously, on the very spot where Jocelyn now stood, and looking upon London for the first time since his accession to the throne of England —well might he exclaim in rapturous accents, as he gazed on the magnificence of his capital, 'At last the richest jewel in a monarch's crown is mine!'"

However much the above description of the view from Stamford Hill may be overdrawn, and whether Jocelyn could descry the cross at Charing from this spot or not, there is at least some foundation for the exclamation which Mr. Harrison Ainsworth has put into the mouth of King James; for it is on record how that on the 7th of May, 1603, his Majesty was here met by the Lord Mayor and aldermen on his first public entry into London after his accession.

The river Lea, which flows at the distance of from one to two miles on our right, all the way from Kingsland, and which here makes its nearest approach to the road that we are travelling, divides the county of Middlesex from that of Essex, as far to the north as Waltham Abbey. Its course on the whole is due south, though somewhat winding, and here and there it divides its water into two or three separate channels, and then re-unites them. Nearly all along its course there is a broad belt of meadow and marsh land on one side of the river, or on both, which is used as pasturage for cattle. The Lea itself, after sweeping past Chingford, Stratford, and Bow, falls into the Thames close by the Victoria Dock. This river in former times was deemed one of considerable importance, as the means of supply in conveying corn, meal, and malt to the metropolis; so much so, in fact, that in the reign of Edward IV. an Act of Parliament was passed for improving the navigation. It has, too, an historical interest, for Drayton, in his "Polyolbion," tells us how that—

"The old Lea brags of the Danish blood."

It is said in Lambarde's "Dictionarium Topographicum" that "it hath of longe tyme borne vessels from London twenty miles towards its head: for in the tyme of King Ælfrede, the Danes entered Leymouthe and fortified at a place adjoyning this river twenty miles from London, where by fortune Kinge Alfred passinge by espied that the channel of the river might be in such sorte weakened, that they should want water to return with their shippes; he caused therefore the water to be abated by two great trenches, and settinge the Londoners upon them he made them batteil, wherein they lost four of their captaines, and a great number of their common souldiers, the rest flyinge into the castell which they had built. Not long after they were so pressed that they forsoke all and left their shippes as a prey to the Londoners; which, breakinge some and burninge other, conveyed the rest to London." He adds that this castle, though it might seem to be Hertford, was on another part of the river's bank; but where it stood is not clearly defined, and must always remain a moot point. Other authors, however, confirm in the main the leading statement of Lambarde, namely, Sir William Dugdale in his "History of the Embanking and Draining the Fens," and Sir John Spelman in his "Life of Alfred the Great." A perusal of the latter work will leave the honest reader in very little doubt but that these trenches are the very same that now branch off from the river between the Temple Mills and Old Ford, and crossing the Essex Road near Stratford, enter the Thames together with the main stream of the Lea.

On those channels of the Lea which are not used for the purposes of navigation there are corn and paper mills, near which are the favourite resorts for the disciples of Izaak Walton's "gentle craft." At many places the fishing is strictly preserved, and admission to these pleasant spots is obtained only by the "silver key" of a yearly subscription. There is a tranquillising influence in such spots, which harmonise best with minds formed as those of John Scott, the Quaker poet of Amwell, and of the author of the "Complete Angler." In fact, Scott has paid his tribute to Izaak Walton, who

> "Oft our fair haunts explored; upon Lea's shore
> Beneath some green tree oft his angle laid,
> His sport suspending to admire their charms."

"Honest Izaak" has been immortalised by his literary labours, which were mainly of a biographical character; but his best known production is the "Complete Angler, or Contemplative Man's Recreation."* This appeared in 1653, and has gone through numerous editions. The motto to the first edition was, "Simon Peter said, I go a fishing; and they said, We also go with thee;" but it was cancelled in subsequent editions. This "pleasant curiosity of fish and fishing," writes his amiable biographer, "is a series of dialogues—no long 'and watery discourse,' but truly a rich entertainment—quaint, humorous, and cheerful, abounding in happy touches of wit and raillery, practical wisdom, sagacious reflections, and snatches of poetry and song. While his lectures on his art are so clear and so curious, his digressions are ever most amusing."

DR. WATTS' MONUMENT, ABNEY PARK CEMETERY.

While he continued in London, his favourite recreation was angling, in which he was the greatest proficient in his time; and indeed so great were his skill and experience in the art that there is

* See Vol. II., p. 533.

VIEWS ON THE RIVER LEA.

1 Ferry House. 2. Tottenham Church from Lea River. 3. Tumbling Weir. 4. Fishing Cottage 5. Tottenham Lock.

scarce any writer on the subject since his time who has not made the rules and practice of Walton his very foundation. It is therefore with the greatest propriety that Langbaine, in his "Lives of the English Dramatic Poets," calls him "the common father of all anglers." The river that he seems mostly to have frequented for this purpose was the Lea, which has its source above Ware, in Hertfordshire, and falls into the Thames, as we have seen, a little below Blackwall; unless we suppose that the vicinity of the New River to the place of his habitation might sometimes tempt him out with his friends—honest Nat and R. Roe, whose loss he so pathetically deplores in his preface of the "Complete Angler"—to "spend an afternoon there." In the above work, the kindness of old Izaak's nature often peeps out, as when he tells his friend and disciple or scholar who had caught his first chub, "it is a good beginning of your art to offer your first fruits to the poor, who will thank both you and God for it." "He was no ascetic, for he liked 'the barley-wine, the good liquor that our honest forefathers did use to drink of,' and he loved such mirth 'as did not make friends ashamed to look on one another the next morning.' His humour is sometimes quite comic, as when, after instructing his listener and companion in the art of impaling a frog upon a hook, and securing the upper part of its leg by one loop to the arming wire, he naïvely adds, 'In so doing, use him as if you love him.'"

According to Izaak Walton, the river Lea affords fine sport to the angler, not only in perch, chub, pike, barbel, dace, roach, gudgeon, and other common fish, but also in trout. He speaks of the Lea meadows as flowery above the average, and even of the milkmaids of the neighbourhood as prettier and more charming than their sisters in other parts; but in this last respect he probably mixed up too much of the poet with the philosopher. His serene heart, in fact, is ever going out in admiration of the clear stream in its shallows, pools, and flowery banks; the shady trees, the odorous honeysuckle, the green pastures, the disporting of the lambs, the hum of the bee, the clouds and sky, and the song of the linnet and the lark, the blackbird and thrush. "The book," writes its reviewer, "will ever be a favourite with all 'that love virtue and angling,' as did its author, who was at peace with himself and all creation excepting otters." Yet, in spite of this, Byron could write of Walton reproachfully in the following couplet—

> "That quaint old cruel coxcomb in his gullet
> Should have a hook and a small trout to pull it."

Rennie, in one of his notes on the "Complete Angler," tells a good story anent this river. An old river Lea angler being daily seen in one particular spot hereabouts, a brother angler conceived that the place must be the resort of abundance of fish, and therefore commenced his operations there one summer morning before daybreak. The usual attendant of the place arrived some hours after, and threw in his line. After a long silence, the first-comer remarked that he was out of luck, not having caught a single fish in this hole, which he had noticed to be such a favourite with his brother of the rod. "Sir," replied the old stager, "I confess that long custom has made me very partial to the spot; but as for fish, I assure you that here I have angled regularly for forty years, and have never had a bite as yet!"

The "Jolly Anglers" inn, at Lea Bridge, a little to the east of Upper Clapton, is of itself sufficient to indicate that the stream hereabouts is largely frequented by the lovers of Walton's "gentle art." It is also, during the summer months, much frequented for the purposes of bathing and boating, and the number of fatal accidents arising from the unskilful management of small craft by youths who can neither row nor swim is lamentably great.

CHAPTER XLV.

TOTTENHAM.

> "It will not be long ere we shall be at Tottenham High Cross; and when we come thither, I will make you some requital of your pains."—*Izaak Walton.*

The Division of the Parish into Wards—Extent and Boundaries of the Parish—Early History of Tottenham—The Manor owned by King David Bruce of Scotland—Other Owners of the Manor—The Village of Tottenham—The Hermitage and Chapel of St. Anne—The "Seven Sisters"—The Village Green—The High Cross—The River Lea at Tottenham—Bleak Hall—Old Almshouses—The "George and Vulture"—The Roman Catholic Chapel of St. Francis de Sales—Bruce Castle—The Parish Church—The Chapel and Well of St. Loy—Bishop's Well—White Hart Lane—Wood Green—Tottenham Wood—Concluding Remarks.

WE descend the sloping ground to the north of Stamford Hill, and following the roadway—the river Lea running parallel with our course through the green fields on our right—we soon enter the village of Tottenham. This village, or, as it is generally called, Tottenham High Cross, is described at some length in the "Ambulator" (1774). It is stated that "the present Duke of Northumberland and the late Lord Coleraine had seats here; and there are also a great number of pretty houses belonging to the citizens of London."

The parish of Tottenham is very extensive, or, at all events, was so, until sundry ecclesiastical districts were formed out of it. It was divided into four "wards," thus enumerated in the "Ambulator:"—"1. Nether Ward, in which stands the parsonage and vicarage; 2. Middle Ward, comprehending Church End and Marsh Street; 3. High Cross Ward, containing the hall, the mill, Page Green, and the High Cross; 4. Wood Green Ward, which comprehends all the rest of the parish, and is considerably bigger than the three other wards put together."

Bedwell, in his "History of Tottenham," describes the parish as being nearly fifteen miles in circumference. "It is divided," he writes, "on the east, from Walthamstow, in Essex, by the river Lea; on the north it meets the parish of Edmonton; on the west it is bounded by Hornsey and Friern-Barnet; and on the south by Hackney and Stoke Newington. The western division is watered by the circuitous progress of the New River; and a little brook, termed the Mosell, which rises at Muswell Hill, passes through the village, and shortly unites with a branch of the Lea."

The first that we hear of Tottenham is in the reign of Edward the Confessor, when it formed part of the possessions of Waltheof, Earl of Huntingdon. He took a prominent part in opposing the Norman invasion, but not long after he joined William, and married Judith, the niece of that king. From that time until his death, although he professed to be on William's side, still he was continually intriguing with the English, and a few years after his marriage he was betrayed by his wife and beheaded. Judith, however, was allowed to keep the manor of Tottenham, or, as it was then called, Toteham, on condition that she should pay to the king every year the value of five hides, equal to about 100 Norman shillings. There is a curious old record in the Domesday Book which mentions this fact, and also that the land consisted of ten carucates, or ploughlands. A carucate is estimated at about 240 acres, and thus the whole estate would be 2,400 acres. The value of the land, including a wood for 500 hogs and a weir worth 3s., amounted to £25 15s. and three ounces of gold. After the death of Judith the manor passed to her daughter Maud, who married a Norman noble, Simon de St. Liz. He died in the reign of Henry I., leaving a son Simon, from whom the king took away the estate and gave it to David, the son of Malcolm III., King of Scotland, who then married Simon's mother Maud. Their son Henry, their grandson Malcolm, and their great-grandson William the Lion, held it until the last joined Prince Henry against his father, Henry II., who ejected William, and restored it to its rightful owner Simon; but after his death the king gave it back to William, and he to his brother David, who then took the title of Earl of Huntingdon. On his death the manor probably fell to the share of his second daughter Isabel, who married the father of Robert Bruce, the competitor with John Baliol for the crown of Scotland, and afterwards king. It was he who made Tottenham his place of residence, and, as we shall presently see, gave the house the name of Bruce Castle, or rather, as it was then called, Le Bruses. On his revolt from Edward I. his property in England was forfeited, and came into the hands of the Crown. After this the manor was split up among different persons, to whom the king gave it in return for some service or other, but it appears that it never went down to the descendants of the owner, but always reverted to the Crown after his death. In the reign of Henry VI. we find that there were several lesser manors, which went by the following names:—Bruce's, Pembroke's, Mocking's, and Dawbeney's. These were named from their owners, and were held on condition that whenever the king went to war in person the owner should furnish him with a pair of silver spurs gilt.

David Bruce, King of Scotland, having thus become possessed of this manor and church, the latter, after it had belonged to the Earls of Northumberland and Chester, was given to the monastery of the Trinity, in London; but King Henry VIII. granted it to William, Lord Howard of Effingham, who being afterwards attainted, it again reverted to the king, who thereupon granted it to the Dean and Chapter of St. Paul's, to whom it still belongs.

In the "Beauties of England and Wales" it is stated that the manor of Tottenham, after having been held for several generations by three distinct families—and called respectively by the names of the manor of Bruses (or Bruce), the manor of Baliols, and the manor of Pembrokes—was in the reign of Edward I. given to William Dawbeny, "in consideration of his military services." King Henry VIII. gave the whole estate to Sir William Compton, groom of his bedchamber, who entertained at Bruce Castle the king and his sister Margaret, the wife of James IV., King of Scotland, who made Tottenham their place of meeting when the Scottish queen came up from the North. The manors thus united have, it is stated, ever since that time passed through the same hands. Early in the seventeenth century they were purchased by Hugh, second Lord Coleraine, from whom they descended to his next brother, the third lord, who compiled an essay towards a "History of Tottenham." His lordship's family name of Hanger may perhaps be still commemorated here by the name of Hanger Lane, though there is another possible derivation of the term from the hanging woods which fringed it. On the death of the third Lord Coleraine, the manor of Tottenham did not devolve upon his eccentric brother, the fourth and last lord, of whom we have already spoken in our account of Chalk Farm,* but were bequeathed to a natural daughter of the third lord; but as the lady was an alien, the estates were escheated to the Crown. The lady, however, having married Mr. James Townsend, an alderman of London, the lands were subsequently granted to that gentleman, and have since changed hands by sale on several occasions.

At Tottenham the first ambassador from the "Emperor of Cathair, Muscovia, and Russeland," who had been wrecked on the coast of Scotland, was met in 1556 by a splendid procession of the members of the Russia Company, then lately founded for carrying on traffic with that country.

The main street of the village of Tottenham is formed of good houses, irregularly built, along each side of the great northern road, with a few smaller streets branching off at right angles on either hand. The situation is unpleasingly flat, and the buildings for the most part straggling and unequal, yet partaking little of a rural character. On the east side of High Street, and at a short distance southward from the Cross, stood formerly the Hermitage and Chapel of St. Anne. It was a small square building, constructed chiefly of brick, and had a narrow strip of ground annexed to it, stretching away along by the highway southward from the building to the "Seven Sisters." The "Hermitage" was a cell dependent on the Monastery of the Holy Trinity in London, and its site is now covered by the "Bull" public-house; whilst on the strip of ground mentioned above a row of houses has been erected called Grove Place.

The "Seven Sisters," as we have already remarked,† is the sign given to two public-houses at Tottenham. In front of that at Page Green, near the entrance of the village, were planted seven elms in a circle, with a walnut-tree in the middle. Of these trees we have given an illustration, when describing the Seven Sisters' Road, which was named after them. It was traditionally asserted that a martyr had been burnt on the spot where the trees were originally planted more than five hundred years ago; but the tradition wants verification.

The centre of Tottenham is occupied by a large triangular enclosure, called the Green. Mr. Harrison Ainsworth, from whose romance of the "Star Chamber" we have quoted in the previous chapter, introduces to our notice some of the rustic scenes which may have been witnessed here at the period at which the plot of his story is laid. The following are some of his remarks:—

"Long before Jocelyn and his companion reached Tottenham, they were made aware, by the ringing of bells from its old ivy-grown church tower, and by other joyful sounds, that some festival was taking place there; and the nature of the festival was at once revealed as they entered the long straggling street, then, as now, constituting the chief part of the pretty little village, and beheld a large assemblage of country folk, in holiday attire, wending their way towards the Green for the purpose of setting up a May-pole upon it, and making the welkin ring with their gladsome shouts. All the youths and maidens of Tottenham and its vicinity, it appeared, had risen before daybreak that morning, and sallied forth into the woods to cut green boughs and gather wild flowers for the ceremonial. At the same time they selected and hewed down a tall, straight tree—the tallest and straightest they could find; and, stripping off its branches, placed it on a wain, and dragged it to the village with the help of an immense team of oxen, numbering as many as forty yoke. Each ox had a garland of flowers fastened to the tip of its horns; and the tall spar itself was twined round with ropes of daffodils, bluebells, cowslips, primroses, and other early flowers, while its summit was surmounted with a floral crown, and festooned with garlands, various-coloured ribands, kerchiefs, and streamers. The foremost yokes of oxen had bells hung round their necks, which they shook as they moved along, adding their blithe melody to the general hilarious sounds. When the festive throng reached the village, all its inhabitants—male and female, old and young—rushed forth to greet them; and such as were able to leave their dwellings for a short while joined in the procession, at the head of which, of course, was borne the May-pole. After it came a band of young men, armed with the necessary implements for planting the

* See *ante*, p. 294. † See *ante*, pp. 380, 381.

shaft in the ground; and after them a troop of maidens, bearing bundles of rushes. Next came the minstrels, playing merrily on tabor, fife, sackbut, rebec, and tambourine. Then followed the Queen of the May, walking by herself—a rustic beauty, hight Gillian Greenford—fancifully and prettily arrayed for the occasion, and attended, at a little distance, by Robin Hood, Maid Marian, Friar Tuck, the hobby-horse, and a band of morris-dancers. Then came the crowd, pell-mell, laughing, shouting, and huzzaing—most of the young men and women bearing green branches of birch and other trees in their hands.

"The spot selected for the May-pole," he adds, "was a piece of greensward in the centre of the village, surrounded by picturesque habitations, and having on one side of it the ancient cross. The latter, however, was but the remnant of the antique structure, the cross having been robbed of its upper angular bar, and otherwise mutilated, at the time of the Reformation, and it was now nothing more than a high wooden pillar, partly cased with lead to protect it from the weather, and supported by four great spurs."

On the eastern side of the street, not far from the centre of the village, and close by the north-east angle of the Green, stands the high cross, whence this particular "ward" or division of the parish receives its second name. The structure forms a very interesting feature in the antiquities of Tottenham. Lysons, in his "Environs of London," states that "the hie crosse" is mentioned in a Court Roll, dated 1456; and Norden, in his "Speculum Britanniæ" (1593–1620), says, "Tottenham High Cross was a hamlet belonging to Tottenham, and hath this adjunct High Cross of a wooden cross there lately raised on a little mound of earth." Bedwell, in his history of the parish, written in 1631, describes the appearance of the cross some fifty years previously as "a columne of wood, covered with a square sheet of leade to shoote the water off every way, underset by four spurres." He adds: "There hath been a cross here of long continuance, even so long as since that decree was made by the Church that every parish should in places most frequented set up a cross, but whether it were such at the first as afterwards it is manifest it was I much doubt of, for that it hath been of an extraordinary height, and from thence the towne gained the addition of *alta crucis*."* Notwithstanding the preservatives spoken of by Bedwell, the cross speedily afterwards sank to decay, for at the commencement of the seventeenth century, Dean Wood, who had a residence close by, "built a plain octangular cross of brick, which," says Mr. Brewer, in the "Beauties of England and Wales" (1816), "yet remains, but has recently experienced considerable alteration. In consequence of a subscription among some of the inhabitants of Tottenham," he adds, "a complete covering of stucco was bestowed in 1809, and at the same time various embellishments, of the character usually termed Gothic, were introduced. These are in the style which prevailed in the Tudor era, and it is to be regretted that the date at which the alterations were effected is not placed in a conspicuous situation. On each face of the octagon is a shield with one of the letters composing the word *Totenham* in the old character." It is perhaps even still more a matter of regret that the "restoration" of the cross was not postponed for half a century, until the public had become a little more enlightened as to the principles of Gothic architecture. In that case it would not probably have been covered with a composition of stucco, but conscientiously renewed in Bath stone.

Bedwell, in speaking of the "Eleanor crosses," does not venture to assert that this is one of the series, but remarks that "it was against the corps should come thro' the towne re-edified and peradventure raised higher."

It will be remembered by the reader of Izaak Walton's "Complete Angler" how, in the opening scene, "Piscator" cries out to his friends "Venator" and "Auceps," who are on their way to the "Thatched House," in Hodsden, "You are well overtaken, gentlemen. A good morning to you. I have stretched my legs up Tottenham Hill to overtake you, hoping your business may occasion you towards Ware;" and how "Auceps," in reply, agrees to bear him company as far as Theobalds, at Cheshunt. In fact, the long street of Tottenham is the direct road not only to Theobalds, but to Enfield and Edmonton, and so on to Ware and Hatfield.

On reaching Tottenham Cross, "Piscator" thus addresses his fellows, "Venator" and the "Scholar:" "And pray let us now rest ourselves in this sweet shady arbour, which Nature herself has woven with her own fine fingers; it is such a contexture of woodbines, sweet-briars, jessamine, and myrtle, and so interwoven as will secure us both from the sun's violent heat and from the approaching shower. And being sat down, I will requite a part of your courtesies with a bottle of sack, milk, oranges, and sugar, which, all put together, make a drink like

* "A Brief Description of the Towne of Tottenham High Cross, in Middlesex, together with an historical narrative of such memorable things as are there to be seen and observed; collected, digested, and written by William Bedwell, Pastor of the parish, 1631."

nectar—indeed, too good for anybody but us anglers. And so, master, here is a full glass to you of that liquor; and when you have pledged me, I will repeat the verses which I promised you." It is to be feared that the "Piscator" of the present day would find this pretty picture of sweet shady arbours, overgrown with jessamine, sweetbriars, and myrtle, to say the least, a little overdrawn.

TOTTENHAM HIGH CROSS, 1820.

Almost every illustrated edition of the "Complete Angler" has an engraving of a fishery and ferry here, called "Bower Banks;" and no wonder, for the river Lea, as it flows by Tottenham, is very charming, especially in its old course about the Mill. The author of "Rambles by Rivers" thus sketches the scene at this point:—"An old pollard willow, with an angler under its shadow—a few cows, perhaps, standing in the water, and enjoying with philosophic quiescence the cooling luxury—perchance a punt in the middle of the river—a bright blue sky overhead, reflected with a softened lustre in the clear stream—an abundance of yellow water-lilies at our feet, and the low banks decked with all gay flowers—these are the materials of the picture; and he who has not his heart gladdened as he gazes on them, has yet to learn that there are things in heaven and earth not dreamt of in his philosophy. Walton was not one of these:

> 'The meanest flow'ret of the vale,
> The simplest note that swells the gale,
> The common sun, the air, the skies,
> To him *were* opening Paradise.'

And only such as, in a measure, can participate in these feelings and sympathies are fitted to wander along Izaak Walton's Lea."

A short distance farther up the stream, at a place called Cook's Ferry, stood Bleak Hall, the house fixed upon as being the one to which "Piscator" took his scholar, and which was then "an honest ale-house, where might be found a cleanly room, lavender in the windows, and twenty ballads stuck about the wall; with a hostess both cleanly, and handsome, and civil." The old house has long been swept away; a portion of it, however, remained standing down into the present century. It consisted of a kitchen, with a room over it (ascended by a staircase on the outside), called the "fisherman's locker," from its having been used as a locker for their tackle. If not the actual place to which Izaak Walton refers, it must long have been a well-known hostel for Lea fishermen. The evidence appears to tell against its identity as the Bleak Hall of old Izaak, but local tradition was, and is, very strong in its favour. The Lea, we need scarcely add, is the only river, next to the Thames, that is engrafted in the affections of the Londoner.

In 1596, an almshouse was founded in the High Street of Tottenham by one Zanchero, a Spaniard, the first confectioner ever known in this kingdom. Near to the Cross there is another row of almshouses, founded by a Mr. Nicholas Richardson, and which date their erection from the early part of the last century.

The "George and Vulture" tavern, in the high road, nearly opposite Bruce Grove, occupies the site of a much older inn, which was frequented by the Londoners in early times for the purpose of recreation. It is mentioned in the "Search after Claret," as far back as the reign of William III., but was probably far older. Its charms are thus described in a newspaper paragraph, immortalised by Mr. Larwood in his "History of Sign-boards:"

BRUCE CASTLE.

> "If lur'd to roam in summer hours,
> Your thought inclines tow'rd Totnam bowers,
> Here end your airing tour, and rest
> Where Cole invites each friendly guest.
> Intent on signs, the prying eye
> The 'George and Vulture' will descry:
> Here the kind landlord glad attends
> To wellcome all his cheerfull Friends,
> Who, leaving City smoke, delight
> To range where vision's scenes invite.

The spacious garden, verdant field,
Pleasures beyond expression yield;
The Angler here to sport inclined,
In his Canal may pastime find.
Next, racy Wine and home-brew'd Ale
The nicest palates may regale;
Nectarious Punch—and (cleanly grac'd)
A Larder stor'd for every taste.
The cautious Fair may sip with glee
The freshest Coffee, finest Tea.
Let none the outward *Vulture* fear;
No *Vulture* host inhabits here:
If too well us'd ye deem ye—then
Then take your revenge, and come again."

On the western side of the chief street, near White Hart Lane, stands in a retired situation, as though retreating from the public gaze, the Roman Catholic Chapel of St. Francis de Sales. It is a small and unpretending structure, in the style of the Dissenting chapels of half a century ago, about forty feet in length by thirty. It was erected by the late Baroness de Montesquieu in 1826–7, on a site purchased by her for that purpose, and was solemnly opened by Bishop Poynter, in the May of the latter year, previous to which time the Roman Catholics here had been content with the use of a room in the house of the resident priest. For more than a century Tottenham and Edmonton have been noted for the number of poor lodging-houses in which lived the Irish labourers who worked in the fields and market gardens around this part. On the outbreak of the first French Revolution their number was increased by an influx of emigrants from the north of France, who brought with them much skilled industry, but more poverty. It was not, therefore, till about 1793 that any regular provision was made in Tottenham for their religious wants. In that year the Abbé Cheireux, afterwards Bishop of Boston, in the United States, and subsequently Archbishop of Bordeaux, and a cardinal, being employed as tutor in a Protestant family in Tottenham, obtained the use of a room in Queen Street, Tottenham Terrace, in order to minister to the spiritual needs of both the Irish and the French poor. On his departure for America, the Abbé Cheireux handed over his charge to another French *emigré* priest, and eventually, about the year 1805, the Abbé Le Tethier erected a modest chapel-house and still more modest presbytery in the same street. This, however, became alienated, through debt or other causes, and the Roman Catholics were left without a chapel or chaplain from the year 1818 down to the time when the present structure was built by the Baroness de Montesquieu, as mentioned above. In 1871, some nuns of the Servite order settled down in a house in Hanger Lane, at the southern end of Tottenham, where they have opened a school and a chapel.

Westward of the main street, near Bruce Grove Station on the branch line of the Great Eastern Railway, is Bruce Castle, which has long been used as a private school. The mansion was rebuilt in the latter part of the seventeenth century, and is a good specimen of Elizabethan domestic architecture. The structure, as stated above, takes its name from a castellated mansion, the residence of Robert Bruce the elder, father of the Scottish king of that name, which in ancient times occupied this site. The original building is said to have been erected by Earl Waltheof, who married Judith, niece to William the Conqueror, who gave him for her portions the earldoms of Northumberland and Huntingdon. Their only daughter, Maud, after the death of her first husband, married David I., King of Scotland, and being heiress of Huntingdon, had in her own right, as appended to that honour, "the manor of Tottenham, in Middlesex." Through her these possessions descended to Robert Bruce, brother of William III., King of Scotland. Bruce contended for the throne of Scotland with John Baliol, who was ultimately adjudged heir to the crown. Upon this adjudication Robert Bruce retired to England, and, settling on his grandfather's estate at Tottenham, repaired the castle, and acquiring an adjacent manor, named it and the castle Bruce. In the reign of Henry VIII. the property, as we have already had occasion to remark, was granted to Sir William Compton, then groom of the king's bedchamber.

It is recorded that, in 1516, Henry VIII. here met his sister Margaret, Queen of Scots. Dr. Robinson, in his "History of Tottenham," says: "It is probable that Sir William Compton rebuilt the house soon after he became possessed of the manor in 1514, and that it was finished to receive the royal guests in 1516, for on the Saturday after Ascension Day in that year King Henry VIII. met his sister, Margaret Queen of Scots, at 'Maister Compton's house, beside Totnam!'" The next royal visitor was Queen Elizabeth, who became the guest of Margaret's grandson, Henry, Lord Compton, so that it would seem that the daughter of the Queen of Scots had married the heir of the Comptons. A passage in Robinson, referring to Queen Elizabeth's visit to Henry, Lord Compton, would seem to throw some doubt on his earlier statement that Sir William Compton rebuilt the house, for in it he observes, "The style of the building, which is of that period—namely, 1570—seems to justify the conjecture that the house was built by Henry, Lord Compton;" but it receives additional strength from the following passage from Lord Coleraine's MS. :—"In respect to its great antiquity more than conveniency, I keep the old brick tower in good repair, although I am not able to discover the founder thereof; and among the other anticaglia of this place I range Sir William Compton's coat of armes, which I took out of the old porch when I raised the tower in the front of the house." It appears, therefore, as if Lord Coleraine's evidence goes to confirm the first statement of Robinson. The coat of arms he referred to is believed to be that which is now affixed on the north side of the house, above the windows of one of the class-rooms.

Among the "Burghley papers" in the British Museum there is a curious letter, which was written by the Marquis of Winchester to Sir W. Cecil, afterwards Lord Burghley. It seems to refer to the occasion of some visit of Queen Elizabeth to Henry, Lord Compton. The following is a copy of it :—

"After my hartie commendacions with like thanks to you for your letter of libertie given me for the repaire of Mr. Compton's House at Totenham, in order as well for the Queene's Highness, as for the owner, which I shall gladlie do. And because my Ladie of Pembroke hereth that th' Officers take the loppes and toppes of the Trees that be felled for reparations for their fees, which indeede ought not to be, and that resteth in your order, and then the wood may be feld to the profit of the reparation, yet the Woodwarde had neede to have something for his labour; and if yt shall please my Ladie to send one honest man to your feodarie and me, he shall see all the tymber that shall be taken, and howe it shalbe employed, and if my Ladie will the house still unrepaired, mynding a better House to be built upon the ground, You and I shall be well content therewith: for that you and I shall do ys for the Quene's honor and Mr. Compton's profitt, otherwise You and I meane not to do any thing, and herein knowe my Lord's pleasure and write to me againe I pray you in that matter, and I shall yelde myself to all that shall be thought for the best. So fare you well. Written this Xth of November 1563.

"Your loving friend
"WINCHESTER.

"To my loving friend
Sir William Cecil Knight
Principall Secretary to the Quene's M[atie]."

The Comptons seem to have held the estate until 1630, when the last Compton died. The next owners were the Hares of Norfolk, but how they got possession of it we are not able to discover. Certain it is that Bedwell, in his book entitled "A Breef Description of Tottenham High-crosse" (written in 1631), mentions that Hugh Hare, who was created Lord Coleraine in 1625, was then in possession of the whole estate. This Hugh Hare was a great favourite of Charles I., who created him an Irish baron when he was only nineteen years of age. On the breaking out of the Civil War, he supplied the king with money and gave up his seat at Longford, in Wiltshire, for a royal garrison. But this was afterwards taken and plundered by the Roundheads, and his other estates were sequestered. However, soon after the Restoration they were all restored. His son, grandson, and great-grandson all held the estate. The last married Miss Rose Duplessis, the daughter of a French clergyman, by whom he had a daughter, Rose. On his death in 1749 a question arose, as we have shown above, as to whether his wife, the first Rose, ought not to forfeit the estate, since she was an alien; and in 1755 the cause was finally determined in favour of the heirs at law. The estate having thus reverted to the Crown, a grant of it was obtained by Mr. Chauncey Townsend, for his son James, who married Miss Duplessis. By her he had a son, James Hare Townsend, who in 1789 had to sell a great part of the estate to pay off his father's debts. It passed through the hands of various owners, and in 1827 was bought by Mr. (afterwards Sir Rowland) Hill, of whom we have already spoken in our account of Hampstead.* Six years later the Messrs. Hill finally removed hither from Hazelwood, near Birmingham, where their school had been first established.

It is utterly impossible to tell how many houses have been in succession built on these grounds, but there must have been three at least, if not more. It is probable that they were not all built on exactly the site where the present house stands, but on some other spot near. This supposition is corroborated by the fact that very frequently when drains are dug at some depth old brick foundations and walls are found. For instance, a few years ago, when the well was being repaired, three or four feet below the surface, the workmen came upon the top of a wall, which extended to the depth of about twelve feet. Near the bottom of this wall a silver coin of the beginning of King Henry VIII.'s reign was found, and on the side of the wall, not so deep down, a gilt button, probably of the time of Queen Anne.

There is no mention of any castle in the Domesday Book at the time when the estate was in the

* See *ante*, p. 490.

possession of Earl Waltheof; nor, indeed, do we find any record of a house until the reign of Edward II. But if Bruce lived here—and he must have done so, or how would the place have received the name?—there must have been a house for him to live in, and therefore we may fairly conjecture that there was a castle at that time. As we mentioned above, the house was rebuilt in the reign of Henry VIII. In the "Antiquities of Tottenham" we find that there formerly hung over the chimney-piece in one of the parlours a picture, which exhibited two other towers, besides the one which is still left. Lord Coleraine says that the house was either rebuilt or new-fronted by the Hare family a little before the Revolution. We suppose that the middle part was only the thickness of the refectory, which was then the entrance-hall; for a few years ago, when a part of the wainscoting of the inner wall in one of the class-rooms was taken down, there were found on the wall inside some dead stalks of a vine or other creeping plant, clearly proving that that had been once the outside wall. But we can find no mention of the other part having been added. The room which is now called the porch-room used to be the porch, and from it a passage led straight through the house into the pleasure-grounds beyond. There used formerly to be a west wing of the house, but it was pulled down, together with the stables and coach-house, about sixty years ago, by Mr. Ede, the then owner. The east wing was added by Alderman Townsend, and in it, tradition says, John Wilkes has been often entertained.

A very peculiar custom prevailed here, the origin of which is not known. At the burial of any of the family the corpse was not suffered to be carried through the gate, but an opening was made in the wall nearest to the church, through which the corpse and mourners passed into the churchyard. "There are still," says Dr. Robinson, "the appearance of several apertures which have been bricked up, and among them is that through which passed the corpse of Mr. James Townsend, the last that was carried from the castle to the mausoleum of the Coleraine family. This aperture has been recently opened, and a Gothic door is now fixed in the place."

Although still called a castle, the building now presents none of the features usually associated with such structures; it is constructed of brick, with stone dressings, and is altogether a spacious edifice. It consists chiefly of a centre, with projecting wings. The old entrance-hall in the centre —the doorway of which has been blocked up, the hall itself being converted into a small sitting-room —is surmounted by a large square tower, surrounded by two external galleries, and crowned by an octagonal turret. The rooms throughout the house are exceptionally good, the boys' dormitories being all lofty and well ventilated. The walls of the dining-room are wainscoted to the ceiling, and are hung with a large number of engraved portraits of old divines and other ancient worthies; and to add to the effect, and to give the place a somewhat baronial character, above the portraits are placed several pairs of spreading antlers. The school-room in itself is a large and lofty apartment at the north-west corner of the house. The school and grounds occupy upwards of twenty acres. The grounds are laid out in the style of a park, in which are some very fine trees; and they include a cricket-ground and a field for football. There is also an old-fashioned walled kitchen-garden, comprising about two acres, near to which is an excellent infirmary for such of the boys as may require medical treatment, entirely detached from the school buildings. A detached tower, of red brick, which covers a deep well—now disused and filled up—is the only surviving relic of the previous edifice which was built by the Comptons early in the sixteenth century. This structure is now used as a larder. A fresh well has been dug close by. In Hone's "Year-Book" there is an engraving of Bruce Castle, reproduced from a view taken in 1686, from which it appears that the main portion of the building has been considerably altered since that time. Among the pictures that adorn the walls of the principal staircase, too, is an oil painting showing the castle as it appeared in the early part of the last century. In this view the upper part of the central portion of the house on either side of the tower is terminated by a gable with one window in each. These gables have now entirely disappeared, the front of the house having been carried up to the level of the top of the gable, and two false windows inserted.

Having been for fifty years managed by Sir Rowland Hill and his family, Bruce Castle School changed hands in 1877. The average number of pupils in the school is about seventy. On Sunday mornings the whole of the pupils attend the service in the parish church, which is close by the north-west corner of the ground, and on Sunday evenings divine service is conducted by the head-master of the school in the house. The pupils have daily access to a well-selected library, containing nearly 3,000 volumes. With reference to the rise and subsequent growth of this library, we may state that it was first started about the commencement of the present century by Mr. Thomas W. Hill, the father of Sir Rowland Hill, and that it was for two or three years so small that it was kept in a master's desk. When the school was removed to Hazelwood, the library was taken there and added to occasionally by the head-master, until 1817, when a school fund was started, part of which was spent every year in new books. Former members of the school used also sometimes to send a book or two, and thus the library kept increasing slowly year by year. In 1827 rewards were first given to those boys who passed a successful examination in books of an instructive nature, and from that time the reading of those books has formed here a part of nearly every boy's education. When, in 1827, the school was first started at Bruce Castle, Mr. Rowland Hill began to form the present library, and when, six years later, the Messrs. Hill finally removed, as we have stated above, to Tottenham, they brought with them a part of the Hazelwood library.

We may add, in conclusion, that the pupils at this school, as a rule, are preparing for the universities, the public schools, or professional life. While very accessible from London, Bruce Castle has all the advantages of the country, and few schools have better in-door and out-door arrangements for the health and comfort of their pupils.

In Bruce Grove, near the Castle, are the Sailmaker's Almshouses, comprising some forty or more neat brick-built dwellings. They were erected in the year 1869, and are in the gift of the Drapers' Company.

The parish church of All Hallows, which stands at a short distance north of Bruce Castle, and is bounded by the little river called the Mosel on the west, north, and east, is an ancient building, in the Gothic or pointed style, and the chief parts may perhaps be ascribed to the fourteenth century. It has at the west end a square embattled tower, of red brick, picturesquely covered with dark ivy of many years' growth.

This tower was supposed by Lord Coleraine to have been more lofty than it was at the time he wrote his history of the parish, for after speaking of the upper windows, he adds: "And as the steeple seems to have been heretofore considerably more lofty, so upon the middle of the outside top of it there stood of old a long cross of wood, covered with lead, fastened into the centre of the roof so strongly as that it was a signification of some cause why the town mark and the parish had the sign of a high cross, which defied all its enemies from Henry VIII.'s days till the unhappy civil wars, when the violent zeal of some cunning Parliamentarians blew up some rascally fellows to set about the pulling down of this cross, which they did with such great difficulty and hazard as that they repented their foolish attempt long afterwards, one breaking his leg and the rest never thriving after the fact, and leaving a stump for the grafting another cross upon it, as a token of their rashness in reformation." It is indeed somewhat remarkable that this cross on the church tower should have escaped the zeal of the early reformers, considering the ado that was made about "superstitious" images and crosses in the latter part of the reign of Henry VIII., and the general destruction of such objects.

From the statement made by Lord Coleraine that the steeple of Tottenham Church was before his time "more lofty," many persons have fallen into the mistake of supposing the extra height to have been beyond its present height. Such a view, however, is at variance with the true sense of his lordship's statement, which describes the windows which had been sunk as the upper windows of the tower, within which the bells (which had not at that time, 1693, been re-cast) undoubtedly hung.

It is very probable that the upper portion of the tower was at one time covered with one of those pyramidal roofs or dwarf kind of steeples peculiar to some of the ancient church towers, upon the apex of which roof or steeple the cross referred to by Lord Coleraine might originally have stood, and which he might fairly describe as being "fastened into the centre of the roof." This steeple might have become out of repair, owing to the treatment it had received by the rebels, and, with its "stump," have been removed lest another cross might afterwards be grafted upon it. Its appearance would then warrant the statement made by Lord Coleraine that it seemed to have been "more lofty." All the old doorways and window-openings in the tower are in the plain pointed style, as is also the massive and well-formed arch which opens from the tower into the church on the east side. The style of this arch, although similar to that of the arches in the nave, differs considerably from them in its mouldings.

On the south side of the church is a large porch, built of brick, with stone dressings. Lord Coleraine, in his account of the parish, noticed above, says, with reference to this porch:—"Long since the building of the great door there has bin an edifice joyned to it, not as a twin, but as a younger brother to the church; therefore I suppose the old porch to this church, being so small or decayed, might by the charity of some great and well-minded person be taken down, and the present large fabrick set up in its stead." The same writer supposes the porch to be "not older than Henry VII.'s time," and states that he had heard that it was built by a widow lady, whom he believes was Joan Gedney, "who was lady of some of the manors before they fell to the Comptons, or by one of the Comptons' ladys." This porch has a small chamber over the entrance, concerning which these remarks appear in Lysons' "Environs:"—"This was originally intended, as I suppose, for a church-house, a building of which traces are to be found in the records of almost every parish. They were, as our vestries are now, places where the inhabitants assembled to transact the parish business." In this room there formerly resided, for many years, an old almswoman, named Elizabeth Fleming; she died in 1790, a veritable centenarian. Of late years this upper chamber was used as a school-room for the children of the parish. There is a hagioscope, or "squint," made in the wall of the church, so that the occupant of this room over the porch might be enabled to see the altar.

The font is octagonal in shape, having ornamental panels enclosing quatrefoils, within which are roses, a three-leafed plant enclosing berries, a pelican, a mermaid, a dragon or wyvern, and a figure representing a human head; there are also corbel heads at the angles beneath the basin. The carving is of the Perpendicular period, and is in a fair state of preservation, although somewhat worn with age and disfigured with paint. The figures, as well as the font, were re-chiselled in 1854 by a local tradesman, at a charge of £5. This font is probably as old as the present church; the roses carved upon it correspond with those on the doorways of the porch, from which we may infer that it was made early in the fifteenth century.

TOTTENHAM CHURCH.

The monuments and brasses are somewhat numerous; but in consequence of the alterations recently made in the building, few of them retain their original position. Some of the more ancient brasses have altogether disappeared. They are fully described in Robinson's "History of Tottenham." The oldest brass still remaining is a small plate to the memory of Thomas Hynnyngham; it bears the date 1499. Mr. George Waight, in his "History of Tottenham," to which we are indebted for much of the information here given, describes a few of the existing monuments, some of which are of peculiar interest. At the east end of the south aisle is one to the memory of Richard

VIEWS IN TOTTENHAM.

Candeler, Esq., who died in 1602, and Eliza his wife, 1622: they are represented kneeling before desks, on which are placed books. Adjoining this monument is another to the memory of Sir Ferdinando Heyborne, Gentleman of the Privy Chamber to Queen Elizabeth and James I., dated 1618, and his wife, the daughter of Richard Candeler, who died in 1612. A mural monument, with effigies, commemorates Sir John Melton, Keeper of the Great Seal for the north of England; he died in 1640. A large and curious monument in the north aisle, ornamented after the fashion of the period in which it was set up, is to the memory of Maria, wife of Sir Robert Barkham, of the county of Lincoln, and daughter of Richard Wilcocks, of Tottenham. She died in 1644. Upon this monument are busts of the deceased and her husband, and beneath are the effigies of their twelve children. A sum of money was left by the family of the deceased for the purpose of keeping this monument in good condition. In the chancel was the gravestone of the Rev. William Bedwell, who was many years vicar of this church, and also rector of St. Ethelburga's, in Bishopsgate Street. The epitaph —which commenced with some account of his daughter, who was married to one Mr. or Dr. Clark, and died December 20th, 1662—concluded as follows:—

> "Here lies likewise interred in
> this chancel the body of Mr. William
> Bedwell her father, some time
> Vicar of this Church, and one of
> King James's translators of the
> Bible, and for Easterne tongues
> as learned a man as most lived
> in these modern times, aged 70,
> dyed May 5th, 1632."

He was the author of the "History of Tottenham" mentioned above, and also of a book called the "Traveller's Calendar."

In 1875–7 the church underwent a thorough "restoration" and enlargement, after the fashion of the time. The additions to the fabric on this occasion consist of one new bay at the east end of the nave and aisles (or rather the old chancel and its aisles), with a new chancel, north and south transepts, an organ-chamber, double vestries, with a furnace-room for heating the church beneath one of them, and a north porch. The old chancel, with the addition of the new bay mentioned above, now becomes part of the nave, and is furnished with seats for the congregation. To meet the case of so greatly enlarged a church, all the new roofs are at a considerably higher level than they were originally. A clerestory, with windows on each side of it, has been put upon the new bay of the nave, the windows being absolutely necessary, as is proved by the unsightly skylights which had in former days been inserted in various parts of the roof. The new work has been carried out in red brick and stone in harmony with the fine red brick and stone south porch. The choir part of the chancel is fitted up with oak and walnut-wood seats and desks, and is paved with tiles. The eastern part, or sanctuary, is arcaded in stone on its sides and east end, with a central reredos behind the altar-table. Marble shafts and marble in various forms are used in this part of the chancel, on the south side of which is a graduated sedilia of two seats, and also a credence, very beautifully designed and executed. A large east window of five lights fills the gable end at a high level. The ceiling above is vaulted in wood and plaster, and is delicately painted in colours, in which a grey-blue predominates, with stars and flowers. The east five-light chancel window, the south three-light transept window, and another three-light window in the new bay of the south aisle, are filled with stained glass, presented by various persons as memorials.

"From the occurrence of a priest with half a hide of land at 'Totanam,' in the Doomsday Survey, the existence of a church may be fairly presumed at least as early as the Conquest, although we have no mention of it as a benefice till the twelfth century, when it was given to the canons of the Holy Trinity by Aldgate, soon after the foundation of their house by David, King of Scotland,* to whom it was appropriated, and a vicarage endowed about the beginning of the thirteenth century by Bishop William de Sanctæ de Mariæ Ecclesiæ."†

"The rudeness of construction and plainness of the oldest parts of the building," observes Mr. George Waight, in his work above mentioned, "make it very probable that the original church, of which they formed part, was built by one of the great lords of the manor, for there is always a marked difference observable between churches built by the lords of the soil and those built by monks and ecclesiastics—*i.e.*, between rectorial churches and vicarial churches. The vicarial churches having been built by the monks, who possessed more architectural skill and probably larger means than the lords of the soil, for that reason, almost uniformly present a greater elegance of design and magnitude than the former. It must be borne in mind that the church of Tottenham did not become vicarial until after it was given by David, King of Scotland, to the canons of the Holy

* Dugd. "Mon.," vol. ii., p. 80. † Newc. "Rep.," vol. i., p. 753.

Trinity, London. Up to that time the church and advowson had been appended to the manor, which had remained entire. There are many things," he adds, "which point to this conclusion; the mention of a priest in the Domesday Survey, the existence of the manorial house called Bruce Castle, the former lordship of the place (the road leading to it being still called Lordship Lane), and the close proximity of the church to both, all testify to the antiquity of the church as a religious foundation. The charter by which David, King of Scotland, granted the church, probably soon after it was built, to the canons of the Holy Trinity, was directed to Gilbert, Bishop of London (surnamed Universalis), who was Bishop of London in the reign of Henry I., from 1128 to 1134, and was confirmed by William de Sancta Maria, who was Bishop of London from the tenth year of Richard I. (1198) to the sixth year of Henry III. (1221)."

A chantry was founded in this church by John Drayton, citizen and goldsmith of London, as appears by his will, dated 27th September, 1456, "to find two priests daily, one to say divine service at St. Paul's, London, and the other at the Church of All Saints, Tottenham, at the altar of the blessed virgin and martyr St. Katherine; and the same priest also, on Wednesdays and Fridays, to perform the like service in the Chapel of St. Anne, called the Hermitage, in this parish, near the king's highway; also for the souls of King Richard II., Anne his queen, and others, his own two wives, parents and benefactors, and all the faithful deceased."

The bells in the old tower are six in number, and one of them, called the Saints' Bell, is ornamented with medallions and other figures and ornamentation. This bell was taken at the siege of Quebec—it having served originally as the alarm-bell of that town—and was given to the parish at the commencement of this century. The old vestry, at the eastern end of the church, was built and endowed by Lord Coleraine, in 1696, upon condition that he and his family should possess the ground beneath as a place of interment; the building was circular, and had originally a dome and an obelisk, but these were removed in 1855, they having become decayed, and ultimately the building was entirely demolished.

Tottenham Grammar School dates from the early part of the last century, when it was endowed under the will of Sarah, Dowager Duchess of Somerset. At one time there is reason to believe that it must have been in a fairly flourishing condition, as among its head-masters we find the name of the learned William Baxter, the nephew of the celebrated Richard Baxter. Of late years it had fallen into disrepute, and had, in fact, become a mere parish elementary school; but about the year 1872 a change of trustees having taken place, steps were taken to place the school upon a more efficient footing. A scheme was accordingly drawn up, the school premises were enlarged, and at the commencement of the year 1877 it was re-opened as a second-grade school.

Down to comparatively recent times, Tottenham could boast of other antiquities besides those we have already described; for in the "Ambulator" (1774) we read that St. Loy's Well, in this parish, is said to be "always full, and never to run over; and the people report many strange cures performed at Bishop's Well." The field in which the first-mentioned well is situated is called "South Field at St. Loy's," in a survey of the parish taken in 1619. It is situated on the west side of the high road, near the footpath leading past the Wesleyan chapel, and across the field to Philip Lane. Bedwell speaks of St. Loy's Well, in his history of the parish, as being in his time "nothing else but a deep pit in the highway, on the west side thereof;" he also adds that "it was within memory cleaned out, and at the bottom was found a fair great stone, which had certain letters or characters on it; but being broken or defaced by the negligence of the workmen, and nobody near that regarded such things, it was not known what they were or meant." The condition of the well has not much improved since Bedwell's time, having become nothing more nor less than "a dirty pool of water, full of mud and rubbish." Dr. Robinson, in his "History of Tottenham" (1840), describes the well as being surrounded by willows, about 500 feet from the highway, and adds that it was bricked up on all sides, square, and about four feet deep. The water of this spring was said to excel, in its medicinal qualities, those of any other near it; and in a foot-note, Robinson says that the properties of the water are similar to the water of Cheltenham springs.

The Chapel or "Offertory" of St. Loy is described by Bedwell as "a poore house, situate on the west side of the great road, a little off from the bridge where the middle ward was determined." It has long since disappeared. St. Loy, or St. Eloy, was one of the greatest oaths which men swore by in the Middle Ages. In Chaucer's "Canterbury Tales," for instance, the carter, encouraging his horses to draw his cart out of a slough, says,

"I pray God save thy body and St. Eloy."

Bishop's Well is described by Bedwell as "a spring issuing out of the side of a hill, in a field opposite to the vicarage, and falling into the Mosel afore it hath run many paces." The ground near it was formerly called Well Field, but now forms part of the cemetery. The water was said never to freeze, and, like that of St. Loy's Well, to be efficacious in the cure of certain bodily ailments.

White Hart Lane, mentioned above, the road leading to Wood Green, has long been built upon. Indeed, in the "Beauties of England and Wales," as far back as 1816, we find it spoken of as containing "several capacious villas, and some modern houses, of less magnitude, which are desirable in every respect, except that of standing in a crowded row. On the left hand of this lane," adds the writer, "at the distance of three quarters of a mile from the village of Tottenham, is the handsome residence of Henry P. Sperling, Esq. This is accounted the manor-house of the Pembrokes, but has, in fact, been long alienated from that estate. The building was, till within these very few years, surrounded by a moat, over which was a drawbridge. The moat was filled up by the present proprietor, probably to the advantage of his grounds, which are of a pleasing and rural character." Pembroke House is stated by Dyson, in his "History of Tottenham," to have been built for Mr. Soames, one of the Lords of the Admiralty, about the year 1636, at which time "the moat was dug and walled in."

At Wood Green are the almshouses belonging to the Printers' Pension, Almshouse, and Orphan Asylum Corporation. The objects of this institution, which was founded in the year 1827, are the maintaining and educating of orphans of deceased members of the printing profession, as well as granting of pensions, ranging from £8 to £25, to aged and infirm printers and their widows. The almshouses are a picturesque block of buildings, with a handsome board-room and offices in the centre, containing, with the two wings, residences for twenty-four inmates. The original portion of the building was erected in 1849, and the additional wings in 1871.

Tottenham Wood, in the fifteenth century, was celebrated for its medicinal spring; it bore the name of St. Dunstan's Well. Of the Wood itself, there are three old proverbs extant. To express a thing impossible, the people here used to say, "You may as well try to move Tottenham Wood," which was of great extent. Another, "Tottenham is turned French," meaning that it is as foolish as other places to leave the customs of England for foreign ones. And a third—

"When Tottenham Wood is all on fire,
Then Tottenham Street is nothing but mire."

This means, when a thick fog-like smoke hangs over Tottenham Wood, it is a sign of rain, and therefore of mud and dirt. We need hardly add that the task of removing Tottenham Wood has been accomplished, and that such part of it as is still unbuilt upon, is under arable cultivation. So much for the familiar "sayings" connected with Tottenham. But there is also a metrical satire which requires some brief mention. This is a mock heroic poem, known as the "Tournament of Tottenham," which appears to be a kind of satire on the dangerous and costly tournaments of the fifteenth and sixteenth centuries, and is supposed by Warton to have been written in the reign of Henry VII. The full title of the work is "The Turnament of Tottenham, or the wooeing, winning, and wedding of Tybbe, the Reeve's daughter there;" and the poem is descriptive of a contest between some five or six lusty bachelors, bearing the aristocratic names of "Perkyn, Hawkya, Dawkya, Tomkyn," &c., from "Hysseldon, Hackenaye," and other country districts, for the hand of the fair Tybbe, a rustic maiden, the daughter of a "reeve," or manciple of the place, whose marriage portion was a gray mare, a spotted sow, a dun cow, and "coppel, a brode hen that was brought out of Kent." The scene is the "Croft" at Tottenham; the rushing of the doughty warriors at each other in the lists, the broken heads and limbs, the falls from their horses, more accustomed to the plough than the jousts, and the winning of the fair Tybbe by the stalwart Perkyn; the carrying home of the defeated and drunken combatants; and finally, the wedding procession to Tottenham Church, in which Perkyn, Tybbe, and the reeve are the foremost characters—all these things are described in a style which excellently takes off the ballad style which has so often been used to portray a genuine tournament of knights, that the reader might almost be pardoned for indulging in the supposition that the affair really happened at Tottenham.

It does honour to the good sense of our nation, as Bishop Percy remarks, that whilst all Europe was captivated by the bewitching charms of chivalry and romance, two of our writers in the ruder times could see through the false glare that surrounded them, and could discover and hold up to the eyes of all what was absurd in them both. Chaucer wrote his "Rhyme of Sir Thopas" in ridicule of the latter, and in the "Turnament of Tottenham" we have a most humorous burlesque of the former. It is well known, of course, that the tournament, as an institution of the Middle Ages, did much to encourage the spirit of duelling —under another name—and that it continued to flourish in spite of the vigorous denunciations of the authorities both of Church and State. Such being the case, the author of the "Tournament" has availed himself of the keen weapon of ridicule in order to show up the absurd custom in its true colours. With this view he here introduces with admirable humour a parcel of country clowns and bumpkins, imitating at the Croft in Tottenham all the solemnities of the tourney. Here we have the regular challenge, the appointed day, the lady for the prize, the formal preparations, the display of armour, the oaths taken on entering the lists, the various accidents of the encounter, the victor leading off the prize, and the magnificent feasting, with all the other solemn fopperies that usually attended the pompous "tournament."

The "Turnament of Tottenham," it may be added, though now rendered popular by its being placed by Bishop Percy in his "Reliques," was first printed from an ancient MS. in 1631, by the Rev. William Bedwell, Rector of Tottenham, who, as stated above, was one of the translators of the Bible, and who tells us that its author was Gilbert Pilkington, thought by some to have been also in his day parson of the parish, and the author of another piece called "Passio Domini." Bedwell, however, though a learned man, does not seem to have appreciated the wit of his predecessor, and really imagines that the verses are a description of a veritable tournament written before the time of Edward III., in whose reign tournaments were prohibited. A perusal of the "Turnament" itself will be sufficient to dispel this matter-of-fact view of the poem, which is, perhaps, the best piece of mock-heroic writing that has come down to us since the "Battle of the Bees," so admirably portrayed by Virgil in his fourth Georgic.

We quote the following stanza, which describes the situation of the contending parties subsequent to the combat, and may serve as a specimen of the production:—

> "To the rich feast came many for the nonce;
> Some came hop-halte, and some tripping on the stones;
> Some with a staffe in his hand, and some two at once;
> Of some were the heads broken, of some the shoulder-bones;
> With sorrow came they hither.
> Wo was Hawkin; wo was Harry;
> Wo was Tymkin; wo was Tirry;
> And so was all the company,
> But yet they came togither."

It may be added that the poem, in its entirety, is given in the various histories of Tottenham, by Bedwell, Oldfield, and Dyson, as well as in Percy's "Reliques of Ancient Poetry."

Before quitting Tottenham, we may state that here was born, in 1557, the learned civilian and statesman, Sir Julius Cæsar, who was some time Master of the Rolls, and as we have already had occasion to observe, lived to such a great age, that he was said to be "kept alive, beyond Nature's course, by the prayers of the many poor whom he daily relieved." He was in attendance on his friend Lord Bacon at the time of his last illness, and was present with him when he died.* In 1598 Sir Julius resided at Mitcham, in Surrey, where he was visited by Queen Elizabeth. He lived near the High Cross, and died in 1636.

Here, in 1842, died William Hone, the author of very many popular works, and among others of the "Every-day Book." "I am going out to Tottenham this morning," writes Charles Dickens, "on a cheerless mission I would willingly have avoided. Hone is dying, and he sent Cruickshank yesterday to beg me to go and see him, as, having read no books but mine of late, he wanted to see me, and shake hands with me 'before he went.'" The request so asked, Charles Dickens performed with his usual tender-heartedness. In a month afterwards he paid a second visit to Tottenham. It was to attend Hone's funeral.

In concluding this chapter, we may be pardoned for referring to the sanitary condition of Tottenham. In 1837, when the Registrar-General's Department was first established, the village was a decidedly healthy place, and its healthiness was further improved by the establishment, about twenty years later, of an excellent system of drainage and water-supply, which reduced for some years the death-rate from fever by nearly one-half. About the year 1860 the population of Tottenham began to increase very rapidly, and owing mainly to the supineness of the leading inhabitants, the Local Board of Health neglected to extend the area of the drainage and water-supply, and likewise supplemented its water-supply from wells in the chalk by land-spring water drawn from highly-manured land. The Board also became remiss in dealing with nuisances. The result was that the death-rate rose rapidly, and by 1870 it was 20 per cent. higher than formerly, while the death-rate from the seven principal zymotic diseases had nearly doubled. Typhoid fever became prevalent, and in 1873 was epidemic. The leading inhabitants becoming alarmed, formed themselves into a sanitary association, elected efficient men on to the Local Board of Health, and devoted themselves to the speedy carrying out of numerous sanitary reforms. Sewers were freely ventilated, additional sewers were constructed, the polluted

---

* See *ante*, p. 405.

land-spring water was excluded from the water-supply, ditches and water-courses were cleansed, nuisances of all kinds were abated. The Local Board issued a handbill to every occupier, urging the need of house-drain ventilation, and, better still, began to insist upon efficient drain ventilation in the case of all new buildings. An immediate improvement in the public health followed upon these measures. The death-rate during 1876 was only 16·7 per 1,000; the rate from the seven principal zymotic diseases only 1·9 per 1,000; and that from fever less than ·2 per 1,000. The water-supply, as shown by the monthly reports furnished to the Registrar-General, stands, in respect of freedom from organic impurity, at the very head of all the waters supplied by the metropolitan water companies. Sanitary reform has not only diminished the number of deaths and the amount of illness, but has also, as a consequence, greatly increased the prosperity of Tottenham.

THE "BELL" AT EDMONTON. (*From an Old View.*)

CHAPTER XLVI.

NORTH TOTTENHAM, EDMONTON, &c.

"Away went Gilpin, neck or nought,
Away went hat and wig."—*Cowper.*

The "Bell" and "Johnny Gilpin's Ride"—Mrs. Gilpin on the Stile—How Cowper came to write "Johnny Gilpin"—A Supplement to the Story—Historic Reminiscences of the "Bell" at Edmonton—Charles Lamb's Visit there—Lamb's Residence at Edmonton—The Grave of Charles Lamb—Edmonton Church—The "Merry Devil of Edmonton"—The Witch of Edmonton—Archbishop Tillotson—Edmonton Fairs—Southgate—Arno's Grove—Bush Hill Park.

We have stated in the preceding chapter that the main road northwards runs through the centre of the village, and indeed forms the principal street of Tottenham High Cross. It continues straight on for some two miles or more towards Edmonton. This bit of roadway has acquired some celebrity, for Londoners at least, as the scene of Johnny Gilpin's famous ride, as related by Cowper. Indeed, we might ask, what traveller has ever refreshed himself or herself at the "Bell," and not thought of Johnny Gilpin, and his ride from London and back, nor sympathised with his worthy spouse on the disasters of that day's outing? The "Bell" inn, where Gilpin and his wife *should* have dined, is on the left-hand side of the road, as we proceed along from Tottenham. The balcony which the house possessed in Cowper's time has been removed, and the place, in fact, otherwise much altered. It has, however, a capacious "banqueting hall," and large pleasure-gardens "abounding with all kinds of shrubs and flowers;" no wonder, therefore, that it is a favourite resort for London holiday-makers. A painting of Johnny Gilpin's ride is fixed outside the tavern, and the house is commonly known as "Gilpin's Bell;" the landlord, however, designates it "The Bell and Johnny Gilpin's Ride."

In his "Library of English Literature," Professor Henry Morley thus tells the story of that ever-popular favourite ballad:—"Lady Austen one evening told Cowper the story of 'John Gilpin,' which, as told by her, tickled his fancy so much that he was kept awake by fits of laughter during great part of the night after hearing it, and must needs turn it into a ballad when he got up. Mrs. Unwin's son sent it to the *Public Advertiser*, where it appeared without an author's name. John Henderson, an actor from Bath, who took the London playgoers by storm in 1777 as Shylock, Hamlet, and Falstaff, was then giving readings at the Freemason's Tavern. He had succeeded almost to Garrick's fame. His feeling was so true, his voice so flexible, that Mrs. Siddons and John Kemble often went to hear him read. Henderson finding 'John Gilpin' in print, but not yet famous, chose it for recitation. Mrs. Siddons heard it with delight, and in the spring of 1785 its success was the event of the season. It was reprinted in many forms, and talked of in all circles; prints of 'John Gilpin,' were familiar in shop-windows; and Cowper, who was finishing the 'Task,' felt that his more serious work would be helped if it were published with this 'John Gilpin,' as an avowed piece by the same author." It is now fairly established as the most popular classic, and almost every English child knows it by heart. Indeed, so famous has the ballad, and consequently the "Bell" at Edmonton, become, that Mr. Mark Boyd tells us in his "Social Gleanings," that some American friends, who had come to England, declared that they had seen the two places most worth a visit in the metropolis, namely, "St. Paul's Cathedral, and the house connected with John Gilpin's famous ride."

EDMONTON CHURCH, 1790.

Mr. John Timbs, in his "Century of Anecdote," gives a similar version of the story of John Gilpin:—"This little poem was composed by Cowper about the year 1782, upon a story told to the poet by Lady Austen, in order to relieve one of the poet's fits of depressive melancholy. Lady Austen, it so happened, remembered the tale from the days of her childhood in the nursery, and its effects on the fancy of Cowper had the air almost of enchantment, for he told her the next morning that he had been kept awake during the greater part of the night by convulsions of irrepressible laughter, brought on by the recollection of her story, and that he had turned the chief facts of it into a ballad. Somehow or other it found its way into the newspapers, and Henderson, the actor, perceiving how true it was to nature, recited it in some of his public readings. Southey, whose judgment on such subjects is worth having and recording, conjectured that possibly the tale might have been first suggested to Cowper by a poem written by Sir Thomas More in his youthful days, entitled 'The Merry Jest of the Serjeant and Freere;' and it is quite within the range of probability that the tale which Lady Austen remembered and related may have originally come from this source, for there is next to nothing really new under the sun."

It has been much disputed, as probably our readers are aware, whether or not "John Gilpin" was an entirely fictitious romance, a creation of Cowper's brain, or whether its author founded his poem upon an adventure, or rather a mis-adventure, in the life of a real personage. The quotation above given from John Timbs, and the opinion of Southey, would certainly seem to give support to the former supposition; but in one of the volumes of the *Gentleman's Magazine* towards the close of the last century there is an entry which certainly looks quite the other way. According to that, the name of the individual who was really the subject of Cowper's inimitable ballad was Jonathan Gilpin, and he died at Bath, in September, 1790. The following notice appears in the *Gentleman's Magazine* for November of that year:—"The gentleman who was so severely ridiculed for bad horsemanship under the title of John Gilpin died, a few days ago, at Bath, and has left an unmarried daughter, with a fortune of £20,000." If this was really the case, then, in all probability, the memorable ride from London to the "Bell" at Edmonton and back again, the loss of wig, and the other accessories of the story, were not matters of pure invention, but some of the stern realities of life to a certain civic dignitary whose name has passed away.

It may not be generally known, though Mr. William Hone has recorded the fact in his amusing "Table-Book," that Cowper afterwards added an amusing little episode to John Gilpin's ride, which was found in the poet's own handwriting among the papers of his friend, Mrs. Unwin, illustrated with a comical sketch by George Romney. The episode consisted of three stanzas, which ran as follows:—

"Then Mrs. Gilpin sweetly said
Unto her children three,
'I'll clamber o'er the style so high,
And you climb after me.'

"But having climbed unto the top,
She could no farther go;
But sat, to every passer-by
A spectacle and show.

"Who said, 'Your spouse and you to-day
Both show your horsemanship;
And if you stay till he comes back
Your horse will need no whip.'"

It is much to be regretted that no more lines of this interesting ballad were discovered, as they were evidently intended to form an addendum to the "Diverting History of Johnny Gilpin," for it is supposed that in the interval between dinner and tea Mrs. Gilpin, finding the time to hang rather heavily on her hands, during her husband's involuntary absence, rambled out with her children into the fields at the back of the "Bell," where she met with the embarrassment recorded on ascending one of those awkward gates and stiles which abound in the neighbourhood of Edmonton and Tottenham. The droll picture of Mrs. Gilpin seated astride on the stile will be found in the pleasant pages of Mr. Hone.

We may state here that the "Bell" at Edmonton was a house of good repute as far back as the days of James I., as will appear from the following extract from John Savile's tractate, entitled, "King James's Entertainment at Theobalds, with his Welcome to London." Having described the vast concourse of people that flocked forth to greet their new sovereign on his approach to the metropolis, honest John says:—"After our breakfast at Edmonton, at the sign of the 'Bell,' we took occasion to note how many would come down in the next hour; so coming up into a chamber next to the street, where we might both best see, and likewise take notice of all passengers, we called for an hour-glass, and after we had disposed of ourselves who should take the number of the horse, and who the foot, we turned the hour-glass, which before it was half run out, we could not possibly truly number them, they came so exceedingly fast; but there we broke off, and made our account of 309 horses, and 137 footmen, which course continued that day from four o'clock in the morning till three o'clock in the afternoon, and the day before also, as the host of the house told us, without intermission." Besides establishing the existence of the renowned "Bell" at this period, the foregoing passage we have quoted is curious in other respects.

Charles Lamb, the last years of whose life were passed at Edmonton, and whose boyhood is so pleasantly connected with Christ's Hospital,* was in the habit of repairing to the "Bell" with any of his friends who may have visited him, when on their return; and here he used to take a parting glass, generally of porter, with them.

Lamb—"that frail good man," as Wordsworth affectionately called him—was the beloved and honoured friend of the leading intellectual lights of his day. From his early school days to his death he was the bosom friend of the poet Coleridge, and the intimate of Leigh Hunt, Rogers, Southey, and Talfourd. By the last-named gentleman his biography, including his letters, &c., was published in 1848. The writings of Lamb, like those of Goldsmith, and especially the "Essays of Elia," mirror forth the gentleness and simplicity of their author's nature. To his wit, Moore's lines on Sheridan most admirably apply :—

"Whose wit, in the combat, as gentle and bright,
Ne'er carried a heart-stain away on its blade."

Macaulay has paid the following tribute to his memory :—"We admire his genius; we love the kind nature which appears in all his writings; and we cherish his memory as much as if we had known him personally." On one occasion Lamb and Coleridge were conversing together on the incidents of the latter's early life, when he was beginning his career in the Church, and Coleridge was describing some of the facts in his usual tone, when he paused, and said, "Pray, Mr. Lamb, did you ever hear me preach?" To this the latter replied, "I never heard you do anything else."

Lucy Aikin, in one of her letters, gives her estimate of the character of Charles Lamb in the following words :—"There is no better English than that of poor Charles Lamb—a true and original genius; the delight of all who knew, and much more of all who read him, and a man whom none who had once seen him could ever forget."

Having already travelled somewhat farther northward than we had at first intended, we must forbear passing on to Enfield, where Lamb appears also at one time to have resided; but we may be pardoned for introducing one or two scraps of correspondence having reference to that fact.

Charles Lamb writes to a friend from Enfield Chase, Oct. 1, 1827: "Dear R——, I am settled, and for life I hope, at Enfield. I have taken the prettiest, compactest house I ever saw." And the same friend writes in similar terms: "I took the stage to Edmonton, and walked thence to Enfield. I found them—*i.e.*, Charles and Mary Lamb—in their new house, a small but comfortable place, and Charles Lamb quite delighted with his retirement. He does not fear the solitude of the situation, though he seems to be almost without an acquaintance (here), and dreads rather than seeks visitors."

In a letter addressed by Lamb, about this time, to his friend Tom Hood, we get a glimpse of the "inner life" of the Lambs at Enfield. "If I have anything in my head," he writes, "I will send it to Mr. Watts. Strictly speaking, he should have had my album-verses, but a very intimate friend importun'd me for the trifles, and I believe I forgot Mr. Watts, or lost sight at the time of his similar *souvenir*. Jamieson conveyed the farce from me to Mrs. C. Kemble; *he* will not be in town before the 27th. Give our kind loves to all at Highgate, and tell them that we have finally torn ourselves outright away from Colebrooke, where I had *no* health, and are about to domiciliate for good at Enfield, where I have experienced *good*.

'Lord, what good hours do we keep!
How quietly we sleep!'

"See the rest in the 'Complete Angler.'

"We have got our books into our new house. I am a dray-horse, if [I] was not ashamed of the undigested, dirty lumber, as I toppled 'em out of the cart, and blest Becky that came with 'em for her having an unstuff'd brain with such rubbish. We shall get in by Michael's Mass. 'Twas with some pain we were evuls'd from Colebrooke. You may find some of our flesh sticking to the door-posts. To change habitations is to die to them; and in my time I have died seven deaths. But I don't know whether every such change does not bring with it a rejuvenescence. 'Tis an enterprise; and shoves back the sense of death's approximating, which, tho' not terrible to me, is at all times particularly distasteful. My house-deaths have generally been periodical, recurring after seven years; but this last is premature by half that time. Cut off in the flower of Colebrook! The Middletonian stream, and all its echoes, mourn. Even minnows dwindle. *A parvis fiunt minima!* I fear to invite Mrs. Hood!"

Lamb, it is stated, was addicted to the practice

* See Vol. II., p. 370.

of smoking, and on being asked one day how he had acquired the habit, he replied, "By striving after it, as other men strive after virtue."

Charles Lamb survived his earliest friend and schoolfellow, Coleridge, only a few months. One morning, it is said, he showed a friend the mourning ring which the author of "Christabel" had left him, and exclaimed sorrowfully, "Poor fellow! I have never ceased to think of him from the day I first heard of his death!" Only five days after he had thus expressed himself—namely, on the 27th of December, 1834—Charles Lamb died, in his sixtieth year.

We leave the house in which he lived and died, Bay Cottage, on the right-hand side of Church Street, as we walk from the main road towards Edmonton Church. It is a small white house, standing back from the roadway, and next door to the large brick-built dwelling, known as the "Lion House," from the heraldic lions supporting shields on the tops of the gate-piers.

Poor Lamb was buried in the old churchyard close by, and the tall upright stone which marks his grave, near the south-west corner of the church, bears upon it the following lines, written by his friend, the Rev. Henry F. Cary, the translator of Dante :—

> "Farewell, dear Friend—that smile, that harmless mirth,
> No more shall gladden our domestic hearth;
> That rising tear, with pain forbid to flow,
> Better than words—no more assuage our woe;
> That hand outstretch'd from small, but well-earn'd store,
> Yield succour to the destitute no more.
> Yet art thou not all lost: through many an age,
> With sterling sense and humour, shall thy page
> Win many an English bosom, pleas'd to see
> That old and happier vein reviv'd in thee;
> This for our earth; and if with friends we share
> Our joys in heaven, we hope to meet thee there."

Mary Lamb continued to live on here after her brother's death. She died at St. John's Wood in 1847, but was buried in the same grave with her brother; so it may truly be said of them, that they "were lovely and pleasant in their lives, and in their death they were not divided."

Church Street has another literary memory, for here, from 1810 till 1816, resided John Keats, whilst serving his apprenticeship to a Mr. Hammond, a surgeon; here he wrote his "Juvenile Poems," which were published in 1817.

The parish church of Edmonton, dedicated to All Saints', is a large edifice, chiefly of Perpendicular architecture. At the west end is a square tower of stone, embattled, and profusely overgrown with ivy. The remainder of the building was encased with brickwork in the year 1772, and, at the same time, most reprehensible liberties were taken with the original character of the fabric. "A bricklayer and a carpenter," says the author of the "Beauties of England and Wales," "at that period possessed influence over the decisions of the vestry. A general casing of brick was evidently advantageous to the former; and the carpenter obtained permission to remove the stone mullions of the venerable windows, and to substitute wooden framework! The interference of higher powers prevented his extending the *job* to the windows of the chancel, which yet retain their ancient character, and would appear to be of the date of the latter part of the fourteenth century." In 1866 the interior of the church was carefully restored, new Perpendicular windows of stained glass being inserted in the chancel, and a south aisle added to it. The nave has a north aisle, separated from it by pointed arches sustained by octangular pillars. There are galleries at the western end, and in the north aisle. The chancel and its side aisles are separated from the nave by a bold arch. Weever mentions several monuments in this church, which do not exist in the present day; and Norden, in his MS. additions to his "Speculum Britanniæ," observes that, "There is a fable of one Peter Fabell that lyeth here, who is sayde to have beguyled the Devyll for monie: he was verye subtile that could deceyve him that is deceyt itselfe." This Peter Fabell is supposed by Weever to have been "some ingenious conceited gentleman, who did use some sleightie tricks for his own disport." There is a scarce pamphlet, entitled "The Life and Death of the Merry Devil of Edmonton, with the Pleasant Pranks of Smug the Smith," &c. In this book we are informed that Peter Fabell was born at Edmonton, and lived and died there in the reign of Henry VII. His story was made the groundwork of a drama, called the "Merry Devil of Edmonton," which is stated to have been "sundry times acted by his Majesties Servants, at the Globe on the Bankeside." Notwithstanding that this drama has the letters "T. B." appended to it as the initials of the author's name, it was long the fashion to attribute it to Shakespeare, just as it was in later times to ascribe it to Michael Drayton. In the prologue to the play we are informed that the "merry devil" was "Peter Fabel, a renowned scholar;" and are further told that—

> "If any here make doubt of such a name
> In Edmonton, yet fresh unto this day,
> Fix'd in the wall of that old ancient church,
> His monument remaineth to be seen."

As we have intimated above, however, this monument has long since disappeared.

Edmonton appears to have produced not only a "merry devil," but also a witch of considerable notoriety—

> "The town of Edmonton has lent the stage
> A Devil and a Witch—both in an age."

If we may believe the compiler of the "Beauties of England and Wales," the wretched and persecuted woman alluded to in the above lines was named Sawyer; and many particulars concerning her may be found in a pamphlet, published in 1621, under the title of "The wonderfull discoverie of Elizabeth Sawyer, a witch, late of Edmonton; her conviction, her condemnation, and death; together with the relation of the Devil's accesse to her, and their conference together. Written by Henry Goodcole, minister of the Word of God, and her continual visitor in the Gaole of Newgate." A play, by Ford and Dekker, was founded on this unhappy female.

At a short distance from the church, on the road leading towards Bush Hill, in a mansion called the Rectory House, Dr. Tillotson resided for several years, whilst Dean of St. Paul's, and occasionally also after he became Archbishop of Canterbury. "The day previous to his consecration as Archbishop," remarks the compiler of Tillotson's works, "he retired hither, and prepared himself, by fasting and prayer, for an entrance on his important and dignified duties with becoming humility of temper."

The ancient fair of Edmonton, with all its mirth and drollery, its swings and roundabouts, its spiced gingerbread, and wild-beast shows, is now a thing of the past. There were, in fact, three fairs annually held within the parish of Edmonton. Two of these, termed Beggar's Bush Fairs, arose from a grant made by James I., when he laid out a part of Enfield Chase into Theobalds Park. The third was called Edmonton Statute Fair, and was formerly held for the hiring of servants; it, however, became perverted to the use of holiday-people, chiefly of the lower ranks, and, in common with similar celebrations of idleness in the vicinity of the metropolis, became a source of great moral degradation.

In 1820, one of the chief attractions of the fair was a travelling menagerie, whose keeper walked into the den of a lioness, and nursed her cubs in his lap. He then paid his respects to the husband and father, a magnificent Barbary lion. After the usual complimentary greetings between them, the man, somewhat roughly, thrust open the monster's jaws, and put his head into his mouth. This he did with impunity. A few days afterwards, having travelled a little farther north with his show, the keeper repeated his performance, and fell a victim to his rashness.

Southgate, the favourite haunt of Leigh Hunt's childhood, is a detached hamlet, or village, belonging to Edmonton, and derives its name from having been the southern gate to Enfield Chase, which stretches away northward. The village of Southgate lies on the road towards Muswell Hill. Christ Church, a handsome edifice of Early-English architecture, dates its erection from 1862, when it was built in place of the old Weld Chapel.

Minchenden House, in the village, was the seat of the Duchess of Chandos early in the present century. It is said that George II., on coming here to visit the duke's father or grandfather, was obliged to pass through Bedstiles Wood, which was a trespass. The man who kept the gate, being ordered to open it for his Majesty, refused, saying, "If he be the D—— himself, he shall pay me before he passes." The king had to pay; but the result was that the duke threw open the road.

Arno's Grove is another mansion of some note in the hamlet of Southgate. It stands on the site of a more ancient structure, termed Arnold's, which some two centuries ago belonged to Sir John Weld. After some intermediate transmissions, it was purchased, early in the last century, by Mr. James Colebrooke, father of Sir George Colebrook, Bart., who eventually inherited the property. Among its subsequent owners was Sir William Mayne, Bart., who was in 1776 raised to the peerage with the title of Lord Newhaven.

Bush Hill Park, in the neighbourhood of Southgate, between Edmonton and Enfield, was formerly the seat of a rich merchant, named Mellish (who was M.P. for Middlesex), and afterwards of Mr. A. Raphael, and of the Moorat family. Its grounds are said to have been laid out by Le Notre. In the hall there was a curious carving in wood, by Grinling Gibbons, representing the stoning of St. Stephen. "It stood for some time," writes Lambert, "in the house of Mr. Gibbons, at Deptford, where it attracted the attention of his scientific neighbour, Mr. Evelyn, the author of 'Silvia,' who was induced by this specimen of his work to recommend him to Charles II. This carving was purchased for the Duke of Chandos, for his seat at Canons, near Edgware, whence it was brought to Bush Hill." The estate is now broken up and built over with villas. In the grounds of an adjoining mansion are the remains of a circular encampment, of considerable dimensions, about which antiquaries are divided in opinion as to whether they formed part of a Roman or a British camp.

OLD BOW BRIDGE.

CHAPTER XLVII.

THE LEA, STRATFORD-LE-BOW, &c.

"Longarum hæc meta viarum."—*Virgil.*

The River Lea—Bow Bridge—Stratford-atte-Bowe, and Chaucer's Allusion thereto—Construction of the Road through Stratford—Alterations and Repairs of the Bridge—Don Antonio Perez, and other Noted Residents at Stratford—The Parish Church of Stratford-le-Bow—The School and Market House—The Parish Workhouse—Bow and Bromley Institute—King John's Palace at Old Ford—St. John's Church—The Town Hall—West Ham Park—West Ham Abbey—Abbey Mill Pumping Station—Stratford New Town—The Great Eastern Railway Works—"Hudson Town"—West Ham Cemetery and Jews' Cemetery—St. Leonard's Convent, Bromley—The Chapel converted into a Parish Church—Bromley Church rebuilt—Allhallows' Church—The Church of St. Michael and all Angels—The Manor House—The Old Palace—Wesley House—The Old Jews' Cemetery—The City of London and Tower Hamlets Cemetery.

In order to make our way to London Bridge, which is our destined starting-point in the next and concluding volume, we may now drop quietly down the river Lea, passing between green and flowery meadows, and re-visiting on our way some of those shady nooks by which, as we have seen in our wanderings northward, Izaak Walton so much loved to lounge when engaged in his favourite pastime of angling. We shall in due course find ourselves at Bow Bridge, which crosses the Lea between Whitechapel Church and Stratford.

The river, after it leaves Clapton and Hackney, passes on by the Temple Mills to Stratford, or as it is frequently called, Stratford-le-Bow, which lies between Hackney and Whitechapel parishes. Here it divides its course into several channels, the principal stream being that which is spanned by Bow Bridge. The name of Stratford evidently points to the existence near this spot of a ford which doubtless connected London with the old Roman road to Camalodunum, whether that were at Maldon or at Colchester. In the course of time, however, the primitive ford was superseded by a bridge, which appears to have been called "Bow" Bridge, from the arches (*arcus*), which supported and really formed the structure; or possibly because it was constructed of a single arch, as suggested by the writers of the "Beauties of England and Wales." Hence the village was called "Stratford-atte-Bowe," under which name it is immortalised by Chaucer, in the Prologue to the "Canterbury Tales," in terms which seem to imply that five centuries ago it was a well-known place of education for young ladies. Most of our readers will remember the comely prioress, how, in the words of the poet—

> "French she spake full fayre and fetisly,
> After the scole of Stratforde-attè-Bowe,
> For French of Paris was to her unknowe."

We may be pardoned for suggesting as a solution of the meaning of this allusion, that in the adjoining parish of Bromley, within a mile of the bridge, stood the Convent of St. Leonard's, usually termed the Priory in Stratford, and that the nuns of that religious house probably taught the French language among other accomplishments to the young ladies of that favourite suburb.

But it is time that we said something about the old bridge, which was really an historic structure. Fortunately we have to guide us, not only the "Survey" of Stow, and the "Collectanea" of Leland, but also a document, the substance of which was given upon oath at an inquisition taken before two justices of the peace in the year 1303, and which is to be found at length in Lysons' "Environs of London."

"The jurors," writes Lysons, "declared that at the time when Matilda, the good Queen of England, lived, the road from London to Essex was by a place called the Old Ford, where there was no bridge, and during great inundations was so extremely dangerous that many passengers lost their lives; which, coming to the good queen's ears, she caused the road to be turned where it now is—namely, between the towns of Stratford and Westham, and of her bounty caused the bridges and road to be made, except the bridge called Chaner's Bridge, which ought to be made by the Abbot of Stratford. They said further, that Hugh Pratt, living near the roads and bridges in the reign of King John, did of his own authority keep them in repair, begging the aid of passengers. After his death his son William did the same for some time, and afterwards, through the interest of Robert Passelowe, the King's Justice, obtained a toll, which enabled him to make an iron railing upon a certain bridge, called Lock Bridge, from which circumstance he altered his name from Pratt to Bridgewryght; and thus were the bridges repaired, till Philip Bagset and the Abbot of Waltham, being hindered from passing that way with their wagons in the late reign, broke down the railing; whereby the said William, being no longer able to repair it, left the bridge in ruins; in which state it remained till Queen Eleanor of her bounty ordered it to be repaired, committing the charge of it to William de Capella, keeper of her chapel. After which, one William Carlton (yet living) repaired all the bridges with the effects of Bartholomew de Castello, deceased. The jurors added that the bridges and roads had always been repaired by 'bounties,' and that there were no lands or tenements charged with their repair except for Chaner's Bridge, which the Abbot of Stratford was bound to keep in repair."

In the early part of the present century Bow Bridge consisted of three arches. It was very narrow, and bore marks of venerable age; but the numerous alterations and repairs of four centuries had obscured its original plan, and, indeed, left it doubtful how much of it was the work of the good Queen Matilda, and, indeed, whether any part of the original structure remained. The bridge was taken down about the year 1835, and superseded by a lighter and wider structure.

Stratford-le-Bow has few historical or personal associations for us to record. It may, however, be remembered that it was the residence of Don Antonio Perez, who endeavoured to obtain the crown of Spain and Portugal, but who, failing in the attempt, fled for refuge to England as an asylum. He is said to have lived here whilst negotiating with Elizabeth for aid in support of his pretensions, and his residence here is rendered all the more probable from the fact that the parish register contains the entry of the burial of a foreigner who is called his treasurer. Another resident in Stratford was Edmund, Lord Sheffield, who distinguished himself so much in the sea-fights off our coast against the Spanish Armada. Lysons states that John Le Neve, the author of "Monumenta Anglicana" and other learned antiquarian works, also had a house within the parish. The exact situation, however, of these two residences is not known.

The church of Stratford-le-Bow was built as a chapel of ease to Stepney early in the fourteenth century, in consequence of a petition from the inhabitants of this place and of Old Ford, stating the distance of their homes from their parish church, and the difficulty of the roads, which in winter were often impassable on account of the floods. In consequence, Baldock, Bishop of London, issued a licence for the erection of a new chapel upon a site taken from "the king's highway" for that purpose. The chapel ultimately blossomed into a separate parish church, and was consecrated as such in 1719. It consists of a chancel, nave, and aisles, separated from the nave by octangular pillars supporting pointed arches.

At the west end is a belfry tower, rather low, with graduated buttresses, and embattled. The edifice, we may add, stands in the middle of the high road, the houses receding slightly from the straight line on either side, so as to allow of a roadway on each side of the church.

A little to the east of the church was formerly a building which had been used at various times as a school and as a market-house. Brewer, in his "History of Middlesex," when speaking of Bow, says: "At a small remove from the church towards the east is a building which appears to have been used as a market-house. A room over the open part of this building had long been occupied as a charity school, on the foundation of Sir John Jolles, established in 1613, and intended for thirty-five boys of Stratford, Bow, and St. Leonard, Bromley." About the year 1830 this building was removed in order to enlarge the churchyard, and a new school-room erected in its stead at Old Ford.

At a short distance, on the north side of the main street, stood the parish workhouse, which evidently was at one time a mansion of handsome proportions, its rooms being ornamented with fine ceilings and carved chimney-pieces. It was pulled down several years ago, its site being converted to business purposes.

On the north side of the high road, at a short distance westward of Bow Church, stands a large and attractive building, the upper part of which, known as the Bow and Bromley Institute, is used occasionally for concerts, lectures, and similar entertainments. The ground floor serves as the Bow Station of the North London Railway, which here runs below the road. In the roadway close by is a statue of Mr. Gladstone, presented by Mr. H. T. Bryant in 1882.

The hamlet of Old Ford is situated a little to the north of Bow. "In this place," write the compilers of the 'Beauties of England and Wales,' "stood an ancient mansion, often termed King John's Palace, but which does not appear to have been at any time vested in the Crown. The site of this mansion was given to Christ's Hospital by a citizen of London named William Williams, in 1665. A brick gallery, which has been recently covered with cement, is now the only relic of the ancient building. The present (1816) lessee of the estate is Henry Manley, Esq., who has here a handsome residence, and has much improved the grounds and neighbourhood." The last vestige of this building was demolished a few years ago.

Stratford—the "ford of the street, or Roman way from London to Colchester"—lies on the east side of the river Lea, and is consequently in the county of Essex. It is also on the Great Eastern Railway, whence the Colchester and the Cambridge, and the Blackwall and Woolwich, and the Woodford and the Tilbury branch lines diverge; and it is a ward of the parish of West Ham. The church, dedicated to St. John, is a large and handsome edifice, in the centre of the town, and is in the Early English style. Its site is on land which, up to the time of its erection, in 1834, had been an unenclosed village green. At first the church was founded as a chapel of ease to the parish church of West Ham; but about 1859 it was constituted a vicarage, and Stratford became a parish of itself.

The Town Hall, in the Broadway, at the corner of West Ham Lane, was opened in 1869. It is a handsome building, in the classic style, and has a frontage of about 100 feet each way. It has a tower about 100 feet in height, and the building is surmounted by various figures and groups of statuary, illustrative of the arts, science, agriculture, manufacture, commerce, &c. The lower part of the building comprises some commodious public offices, and on the first floor is a spacious hall, artistically decorated.

At a short distance eastward is West Ham Park, a large plot of ground open for the purpose of recreation for the inhabitants of this district. It was formed a short time ago, under the auspices of Sir Antonio Brady, and occupies what was formerly Upton Park, the seat and property of the Gurneys. The mansion has been taken down. The park was laid out with the aid of City funds. In December, 1876, a grant was voted—£1,500 for necessary works carried out, and £675 for the annual maintenance of the grounds.

Stratford (or West Ham) Abbey was founded here in 1135, for monks of the Cistercian order, the abbot of which was a lord of Parliament. There are considerable remains of the building.

Abbey Mill Pumping Station, close by, is an extensive range of works, in connection with the main drainage of North London. As the works here are very similar to those already described in connection with the Pumping Station at Chelsea,* there is no occasion for entering upon a further account of them.

Stratford being, as stated above, the point where the two main branches of the Great Eastern Railway leading respectively to Cambridge and Colchester diverge, has of late years given birth to a new town, which has become quite a railway

---

* See *ante*, pp. 41, 42.

colony. Here the company has its chief depôt for carriages, engines, and rolling stock, and yards for their repairs. The works, which were established here about the year 1847, cover a very large extent of ground, and give employment to upwards of 2,500 hands, independently of about 600 others engaged in the running sheds. The various buildings used as workshops for the different branches of work required to be done, either in the construction or the repair of engines, &c., are large and well lighted, and embrace foundries for casting, forges, fitting rooms, braziers' shops, carpenters' shops, saw-mills, &c. The principal erecting shops are about 120 yards in length, by sixty in breadth. The machinery throughout is of the most perfect description, and adapted for almost all kinds of work; one shop alone contains upwards of 100 machines for the performance of the most delicate work. One of the latest and most useful pieces of machinery in operation in the smiths' shop is the hydraulic riveting-machine. To give some idea of the amount of labour accomplished in these works, we may state that about 500 engines, 3,000 carriages, and 10,000 wagons are here kept in constant repair, and that the sum paid weekly in wages in the locomotive department alone amounts, on an average, to about £6,000.

The new town which has sprung up in the neighbourhood of the works is the residence of several hundreds of skilled *employés*—engineers, drivers, and others. At first it was called Hudson Town, in compliment to the "Railway King;" but when he lost his crown, the name fell into disuse. In 1871 the New Town numbered some 23,000 souls; and now probably the population has nearly doubled itself. The town, it may be added, has its literary institution, a "temperance" public-house, besides numerous places of worship.

At a short distance eastward of the railway works, by the side of Forest Road, which runs parallel with the Colchester line, stands an industrial school, with spacious grounds attached, in the rear of which is the West Ham Cemetery, and the Jews' Cemetery. In the latter, which covers about eleven acres of ground, and was formed in 1858, on the closing of the Jews' Cemetery at Mile End, are the vaults of the Goldsmid and the Lucas families, of Sir David Salomons, and other leading members of the Jewish community, together with a dome-crowned mausoleum for the members of the house of Rothschild.

Adjoining Bow on the south-east, in the parish of Bromley, was, as above-mentioned, a convent dedicated to St. Leonard, stated by some historians to have been founded in the reign of William the Conqueror, by William, Bishop of London, for a prioress and nine nuns; other writers, however, are of opinion that it was founded at a much earlier period. Indeed, when, or by whom, the convent was really founded, seems a very difficult matter now to decide. Stow says it was founded by Henry II., in the first year of his reign (1154); but Dugdale, in the "Monasticon," says, "This is a mistake, it was in being before." Weever fixed the foundation still later, by saying that "this religious structure was sometime a monastery replenished with white monks, dedicated to the honour of our Saviour Jesus Christ, and Saint Leonard; founded by Henry II., in the twenty-third year of his reign." But Strype, in his "Survey of London," says, respecting this statement of Weever:—"How to reconcile the said antiquary with an elder than he, namely, John Leland, and the 'Monasticon Anglicanum,' I cannot tell, for Weever writes that this monastery was replenished with white monks, and founded by King Henry II., in the twenty-third year of his reign; whereas Leland and the 'Monasticon' reports it a religious house for nuns, founded by William, Bishop of London, that lived in the Conqueror's time," which was nearly a century earlier. Lysons, in his "Environs of London," attempts to unravel the apparently opposite statements of Stow, Weever, Leland, Dugdale, and others, by supposing Weever to have been altogether in error, he having confounded the Abbey of Monks at Stratford (the remaining vestiges of which is now called West Ham Abbey), in Essex, with the Convent of Nuns, in Middlesex, which convent, says Lysons, was invariably said in ancient wills to have been at Stratford, Bow, on account of its contiguity to that place. And he further says, respecting these two religious houses: "It is difficult to distinguish them in the calendars in the Tower; nor can it be always done without referring to the original will, where the word 'Prioresse' will determine the grants which belong to this house at Bromley, even if 'Beati Leonardi' should not follow."

Weever states that the convent of which he was speaking was in Middlesex, and dedicated to St. Leonard; whereas, the convent at Stratford he knew to be in Essex, which he says that he visited himself "after going over 'Bow Bridge,' in his journey towards West Ham." Leland, who was engaged in making historical collections relating to religious houses, by order of Henry VIII., is reported to have met with but little encouragement, and to have died insane in the neighbourhood of St. Paul's; "uncertain," says Fuller, "whether his brains were broken with weight of work or want of wages." This report of Leland's—for such it really is—was printed in Latin, and entitled "Antiquarii de rebus;" and in it he says, respecting the Priory at Bromley, "Gul. Episcopus London fundator." Historians generally have followed this dictum, since Leland wrote, and ascribed the first foundation, both of the structure and religious society of St. Leonard, to William, Bishop of London, in the Conqueror's reign. But Speed, in his "History of England and its Monasteries," speaks of the Norman bishop, with respect to the Priory at Bromley, as a "benefactor" only; and this is quoted against Leland in the "Monasticon." Mr. Dunstan, in his "History of Bromley and St. Leonard," says: "That William, Bishop of London, was a benefactor there can be no doubt; nay, more, it is probable that he enlarged the original priory about the period mentioned. He might also have much enlarged the Lady Chapel attached to the priory which was dedicated to St. Mary; and this will account for the mixed style of the old church, it having been partly of Gothic, partly of Saxon, and partly of Norman architecture, which would indicate that the structure was not all the work of one hand, nor even of one age; for whilst the round-headed arches in one part were both Saxon and Norman, the pointed arches, yea, even the main or principal doorway, and heavy buttresses, were purely Gothic, and therefore of more ancient date, in the other. It is very probable," he continues, "that William, Bishop of London, might have removed some portions of the original chapel, and added others of more extensive and lofty dimensions, suited to the style of Norman architecture." This hypothesis is particularly strengthened by the fact that when the old chapel or church was taken down in 1842, a considerable quantity of old building materials, chiefly consisting of very ancient wrought stone, was found embedded in various parts of the walls; evidently the fragments of some very ancient religious structure, which probably had occupied the same, or nearly the same site, anterior to the episcopacy of William, in the Conqueror's reign. Moreover, the arches which were found blocked up and plastered over, and covered with many generations of whitewash within, and rough-coat without, in 1825, were all of the Gothic style, and evidently led into some building (as Lysons conceives) on the south side; whereas, according to Newcourt and others, the nunnery or convent in the days of Henry VIII. was at the west end of the chapel; and the lofty arch at the western end of the church contained the screen which separated the chapel from the convent and cloisters.

"Speed, therefore, views the antiquity of the Convent of St. Leonard as being anterior to that of Henry II., as mentioned by Stow and Weever, and considers Henry II. as a benefactor only; and in the same light he considers all the others whose benefactions and confirmations have been named, including William, Bishop of London, among the rest. And, therefore, in tracing that antiquity to a reasonable, nay, to a probable source, it does appear from the many foregoing considerations that the original foundation of the Convent or Priory of St. Leonard at Bromley may, with the greatest propriety, be attributed to the time of Edgar's reign, about one hundred years before William the Conqueror landed on the British shores—namely, somewhere about the middle of the tenth century, or nearly coeval with the re-establishment of the monastery at Westminster." All trace of the old priory buildings, with the exception of the chapel, has long since passed away. The chapel was dedicated to St. Mary, and at the dissolution of the religious houses it was converted into a parochial church. Lysons says that "the chapel of St. Mary, with the convent of St. Leonard, Bromley, is mentioned in several ancient wills." The fabric consisted of a nave and chancel, and the latter was separated from the former by a chancel-screen and by being raised one step. The principal entrance, at the western end, was in the same situation as that in the present building, but consisted of a Gothic arched doorway. This doorway, it is conjectured, was inserted when the old chapel first became appropriated as a parish church, as upon the removal of the north wall there was found, bricked up and plastered over, a very ancient doorway of small dimensions and of Norman architecture. The chancel of the old church occupied precisely the same position with that of the present church, as portions of the walls of the old building are now standing, both in the north and south-eastern ends of the present church. In the chancel are five stone stalls, or *sedilia*, through one of which was a small doorway opening at once into the churchyard. At the western end of the nave was a capacious gallery, and the body of the church was fitted up with pews of the orthodox fashion. In 1692 the chancel was lengthened by Sir William Benson, the then lord of the manor, "by the addition of a projecting recess in which was placed the communion-table." At the west end of the church was a large round-headed arch, ornamented with lozenge and other Saxon or early Norman mouldings; this was much disfigured by the galleries inside, and also by the vestry-room outside. It has been suggested that the church as it remained down to the present period was only the chancel and lady chapel of a much larger edifice; and that the arch here spoken of was that which separated it from a nave, of which every trace has long since perished. In 1843 the new church was opened, the old fabric having been demolished piecemeal. It is a plain brick-built structure, consisting of a nave, chancel, and side-aisles, with a tower and dwarf spire at the south-west corner. The style of architecture adopted is that of the Norman period, and some of the windows are enriched with coloured glass.

The font is of Norman design, and of the usual size; it is said to have been for many years expelled from the church, and to have lain in the churchyard. In 1825, when the old church was repaired and "beautified," the churchwardens had the antique device on the font re-cut, and it was placed upon a Gothic pedestal. Although it was so far restored to its original position, it appears to have been discarded by the officiating minister; a small portable font having been used for many years. It has, however, now been fully re-installed, and the Gothic character of the pedestal changed into Norman.

The old church was particularly rich in monuments and funeral hatchments. In the nave formerly lay a large stone which contained the brasses of a man and woman, with much ornamental work over their heads. "They seem," says Strype, "to be some nobleman and his wife interred in this religious house. Perhaps the Earl [John De Bohun] and his wife, already mentioned." If so, it would have dated from about 1336. The stone was afterwards removed to the entrance of the old church, and formed a part of the floor; it is now placed in the floor of the tower. Against the south wall of the church was a large mural monument of marble, to the memory of William Ferrars, and dated 1625. On the erection of the new church this monument was placed against the north wall. Busts of the deceased and his wife, who was Jane, daughter of Sir Peter Van-Lore, are represented under arches supported by pillars of the Corinthian order. The man is habited in a doublet and ruff, and the hands of both are united, resting on a skull. In a panel over the effigies is the motto—

> "Live well, and dye never,
> Dye well, and live ever."

A curious and interesting monument is that of Abraham Jacob, Esq., who died in the year 1629. The figures of himself and his wife are represented kneeling under arches, the monument being adorned with the arms of the family and its alliances. The monument is particularly chaste and emblematical. The principal feature in the ornamentation is the representation of a vine, on the leaves of which are written the names of his twelve children. The names of five that were married, and their respective alliances, are expressed by the quartering of their several coats of arms; whilst the younger offshoots indicate the fruits of the respective unions, on the leaves of which offshoots are inscribed the names of their children. The names of the seven unmarried remain above on the leaves of the old vine. This monument was erected by Sir John Jacob, who, after the death of his father, Abraham Jacob, had purchased the manor and advowson of Bromley, in 1634. He is said to have been a very rich and loyal citizen, and one of the "farmers of the customs." He was a great sufferer during the Civil War, and was at one time confined as a prisoner in Crosby House.

Bromley possesses also three or four other churches, besides chapels and meeting-houses for members of various denominations. Allhallows' Church, an edifice of Early English architecture, was built in 1874, from the proceeds of the sale of the church of Allhallows Staining, Mark Lane, and is in the patronage of the Grocers' Company. The large church of St. Michael and All Angels, which is of similar architecture, and consecrated in 1865, contains sittings for about 1,300 worshippers.

About the middle of the seventeenth century Sir John Jacob built a "large brick edifice" on the site of the old priory. The house was surrounded by a small park and gardens, the east side of which was washed by the river Lea. The building, which was called the Manor House, was demolished early in the present century, and its site covered by rows of small cottages, whilst some portion of the grounds was added to the churchyard.

That Bromley in its time has had a fair share of aristocratic inhabitants may be seen from the fact that, in the parish rate-books of the seventeenth century, besides the name of Sir J. Jacob, appear those of Sir Henry Ferrers, Sir William Turner, Sir John Poole, Sir Nicholas Crisp, Sir J. Fleetwood, Sir John Chambers, Sir Richard Mundy, Lady Stanhope, Lady Munden, and several other titled personages.

At a short distance westward of the church, a large brick-built mansion—one of the former glories of the place—is still standing, but cut up into three or four tenements. It is commonly known as the Old Palace, and is sometimes called Queen Anne's Palace. The building is very lofty, and has a slightly projecting wing at either end.

The interior bears numerous traces of its original splendour in the shape of stuccoed ceilings, carved panellings and chimney-pieces, as well as marble floors. A long row of wooden houses standing at right angles with the mansion, and forming one side of another street, occupies the site of the ancient stables. Another curious old house in this street, with the words "Wesley House" painted over the doorway, is said to have been one of the first meeting-houses in which John Wesley preached.

Before quitting Bromley, we must not omit to mention the bowling-green, the village stocks, the whipping-post, the pond and ducking-stool, and the parish pound, all of which remained in full operation down to the latter part of the last century.

Adjoining Bromley, and at the eastern end of the Mile End Road, not far from Bow and Old Ford, is the disused Jewish Cemetery, formerly belonging to the Great German Synagogue in Duke's Place. Here are buried nearly all the members of the Jewish religion who have been connected with the City and the East End of London. Among them lies Baron Nathan Rothschild, the great millionaire, and head of the well-known banking and financial house which bears his name. He died in 1836, and his funeral was perhaps the most imposing ever witnessed in these districts. This cemetery was closed in 1858, on the opening of the new Jewish Cemetery near Stratford New Town, as mentioned above. The burial-grounds for Jews are mostly laid out and planted in a manner similar to other cemeteries. Formerly their burial-place was "outside the City Wall, at Leyrestowe, without Cripelgate."

In this neighbourhood—at South Grove, Mile End—is the Cemetery of the City of London and Tower Hamlets Company. It occupies about thirty acres of ground, north of Bow Common, and is skirted on the south-east side by a branch of the Great Eastern Railway, on its way from Stepney Station to Bow Road and Stratford. The cemetery, which is altogether a dreary place, now holds the remains of many thousands of persons, mostly of the poorer classes, many of whom occupy nameless graves.

It now only remains to remind our readers that in the course of the present volume we have endeavoured to act as their guides over a far larger extent of ground than that which we traversed in all our previous volumes. We have lounged in their company about the old mansions of Chelsea and Kensington; we have wandered with them through the green fields of Bayswater and Paddington, of Marylebone and the Regent's Park; we have climbed with them the "northern heights" of Hampstead and Highgate Hills; and lastly, we have reconnoitred the northern outskirts of Dalston and Hackney, Stoke Newington and Tottenham; and roamed hand in hand with them the pleasant meadows that fringe the river Lea. Here we must leave our readers for a time, purposing in the following volume to take them through quite another tract of country, not romantic in its outward features, but full of historic interest, on the south bank of the Thames, feeling assured that but scanty justice will have been done to "London, Old and New," unless we include in our perambulations both Southwark and Lambeth, Bermondsey and Deptford, Kennington and Walworth, Wandsworth and Putney, Fulham and Hammersmith; in each, and all of which, once rural villages, though now large and populous towns and busy "hives of industry," we shall studiously endeavour so to blend the present with the past as to avoid, and, if possible, to escape the risk of proving ourselves dull and profitless companions.